AMERICAN
SPORTS

2nd Edition

AMERICAN SPORTS

From the Age of Folk Games to the Age of Televised Sports

Benjamin G. Rader
University of Nebraska, Lincoln

PRENTICE HALL, Englewood Cliffs, New Jersey 07632

Library of Congress Cataloging-in-Publication Data

Rader, Benjamin G.
  American sports : from the age of folk games to the age of
televised sports / Benjamin G. Rader.
      p.   cm.
  Includes bibliographical references.
  ISBN 0-13-029133-1
  1. Sports—United States—History.   I. Title
GV583.R3 1990
796'.0973—dc20   89-37117
                                                                CIP

Editorial/production supervision and
  interior design: Joe O'Donnell
Cover design: Photo Plus Art
Cover photo: UPI/BETTMANN NEWSPHOTOS
Manufacturing buyer: Carol Bystrom

 ©1990, 1983 by Prentice-Hall, Inc.
A Division of Simon & Schuster
Englewood Cliffs, New Jersey 07632

Printed in the United States of America

10 9 8 7 6 5 4 3 2 1

ISBN 0-13-029133-1

Prentice-Hall International (UK) Limited, *London*
Prentice-Hall of Australia Pty. Limited, *Sydney*
Prentice-Hall Canada Inc., *Toronto*
Prentice-Hall Hispanoamericana, S.A., *Mexico*
Prentice-Hall of India Private Limited, *New Delhi*
Prentice-Hall of Japan, Inc., *Tokyo*
Simon & Schuster Asia Pte. Ltd., *Singapore*
Editora Prentice-Hall do Brasil, Ltda., *Rio de Janeiro*

Acknowledgments appear on p. 347, which constitutes
a continuation of the copyright page.

To Barbara Koch Rader

CONTENTS

vii

PART III
The Ascendancy of Organized Sports, 1890-1950

PART IV
The Age of Televised Sports, 1950-Present

PREFACE

Although revising a successful book can entail the risk of robbing the original of its strengths, the case for a new edition of *American Sports* is compelling. Not only did the book's content need updating, but more importantly, it needed to reflect the proliferation of scholarship in sports history. In the first edition (published in 1983) I warned the reader that "vast gaps exist in our knowledge of the history of American sport." Since then, I am happy to report, astonishing progress has been made in closing the knowledge lacuna. This edition, I hope, reflects the fruits of this new scholarship.

As in the first edition, I have attempted to explain how and why the informal games of the colonial Americans evolved into the familiar sports of today. On one level, the task has required an examination of the fundamental changes in the organization, rules, management, finances, and ethos of the games. On another level, it has entailed an examination of the social, cultural, and economic circumstances that have shaped American sports history.

American Sports presents one way (certainly not the only way) of generalizing about the transformation of American folk games into modern sports. The central theme, to state it simply, is that American sports passed through four principal stages: The Age of Folk Games, The Rise of Organized Sports, The Ascendancy of Organized Sports, and The Age of Televised Sports. Such a division into eras is not hard and fast. Baseball, for instance, became a full-fledged spectator sport well before 1890 while tennis did not achieve this position until the 1970s. Even today the remnants of folk games can be found in the play of children. Each stage was evolutionary rather than discrete, each enveloped and expanded upon the preceding one. Thus, the beginning of one age closely resembled the end of the preceding stage.

Another caveat is in order. While I acknowledge the significance and the interconnections between a wide variety of leisure activities and what we commonly call sports, I have mainly limited my treatment to human physical contests that in due time enjoyed large audiences, were governed by rules enforced by bureaucracies, and involved high degrees of specialization. Some readers will be disappointed to find almost no discussion of their favorite sport; fishing, hunting, bridge, and chess have been excluded entirely. Although horse and auto racing attract more live fans today than do baseball, football, and basketball, I have dealt with them only when they helped to elucidate the book's larger theme. I trust that such strictures have kept the book from becoming inordinately long while permitting me to elaborate the main points more fully than would otherwise be possible.

ACKNOWLEDGMENTS

My debts to various persons for this revision are almost as weighty as for the first edition. They must include nearly all of the members of the North American Society for Sport History, a group that warmly welcomed a complete stranger into their midst some ten years ago. For fear that I will overlook someone who made a valuable suggestion or directed me to an important source, I hope they will understand why I do not attempt to list all of them here. Nonetheless, I would be remiss if I did not acknowledge by name Melvin L. Adelman, William J. Baker, William H. Beezley, Janice A. Beran, Michael Ebner, Larry Gerlach, Elliot J. Gorn, Stephen H. Hardy, Joan S. Hult, J. Thomas Jable, Roger Kirby, Timothy Mahoney, Lawrence J. Malley, Patrick Miller, Mary L. Remley, Steven A. Riess, Randy Roberts, Ronald A. Smith, Nancy L. Struna, Jules Tygeil, David Wiggins, and Kenneth Winkle. I am especially indebted to Peter Maslowski for reading critically the entire book. More than any other person, my wife, Barbara, aided in the formation of many of the ideas that have found their way into this book. For that and for much more, I remain profoundly grateful to her.

Benjamin G. Rader

1

THE FOLK GAMES
OF EARLY AMERICA, 1607–1800

Before dawn on Christmas Day 1621, William Bradford, governor of the Plymouth Colony, called all the able-bodied men to their work. To most of the colonists, Bradford's request came as no surprise. The Protestant group, later called Pilgrims, to which Bradford belonged did not celebrate Christmas. Christmas to them was a pagan holiday, a part of the Roman Catholic tradition, and thus not authorized by the Holy Scriptures. A few of the men who had recently arrived objected to Bradford's order. Their consciences, they informed the governor, forbade them to toil on the day of Christ's birth. Bradford briefly remonstrated with the newcomers, but because they were not yet familiar with the "true way" and there was much work to be done, Bradford excused them. He would try to convince them later. He quickly departed with a group of the original settlers and took up the work at hand.

Bradford's group returned at noon. To the governor's astonishment, the newcomers were shouting, laughing, and running about the single street of Plymouth "openly at play." "Some were pitching the bar," Bradford later wrote, "and some [were playing] at stool-ball and such like sports."[1] Bradford knew well these common folk games of the seventeenth-century English villages. (Stool-ball was an antecedent of modern cricket.) But the doughty governor was angry. He seized the players' "implements" and ordered them off the street. As work on Christmas Day violated the consciences of the newcomers, Bradford

[1]William Bradford, *Of Plymouth Plantation, 1620–1647*, ed. by Samuel Eliot Morison (New York, 1952), p. 97.

1

said, so it was that sport on Christmas Day violated the conscience of the governor.

This incident, though of little importance in itself, illustrates several of the fundamental forces that shaped the pastimes of colonial Americans. Had they been able, most of the colonists would have preferred to continue playing the same games that they had left behind in England. Throughout the colonial era (1607–1775), the settlers' memories of English pastimes, when reinforced by streams of new immigrants, encouraged the retention of the Mother Country's games. Nonetheless, the Old World pastimes encountered opposition; William Bradford was only one of many religious zealots who frowned upon England's currently popular forms of recreation. Apart from religious suspicion, two other salient facts constricted efforts to replicate Old World pastimes. First, only a few English aristocrats came to the New World (and those who did remained only briefly). Until a native gentry emerged in the eighteenth century, efforts to ape the sports of the English upper classes came to naught. Second, nearly all settlers (except in New England) were dispersed over the countryside, which worked against the re-creation of village folk games in the New World.

The net effect of these considerations was the emergence in the colonies of a sporting world that, although broadly similar to that of England, differed in significant ways. During most of the seventeenth century, the colonists were unable to reproduce anything approaching the rich recreational life of the Mother Country. But in the eighteenth century, as the colonies acquired more population and wealth, both an upper class, or gentry style, and a common people's, or vernacular style, of recreation emerged. Each of these styles had special meanings and uses for their respective patrons. But because of New World circumstances neither style had precise counterparts in England.[2]

ENGLISH VILLAGE PASTIMES

The American colonists inherited from seventeenth-century England a dual heritage of pastimes. One flourished among the common people of the country villages while the other arose among the privileged upper classes. The nobility and the gentry took their cues from the monarchs. As patrons and sometimes as actual participants, the Tudor and Stuart monarchs were avid sportsmen. James I, the English king from 1603 to 1625, was an especially vigorous promoter of sport. He advised his son to banish "the mother of all vice"—idleness—by resorting frequently to running, wrestling, court tennis, and hunting. Following the example of the monarchs, certain sporting activities became an integral part of life in the upper strata. Hunting was an important privilege especially reserved

---

[2]No satisfactory monographic synthesis of colonial recreation exists, but I have found Nancy L. Struna's summary, "Sport and Society in Early America," in the *International Journal of the History of Sport* 5 (1988), 292–311, to be especially useful.

for the well-born; only they were allowed to hunt deer, for example. They employed both hounds and hawks to ferret out their prey. When the seventeenth century opened, horse racing was in its nascent stage, but it too was soon to become a major upper class sporting enterprise. Yet, initially the influence of English upper-class pastimes on the American colonists was negligible. Until the eighteenth century few colonists possessed enough wealth or leisure time to imitate the spare-time activities of the English nobility and gentry.[3]

English agricultural villages furnished an equally important recreational tradition. Most of the colonists were of the "middling sort" who emigrated from the small villages. Scattered two or three miles apart, the villages served as the homes for ordinary tradesmen, craftsmen, and farmers. The yeoman farmers often lived in towns and tilled the land around the villages. With a limited supply of arable land and an absence of the knowledge required to increase productivity, there was little incentive for hard work. Only the harvest season required intensive labor; then the entire village, including women, children, and artisans, might join the farmers in bringing in the crops. The villagers invariably concluded the harvest season with a festival of thanks accompanied by hearty eating, drinking, dancing, and folk games.

The legend of a "merrie ole England" rested on the communal life of these small villages. The festivities, which usually centered around the parish church, expressed and reinforced communal solidarity. The ecclesiastical calendar freed the common people to celebrate the major events in the life of Christ and commemorate numerous saints and martyrs. Yet the manner of celebration combined both Christian doctrine and pagan customs. Christianity had never completely erased the old folk customs that extended back into the mists of English history. For instance, May Day, perhaps the favorite holiday of the villages, originated as a rite of spring. Villagers believed that the return of spring depended upon the proper veneration of a phallic symbol. Accordingly, English young people trekked to the woods after midnight on May first, cut down a tree, and brought it back to the village. There they erected a maypole amid much ceremony, fastened long ribbons to the top of the pole, and danced about it merrily. Puritan critics saw the ancient rite as a form of idolatry and as a source of loose morals. "Of forty, three-score, or a hundred maids going to the wood over night," Phillip Stubbes, a Puritan and an archenemy of the traditional customs, reported, "there have scarcely the third part of them returned home again undefiled."[4]

[3]See esp. Joachim K. Ruhl, "Religion and Amusements in Sixteenth- and Seventeenth-Century England," *British Journal of Sports History*, 1 (1984), 125–65; Joseph Strutt, *The Sport and Pastimes of the People of England* (London, 1838); Dennis Brailsford, *Sport and Society: Elizabeth to Anne* (London, 1969); Christopher Hill, *Society and Puritanism in Pre-Revolutionary England* 2nd ed. (New York, 1967), Chap. 5; Robert W. Malcolmson, *Popular Recreations in English Society,1700–1850* (London, 1973); and E.P. Thompson, "Patrician Society, Plebeian Culture," *Journal of Social History*, 7 (Summer 1974), 382–405.

[4]Quoted in Winton U. Solberg, *Redeem the Time: The Puritan Sabbath in Early America* (Cambridge, MA, 1977), p. 48.

The villages celebrated many other holidays. One of the most popular holidays was the annual parish feast, often called a wake or revel. At the wakes the entire village gathered to feast, drink, dance, and engage in the rustic games of their forefathers. Wakes began on Sundays and sometimes lasted the entire week. Seasonal holidays, which were equally popular, included the Christmas season, Plough Monday, Shrove Tuesday, and the Easter season. Country fairs, which mingled business with pleasure, added to the long list of opportunities for the common people in the villages to engage in merrymaking. Combining Sundays, holy days, and seasonal holidays, the typical seventeenth-century rural village may have celebrated over one hundred days of the year, almost one holiday for each two days of work. No doubt the frequent celebrations relieved some of the grimness of seventeenth-century English life.

Each of the holidays featured a wide assortment of folk games, some of which were quasi-athletic in nature. The villagers played games of chance, games of skill, individual games, team games, games in which most of the residents participated, and games in which most were spectators. Many parishes enjoyed stool-ball, footraces, quoits (in which a contestant attempted to throw an iron ring over a peg), skittles, and ninepins (both forms of bowling). Unlike modern sports, the rules for these games sprang from unwritten customs and might differ sharply from one parish to the next. Boisterousness, gusto, and physical roughness often accompanied the playing of all the games. The villagers took special delight in violent games and spectacles, such as bear and bull baiting, cockfighting, football, hurling, and public executions. They relished contests of brute strength, especially wrestling and cudgeling. In cudgeling the contestant used a long, heavy stick with the intention of "breaking the head," or drawing blood from his opponent. The violent contest affirmed a masculine ethos of physical courage and individual prowess.

Football was perhaps the most exciting team game of the villagers. Unlike modern football (soccer), rugby, or American football, all of which are offsprings of the medieval game, the village sport was often an ad hoc affair with an unspecified number of players. Villagers played impromptu matches in the streets or nearby empty fields. The holidays might feature big matches between the residents of two villages. Depending upon local customs, the game might emphasize kicking, running, or throwing the ball. (The ball was usually an inflated animal bladder that was sometimes encased in leather.) Ostensibly, the object of the game was to move the ball across a previously defined goal line. Once a team had accomplished this feat, the game ended, though darkness also probably halted many matches.

Football vividly illustrates the contrasts between the folk games of the villagers and modern sports. Apart from the absence of referees, standardized rules, well-defined playing positions, and a set number of players on each side, the medieval game, by modern standards, constituted nothing less than a savage brawl. The players kicked, wrestled, struck with their fists, and sometimes bit their opponents. Damaged property, bloodied bodies, torn clothing, broken limbs, and sometimes death accompanied the contests. Between 1314 and 1617 English monarchs and local magistrates banned the game on at least thirty separate occasions, none of which successfully deterred the popularity of football. Apparently football offered the villagers an opportunity to channel their violent tendencies into a form of ritualized combat. It also seemed to promote village unity. "At the seasons of football and cockfighting" many parishes, according to a report in 1712, "reassume their national hatred of each other. My tenant in the country is verily persuaded, that the parish of the enemy had not one honest man in it."[5]

SEVENTEENTH CENTURY ENGLISH REFORMERS

During the late sixteenth and early seventeenth centuries, even before the first permanent English settlements had been established in North America, village recreation became a major source of conflict in England. On the one side were the defenders of traditional modes of life. The common people of the villages wanted to retain the ancient rituals, the old holidays, and the customary pastimes. They received additional support for the preservation of the old ways from the more moderate clergymen, some members of the nobility, and from the Stuart monarchs, James I and Charles I. On the other side were the reformers who sought to impose a new moral discipline upon England. The reformers came mostly from the ranks of the prospering merchants and smaller gentry. These groups benefited from the raging inflation that had been induced by the influx of precious metals from the Americas, but inflation had simultaneously created hordes of landless vagrants. Fearful of social disorder and concerned with the absence of godliness among the villagers, the upwardly mobile economic groups launched all-out campaigns in behalf of harder work, a strict Sabbath, and the suppression of traditional amusements.[6]

Religious conviction was also an important component of the reformers' mentality. Usually Puritans in religious persuasion, the reformers wanted to purify and reform the Church of England. They wanted to rid it entirely of Roman Catholic ritual, pageantry, symbols, and the older magical and sacramental modes of thought. To them, Henry VIII, who had made the break from Rome in the 1530s, and the monarchs succeeding him, had failed to carry the Protestant Reformation to its conclusion. The Puritans wanted to reform personal behavior. Glorifying God by the diligent pursuit of one's calling, or work, ought to be the ultimate, all-absorbing end of each person's earthly existence. Every Puritan should strive to become, in Ralph Barton Perry's apt metaphor, a "moral athlete."[7] Play should never be an end in itself. They viewed play as

[5]Quoted in Malcolmson, *Popular Recreations*, p. 83. See also Eric Dunning and Kenneth Sheard, *Barbarians, Gentlemen, and Players: A Sociological Study of the Development of Rugby Football* (Oxford, 1979), pp. 21–45.

[6]See Hill, *Society and Puritanism*, pp. 168, 208–10, and David Underdown, *Revel, Riot, and Rebellion: Politics and Culture in England, 1603–1660* (Oxford, 1985).

[7]Ralph Barton Perry, *Puritanism and Democracy* (New York, 1964), Chap. 10.

frivolous and unproductive, unless it was resorted to in order to refresh oneself for the execution of one's calling. Long after the main theological superstructure of Puritanism had collapsed, its heirs continued to experience agonizing guilt from engaging in playful activity. "I was not sent to this world to spend my days in sports, diversions, and pleasures," wrote John Adams in the middle of the eighteenth century. "I was born for business; for both activity and study."[8]

Sunday merriments especially enraged the reformers. Throughout England in the early years of the seventeenth century the local magistrates and churchmen of a reform temper mounted campaigns to suppress all recreation on the Sabbath. But they encountered angry opposition from the common people, high authorities in the Church of England, many of the gentry, and the king himself, all of whom wanted to preserve a more traditional Sabbath. In response to the assaults on Sunday recreation by the Puritans, King James I issued the Declaration (Book) of Sports in 1618. (Fifteen years later Charles I reissued the proclamation in an extended form.) The Book of Sports, which was to be read from every pulpit in England, gave royal sanction to specific village pastimes as well as the custom of holding parish feasts. The King asserted that "after the end of divine service our good people [should] not be disturbed . . . or discouraged from any lawful recreation, nor from having of May-games, Whitson Ales, and Morris-dances, and the setting up of May-poles and other sports." James rhetorically asked: "For when shall the common people have leave to exercise if not upon Sunday and holidays, seeing they must apply their labor and win their living in all working days?"[9] Those clergymen of a Puritan persuasion who declined to read the royal proclamation from the pulpit found themselves censured, suspended, or deprived of their positions.

The Puritan, middle-class majority in Parliament repeatedly attempted to rescind the Book of Sports, only to be blocked by the monarchs. Finally, in 1641, during the Puritan Revolution, Parliament imposed a rigid Sabbath upon all of England. Restoration of the monarchy and the established church in 1660 brought a partial return of Sunday merriments, the celebration of traditional festivals, and the playing of folk games. Yet the Puritan Revolution had bequeathed to England, Scotland, and the American colonies "the peculiar British Sunday," one devoid of much of the holiday spirit that had prevailed in the England of the Middle Ages and one that stood in sharp contrast to practices of the continental countries of Europe.

THE PROTESTANT REFORMERS IN THE NEW WORLD

As they had in England, the Protestant reformers who fled to the New World tried to legislate a strict observance of the Sabbath, abolish holy days, and restrict

---

[8]Quoted in Philip Greven, *The Protestant Temperament: Patterns of Child-Rearing, Religious Experience, and the Self in Early America* (New York, 1977), p. 253.
[9]Quoted in Malcolmson, *Popular Recreations*, p. 7.

or suppress the old village pastimes. The New England Puritans eliminated the celebration of all of the old holy days; for example, in 1640, Massachusetts imposed a fine upon anyone who fasted, feasted, or refused to work on Christmas Day. Beginning on Saturday night and ending at sundown on Sunday, the New England colonies permitted no labor, recreation, travel, "idle conversation," or even "unnecessary and unseasonable walking in the streets and fields." In 1656 a Captain Kemble of Boston had to sit in the stocks for two hours for "lewd and unseemly conduct." After having been at sea for three years the indiscreet captain had publicly kissed his wife on the Sabbath. Even as late as the 1730s, Joseph Bennett, an English traveler, observed that in Boston the Lord's Day was the "strictest kept that ever I yet saw anywhere."[10]

The Middle and Southern colonies enacted equally severe Sabbatarian laws. One of the first acts of the Virginia House of Burgesses in 1619 was to ban all Sunday amusements, although the absence of arduous religious convictions and the dispersal of settlers made such laws difficult to enforce there. Similar laws existed in early Maryland. In William Penn's Quaker colony of Pennsylvania, the assembly in 1682 banned all "rude and riotous sports." Likewise in New Netherlands, the Dutch in 1656 prohibited dancing, playing ball, cards, "tennis," cricket, and ninepins on Sunday morning. The Sabbatarian legislation of colonial America left an enduring legacy, one that was reinforced by periodic revivals over the next two centuries and continues to exist, albeit in a much more tolerant form, to this day.[11]

While those of a Puritan temperament obtained numerous laws, especially in the New England colonies, preventing the people from engaging in the traditional village forms of play, the doctrine of the calling did not logically lead to the prohibition of all recreation. On the contrary, diversions that clearly contributed to the fulfillment of one's calling were justified and approved. "We daily need some respite and diversion, without which we dull our powers; a little intermission sharpens 'em again," wrote one Puritan minister. Recreation, wrote another prominent divine, "must tend also to glorify God . . . the scope and end of all recreation is, that God may be honored in and by them."[12] New England parents also allowed their children to play with dolls and toys. When young boys had the leisure time and were orderly, authorities usually permitted them to play informal football, ball and bat, and stool-ball matches. Nonetheless, the conscientious Puritan always worried that recreation would become an end in itself. To the Puritans, play often stimulated the passions, leading to deceit, feasting, dancing, gambling, sexual immorality, and the neglect of one's calling.

---

[10]Quoted in John C. Miller, *The First Frontier Life in Colonial A: ierica* (New York, 1966), p. 87.

[11]See Solberg, *Redeem the Time*, and Thomas Jable, "Pennsylvania's Early Blue Laws: A Quaker Experiment in the Suppression of Sport and Amusement, 1682–1740," *Journal of Sport History*, 1 (1974), 107–21.

[12]Perry Miller and Thomas H. Johnson, eds., *The Puritans: A Sourcebook of Their Writings*, 2 vols. (New York, 1963), II, 392. For a lucid discussion of the Puritan position on recreation, see esp. Ruhl, "Religion and Amusements."

Although a large, vocal minority of the settlers to the New World came as Protestant reformers, the power that religion exercised over the lives of the colonists ebbed and flowed. Puritanism in New England and elsewhere declined in influence during the latter half of the seventeenth and first two decades of the eighteenth centuries. Then in the 1730s and 1740s, the Great Awakening, a religious revival of unprecedented proportions, swept through the colonies. If anything, the evangelicals, as the participants in the revivals were called, took a dimmer view of sports than had the first Puritan settlers. They required the absolute submission of the self—first to the parents, and then, through a searing conversion experience, to an omnipotent God.

After the spiritual rebirth, the evangelicals released their suppressed rage by launching crusades against the evils of the secular world and those who adhered to a more moderate religious persuasion. The evangelicals demanded absolute purity in the church and in individual behavior. They attacked unmercifully the customs, habits, and life styles of the nonevangelicals. For example, George Fox, the founder of the Society of the Friends (Quakers), traveled throughout England "in warning . . . and in testifying against their wakes or feasts, their May-games, sports, plays, and shows which trained up people to vanity and looseness, and led them from the fear of God, and the days they had set forth for holy-days were usually times wherein they most dishonored God by these things."[13] George Whitefield, a phenomenally successful evangelist during the Great Awakening, stopped in Annapolis, Maryland, in 1739, where he met the governor, local ministers, and several gentlemen. "Some of the company, I believe, thought I was too strict, and were very strenuous in defense of what they called innocent diversions; but when I told them everything was sinful which was not done with a single eye to God's glory, and that such entertainments not only discovered a levity of mind, but were contrary to the whole tenor of the Gospel of Christ, they seemed somewhat convinced. . . ."[14] Although the evangelicals rarely were able to enforce their strict piety in the communities in which they lived, they long remained opponents of sport in any form.

THE GAMES OF THE COMMON PEOPLE

The folk games of the Mother Country never prospered in the New World. Although New England settlers lived mostly in villages (as in England), the authorities savagely repressed efforts to retain Old World communal festivities. They did not permit the erection of Maypoles, the celebration of holy days, and frivolities on Sunday. Days of thanksgiving, election days, commencements, public punishments, and funerals did provide occasions for townspeople to gather at a single place, but the playing of folk games rarely if ever accompanied

[13]Quoted in Greven, *The Protestant Temperament*, p. 144.
[14]Ibid., p. 145. See also Rhys Isaac, *The Transformation of Virginia, 1740–1790* (Chapel Hill, NC, 1982).

NATIVE AMERICANS PLAYING LACROSSE, 1763
An artist depicted a game of lacrosse between the Ojibway and Sac tribes outside of Fort Michillinmackinac (Michigan) in 1763. When the troops came outside the fort to witness the contest, the Indian warriors rushed inside, massacred the inhabitants, and burned the fort to the ground. Played by at least 48 North American tribes, some European settlers took up the game in the nineteenth century.

these events. In the last quarter of the seventeenth century, training days, the days in which colonial militia units mustered, resembled in some ways the holidays of the English village parishes. Perhaps because the training days had no association with the customs of the Church of England, the troops sometimes engaged in feats of drinking, foot races, jumping, and shooting-at-the-mark. In Connecticut, according to a traveler in 1704, the winner of a target-shooting contest on training day won several yards of red ribbon and a "great applause, as even the winner of the Olympic games."[15]

Yet, in general, New Englanders dissociated games from the communal life of the towns. Without a doubt, at home and in other private places free from the censure of critical neighbors, individuals and small groups indulged in the pastimes of the Mother Country. The passage of nearly identical laws throughout the colonies against certain pastimes is an indication of efforts to preserve traditional pastimes. In the last two decades of the seventeenth century a noticeable decline in piety, the arrival of new immigrants, and the insistence of the British government on religious toleration all contributed to a more hospitable climate for recreation. Apart from a few reports of boys playing football and other games in the streets of Boston, there is only one extant record (in 1685) of an adult male football match in the colonial era. Not until after the American Revolution are there other indications of men participating in football. Late in the seventeenth century and throughout the eighteenth century, authorities usually tolerated the playing of games such as billiards, skittles, and shuttlecock by inhabitants in their homes but not in public places.[16]

[15]Sara Kemble Knight, *The Journal of Madam Knight* (Boston, 1971), p. 20. See also H. Telfer Mook, "Training Days in New England," *New England Quarterly,* 11 (1938), 687–97.

[16]See Nancy L. Struna, "Sport and Societal Values: Massachusetts Bay," *Quest* 27 (1977), 40; Albert Bushnell Hart, ed. *Commonwealth History of Massachusetts* 5 vols. (New York, 1927–1930), II, 280; W. Winterbotham, *An Historical...View of the American United States,* 4 vols. (London, 1976), II, 17; and William Bentley, *The Diary of William Bentley, D.D.,* 4 vols. (Gloucester, MA, 1962), I, 253–54.

Traditional pastimes fared only somewhat better in the South. Although the Southern Colonies did not suffer the liability of long, cold winters or (until the 1740s) strong religious hostility toward the old pastimes, the pattern of village settlement never gained a foothold there. Encouraged by the availability of land, they tended to settle along the Atlantic Coast and up the navigable rivers. Instead of residing in towns, they lived on the land that they farmed. Such a dispersal of population encouraged social isolation and extreme individualism. Because of the sheer distance between settlers, the Church of England (or Anglican Church), the established church of the region, could not recreate the old English parish. Thus observance of the ecclesiastical calendar, along with the timeless rituals, vanished from southern churches. Nor did the middle colonies copy the New England or Old World pattern of settlement; population dispersal, along with the predominance of the Quakers in Pennsylvania, discouraged communal celebrations there as well.

Nevertheless, as conditions stabilized and settlement became denser in the eighteenth century, the common people either developed their own style of recreation or tried to replicate Old World customs. Farmers in both the southern and middle colonies held harvest festivals; annual county fairs were popular. The Hanover County Fair in Virginia, established in 1737, included a great feast accompanied by the music of drums, trumpets, and oboes. The fair sponsored contests with a wide variety of prizes: five pounds for a horse race, a cudgeling match for a hat, a fiddling contest for a violin, a quire of ballads to be sung for, a wrestling match for a pair of silver buckles, and a "pair of handsome silk stockings . . . [to] be given to the handsomest young country maid that appears in the field."[17] Horse races sponsored by the great planters also attracted large numbers of the common people as spectators and wagerers.

Vernacular recreation flowered most successfully in the ubiquitous taverns or inns. Scattered a few miles apart throughout the colonies, the taverns provided multiple services. To travelers, they furnished food, drink, and sleeping quarters. Merchants, artisans, and common workingmen gathered at the taverns to discuss topics of mutual interest and to escape daily cares. Convivial drinking was an especially popular form of release. Even Puritan clergymen who assailed drunkenness rarely objected to moderate drinking. Boston itself had 177 innkeepers and retailers of liquor in 1737, roughly one dealer for every twenty-five adult males. "In most country towns," John Adams reported of New England in 1761, "you will find almost every other house with a sign of entertainment before it. . . . If you sit the evening, you will find the house full of people drinking drams, flip, toddy, carousing, swearing."[18] Yet rarely did the imbibers become roaring drunk; they usually consumed small quantities of mild sedatives such as beer, ale, or grog.

[17]Quoted in Edmund S. Morgan, *Virginians at Home: Family Life in the Eighteenth Century* (New York, 1952), p. 88. For colonial fairs elsewhere see Harry B. Weiss and Grace M. Weiss, *Early Sports and Pastimes in New Jersey* (Trenton, NJ, 1960), pp. 10–13.

[18]John Adams, *The Works of John Adams*, 5 vols. (Boston, 1840), II, 125–26.

Although nearly all the colonies had specific laws prohibiting "inn games," tavern patrons frequently combined games and wagering with drink and lively conversation. Taverns have "become the common . . . rendezvous of the very dregs of the people," complained a Virginia clergyman in 1751, "where not only time and money are vainly and unprofitably squandered away, but (what is yet worse) where prohibited and unlawful games, sports, and pastimes are used, followed and practiced, almost without intermission, namely cards, dice, horse-racing, and cock-fighting, together with vices and enormities of every other kind."[19] The clergyman might have added animal baiting and skittles (a form of bowling) as among the more popular tavern amusements.

Of the major colonial towns only New York had a recreational life approximating that of the Mother Country's London or Bristol. (Colonial cities were quite small; the first systematic population count, the Census of 1790, revealed that in the nation only five cities had a population of 10,000 or more.) With a far larger non-English population and without the harsh religious restraints of Boston and Philadelphia, New York was the most cosmopolitan of colonial towns. Prior to 1664, when the English acquired New York, the Dutch had bowled, held boat races, and played *kolven*, which some scholars translate as "golf." Apparently *kolven* was still being played a century later, for in 1766 James Rivington advertised for sale "gouff clubs," as well as shuttlecocks, cricket balls, and racquets. Although the Dutch governor prohibited horse racing within the city limits in 1657, New York's first English governor in 1664 established the first organized horse races at the Newmarket Course on Hempstead Plains, Long Island. Periodically thereafter horse racing generated excitement; apparently its success or failure depended upon the enthusiasm and patronage of the royal governor and his entourage.

SKITTLES OUTSIDE A COLONIAL TAVERN
Skittles was a folk game initially played out-of-doors, usually next to the ubiquitous colonial taverns. Modern ten-pin bowling had its origins in skittles and similar games.

[19]Quoted in Morgan, *Virginians at Home*, p. 87. See also Ruth E. Painter, "Tavern Amusements in Eighteenth Century America," *The Leisure Class in America*, ed. by Leon Stein (New York, 1975).

The Dutch seem to have been responsible for introducing the unique blood sport of "gander pulling" to the colonies. In this contest the neck of a goose would be liberally greased and the hapless animal would be hung by its feet from a rope stretched between two trees or tied to a tree limb. Sometimes the goose was hung over a stream and the contestant would, while passing by on a boat, try to jerk the goose's head off. If he failed, a dunking followed. At other times a horseman would attempt the same feat while riding at full gallop. As a prize the winner got the goose. Varieties of gander pulling, which was to become popular in frontier regions, spread southward to Georgia and continued into the nineteenth century.[20]

Although the eighteenth century witnessed the establishment of rudimentary forms of vernacular recreation, it fell far short of being "merrie old England" reproduced. Population dispersal and religious antipathy slowed the potential growth of vernacular pastimes. The Great Awakening (the religious revivals of the 1730s and 1740s) had far-reaching consequences for all the colonies, even in the traditionally freer South. In 1774, a Virginia "gentleman" explained to Philip Fithian the effects of the growing evangelical temperament on recreation. "The Anabaptists [an evangelical group] in Louden County are growing very numerous and seem to be growing in afluence [sic]; . . . quite destroying pleasure in the country; for they encourage ardent pray'r; strong and constant faith, & the entire banishment of gaming, dancing & Sabbath-day diversions."[21] A substantial growth in the pastimes of the common people awaited the vast social changes of the nineteenth century.

PASTIMES OF THE GENTRY

In the eighteenth century a separate world of leisure evolved among the emerging colonial gentry. Given the absence of a legal aristocracy in the colonies, wealth was the main requirement for those claiming to be "gentlemen." By the opening years of the eighteenth century two groups possessed the wealth requisite for gentry status: the prosperous merchants in the larger cities and the large planters in the Southern Tidewater Region. The city merchants built lavish homes, retained servants, entertained generously, and often became part of the entourage of the royal governor. The planters built splendid mansions that often included special rooms for dancing and billiard-playing; they ate with silver decorated with the family's coat of arms and managed their estates with the confidence of Oriental potentates. Most of the gentry were members of the Church of England: They worried little about the fate of their souls and were supremely confident

[20]For gander-pulling and its early history see John Durant and Otto Bettmann, *Pictorial History of American Sports: Colonial Times to the Present* (Cranbury, NJ, 1965), p. 7, and Jennie Holliman, *American Sports, 1785–1835* (Durham, NC, 1931), pp. 146–47.

[21]Hunter Dickinson Farish, ed., *Journal & Letters of Philip Vickers Fithian, 1773–1774* (Williamsburg, VA, 1943), p. 96.

that God would award them salvation just as he had rewarded them with material abundance.[22]

The gentry dominated all aspects of public life in their respective colonies. They assumed an inherent inequality among men, believing that some were destined to govern while others were foreordained to carry out the meaner tasks required by society. In both England and the colonies, nearly all social groups accepted the principle that "inferiors" ought to defer socially and politically to their "superiors." Certain pastimes identified one as having the leisure time and wealth for gentry status. Colonial merchants usually preferred formal dinners, dancing, and card playing to physical contests. On the other hand, southern planters not only entertained each other extravagantly, they enjoyed horse racing, cockfighting, gambling, and hunting. The case of James Bullocke, a common tailor, provides striking evidence of the gentry's social sensitivity. In 1674 Bullocke scandalized the gentry of York County, Virginia, by presuming to enter his horse in a race for 2,000 pounds of tobacco against a horse owned by a "gentleman," Dr. Matthew Slader. For such a presumption the county court fined the tailor 200 pounds of tobacco and asserted that horse racing was "a sport for gentlemen only."[23]

The experiences of William Byrd II (1674–1744), a prominent Virginia planter, provide insight into the leisure life of the southern gentry. William Byrd the elder had established the family's wealth by a good marriage, land speculation, political connections, a lucrative trade in guns and rum with the Indians, and tobacco farming in which black slaves furnished the labor. He, like other wealthy planters, thought his son should be given every opportunity to acquire the polish and culture of an English gentleman. Thus he sent William the younger to England where he attended the Felsted Grammar School in Essex and the Middle Temple in London. In due course his son was admitted to the bar. Apart from acquiring the tastes and manners of a young English gentleman, the younger Byrd also learned something of business and trade while in Europe. When he inherited his father's vast estate in 1705 at the age of thirty, he was already a man of distinction. He had served in Virginia's House of Burgesses and represented the colony as its agent in London.

Byrd exemplified the most refined qualities of the southern gentry. He rebuilt the family mansion at Westover, furnished it with the finest Georgian furniture, and constructed an extensive formal garden that fronted the James River. He collected the second largest library in the American colonies, read both Greek and Latin, wrote an urbane account of his expedition to survey the

---

[22]See C. Robert Barnett, "Recreational Patterns of the Colonial Virginia Aristocrat," *Journal of the West Virginia Historical Association*, 2 (1978), 1–11; Jane Carson, *Colonial Virginians at Play* (Charlottesville, VA, 1965); Greven, *The Protestant Temperament*; and Louis B. Wright, *The First Gentlemen of Virginia: Intellectual Qualities of the Early Colonial Ruling Class* (San Marino, CA, 1940).

[23]Quoted in T. H. Breen, "Horses and Gentlemen: The Cultural Significance of Gambling Among the Gentry in Virginia," *William and Mary Quarterly*, 34 (1977), 250.

boundary between Virginia and North Carolina, and dabbled enough in science to be admitted to the Royal Society in England. Like most of his fellow planters, Byrd worried much less about religious matters than the evangelicals, but he always attended church services and said his prayers regularly.

Byrd participated enthusiastically in all the pastimes common to the English gentry.[24] One of his favorites was billiards. He played with fellow planters, his wife, and his son. He also loved to try his hand at bowls. In 1721 he constructed his own green at his Westover plantation. Every summer for twenty years guests spent pleasant afternoons with Byrd, attempting to roll the imperfectly balanced balls—bowls—as near the "jack" as possible. On rare occasions Byrd played ninepins or skittles. However, skittles was usually played only by the lower classes in alleyways or taverns.

Before Byrd had laid out a bowling green, he often played cricket. According to his diary, in the early spring of 1710 he played regularly with neighboring planters on both sides of the James River. The version of cricket played by Byrd and his friends was quite different from the modern game. The wicket was simply two posts about a foot high and a foot apart; the space between was called the "popping hole." The striker ran to the popping hole and tried to hit the ball before the wicket keeper rolled the ball into the hole. In the colonial game as well as the English game of that time, any number of persons could play, and rules of play were passed on orally.

While some of the southern gentry had an interest in physical contests like billiards, bowls, and cricket, the gentry's involvement in gambling, cockfighting, and horse racing had a more profound impact upon the future of American sports. Wherever a few of the great planters gathered, someone always produced a deck of cards, a backgammon board, or a pair of dice. Indeed, these men occasionally risked large sums of money and tobacco—sometimes a year's earnings or more—on almost any proposition that involved an element of chance. While William Byrd II wagered only modest amounts, his intemperate son was an inveterate gambler. As a consequence of his gambling, William Byrd III eventually bankrupted the family estate and committed suicide.

Above all, the gentry had a passion for horse racing. Until the mid-eighteenth century, the quarterhorse race, a sprint of two horses over a quarter-mile dirt track, excited the most interest. A race might result from either a regularly scheduled contest on a Saturday afternoon on an established track or an impromptu challenge run on a country road or in an open field. Each contestant backed his horse with a wager and might make side bets with spectators. Likewise spectators often bet with each other on the outcome.

In the last half of the eighteenth century, the gentry turned from the native quarterhorse to English thoroughbred racing. Thoroughbred racing tested "bottom," that is speed over a mile or several miles rather than a quarter mile. But in contrast to the English, the colonial gentry apparently encouraged thor-

[24]See Louis B. Wright and Marion Tinling, eds., *The Secret Diary of William Byrd of Westover, 1709–1712* (Richmond, VA, 1941).

oughbred racing as a public spectacle. In England, the straight-a-way courses permitted exciting perspectives only in the vicinity of the finishing line; only the upper strata attended the races. But the colonial gentry raced their horses on mile-long circular tracks, thereby permitting a good view to all the spectators. Men of all ranks attended their races. The gentry also formed jockey clubs in Virginia, Maryland, and South Carolina. Thoroughbred racing was the first organized sport in the colonies.[25]

The gentry's passion for games and gambling held wider meaning for southern society. First, it nurtured a body of social conventions that set the gentry apart from the more boisterous games of the common people. Although the great planters extolled reckless courage and physical prowess, in the eighteenth century they replaced unregulated brawling with genteel forms of boxing or the potentially deadly duel. Properly fought duels embodied cool restraint rather than the uninhibited rough-and-tumble fighting of the common people. Such conventions not only reinforced gentry values but served as behavioral guides for latter-day sporting elites. Second, by promoting great public displays, such as horse racing, the planters helped convince subordinate groups that gentry life was something to be esteemed. For the onlookers, which often included both the common white people and the slaves, horse racing among the gentry was a form of high social drama. And by conceding the superiority of gentry culture, the common people were more likely to acquiesce to the gentry's control of the political and economic life of the colonies.[26]

REPUBLICANISM AND RECREATION

The republican ideology that flowed from the Revolutionary Era (roughly from 1774 to 1789) reinforced traditional suspicions toward the pastimes of the Old World. According to republican ideology, a republic—a political system without a monarchy and with sovereignty residing with the people—could not be founded upon the idle amusements of the decadent monarchies of Europe. For a republic to survive, the citizens had to be especially virtuous. They had to abstain from luxury, practice frugality, and avoid dissipation. The First Continental Congress, meeting in 1774 when war with the Mother Country loomed on the horizon, resolved that the colonies "discountenance and discourage every species of extravagance and dissipation, especially all horse-racing, and all kinds of gaming, cock fighting, exhibition of shows, plays, and other expensive diversions and amusements."[27] Wherever they could, the Sons of Liberty, an extralegal

[25]See Carson, *Virginians at Play,* pp. 105–32.

[26]Nancy L. Struna, "The Formalizing of Sport and the Formation of an Elite: The Chesapeake Gentry, 1650–1720s," *Journal of Sport History,* 13 (Winter 1986), 212–34, and Breen, "Horses and Gentlemen."

[27]Henry Steele Commager, ed. *Documents of American History,* 2 vols. (Englewood Cliffs, NJ, 1973), I, 86. For republican ideology, see esp. Gordon S. Wood, *The Creation of the American Republic, 1776–1787* (Chapel Hill, NC, 1969).

citizens organization, attempted to impose such strictures on the population for the duration of the Revolution. During the Revolution, all of the states likewise adopted strict sumptuary legislation designed to curtail personal extravagance and luxury. As Samuel Adams put it, each state ought to strive to become a "Christian Sparta."

After the war, Thomas Jefferson, republicanism's leading champion, blamed the English gentry for the tendency of young American "gentlemen" to gamble, drink excessively, patronize prostitutes, and engage in riotous sports. If the young American "goes to England," Jefferson wrote, "he learns drinking, horse racing, and boxing." In addition, "he is led, by the strongest of human passions, into a spirit of female intrigue . . . or a passion for whores, destructive of his health, and in both cases learns to consider fidelity to the marriage bed as an ungentlemanly practice."[28] In this letter Jefferson aptly spelled out a fundamental republican fear, namely that the indulgences of the European upper classes threatened to spread like a cancer, destroying in the new nation the virtue and simplicity essential to the republic's existence. Nothing haunted the imaginations of the republicans more than an idle, pleasure-loving aristocracy. In the nineteenth century, when the republicanism of the revolutionary era eventually lost much of its crusading zeal and took on new meanings, it continued to act as a restraint upon uninhibited behavior.

As provincial outposts of the British Empire, the colonial pastimes were the result of the interaction between the customs that the people brought with them and New World circumstances. The gentry, especially the southern gentry, were able to copy to some degree the leisure activities of the English upper classes. On the other hand, common people in the colonies had to sacrifice their heritage of village games. The dispersion of the settlers, the need for hard work, and the religious sentiments of many of the settlers made it impossible for them to transplant intact the English folk games. Neither did the Native Americans (Indians) nor the imported African slaves greatly affect the pastimes of the English settlers. The English colonists, unlike the Spanish and the French in the New World, assimilated little of the Native American culture. Because of having endured the severe shock of forced dislocation and the institution of slavery, the black influence on recreation of the English colonists was also minimal.

---

[28]Quoted in Henry Steele Commager, ed., *Living Ideas in America*, new ed. (New York, 1964), pp. 555–56.

2

THE RISE
OF
ORGANIZED SPORTS, 1800–1890

Baseball excitement in the greater New York City area reached a fever pitch in 1858 when an all-star Brooklyn team met the New York all-stars for a two best games out of three championship series. After lengthy negotiations, the teams selected the Fashion Race Course (a horseracing track with a stone grandstand) on Long Island as the site of the series. Despite a fifty-cent admission charge, fans came to the first game in droves; 1,500 of them crowded into carriages, omnibusses, and the special trains of the Flushing Railroad. According to a press report, the spectators included "a galaxy of youth and beauty in female form, who . . . nerved the players to their task."[1] New York responded by taking the first game, 22–18; in the second game Brooklyn evened the series, 29–8; but the New Yorkers captured the championship in the third contest, 29–18.

Only two decades earlier, one would have witnessed a quite different kind of ball game. Then, a group of boys might gather for an impromptu contest on a Saturday afternoon on an empty city lot or local cow pasture. The boys usually made the ball on the spot; one of the youngsters might offer a woolen sock to be unravelled and wound around a bullet or a cork. No one worried about the number of bases or the distances between them. There was no umpire; the objective of the pitcher was to throw a ball so that it could be hit by the batter. None but the players watched the contest, the results were rarely known outside of that circle, and no one bothered to keep any records for posterity.

[1]Quoted in Harold Seymour, *Baseball*, 2 vols (New York, 1960, 1971), I, 25.

The contrast between these two baseball games reflected a remarkable transformation in American sports. During the middle decades of the nineteenth century, informal games began to give way to highly organized forms of sports. The modern sports included formal organizations, written rules, competitions that frequently extended beyond local areas, higher levels of athletic specialization, a sharper division between spectators and players, the attention of the media, and the careful preservation of records.[2] By 1890, organized sports had grown prolifically. Clubs devoted to sports existed in towns both small and large, professional baseball teams captivated millions, and John L. Sullivan had become the nation's first athletic hero.

Great changes in nineteenth-century American life spawned the growth and modernization of sports. They included revolutions in communication and transportation, rising incomes, growing amounts of leisure time, and the rapid growth of cities. Simultaneously, radical changes in the workplace and in society at large undercut traditional sources of excitement, job satisfactions, and senses of belonging. The urban elite and the working class (both white collar and blue collar) often sought to satisfy these yearnings by preserving older, or creating entirely new, leisure activities. Sports became an integral part of a new universe of urban leisure. On the other hand, the Victorians, an assortment of industrious laborers, merchants, businessmen, and manufacturers, who were often of an evangelical Protestant religious temperament, frowned on all "idle" amusements, including sport when engaged in for its own sake or when associated with uninhibited display, drinking, and gambling.

By the end of the nineteenth century, these groups were no longer so singularly important to sport history. By then, organized sport was becoming firmly entrenched in the national culture. Even proper Victorians had begun to embrace certain types of sport; under wholesome auspices, they asserted, sports could relieve anxieties arising from overwork, discourage impulsive behavior, and inculcate such traits as leadership and cooperation. Also by the 1890s, many Americans, regardless of their incomes, occupations, or social class, spent their leisure time in the selection and purchase of amusements. They bought tickets to professional baseball games, prize fights, and intercollegiate football games. For them, sports then became principally a matter of personal consumption.

CONQUERING DISTANCE AND TIME

A population dispersed over enormous distances was perhaps the single greatest obstacle to the growth of American sports. During the nineteenth century the people continued to spread out over the North American continent. During the

---

[2]Modernization theory informs Allen Guttmann's global work, *From Ritual to Record: The Nature of Modern Sports* (New York, 1978), and his treatment of the rise of sports in the United States in *A Whole New Ball Game: An Interpretation of American Sports* (Chapel Hill, 1988). Melvin L. Adelman's *A Sporting Time: New York City and the Rise of Modern Athletics, 1820–70* (Urbana, 1986) is a premier study of the application of modernization theory to a specific city.

same century, improvements in communication and transportation plus the growth of cities greatly aided in the solution to the problem of spatial separation.[3]

Although American sports had deep roots in villages and rural life, the cities provided the main home for the rise of organized sports. In the nineteenth century, cities grew both in sheer number and in size at a startling pace. In 1800, the Census recorded only 33 cities and towns having over 2,500 residents; a century later the figure leaped to 1,737. In 1800, only New York City had in excess of 50,000 residents, but by the end of the century some 83 cities had achieved these numbers.

City life facilitated the growth of sports in multiple ways. Not only could people gather easily for the playing and watching of contests, but news of sporting events could be conveyed far more quickly than in the countryside. Moreover, city life encouraged the substitution of modern sport for traditional amusements. These substitutes ranged from commercial spectacles in which people participated vicariously to the formation of voluntary associations or clubs by which urbanites could participate directly in games. Sports teams and athletic heroes became powerful urban symbols—they could serve as rallying points for all of a city's residents.

Transportation improvements also had a direct impact on sports. Technological breakthroughs came in great waves. First was the steamboat, which after 1815 began to prove its value on western rivers and lakes. By 1860 more than a thousand paddle-wheelers carried freight and passengers up and down the Mississippi River. For a time, as steamboat captains tried to demonstrate the superiority of their boats and of their personal skills, steamboat racing was a kind of sport, albeit a dangerous one since overheated steam engines frequently exploded, killing passengers and crewmen. Steamboats aided the growth of sports in other, more important ways; the steamers transported both horses and spectators to horse races. Steamboats carried early prize fight crowds to matches fought alongside rivers away from the vigilence of the local legal authorities. For example, in 1842, five steamers carried some 2,000 spectators to the New York Narrows to watch Yankee Sullivan subdue Tom Secor.

Railroads soon supplanted the steamers in importance. In 1830 travel from Detroit to New York took at least two weeks; by 1857, the trip required only an overnight train ride. By tying nearly every hamlet in the nation into a giant transportation grid, railroads sharply reduced the importance of space and time to the growth of sports. As early as 1838 Wade Hampton of Virginia used the railroad to transport race horses to Charleston; in 1842, the Long Island Railroad

[3]In addition to Adelman, *A Sporting Time*, see John R. Betts, "The Technological Revolution and the Rise of Sports, 1850–1900," *Mississippi Valley Historical Review*, 40 (1953), 231–56; John R. Betts, "Sporting Journalism in 19th Century America," *American Quarterly*, 5 (1953), 39–56; Francis G. Couvaras, *The Remaking of Pittsburgh: Class and Culture in an Industrializing City, 1877–1919* (Albany, 1984); Stephen Hardy, "The City and the Rise of American Sport: 1820–1920," *Exercise and Sport Science Review*, 9 (1981), 183–219; Stephen Hardy, *How Boston Played: Sport, Recreation, and Community, 1865–1915* (Boston, 1982); Steven A. Riess, *City Games: The Evolution of American Urban Society and the Rise of Sports*, (Urbana and Chicago, 1989); Dale A. Somers, *The Rise of Sports in New Orleans, 1850–1900* (Baton Rouge, LA, 1972).

reportedly carried some 30,000 passengers to the Fashion-Peytona horse race. The infant sport of baseball especially benefited from the railroads. In 1860, the Excelsior Club of Brooklyn toured upper New York State by rail, and, in 1866, a tournament in Rockford, Illinois, attracted clubs from Detroit, Milwaukee, Dubuque, and Chicago. Only a rapidly expanding railroad network made possible the founding of the National League of professional baseball in 1876, which included franchises in a tier of cities in the Northeast extending from New York to St. Louis. Major league baseball continued to use rail transport until the 1950s, when air travel supplanted it.

A series of transportation innovations within cities abetted the growth of sports. By the 1870s horse-drawn steetcars, steam railways, and cable cars had replaced horse-drawn omnibusses. Electric trolleys, which began to replace earlier forms of mass transit in the 1890s, sped through city streets at astonishing speeds of ten to twelve miles per hour! During the late nineteenth and the first half of the twentieth centuries rapid urban transit systems carried millions of spectators to sporting events. In the twentieth century, conquering space for the purposes of sports depended increasingly upon the automobile (which began to be used widely in the 1910s) and the airplane (which became important to sport in the 1950s).

Innovations in communications and a growing time-consciousness were also significant preconditions to the growth and modernization of sports. In the colonial era, reports of sporting events were usually restricted to word-of-mouth; thus the news of a contest spread slowly and rarely beyond a local area. The mass production of watches in the early nineteenth century and a greater awareness of clock time made it possible to schedule and advertise in advance the precise starting time of sporting events. The inventions in the nineteenth century of the telegraph and telephone, and the improvement of the printing press inaugurated a new age of communications. The telegraph and telephone made it possible to communicate sporting news instantaneously over long distances.

Communication improvements came in rapid succession. By 1853, only nine years after the stringing of the first experimental telegraph line, over 23,000 miles of line had been built. As early as 1867, Philadelphians, "some of them venerable in years," jammed telegraph and newspaper offices to learn if their beloved Athletics had crushed the Unions of Morrisania, New Jersey, in a baseball match. Within thirty years after its development in the 1870s, a telephone system extended from the Atlantic Coast to Chicago. Improvements in printing made equally rapid strides; by 1846 presses could print 20,000 sheets per hour, thereby making it possible to sell newspapers for a penny apiece. Daily newspapers suddenly came within the reach and purchasing power of ordinary people.

Two kinds of print media encouraged public interest in sports: the regular daily newspapers and the weekly specialized sheet devoted to covering all aspects of nineteenth-century leisure life. Throughout the century, specialized weeklies carried news of the theater, odd happenings, and sporting contests. John Stuart Skinner pioneered in sporting journalism with articles on the turf in the *American Farmer* (1819) and the *American Turf Register and Sport Magazine* (1829).

William T. Porter's *Spirit of the Times,* a weekly, which began publication in 1831, became the nation's premier sporting sheet; by 1856 it claimed to have 40,000 subscribers scattered throughout the nation. Unpaid, largely untutored authors sent in reports of sports, games, and curiosities. In the last half of the century, the New York *Clipper* (1853) and *The Sporting News* (1886) popularized baseball while the *National Police Gazette* (1945), which gaudily covered sports plus other forms of entertainment, became the widest-selling weekly in the nation. Most sporting periodicals appeared briefly and sporadically, but their sheer numbers increased from three in the 1840s to 48 in the 1890s. That these sheets devoted as much (or often more) attention to the theater than to sports was indicative of the close connections between various forms of nineteenth-century commercial leisure.

In part because of the widespread suspicion of the value of sport, the modern sports page found in the daily newspaper evolved slowly. As early as the 1830s papers reported occasionally the results of horse races and prize fights. When Fashion met Peytonia in an 1845 horse race, the *New York Herald* sent eight reporters to cover the event. As interest in sport increased sharply in the 1850s, daily newspapers provided additional coverage, but it was not until the 1880s that the daily press recognized the value of continuous sports reporting. By then, the major metropolitan dailies began to assign reporters exclusively to sports. In the 1880s and the 1890s, the great circulation wars between the dailies, especially in New York City, encouraged "yellow journalism," the sensational reporting of crimes and sports. Yet, most daily papers did not set aside a regular section for sports until the 1920s.

VICTORIAN CULTURE

Improvements in transportation and communication had helped to overcome the major obstacles of space and time to the rapid growth of nineteenth century sport. But in Victorian culture sportsmen confronted an equally, or perhaps even more, formidable challenge. Throughout most of the nineteenth century, the Victorians, who came mostly from the middle-income ranks, praised the values of hard work, thrift, religious duty, sexual control, sobriety, and punctuality.[4] Led by the evangelical clergy, the Victorians frequently launched crusades against drink, gambling, sexual promiscuity, and all forms of impulsive behavior. They associated these vices with the "dissolute aristocracy" from above (the urban wealthy, especially the parvenu) and the "unproductive rabble" from below (the working class).

The rapid erosion of older class restraints, pell-mell geographic mobility, the unregulated pursuit of material gain, and the profound transformation of the nation's economy fractured larger kinship groups, corroded links between generations, destroyed an identity with a special place, undermined traditional

[4]The literature relevant to Victorianism is immense, but one may begin with Daniel Walker Howe, ed. *Victorian America* (Philadelphia, 1976).

modes of work, and encouraged impersonal relationships between people. Contrary to the expectations of many, the unleashing of traditional social boundaries in the nineteenth century did not lead to orgies of self-destructive behavior or anarchy. Instead, a new social order emerged, anchored upon the traditional institutions of the family, church, and community, but one also based upon the formation of innumerable voluntary associations and the nurture of a new kind of moral discipline.

This new moral discipline, which can be described as Victorian, (or as "modern," because of its suitability for achieving success in the new economy), stemmed in part from the survival in the nineteenth century of an older ideology, the republican ideology of the revolutionary era. The relentless quest for wealth, sharp social cleavages, and ostentatiousness contradicted the republican vision of a nation of small, independent, self-restrained producers. In a short story published in the 1830s, Sarah Hale had one of her heroes experiment with the elegant leisure of a Saratoga resort; afterwards he concluded that "this trifling away of time when there is so much to be done, so many improvements necessary in our country, is inconsistent with that principle of being useful, which every republican ought to cherish."[5] As in the revolutionary era, republicans continued to urge abstention from luxury, hedonism, and extravagance.

The republican concern for self-control received an immense transfusion of energy and ardor from a reinvigorated evangelical Protestantism. While organized religion had suffered a temporary lull in the aftermath of the American Revolution, it rebounded with renewed vigor in the first half of the nineteenth century. Great revivals, sometimes collectively called the Second Great Awakening, swept the country at the beginning of the nineteenth century, the decades of the 1820s, 1830s, and 1840s, and again in 1857. Between 1800 and the Civil War, the number of evangelical churches grew twice as fast as the population. Since evangelical Protestants controlled most of the pulpits, voluntary societies, newspapers and magazines, and the public schoolrooms, their influence extended everywhere—into the small towns and the countryside, as well as the cities.

Evangelical Protestants abhorred impulsive behavior and championed self-restraint. Philip Schaff, a visiting theologian from Europe, explained that the ideal American "holds his passion in check; is the master of his sensual nature; obeys natural laws, not under pressure from without, but from inward impulse, cheerfully and joyfully." Since the evangelicals could no longer depend on class deference, an established church, nor the small, close-knit geographic community to insure social order, they frequently turned to the individual conscience. They tried to instill in each individual an internal set of values so that the person would no longer be left to his or her own volition. Ideally, each would be guided by an internal moral gyroscope through the bewildering changes that were transforming American society.

[5]Quoted in Daniel T. Rodgers, *The Work Ethic in Industrial America* (Chicago, 1978), p. 10.

Religious activism helped separate the "respectable" from the "disreputable" people. The revivals appealed most to "men on the make," to rising manufacturers, merchants, shopkeepers, skilled workingmen, and professional men. Such men sought to be known for their self-control, sobriety, and hard work. They equated work with godly virtue; they viewed idleness with horror and the idler with utter contempt. Worried by the impulsive behaviors of both the workingmen and the wealthiest Americans, as well as perhaps their own suppressed yearnings for uninhibited experience, they perceived impulsive behavior as the principal threat to social stability.

Adherents of the new moral discipline assigned special responsibilities to women. Increasingly relieved from the tasks of the household economy and assumed to be more delicate and sensitive than men, women ideally occupied a "separate women's sphere," a term that conjures up images of rigid social boundaries being drawn around the lives of female family members. Within that sphere, Victorian women were expected to cultivate compassion, gentleness, piety, and benevolence. Serving as models of proper behavior and acting in quiet ways, women were asked to exercise a large but unobtrusive influence over the community. They assumed the responsibility of nurturing the children and for restraining the behavior of men.[6]

THE VICTORIAN QUEST FOR "RATIONAL RECREATION"

Throughout the nineteenth century, those with a Victorian temperament had grave reservations about the playing and watching of sports. Apart from seeing sports as encouraging impulsive behavior, many saw it as a waste of valuable time. Some of the more religious Victorians were inclined to accept the ancient belief that the mortification of the flesh enhanced one's spirituality. Yet many Victorians did recognize the importance of a healthy body and leisure time properly used. Consequently, in the middle decades of the nineteenth century, a small group of clergymen, essayists, and journalists began to fashion an ideology of "rational recreation" that endorsed limited participation in certain sports while continuing to condemn the amusements of the wealthy and the working class.[7]

The Victorian ideals of rational recreation grew out of the Puritan tradition. As noted in Chapter 1, the Puritans and their evangelical Protestant heirs loathed idleness and considered sinful any activity that reduced the effectiveness

[6]See Linda K. Kerber, "Separate Spheres, Female Worlds, Woman's Place: The Rhetoric of Women's History," *Journal of American History*, 75 (1988), 9–39.

[7]Adelman, *A Sporting Time*, pp. 269–89, examines the ideology of sport developed by the New York press. See ibid., p. 362n, for citations of other works treating the Victorian quest for rational recreation. Also see Bruce Haley, *The Healthy Body in Victorian Culture* (Cambridge, MA, 1978); Patrick Bryant Miller, "Athletes in Academe: College Sports and American Culture, 1850–1920," unpub. Ph.D. diss., University of California, Berkeley, 1987, Chap. 1; James C. Whorton, *Crusaders for Fitness: The History of American Health Reformers* (Princeton, NJ, 1982); Harvey Green, *Fit For America: Health, Fitness, Sport, and American Society* (New York, 1986).

in executing one's calling. They approved only of play that was "recreational," that is, instrumental in aiding one or one's community to fulfill the more serious obligations of either secular or spiritual work. This conception of recreation led the Puritans to campaign against all forms of play that were not properly subordinated to higher ends.

The boundlessness of nineteenth-century society, especially the growth of cities, gave a new sense of urgency to efforts by Victorians to devise a morally defensible system of recreation—one that was "rational." In earlier times, work and leisure had often merged: cornhusking, for example, might consist of both work and play. But the new workplaces of the nineteenth century tended to segregate work and play. The use of spare time then became more discretionary, freeing the person to use leisure time as he or she saw fit. Entrepreneurs soon seized the opportunities provided by the new division of labor and leisure. They quickly filled the void by providing urban audiences with theaters, circuses, dance halls, saloons, and organized sports. Victorians universally condemned the new commercial amusements; they associated them with a loss of self-control, bold display, swearing, gambling, drinking, and sexual licentiousness.

Victorian reformers sought a variety of alternatives, most of which did not entail competitive sports. Some simply advised avoidance of the new amusements while others advocated vigorous physical exercises. For example, Frederick W. Sawyer, in *A Plea for Amusements*, (1847) proposed as substitutes for commercial amusements "athletic institutes" for gymnastic exercises that "would be established in all our towns and cities, for the free use of the people." We should "see to it," added Sawyer, "that we have enough healthy sources of recreation to empty the gambling rooms, the tippling shops, and the brothels."[8] Exercises had the added benefit of strengthening the body. Invidious comparisons between the allegedly robust physical fitness of Englishmen and frailty of urban Americans became a favorite refrain of the reformers. "I am satisfied that such a set of . . . stiff-jointed, soft-muscled, paste-complexioned youth as we [Americans] can boast in our Atlantic cities never before sprang from the loins of Anglo-Saxon lineage," declared the genteel physician, Oliver Wendell Holmes, Sr.[9] To the reformers, only vigorous physical exercise could counter the sedentary life of the city and help to deter intemperate behavior.

In the 1850s, physical robustness as a vital part of rational recreation received reinforcement from a tiny but growing muscular Christianity movement. Influenced by the English writers Thomas Hughes and Charles Kingsley, American physicians, clerics, and essayists, joined by many newspaper editors, launched a crusade to reverse the popular impression that physical vigor and spirituality were incompatible. The tireless American champion of muscular moralism, Thomas Wentworth Higginson, asked for a renaissance of the Greek ideal of a symmetrical life that gave equal

[8]Quoted in Hardy, *How Boston Played*, p. 50.
[9]Oliver Wendell Holmes, "The Autocrat at the Breakfast Table," *Atlantic Monthly*, 1 (1858), 881.

attention to both physical and spiritual growth. "Physical health," Higginson added, was "a necessary condition of all permanent success."[10] In linking success to a strenuous boyhood, Higginson introduced a major motif of advice-to-boys books after the Civil War.

While nearly all Victorian reformers endorsed physical exercises as consistent with spirituality and as an antidote to commercial amusements and frail bodies, they enjoyed little immediate success. An effort to introduce German gymnastics into New England schools in the 1820s and 1830s, for example, failed to take permanent roots. The advocacy of regular calisthenics for young women by such genteel reformers as Catherine Beecher in the antebellum era also won few converts but perhaps laid the groundwork for later acceptance. Most antebellum educators believed that the schools should be concerned solely with the intellectual and moral development of their charges, though the students themselves frequently engaged in informal sports. Only after the Civil War, in the 1870s and 1880s, did physical education in the schools and colleges achieve a few notable successes. In the same era, the fast-growing Young Men's Christian Association began to make gymnastics and other physical exercises a large part of its program.

NINETEENTH CENTURY WORKPLACES

Most Americans, whether in the countryside or in the cities, did not share the Victorian concern for rational recreation. In those parts of the nation relatively untouched by the great changes in the nineteenth century—the rural areas, along the advancing frontier, and much of the South—the playing of folk games continued much as in the past. The sportlike activities found in these regions usually sprang from daily work or common custom. Since fishing and hunting could be vital to survival, such contests as shooting-at-the-mark were especially popular. Prizes might include a jug of whiskey, a turkey, or a side of beef. Other kinds of quasi-athletic contests, such as throwing, running, jumping, rail-splitting, and wrestling often accompanied shooting matches. In the late eighteenth and early nineteenth centuries, "rough and tumble" fighting, a form of combat that might include kicking, biting, kneeing, hair-pulling, emasculation, and "gouging"—tearing an opponent's eye out of it socket—was popular along the Southern frontier.[11] Vestiges of these informal, individual, and sometimes violent folk games survived in the more isolated rural regions of the United States well into the twentieth century.

Likewise, Victorian attitudes failed to crush the sporting life of urban America. Large numbers from both the elite and the working class rejected Victorian strictures. Persons from either rank supported a "sporting fraternity,"

[10]Thomas Wentworth Higginson, "Saints and Their Bodies," ibid, 585-86.
[11]See Elliot J. Gorn, " 'Gouge and Bite, Pull Hair and Scratch:' The Social Significance of Fighting in the Southern Backcountry," *American Historical Review*, 90 (1985), 18–43.

an informal group of urban professional sportsmen who became instrumental as early as the 1840s in the promotion of such sporting spectacles as prize fighting, pedestrianism, blood sports, and horse racing. Gambling, drinking, and spectatorship usually accompanied these spectacles. During the 1850s, the artisans, the most skilled of the blue collar workers, and the clerks, those at the bottom of the white collar hierarchy, formed hundreds of baseball clubs. After the Civil War, the sport grew in popularity. Featuring both amateur and professional teams, baseball became the "National Game." Likewise, in the post-bellum era, members of the urban elite organized dozens of socially-exclusive athletic clubs that promoted track and field, tennis, and golf.

Fundamental changes in nineteenth century workplaces provided a basis for working-class support of sports. Even in the late colonial era, 20 to 30 percent of the urban population consisted of those who made their living from casual, often seasonal work. They performed such backbreaking chores as the loading and unloading of ships and wagons. In the nineteenth century, when the handicraft mode of producing goods gradually gave way to factory production, the size of the unskilled and semiskilled workforce increased markedly.[12]

At the beginning of the nineteenth century, nearly all goods—shoes, clothing, carriages, furniture, and hardware products, for example—were made in the small shops of independent artisans. Customers simply asked an artisan to fashion a pair of shoes or a chair according to their special wishes. Using skills passed down through many generations, the typical artisan was, in effect, simultaneously both a small manufacturer and a businessman. Completely responsible for the final product, artisans took fierce pride in the quality of their work.

The factory system did not suddenly or completely annihilate the skilled handicraft mode of production. As late as 1840, the majority of those artisans employed in the business trades, shoemaking, printing, furniture-making, carriage-making, metal-working, and brewing continued to work in small shops. But the long-term trend away from the small shop was unmistakable. Masters with foresight and capital enlarged their workforces, employed machinery, and broke down the work into simpler tasks. The resulting factory system required fewer skills of the artisans and a larger unskilled or semiskilled workforce. The roles of employer and employee became sharply segregated. Masters, journeymen, and apprentices no longer worked side-by-side nor were their relationships any longer governed by custom; the factory substituted rigid discipline for the casual work patterns of an earlier era. No longer did young apprentices or journeymen live in the household of the master craftsman; increasing numbers lived in boarding houses.

[12]On artisans, in addition to Couvaras, *The Remaking of Pittsburgh,* see especially, Paul Faler, "Cultural Aspects of the Industrial Revolution: Lynn, Massachusetts, Shoemakers and Industrial Morality, 1826–1860," *Labor History,* 15 (1974), 337–66; Susan Hirsch, *Roots of the American Working Class: The Industrializing Crafts in Newark, 1800–1860* (Philadelphia, 1978); Bruce Laurie, *Working People of Philadelphia, 1800–1850* (Philadelphia, 1980); Steven J. Ross, *Workers on the Edge: Work, Leisure, and Politics in Industrializing Cincinnati, 1788–1890* (New York, 1985); Sean Willentz, *Chants Democratic: New York City & the Rise of the American Working Class, 1788–1850* (New York, 1984).

The workplace of white collar workers, especially clerks, likewise under-went radical change. In the first quarter of the nineteenth century working as a clerk was in effect a training period for those sons of the elite who aspired to become business or professional men. Employed in thousands of small offices, they served as copyists of correspondence and business documents, bookkeep-ers, collectors of invoices and receipts, and in dozens of other roles. In these capacities clerks could learn about all aspects of a business and, with only two or three clerks per office, they had frequent and intense personal interactions with their employers.[13]

By midcentury, the system of apprenticeship-clerking had begun to falter. The rapid growth of the economy resulted in the expansion of the size of business and manufacturing concerns, and consequently, the need for thousands of additional clerks. To meet the demand, businesses recruited clerks from the ranks of educated classes in both the countryside and the city. At the same time business firms began to reorganize their offices; they subdivided the work of clerks. Rather than serving as jacks-of-all-trades, clerks were employed for spe-cific tasks such as copyist or bookkeeper. With little opportunity for advance-ment, clerking for the overwhelming majority of young men became a dead-end job. The division of labor into simpler tasks and the introduction of the typewriter in the 1880s and 1890s resulted in the replacement of most male clerks by female office workers.

The latter half of the nineteenth century also witnessed the spectacular growth of other salaried, white-collar occupations. By 1910, there were eight times as many clerks, professional men (such as accountants, lawyers, and engineers), salespersons, and lower management personnel in corporations as there had been in 1870. Although many of the new positions paid well, much of the work was sedentary, routine, and lacking a capacity to offer intrinsic satisfac-tion. Like the artisans who had become ordinary laborers earlier in the century, the new white collar workers found themselves increasingly dependent on others.

THE VICTORIAN COUNTERCULTURE

Changing experiences in the workplace, the home, and the community spawned the creation of a Victorian counterculture.[14] While substantial numbers of both blue collar and white collar workers accepted the Victorian values of their

[13]On clerks, see Margery W. Davies, *Woman's Place Is at the Typewriter: Office Work and Office Workers 1870–1930* (Philadelphia, 1982), esp. Chaps. 2 and 3; and Allan Stanley Horlick, *Country Boys and Merchant Princes: The Social Control of Young Men in New York* (Lewisburg, PA, 1975).

[14]In addition to the works cited in notes 12 and 13, see Elliot J. Gorn, *The Manly Art: Bare-Knuckle Prize Fighting in America* (Ithaca, 1986); Morse Pecham, "Victorian Countercul-ture," *Victorian Studies*, 18 (1975), 257–76; Ned Polsky, *Hustlers, Beats, and Others* (Chicago, 1967), Chap. 1.

employers, many others received them lukewarmly or rejected them completely. These workers responded to the new conditions by placing a higher value on play, gratification, gusto, and display than on hard work, self-control, and punctuality. Many of the workers sought to gain greater personal satisfaction, excitement, and a sense of belonging from their leisure activities rather than from their work or the morally uplifting associations of the Victorians. Their recreation often consisted of talking, drinking, gambling, and commercial spectacles, activities reminiscent of preindustrial, preurban patterns of life.

Bachelors, whether employed as clerks, artisans, or manual laborers, or whether owners of small businesses, were more likely to reject Victorian values than were married men. From both the countryside and Europe more men than women swarmed into the growing cities; consequently, all cities had a disproportionate number of unmarried, younger adult males. Nationwide, the percentage of the unwedded in the nineteenth century was much higher than today. At mid-century nearly 40 percent of the men between the ages of twenty-five and thirty-five were unmarried; after that date the percentage slowly declined. Bachelors, along with many married, working-class males, spent most of their leisure time with other males. Without close ties to wives or their families, many members of this "bachelor subculture" sought sensual gratification, friendship, and a sense of community in saloons, gambling halls, billiard rooms, cockpits, boxing rings, or the race track.

Massive waves of immigrants from Europe in the nineteenth and early twentieth centuries gave support to the Victorian counterculture. Each newly arrived ethnic group from the peasant societies of Europe (most notably the Irish, Italians, and East Europeans) brought with them attitudes toward time-thrift, self-control, and temperance at odds with Victorianism. The new ethnics, along with many old-stock workingmen, were slow to acquiesce to the regimen of the new economy; they tried to preserve the traditional holidays, preindustrial work habits, and "grog" privileges (the right to drink light alcoholic beverages during the workday). The Pennsylvania iron workers, for example, frequently took off from work to hunt, harvest, "frolic," or celebrate weddings, funerals, and Old World holidays. Manufacturers repeatedly complained of absenteeism and the lack of temperance among their employees. Astonishing rates of job turnovers (as much as 100 percent annually in some factories) also testified to worker resistance to the new industrial discipline.

Those of Irish origins were especially important to the sporting fraternity. A high percentage of bachelors, delayed marriages, rigorous norms of premarital chastity, and traditions of segregation of the sexes made all-male groups more important to Irish-Americans than to any other ethnic group. Whether married or unmarried, a male's status within the larger Irish community tended to rest on his membership and active participation in the life of the bachelor subculture. Thus many of the "bachelors" were actually married men, who spent nearly all their leisure time with other males. Gathering in saloons to drink, gossip, tell stories, exchange information, and engage in business or political transactions, adult bachelors conducted the rites of passage for countless

Irish youths. They promoted a gay, carefree life; they placed a high value on success in fighting, sports, physical prowess, and the political arena.[15]

Face-to-face associations revolving around billiard halls, volunteer fire departments, fraternal societies, labor unions, gambling halls, saloons, theaters, livery stables, and street gangs engendered a sense of group identity among the young workingmen, ethnic males, and bachelors (many were, of course, all three of these at once) who were the main supporters of the Victorian counterculture. A rich associative life aided these men in coping with the rigors of industrial discipline and the ravages of urban life.

No formal association exceeded the importance of the volunteer fire departments. As the need for fire protection grew in the nineteenth century, ethnics (especially the Irish), artisans, clerks, and petty shopkeepers formed hundreds of volunteer companies. When a fire call went out, the men instantly dropped their work (sometimes to the chagrin of their employers), donned brightly hued shirts, and rushed to beat competing companies to the blaze. In the fire companies, the lusty volunteers found all-male companionship, a sense of personal worth, an arena for the expression of manliness, and the excitement of team competition. A few lines from a swaggering song written by a Philadelphia fireman reflects the larger fraternal functions of the volunteer fire company:

> Then arouse ye gallant Rams,
> And by the Wecca stand,
> And show our friends and foes,
> That we're a sporting band. . . .
>
> Then come ye boys of pleasure,
> Wherever you may be,
> Come join the sporting Rams,
> The boys of fun and glee.[16]

The "boys of pleasure" also found "fun and glee" in drinking and gambling. In colonial times, gambling had been a popular pastime, especially among the Southern gentry, but to nineteenth century Victorians, gambling was a sin that led down the path to total degradation. Unleashing all restraints, the traveler, who began with such seemingly innocent diversions as checkers and whist, quickly passed on to wagering on horses and prize fights to end his days in "drunken debauches and murder."

Yet Victorian hostility failed to curb the growth of gambling. By 1840 almost any coffee house, billiard parlor, or saloon might harbor a gambling establishment. Many of the sporting spectacles arose from spirited arguments over the merits of a horse, a prize fighter, or a pedestrian. A wager and the scheduling of a contest then ensued. Spectators wagered on all spectacles, includ-

---

[15]See Richard Stivers, *A Hair of the Dog: Irish Drinking and American Stereotype* (University Park, PA, 1976), esp. Chaps. 5 and 6.

[16]Quoted in Laurie, *Working People*, pp. 60–61.

ing some of the earliest baseball matches. Few experiences equalled the intensity of wagering; for spectator, promoter, and athlete alike, winning a bet might be far more important than the thrill of winning the contest itself. In wagering, one risked not only money but one's self-esteem as well. By choosing to bet on a particular team or prize fighter, the bettor might be making a statement of ethnic or occupational pride. Furthermore, successful wagering offered an opportunity to display skills for men who increasingly found such opportunities denied in their workplaces.

Drinking was an equally important working-class activity. Unlike proper Victorians, many working class men prized drinking for its capacity to provide an escape from the trials of daily living and to promote fraternal goodwill. The focal point for drinking was the saloon, which grew faster in number than the population in the nineteenth century. Saloons varied in the richness of their decor and the wealth of their clientele; there, workingmen could communally enjoy upperclass comforts. By midcentury, the more elegant saloons had brilliantly lighted windows flanked by wicker doors that swung open easily for men of all ages. Inside a patron might see variegated lampshades, frescoed ceilings, a gilded bar with a glittering mirror behind it, and paintings of famous race horses, prize fighters, and voluptuous, scantily-clad women. At particular bars, men created informal cliques; they drank, told stories, argued, sang songs, and cemented friendships.

The saloon served as an ideal retreat for those workingmen who were interested in sports. An advertisement of William Clark summarized some of the social functions of the metropolitan saloon: "Ales, wines, liquors, segars, and refreshments. All the sporting news of the day to be learned here, where files of the *Clipper*, and other sporting papers are kept. Here also may be seen numberless portraits of English and American pugilists. . . . A room of other facilities

A WORKING CLASS SALOON
This working class western saloon, located in Abie, Nebraska, sports Fourth of July decorations. Notice the absence of women. Until well into the twentieth century, saloons served as a major rendezvous for the sporting fraternity.

are also at all times in readiness for giving lessons in sparring under the supervision of the proprietor. Drop in, and take a peep."[17] Saloonkeepers promoted a host of recreations: they arranged dog fights, rat-baitings, cock-fights, and prizefights. Pugilists and their backers almost invariably worked out of local saloons; prizefighters themselves often owned or managed bars. Saloons served as poolrooms; keepers posted the odds on horse races and, after mid-century, on baseball matches. In the latter half of the century, saloons sometimes had telegraph hookups so they could post the latest sporting results instantly.

By the 1850s, in New York City and other large cities, both workingmen and young slummers from the social elites might gather at special halls that featured a regular fare of cockfighting, dogfighting, rattings, and other forms of low entertainment. Of the several halls in New York, the best-known in the 1860s was Kit Burns's Sportsman Hall. Shaped as an amphitheatre, the hall could seat up to 400 spectators. Apart from watching and wagering on how long it would take a dog to kill a pit full of rats, the spectator might pay a quarter to see "Jack the Rat" decapitate a rat or a dime to witness him bite off the head of a mouse. Frederick Van Wyck, of the distinguished Knickerbocker family, suggested that attendance at such events was a "rite of passage" for certain youth of the upper social ranks. At Tommy Norris's livery stable, he reported seeing a ratting, a cockfight, a goatfight, and boxing match between two women who were nude above the waist. "Certainly for a lad of 17, such as I," reported Van Wyck, "a night with Tommy Norris and his attraction was quite a night."[18]

THE COUNTERCULTURE AND NINETEENTH-CENTURY SPORTING GROUPS

Some nineteenth-century sporting groups had closer ties with the Victorian counterculture than did others. For example, the life of the sporting fraternity, or "the fancy," existed entirely outside the confines of Victorian respectability. Although the sporting fraternity never constituted a formal organization, the word "fraternity" implied shared values, solidarity, and a literal brotherhood. In the promotion and viewing of sports as well as in associated activities such as drinking and gambling, the fraternity hoped to consumate the same intensely shared experiences and sense of belonging that existed ideally among blood brothers. As in a family, the fraternity developed its own set of special under-standings, its own argot, its own set of acceptable behaviors, and its own concept of honor.

The sporting fraternity tried to retain in an urban setting some of the spirit of traditional folk games. Like earlier folk games, the blood sports, prize fights, billiard matches, horse races, and pedestrian races of the fraternity

[17]Quoted in John Rickards Betts, *America's Sporting Heritage* (Reading, MA, 1974), p. 162. On the role of the saloon in working class life, see esp. Roy Rosenzweig, *Eight Hours For What We Will: Workers and Leisure in an Industrial City, 1870–1920* (New York, 1983).
[18]Quoted in Adelman, *A Sporting Time*, p. 242.

A RATTING PIT
The spectators of ratting normally wagered on how long it would take a dog to kill a pit full
of rats. Ratting, along with cockfighting, and bear- and bull-baiting, was an ancient blood
sport that survived within the Victorian counterculture of the nineteenth century.

attracted urbanites of all sorts. The spectacles often included uninhibited
expressions of emotions, drinking, and gambling. The spectators themselves
were an integral part of the spectacle; viewing and interacting with one another
supplemented the excitement of the contest itself. Yet unlike folk games, urban
spectacles arose almost entirely from the efforts of professional promoters
within the fraternity rather than from the community at large.

The sporting fraternity extended to both sides of the Atlantic. The English
contingent of the fraternity, having begun organized, commercial spectacles
earlier than did the Americans, exercised a large influence on the character of the
American spectacles. Americans conducted their horse races in strict accordance
with the rules at New Market, their prize fights by the London prize ring rules,
and copied the latest London modes of wagering on contests. England furnished
much of the sporting equipment for the new republic; many of the sporting
books, magazines, and prints came from England. All of the American sporting
newspapers gave extensive coverage to the latest sporting news from Great
Britain. By the 1820s a bevy of professional English (and Irish) athletes regularly
visited the United States to demonstrate their skills and compete for stakes; soon
American athletes began to frequent English shores for the same purpose.[19]

Most members of the wealthiest classes restricted their sports to socially
exclusive clubs that had little or no direct association with the counterculture.
However, a small number of the landed wealthy from both North and South as

[19]See Jennie Holliman, *American Sports, 1785–1835* (Durham, NC, 1931), pp. 5–10.

well as prosperous merchants tried to preserve in the nineteenth century the ethos of earlier gentry pastimes, especially field sports and horse racing. Although more cautious than their counterparts in England, a hedonistic fringe of younger men in the elite also sometimes engaged in sport slumming—participation in the low sports of the common people. In the latter half of the nineteenth century, upper class inhibitions further weakened. The urban parvenu then became especially conspicuous for their presence at and involvement in the commercial spectacles of the sporting fraternity.

The exact relationship between the ball-playing fraternity and the counterculture is more difficult to determine. In the 1850s, the young artisans, clerks, and small businessmen who founded the first ball clubs, repeatedly attempted to reassure concerned Victorians that their activities promoted proper behavior. As *Porter's Spirit of the Times* put it in 1857, the ball player "must be sober and temperate. Patience, fortitude, self-denial, order, obediance, and good-humor, with an unruffled temper, are indispensable.... Such a game ... teaches a love of order, discipline, and fair play."[20] No one could have developed a more satisfactory list of Victorian virtues.

Yet the players were young men. They frequently lived apart from family influences and were therefore more likely to indulge in the leisure activities of the counterculture. From its earliest history, retreating to saloons and drinking liquor after the games was frequent among the ball-playing fraternity. In 1858, *Porter's Spirit*, the same sporting sheet that a year earlier had identified baseball with Victorian values, noted that a marked feature of post-game celebrations was "the indulgence of a prurient taste for indecent anecdotes and songs—a taste only to be gratified at the expense of true dignity and self-respect."[21] After the Civil War, when the sport became more commercialized, wagering on ball games became commonplace. Circus-master P. T. Barnum went so far as to say that "Idleness, Base-Ball and Billiards" had caused the economic panic of 1873.[22] In the latter half of the nineteenth century, the professional game became an integral part of the larger world of commercial entertainment.

While proper Victorians generally avoided all active association with the counterculture, few nineteenth-century males could totally resist the occasional temptation to attend and even wager on a sporting event. "Without intending it by any means," apologized Philip Hone in his diary in 1835, " ... I found myself with Robert in the barouche [carriage], enveloped in clouds of dust ... on the road to the [pedestrian] race course, jostled by every description of vehicle conveying every description of people."[23] The treatment accorded sporting spectacles by the newspapers suggests that there were large numbers of

---

[20]*Porter's Spirit of the Times*, 2 (May 30, 1857), 19.

[21]Ibid, 5 (Oct. 9, 1858), 84.

[22]Quoted in Byran D. Palmer, *A Culture in Conflict: Skilled Workers and Industrial Capitalism in Hamilton, Ontario, 1860–1914* (Montreal, 1979), p. 26.

[23]Allan Nevins, ed., *The Diary of Philip Hone, 1828–1851*, 2 vols. (New York, 1927), I, 156–57.

vicarious sportsmen who never deigned to attend sporting events but nonethe-less assiduously followed the sporting scene. Newspapers often printed both detailed accounts of spectacles plus pious denunciations of their immorality. The typical Victorian apparently experienced the sporting world with ambiva-lent feelings, a secretly harbored awe and fascination mixed with publicly expressed horror and disgust.

3

SPORTING SPECTACLES IN THE ANTEBELLUM ERA

The 1840s and 1850s witnessed a remarkably sudden growth in American sports. In those decades, thousands of spectators gathered at tracks in virtually every state in the Union to watch pedestrian (foot) races; equal numbers thronged the nation's harbor, lake, and river banks to watch boat races. Although a championship prize fight (being illegal everywhere and hastily scheduled at unpredetermined sites) attracted at most two thousand spectators, literally tens of thousands more heard oral accounts or read about them in the newspapers. Prior to 1845, no record exists of an organized baseball club in the nation, but within fifteen years several hundred clubs had been formed, and over ten thousand boys and young men played in club matches.[1]

Two cultural groupings, each described by contemporaries as "fraternities," were of critical importance to the sporting "take-off" of the 1840s and 1850s. One was popularly known as the sporting fraternity and the other as the ball-playing fraternity. Members of the informal ball-playing fraternity organized voluntary associations, or clubs, for the playing of baseball or cricket. The baseball club members wrote and revised the rules of play, appointed officials, scheduled matches, and in 1858 formed a national association. The fraternity provided its membership with the direct excitement of playing ball games and with the indirect benefits arising from male comraderie and exhibitions of manliness. (See Chapter 5).

[1]The most comprehensive and analytical treatment of antebellum sport is Melvin L. Adelman, *A Sporting Time: New York City and the Rise of Modern Athletics, 1820–70* (Urbana, 1986).

A second, equally informal group, the sporting fraternity (or "the fancy"), was largely responsible for the great sporting spectacles of the antebellum era. Unlike the ball-playing fraternity of the 1840s and 1850s, monetary gain was a central ingredient in the sporting life of the fancy. Fraternity "members" earned money by wagering, providing liquor, and sometimes by imposing gate receipts on sporting events. The athletes themselves benefited from stakes, a sum of money given to the winner by promoters. As a vital part of the larger Victorian counterculture, the fraternity offered antebellum Americans (in particular, the younger, male population) a sense of belonging, excitement, sensual gratification, and a refuge from femininity, domesticity, and the demanding routines of the new economy. The sporting spectacles of the fancy represented an adaptation of the older folk games and pastimes to an urban setting.

THE SPORTING LIFE OF JOHN COX STEVENS

The career of John Cox Stevens vividly illuminates the complex relationships between an upper-class sportsman and antebellum sporting spectacles. At one time or another, Stevens patronized, promoted, and/or wagered upon horse, pedestrian, and yacht racing; he also furnished the playing grounds for the nation's first organized baseball matches. Stevens cultivated an aristocratic lifestyle that was more extravagant and expressive than that of the simple republican gentry of the Revolutionary era but not as collossally ostentatious as that of the post-Civil War parvenus. He, along with a set of fast-moving friends, engaged in a continuous round of expensive parties and dazzling excursions. Philip Hone compared the full course dinners given by Stevens with those prepared at the "Palais Bourbon in Paris."[2] Yet Stevens retained a certain distance between himself and the Victorian counterculture. He never patronized prize fighting, for example, and although he loved the theater, he did not associate with theater people. That he also looked at sports as an arena of entrepreneurial opportunity rather than simply as an upper-class diversion helped to identify him with the hard-working business ethic of the nineteenth century.

Stevens first attracted the attention of the sporting world by his involvement in horse racing. The American Revolution had temporarily set back racing, but after the war the turf quickly resumed its former popularity. The center of thoroughbred racing shifted from the Tidewater region of Virginia and Maryland to New York City, the Southwest, and especially to the states of Kentucky and Tennessee. Unlike other sporting spectacles of the antebellum era, horse racing was well organized by the 1830s with regular racing schedules. The economic panic of 1837, charges of corruption and chicanery, and increasing sectional tensions between the North and the South slowed the growth of racing, but after the Civil War the turf rebounded in a more prosperous form.

---

[2]Allan Nevins, ed., *The Diary of Philip Hone, 1828–1851,* 2 vols. (New York, 1927), II, 861. For Stevens, see also John Dizikes, *Sportsmen and Gamesmen* (Boston, 1981), Chap. 5.

JOHN COX STEVENS (1785–1857)
A wealthy New Yorker with a passion for horse racing and yachting,
Stevens was probably the nation's premier antebellum patron of sports.
His yacht, *America*, won a famous race against the best of Britain's
yachts in 1851. Subsequently, the cup—"the *America's* Cup"—won by
Stevens became the most coveted prize of international yacht racing.

In the 1820s Stevens established himself as the North's leading horseman. From his stables located in Hoboken, Stevens raced horses frequently in
New Jersey and New York. For twenty-one consecutive years he served as either
president or vice president of the New York Jockey Club. He wagered heavily
on American Eclipse in the "race of the century" held at the Union Course on
Long Island in 1823. So certain of victory were Stevens and one of his brothers
"that, after their purses were exhausted, they took their watches from their
pockets and diamond breastpins from their bosoms, and bet them on the
result."[3] Fortunately for Stevens, American Eclipse, a northern horse, bested Sir
Henry from the South in two of three four-mile heats. From 50,000 to 100,000
fans had watched the race. In partnership with some of his in-laws from the
"aristocratic" Livingston family, Stevens purchased Eclipse (for $10,000) and Sir
Henry (for $3,000). Stevens then put the two horses out for stud at his Hoboken
stables. Between 1829 and 1835, Stevens's most famous horse, Black Maria, won
thirteen of the twenty-five races that she entered. In the 1830s Stevens sold his
stable and turned his attention to other diversions.

In 1831 Stevens and his brother opened a large amusement park, called
the Elysian Fields, on their waterfront estate at Hoboken. At a "fête champêtre"
given by the Stevens brothers to advertise the fields, two hundred "gentlemen"
attended, including the New York City mayor and aldermen. Later in the day
the New York and Jersey City boat clubs, their members "dressed in white
jackets and trousers, round ship's hats, and checked shirts," came to share the
"abundant champagne" and plentiful gourmet food.[4] Conveniently located
across the river from New York City, the Elysian Fields became a center of the
area's sporting life. It was the home at one time or another of the New York

[3]Archibald Douglas Turnbull, *John Stevens: An American Record* (New York, 1928), p. 486.
[4]Nevins, *Diary of Philip Hone*, I, 46. See also Brian Danforth, "Hoboken and the Affluent New
Yorker's Search for Recreation" *New Jersey History*, 95 (1977), 133–44.

Yacht Club, the St. George Cricket Club, the country's first organized baseball matches, and the playing area of the New York Athletic Club. Initially, the fields offered a retreat for the rich, but eventually thousands of ordinary pleasure seekers crossed the Hudson every weekend in the summer months to enjoy its delights.

Stevens was likewise responsible for the *America's* Cup yacht race. On July 30, 1844, he founded the New York Yacht Club aboard his schooner, *Gimcrack*. After drawing up the bylaws for the club and electing Stevens as commodore, the original nine members promptly set sail for Newport, Rhode Island. A "succession of gentlemen ranking high in the social and financial circles" of the city soon joined the club.[5] Membership in the club came to be the equivalent of acceptance in the very top rung of the New York City elite. Stevens erected a handsome Gothic clubhouse at the Elysian Fields, where the club held regular balls and feasts (with turtle being the favorite dish). The club prescribed expensive uniforms and sponsored extensive social cruises to such spots as Bar Harbor, Maine, and Cape Hatteras, North Carolina. In the postbellum era, the club's annual regatta at Newport became the "social event" of the summer season.

In 1851, Stevens organized a syndicate to build a special boat for the express purpose of challenging members of the Royal Yacht Squadron of Great Britain to a race. George Steers, a young shipbuilder, designed and supervised the construction of the yacht, christened *America*. On August 22 the *America* easily defeated eighteen British yachts in a race around the Isle of Wight to win a coveted cup donated by the Royal Yacht Squadron. Queen Victoria visited the yacht and congratulated Stevens on the Yankee performance. The victory by the New Yorkers over the distinguished British yachtsmen encouraged the formation of exclusive clubs in other cities along the Eastern seaboard. In 1857 the syndicate that owned *America* presented the cup to the New York Yacht Club on the condition that it should be contested for by yachtsmen from abroad. Through 1986, twenty-six international challenge matches had been held for the *America's* Cup, all but one won by American yachts. Until recently, yachting has remained one of the most exclusive of American sports.

PEDESTRIAN RACING

Stevens was also one of the first promoters of professional footracing, or pedestrianism, as the sport was then called. In the 1820s a few sportsmen, taking their cues from England, had offered small purses for both long distance runners and walkers. Stevens shocked the sporting set in 1835 by offering $1,000 to any pedestrian who could run ten miles in less than one hour; if only one runner accomplished the feat he would be awarded an additional $300. The race had grown out of a wager between Stevens and a friend, Samuel L. Gouveneur.

---

[5]Charles A. Peverelly, *The Book of American Pastimes* (New York, 1866), p. 19.

DEERFOOT, THE FAMOUS SENECA PEDESTRIAN, 1835
The commercial spectacle of pedestrianism attracted native-American, free
African-American, old-stock white American, and European athletes. A sport outside the
confines of Victorian respectability, the peds ran for prize money, and the spectators
wagered on the outcome.

Stevens insured that even if he lost his bet and the purse, he would turn a profit. He encouraged the newspapers to report the feats of English runners, advertised freely, attracted an international field of peds, and charged an admission.

The Great Race proved almost as spectacular as earlier horse races. At least 20,000 persons crowded into the stands, the infield, and onto the track of the Union Race Course. Patrick Mahoney, a butcher from County Kerry, Ireland, who was dressed in a green shirt with black slippers set a torrid pace for the first five miles; five of the nine runners reached the halfway mark in less than one half hour. After seven miles only the four favorite peds were still in the field. To the delight of the pro-American crowd, Henry Stannard, a farmer from Connecticut who wore black pantaloons, pulled away from the others to finish in 59 minutes and 48 seconds. Stannard was the only runner to finish in less than one hour. After his victory, he promptly mounted a horse, rode around the track to the cheers of the spectators, and made a short victory speech.[6]

[6]See George Moss, "The Long Distance Runners in Ante-Bellum America," *Journal of Popular Culture*, 8 (1974), 370–82, and John Cumming, *Runners and Walkers* (Chicago, 1981).

The interest aroused by the Great Race of 1835, nationalistic rivalries promoted by pedestrianism, and the wagering potentialities of footracing all helped make pedestrianism one of the most popular sports in the antebellum era. In 1844 the owners of the Beacon (horse) Race Course in Hoboken, New Jersey, staged a spectacular series of long-distance races that won national and international attention. For the first race, which attracted a large field of peds competing for a purse of $1,000, the New York *Herald* noted that "nothing is talked of now, in the sport circle, but this race," while the *Spirit of the Times* predicted that "all the world and his wife will be assembled." An estimated 30,000 spectators did attend. For the next race the promoters exploited ethnic and nationalistic sentiments. They lured 37 peds into the field, including three Englishmen, three Irishmen, and John Steeprock, a Seneca Indian. To the delight of the spectators, John Gildersleeve, a New York chairbuilder, won. "It was a trial of the Indian against the white man, on the point in which the red man most boasts his superiority," wrote an American newspaper reporter. "It was the trial of the peculiar American *physique* against the long held supremacy of the English muscular endurance."[7] Unfortunately for this interpretation, English peds proceeded to win the next three races at the Beacon course.

The excitement generated at the Beacon Course races of 1844 touched off a nationwide enthusiasm for pedestrianism. "During the next ten to fifteen years," noted an observer, "there were more athletes competing and more races than ever before. People in virtually every state in the union attended professional footraces."[8] Promoters devised all sorts of ingenious races. Sometimes runners ran against time, sometimes against both time and other runners, and sometimes even against a horse (with the human given a headstart). Sprints, hurdle races, and walking contests also took place. Besides prize money offered by promoters, the professional peds issued challenges in the sporting journals. A carnival-like atmosphere usually surrounded the races, and sometimes those wagering on the contests resorted to force in an attempt to insure that their favorite ped won.

Although associated with the sporting fraternity and charges of fixing, pedestrianism continued to enjoy some popularity after the Civil War. The 26-day walk of Edward P. Weston from Portland, Maine, to Chicago in 1867 for a purse of $1,000 touched off a revival of long-distance races. In the 1870s, long-distance walking races, known as "go-as-you-please" races, drew large crowds, especially in New York City. In the go-as-you-please races, the peds attempted to cover as many miles as they could on an indoor track within a set time, usually six days. In six days they sometimes walked over 500 miles. In the 1880s, professional footracing declined rapidly, replaced in popularity by the amateur track and field contests of colleges and socially exclusive metropolitan athletic clubs.

[7]Quotations from Adelman, *A Sporting Time*, p. 213, 214.
[8]Quoted in Melvin Leonard Adelman, "The Development of Modern Athletics in New York City, 1820–1870," unpub. Ph.D. diss., University of Illinois, 1980, p. 535.

ROWING AND BILLIARDS

Rowing had its origins in the colonial era. Workers in rivers and harbors along the Eastern seaboard sometimes competed, and in the early nineteenth century newspapers began to carry notices of their races. An international race in 1824 stimulated nationwide interest. George Harris, captain of a British frigate, matched his crew of rowers against the Whitehall boatmen of New York City for a stake of $1,000. The British crew, which had won eight races in the West Indies and was supposed to have no rivals on the Thames, lost to the Americans by 300 yards. (Unlike modern shells, the crafts used ranged from eighteen to twenty-seven feet in length and were usually manned by four oarsmen.) Some 20,000 to 50,000 spectators assembled along the Hudson River, and large sums of money exchanged hands among the many wagerers. By the 1830s a boating mania virtually swept the country. "The beauty and the fashion of the city were there," according to an account of a regatta held in Louisville on July 4, 1839, "ladies and gentlemen, loafers and laborers, white folks and 'niggers' . . . and all the paraphernalia of city life . . . formed the constituent parts of the heterogeneous mass that stood jammed and crowded upon the levee."[9]

Unlike pedestrianism, rowing featured both professional and amateur oarsmen. In 1834 New York City amateur clubs, composed exclusively of wealthy "young men of fashion," formed the Castle Garden Amateur Boat Club Association. The association sought to be a regulatory body; it expressly forbade "any club to row for money, or take part in a Regatta or Races with any club or clubs independent of those belonging to the Association." The association's annual regatta, "attended by the city's elites," Melvin Aderman has concluded, "was as much a display of fashion as it was a display of skill. Each club appeared with its distinct colors and uniforms, and every year the Wave Club, the best crew and quite possibly the wealthiest, came with a new boat constructed by Clarkson Crotus, the leading builder of the day."[10] Nonetheless, enthusiasm for rowing among the city's elites was short-lived; in 1842 the Castle Garden association scheduled its last regatta.

In the mid-1850s rowing enjoyed a revival led by professional oarsmen. Professional races involved single or double sculls, but regattas in the East sometimes included four-oared barges and lapstreak gigs. Beginning in 1854 Boston held annual regattas that featured challenge matches between Irish longshoremen and the Brahmin "Beacon Street swells." In the late 1850s in New York City, throngs estimated at 10,000 or more witnessed the annual regattas of the Empire City Regatta Club or the New York Regatta Club, two organizations that had been formed to promote professional racing. In the East an informal professional racing circuit developed. Rowing fever spread to inland cities, to

[9]*Spirit of the Times,* July 10, 1839.

[10]Adelman, "The Development of Modern Athletics," p. 482. See apart from Adelman, *A Sporting Time,* Peverelly, *Book of American Pastimes,* and Robert F. Kelley, *American Rowing: Its Background and Traditions* (New York, 1932).

Pittsburgh, Chicago, Milwaukee, St. Louis, and Louisville, where crowds of up to 20,000 watched races. As had the pedestrians, professional scullers often published challenges in the newspapers. After the Civil War, amateur rowing, rooted this time in both private clubs and the nation's colleges, began to supplant professional rowing in popularity.

In the antebellum era, billiards developed a dual character, one part springing from the "rich and the well-born," the other from the Victorian counterculture.[11] Only "gentlemen" of means played the polite version found in private residences or in exclusive men's clubs. Unattached, transient males, workingmen, ethnics, and a few slummers, on the other hand, frequented the public parlors. Inexpensive to play and proffering opportunities for gambling, male companionship, and displays of skill, billiards became an integral part of the recreational life of the inner cities. Apart from parlors devoted exclusively to the game, saloons often provided for their customers one or more billiard tables.

Beginning in the 1850s, Michael Phelan, the sport's "dominant personality and promoter in America," attempted to popularize and improve the image of billiards. Nationwide attention focused on the first billiard "championship" of the United States held in 1859 at Fireman's Hall in Detroit. The two contestants, Michael Phelan and John Seereiter, played before a large "genteel audience," which included several ladies. The terms of the match involved unusually large sums of money, a $5,000 side bet plus $5,000 by the promoters and a portion of the gate receipts to the winner. Play began at 7:30 P.M. and lasted until five o'clock the next morning. Seereiter had the highest run, but Phelan won the match and walked away with a reported sum of $15,000. Phelan, author of several books on billiards, remained the most active promoter of the sport until his death in 1871. Never again did championship billiard matches attract as much public attention or betting.

THE ORIGINS OF AMERICAN PRIZE FIGHTING

As with most of the popular antebellum spectacles, American prize fighting had its origins in England.[12] In the last decades of the eighteenth and the first two decades of the nineteenth century stories of great champions came from England to America, but they inspired little immediate enthusiasm for fighting in the new republic. Occasional but unpublicized matches occurred as early as the eighteenth century. There are legends of planters who pitted their best fighting slaves against those of neighboring plantations. One instance may have been Tom Molineaux, a Maryland- or Virginia-born slave, who, according to the folklore of the ring, won his freedom near the turn of the nineteenth century by defeating a

---

[11]See esp. Adelman, *A Sporting Time*, and Ned Polsky, *Hustlers, Beats, and Others* (Chicago, 1967), Chap. 1.

[12]The paragraphs that follow rely mainly on Elliot J. Gorn, *The Manly Art: Bare-Knuckle Prize Fighting in America* (Ithaca, 1986), but also see the relevant sections of Adelman, *A Sporting Time*.

fellow slave. Upon release from bondage, Molineaux eventually appeared in New York City where he may have fought a few impromptu, surreptitious bouts. American newspapers gave Molineaux only passing mention in 1811 when he was bested in London (in a rematch) by the reigning English champion, Tom Crib. Molineaux continued to fight in England but never returned to the United States.

In the 1820s and 1830s a small pugilistic fraternity began to establish the foundations for the future popularity of American fighting. Comprised mostly of gamblers, saloon owners, and hustlers, the informal fraternity welcomed Irish and English boxers to American shores. Both foreign and native-born fighters and their promoters capitalized upon ethnic rivalries. Few occasions equalled a prize fight in arousing feelings of intense ethnic loyalties. During the same decades, English and Irish "professors of pugilism" also offered (without many takers) sparring lessons to the nation's upper crust.

During the 1840s and 1850s, the same decades that witnessed a "take-off" in the popularity of pedestrian races, boat races, and ball-playing, prize-fighting may have become the nation's "single most important spectator sport."[13] By the mid-1850s, pugilism had spread far beyond the New York City environs to mid-western river towns, most notably New Orleans and St. Louis. Reports of scores of fights appeared in the newspapers; in New York City, the capital of pugilism, the papers carried accounts of three or four local sparring matches each week. And a series of sensational championship fights—Tom Hyer vs. Yankee Sullivan (1849), Yankee Sullivan vs. John Morrissey (1853), John Morrissey vs. John C. Heenan (1857), and John C. Heenan vs. Tom Sayers (1860)—captivated millions.

The ascendancy in the 1850s of John Morrissey, "Old Smoke," as the champion, represented the working class, ethnic version of the American success dream. Born in Ireland and immigrating as a three-year-old lad with his impoverished family to Troy, New York, Morrissey combined fighting, gambling, and politics to move up the economic ladder. While holding a series of jobs as a manual worker, Morrissey acquired a reputation as a brutal street brawler. In 1853 he defeated Yankee Sullivan at Boston Corners in New York for $2,000 in prize money and the unofficial American championship; four years later in a widely publicized fight, he bested John C. Heenan, another Irishman.

He then retired from the ring and devoted his full attention to politics and the development of his gambling enterprises. Out of the earnings of his first fight he established a gaming house in New York City, which by 1860 became the most celebrated parlor in the city. Within five years he had an interest in at least five other gambling halls and was the largest single shareholder in a million-dollar lottery business. He also helped to make Saratoga, New York, the nation's most elegant resort. At Saratoga, he built both the first horse race track (in 1864), and (in 1867) a lavish gambling parlor and restaurant, which, in effect, transformed Saratoga from a fashionable spa into an American version of Monte Carlo. He hobnobbed with some of New York's new rich, but his popularity with

[13]Gorn, *The Manly Art*, p. 83.

workingmen also made him a successful politician. Before his death in 1878, he served two terms in the U.S. Congress.

After Morrissey's retirement from the ring, John C. Heenan assumed the championship mantle. Few challengers stepped forward, so Heenan traveled about the country giving exhibitions with theater troupes. In 1860, he met Tom Sayers, the English champion, in a bout outside London. On both sides of the Atlantic, the Heenan–Sayers bout excited far more interest than had any prior fight. It attracted people of all sorts; members of the English aristocracy joined the riffraff in watching the two-hour bloodbath. In the seventh round, Sayers, who weighed a mere 150 pounds compared to Heenan's 190 pounds, pulled a muscle in his right arm but continued to stage a masterful defense. Finally, with both fighters bloody and exhausted, the crowd out of control, and the constables about to stop the bout, the referee called the match a draw. In the United States, interest in the fight overshadowed news about the sectional conflict that would soon lead to the Civil War. For that moment, the fight may have deflected the nation's deep internal divisions. Even respectable Victorians saw the bout as an opportunity to once again twist the British lion's tail. And citizens in both nations identified their fighters with national virility.

THE MEANINGS OF PRIZE FIGHTING

No sport exceeded prize fighting in its capacity to mirror the larger cultural conflicts of antebellum America. In the first place, boxing reflected ethnic divisions within the working class itself. For example, in the 1850s American-born and Irish-born workers clashed on many fronts. The Irish were mostly Roman Catholic; the native-born were mostly Protestant. Experiencing a decline in the need for crafts or skills and a loss of autonomy in the workplace, native workers often blamed the presence of foreigners for their plight. Competition for jobs and political power further kindled religious and ethnic hostilities. Prize fights dramatized these rivalries: The Irish, the English, and the old-stock American-born fighters represented their respective ethnoreligious groups in symbolic contests for supremacy and honor.

In the second place, pugilism manifestly mocked Victorian values, especially the cardinal virtue of self-restraint. The prevailing rules permitted a battle just short of unregulated combat. Under the Broughton (1743) and London (1838) prize ring rules, fighters fought with their bare fists; wrestling skills and brute strength were more important to success than finesse in boxing. A round ended only when a man was struck down by an opponent's fists, thrown to the turf with a wrestling hold, or deliberately fell to the ground to avoid further punishment. Once downed, a fighter had thirty seconds to recover before "toeing the mark," or "coming to scratch," terms that referred to a line drawn through the center of the ring. A fight ended only when a fighter was unable to come to scratch or conceded defeat. Under these rules, fights could be savagely brutal, even fatal. In 1842, Thomas McCoy and Christopher Lilly pummelled one another for two hours and forty minutes before McCoy, drowning in his own blood, fell dead.

Unrestrained spectator behavior often accompanied prize fights. Fights were illegal everywhere, so the "fancy" had to schedule them in remote places—in the backrooms of saloons, on barges, or in remote rural areas—and be ever-watchful for the vigilant legal authorities. The fights attracted the roughest elements of American society, including pickpockets, hustlers, drunks, and bullies, Abundant liquor abetted the release of inhibitions. Ethnic hostilities and opposing wagers often led to disruptions. Those who sensed that their bets were in jeopardy or those who felt their favorite had been unfairly treated sometimes joined the fray by swinging their fists, flashing Bowie knives, or brandishing pistols.

Such absences of restraint deeply concerned and offended Victorian America. Victorians especially feared the consequences for the young. "What will become of the morals of the rising generation—our apprentices, youth from school, servants, male and female, if they have opportunity to mingle in these scenes of riot, brutality, and systematic violations of order and decency?" asked the *New York Spectator*.[14] To the Victorians, the uncontrolled behavior associated with the ring contributed to a disrespect for law and order and to casual attitudes about time, leisure, and money.

The ring inverted Victorian ideals about money and success as well. To Victorians, the accumulation of money represented and validated years of hard work and self-restraint by its possessor. The prize fighter and gambler, on the other hand, might earn hundreds of dollars by winning a single bout or bet; such a single stroke of success openly mocked the Victorian ideals of frugality, sobriety, and hard work. Rather than as evidence of a man's character, sporting men valued money as a means of promoting conviviality; they liked to be known for their lavish generosity. To patrons of the ring, prize fighting, saloon keeping, and gambling were valued alternative avenues to success. In fact, those who achieved success in the world of entertainment were more highly esteemed by the sporting fraternity than were hard-driving businessmen in other sectors of the economy.

The entrepreneurial opportunities afforded by the ring as well as other forms of commercial entertainment especially attracted those Americans of Irish origins. Having English as a native tongue, being unencumbered by Victorian inhibitions, and finding opportunities blocked to more respectable occupations, many Irish naturally turned to careers that satisfied the urban hunger for gaming, drink, and sport. Such careers required little education and could produce quick rewards in a society that placed a high value on material success.

Working class Irish males held fighting ability in the highest esteem. Survival for an Irish boy in the slums could depend more on his ability to use his fists than on his intelligence. Fisticuffs was a favorite means of both settling disputes in the ghetto and maintaining one's standing among fellow juveniles. Street fighting prepared youths for careers as pugilists, criminals, or policemen.

[14]Quoted in ibid, p. 61.

(In antebellum New York City, local political factions employed "shoulder hitters" to intimidate rivals on election day.) If a youth became a successful prize fighter, he furnished a role model for the others. To the youngsters in the tenement districts, the prize fighter embodied not only the survival values of the slums—but received handsome rewards as well. Throughout the nineteenth and into the early twentieth century, Irish boxers dominated the ring, but were replaced in turn by Jews in the 1920s, Italians in the 1930s, and blacks and Latin Americans in the 1940s and since. The prize ring perfectly reflected the order of ascent for ethnic groups from the urban ghettos.[15]

Likewise, ring supporters valued a conception of masculinity at odds with Victorianism. To Victorians, the ideal man labored diligently, kept a tight rein on his impulses, and supported family life. But the changing role of the home from a productive economic unit (the household economy) to a domestic-feminine enclave and the radical changes in the nineteenth-century workplaces undermined opportunities for proving manhood. Workingmen might demonstrate their heterosexual virility by patronizing prostitutes, but they more often confirmed their manliness in the company of other men. In gender-segregated leisure activities, they exhibited toughness, physical prowess, and generosity. To these men, the prize fighter, with his immense strength, muscular body, and swift, decisive answers, represented an appealing alternative to the effeminate, self-effacing Victorian ideal of manhood.

The excitement generated by commercial sporting spectacles in the 1850s is likely to give an exaggerated view of the importance of sport in the antebellum era. Even the nation's upper crust rarely gave over much of their time to recreation; they paid even less attention to sports. Only a few resorted to fashionable summer spots where they might engage in such nonstrenuous activities as cheering at the race track or playing billiards. Neither did the members of middle-income groups endanger their health by too much physical exertion. As the main supporters of Victorian values, they rarely played cards, danced, or engaged in athletics. "Bank clerks, young merchants, mercantile aspirants," declared *Harper's Weekly* in 1857, "all seem to think time devoted to any exercise wasted, and the model clerk him who drudges six days every week at his desk without an hour of physical labor."[16]

Pleas by antebellum health reformers for women to engage in moderate exercise also went largely for naught. Ignoring the fact that many women engaged in such backbreaking chores as farm labor, factory work, cleaning, and child-bearing, at mid-nineteenth century women of all social ranks were expected to be models of physical inactivity. Constricted by an eighteen-inch corsetted waist, "a sea of petticoats," and a floor-length dress, the ideal woman, according to the novels, magazines, and thousands of lithographs of the day, was pale,

---

[15]In addition to ibid, see also S. Kirson Weinberg and Henry Arond, "The Occupational Culture of the Boxer," *American Journal of Sociology*, 57 (1952), 460–69.

[16]*Harper's Weekly* 3 (Oct. 15, 1859), 658.

fragile, and genteel. Consistent with this ideal, American women, wrote an English visitor in 1855, regarded "anyone who proposed vigorous physical exercise as a madman." Even walking was "suited only to such females as are compelled by necessity to labor for their bodily sustenance," wrote another observer. "A woman properly educated and with feeling suitable to her sex, would as soon be . . . in the pulpit" as "pitching quoits or engaged in a game of nine-pins," wrote one sarcastic commentator. "Womanhood is as lovely in one place as the other."[17]

Yet despite all obstacles during the antebellum era the foundations were established for a great "take-off" of organized sports. In terms of per capita wealth the nation would soon overtake England. A transportation and communication revolution was underway. The increased application of machinery to production promised more leisure time while it simultaneously eroded satisfactions traditionally found in work. Larger cities were beginning to dot the landscape. And already thriving was a sporting fraternity that offered an alternative life style to the strictures of Victorian America. Likewise, before the Civil War, the baseball-playing fraternity had established firm roots in the nation's larger cities.

[17]Quotations form Lois W. Banner, *American Beauty* (New York, 1983), p. 54, and Robert Riegel, *Young America, 1830–1840* (Norman, OK, 1949), p. 347.

4

THE OUTSIDERS
IN THE
POSTBELLUM ERA

In the post-Civil War era, the social "outsiders" (those recent immigrants, blacks, unmarried or displaced males, and workingmen who were outside of the mainstream of Victorian life) constructed two distinct sporting universes.[1] One centered on the formation of voluntary associations or clubs in which sports were a conspicuous activity. The sport clubs aided in the formation of ethnic and black subcommunities, in some measure helped to counteract social dislocations, and assisted outsiders in the preservation of traditional cultural patterns.

The second revolved around the Victorian counterculture. Although the counterculture had its origins in the antebellum era, it continued after the Civil War to provide the outsiders with a sense of excitement, meaning, and personal belonging. By promoting professional billiards, bowling, cycling, wrestling, and boxing, certain of the outsiders, especially the Irish-Americans, also profited from the entrepreneurial opportunities arising from the growing urban appetite for "illicit" amusements. Ethnic athletes sometimes found in professional sports, particularly in prize fighting and baseball, opportunities to improve their social and economic lot. Blacks, on the other hand, encountered barriers in professional sports nearly as impenetrable as those they faced in the skilled professions.

[1]Steven A. Riess, *City Games: The Evolution of American Urban Society and the Rise of Sports* (Urbana and Chicago, 1989), esp. Chap. 3, contains valuable discussions of many aspects of this chapter.

PRIZE FIGHTING IN POSTBELLUM AMERICA

Although the Civil War (1861–1865) brought to a close "The Age of Heroes"—the age that produced champion pugilists Yankee Sullivan, John Morrissey, and John C. Heenan—the war may have increased public interest in the ring as well as in other sports. By bringing together in military units massive numbers of young men, the war replicated conditions similar to those that existed among the young workingmen in the cities. Seeking to escape boredom and to establish an identity in an all-male milieu, the soldiers frequently turned to boxing, baseball, running, wrestling, and shooting matches. No doubt the war introduced many young men to the delights of playing and watching organized sports.

The troops especially relished sports featuring toughness and physical prowess. They eagerly subscribed to the purses needed to stage in-camp matches between boxers-turned-soldiers. In addition, boxing matches in many units became a favorite way of settling festering feuds between soldiers. "It was not safe to quarrel unless one wanted to fight," recalled Edmund Randolph Brown of the 27th Indiana Volunteer Infantry. "A ring was often formed with the two quarreling fellows inside, and they were almost compelled to knock it out or cease quarreling."[2] Such matches provided a rule-controlled, expeditious resolution of personal conflicts. Moreover, at least two reported instances of troops temporarily laying down their weapons to enjoy pugilistic encounters between their Union and Confederate comrades suggested the possibility of substituting nonlethal, individual combat for the carnage of actual warfare.

Yet the popularity of boxing among soldiers failed to prevent a general decline in professional fighting during the 1860s and 1870s. Externally, the prize ring suffered from the increased vigilance of legal authorities. In New York City, the center of antebellum prize fighting, the "fancy" could no longer take it for granted that they would be shielded from the law by local politicians. Internally, charges of fixes, dishonest referees, and failures of boxers to fight aggressively shattered the sporting fraternity's confidence in the integrity of the ring. Even so-called championship matches turned into farces. For example, in 1871, before the bout was interrupted by the sheriff and the militia, Jem Mace and Joe Coburn "fought" for an hour and seventeen minutes without landing a single blow. Increasingly, or so it seemed to contemporaries, members of enraged mobs attacked bout referees, the fighters, or each other. Given the risks to personal safety, only the more courageous or foolhardy attended prize fights.

In the 1880s, several circumstances joined to usher in a new era in prize fighting. One was *The National Police Gazette*, published and edited by Richard Kyle Fox. Printed on shocking pink paper and distributed at discount rates to

---

[2]Quoted in Elliott J. Gorn, *The Manly Art: Bare-Knuckle Prize Fighting in America* (Ithaca, 1986), p. 163. The following paragraphs rely heavily upon Gorn, but see also Michael T. Isenberg, *John L. Sullivan and His America* (Urbana and Chicago, 1987).

such all-male domains as barbershops, livery stables, saloons, private men's clubs, and volunteer fire departments, the notorious weekly *Gazette* exploited to the fullest the nation's racial bigotry, secret sexual lusts, and thirst for the sensational. Fox featured engravings of show girls in tights, and printed scandals, atrocities, advertisements for contraceptives, and promotions of bizarre contests. He offered belts and other prizes for winners of championships in (among others) prize fighting, female weight-lifting, teeth-lifting, and one-legged clog dancing. But his favorite sport was prize fighting. With little success, he repeatedly pleaded for the legalization of the fight game. By launching a campaign to unseat John L. Sullivan as heavyweight king and by randomly awarding belts and naming champions in different weight divisions in boxing, Fox attracted national attention to pugilism and even brought a modicum of order to the intrinsically chaotic sport.

Key metropolitan saloons supplemented Fox's efforts to promote prize fighting. In the 1870s and 1880s one of the most important was Harry Hill's saloon, located on notorious Bleeker Street in New York City. Described by reformers as "the most dangerous and demoralizing establishment in the city" and as "the last resort of a low class of prostitutes, and the ruffians and idlers who support the prize ring," politicians, wealthy slummers, gamblers, show people, fight managers, and pugilists all made Hill's their headquarters.[3] Hill's place was more than a saloon; it consisted of a long serving bar upstairs, a standing bar downstairs, a wine room, a music hall, and a room with a boxing and wrestling ring. "If you were anybody at all in New York nightlife in the seventies and eighties," wrote one observer, "you got into Harry Hill's as often as possible. Here boxing and wrestling were held and articles were signed for bigger matches elsewhere, shows were cast, [and] large bets were made."[4] In the early 1880s William Muldoon, the most renowned Greco-Roman wrestler of the day, and John L. Sullivan, the prize fighting champion, both worked out of Hill's saloon. Harry Hill himself was the best known and most esteemed stakeholder and boxing referee in the country. Though usually less lavish, saloons in other large cities served the sporting fraternity in a similar fashion.

Athletic clubs, whether elitist or composed specifically of fight promoters, also contributed to the new era of the ring. A growing interest in boxing among the membership of wealthy athletic clubs, especially in New York, New Orleans, and San Francisco, improved the image of the fight game. Within the confines of exclusive athletic clubs, countless young men of high social standing took sparring lessons from "professors of pugilism." The New York Athletic Club, for example, hired Mike Donovan, the middleweight champion, to teach "gentlemen eminent in science, literature, art, social and commercial life" the finer principles of the "manly art."[5] The New York club also scheduled the first

---

[3]Quoted in Gorn, *The Manly Art*, p. 183.

[4]Donald Barr Chidsey, *John the Great: The Times and Life of a Remarkable American* (Garden City, NY, 1942), p. 13.

[5]Quoted in Gorn, *The Manly Art*, p. 199.

national amateur boxing championships. Sometimes the wealthy slummers from the athletic clubs joined in an uneasy alliance with Irish politicians in campaigns to modify state laws or city ordinances that banned prize fighting.[6]

The entrance of athletic clubs into the fight game altered the nature of the sport. The clubs encouraged the practice of fighting for a specified number of rounds, though round limitations did not become a universal practice until the 1920s. Moreover, the clubs joined Richard Kyle Fox in promoting weight divisions; by the mid-1880s, Fox was naming national champions, often with shadowy claims, for six distinct weight divisions. Finally, by bringing the matches indoors, charging admissions, and offering specific purses to the winners, the clubs altered the traditional mode of fight promotion.

The clubs also prompted the growing acceptance of the Marquis of Queensberry rules. Drafted under the patronage of the Marquis of Queensberry in 1865, the rules required the use of gloves, limited rounds to three minutes, provided for ten-second knockouts, and prohibited wrestling holds. The use of gloves gave boxing the appearance of curbing animality, thereby making the sport more publicly acceptable. Yet the new rules may have made the sport even more brutal, since gloves protected the bones of the hands from breaking (thus permitting the fighter to hit harder with impunity) and added weight to each punch. The banning of wrestling holds, the ten-second knockout rule, and the imposition of round limitations encouraged a faster-paced, more commercially appealing spectacle. A major breakthrough in the use of the new rules came in 1890 when New Orleans passed a new ordinance permitting gloved fights sponsored by athletic clubs. The ordinance paved the way for the first gloved championship fight between John L. Sullivan and James J. Corbett, held in 1892.

ENTER JOHN L. SULLIVAN

Into the new era of prize fighting stepped a new champion heavyweight whose contribution to boxing may have exceeded that of Fox, the saloons, the athletic clubs, and the use of the Queensberry rules. Born in Boston to Irish immigrant parents, John L. Sullivan achieved a celebrity status perhaps unequalled by any other public figure of his time. After trying his hand at the various manual jobs available to an Irish youth in the 1870s, he discovered his talent for boxing. In exhibition matches in Boston theaters and music halls he soon developed a reputation as a slugger. In 1882, he defeated the reigning champion, Paddy Ryan, whom he knocked out in the second round at Mississippi City, Louisiana, for a stake of $5,000 and a side bet of $1,000.

[6]See Zane Hollander, ed., *Madison Square Garden: A Century of Sport and Spectacle on the World's Most Versatile Stage* (New York, 1975), pp. 93–197; and Steven A. Riess, "In the Ring and Out: Professional Boxing in New York, 1896–1920," in Donald Spivey, ed., *Sport in America: New Historical Perspectives* (Westport, CT, 1985), 95–128.

JOHN L. SULLIVAN (1858–1918)
John L. Sullivan, perhaps the nation's first truly national sports hero, was the heavyweight champion prize fighter between 1882 and 1892. His career spanned a transition in prize fighting from a folk, countercultural contest to a form of commercial entertainment.

The public adored the new champion. Shortly after winning the title, Sullivan began the first of several nationwide tours. He offered the astonishing sum of $1,000 to any one who could stand up to him for four rounds. Reportedly only one person performed the feat; scores of others succumbed to Sullivan's mighty blows. Sullivan used gloves in these exhibitions, thereby both saving his hands from damage and adhering to local ordinances against bare-knuckle fighting. When no local hero stepped forward for punishment (as frequently was the case) Sullivan sparred with a member of his own traveling troupe, which typically included other boxers as well as wrestlers, clowns, and jugglers. The tour, Sullivan's love of fighting, and his flamboyant lifestyle raised the "Boston Strong Boy" to the pinnacle of national popularity. Among patrons of the sporting underworld and proper Victorians alike his name became a household word.

In the meantime, Sullivan continued to defend his title. Between 1884 and 1886 he added fourteen official victories to his record, and Richard Kyle Fox launched a worldwide search to find a worthy challenger. Sullivan avoided only the black boxers, one of whom (Peter Jackson) might have sent him to defeat. In the late 1880s Sullivan's fortunes turned sour; he suffered from alcoholism and poor health, and, while on a European sojourn in 1888, fought the English champion, Charlie Mitchell, to an embarrassing draw. The next year Sullivan met Jake Kilrain in the last bout of the bare-knuckle era. Whipped into tip-top shape for the match by wrestler-trainer William Muldoon, Sullivan dueled Kilrain under the blazing sun in Richburg, Mississippi, for 75 rounds before Kilrain's seconds finally threw in the sponge. During the bout, Sullivan's backers reportedly fortified him with copious drafts of tea mixed with whiskey. In the 45th round, Sullivan began to heave up the concoction, leading one wag to claim that the champion's stomach "rejected the tea but held the whiskey." Public interest in the bout knew few bounds. "Never, during even a Presidential election, has there been so much excitement as there is here now," concluded the *New York Times*.[7] Excitement mounted even higher in 1892 when Sullivan defended his title against James J. Corbett in New Orleans. Having relapsed into his old ways of drinking and eating too much and handicapped by age, Sullivan put on a poor show. In the 21st round Corbett "shot his right across the jaw and Sullivan fell like an ox."[8]

The Sullivan–Corbett match marked a series of important "firsts" in the history of prizefighting. Locked in circulation wars with one another, major daily newspapers switched from their usual condemnation to open support of the ring. Rather than signing the articles for the fight in a saloon or in the offices of the *National Police Gazette*, representatives of the two boxers met in the offices of Joseph Pulitzer's *New York World*. As a heavyweight championship bout, the fight was the first to be held indoors under electric lights, to use gloves, to employ the Marquis of Queensberry rules, and to be sponsored by an athletic club. Corbett himself lent to the ring a new aura of respectability. Although of Irish extraction, Corbett had not fought his way up from the streets; he had attended college, held a white collar job as a bank clerk, and learned his boxing skills in an elite athletic club. Hence, the sobriquet "Gentleman Jim." These departures reflected boxing's transition away from its folk, countercultural origins to a form of mass, commercial entertainment.

Sullivan was probably the first truly national sports hero. His climb to fame fulfilled the mythology of rugged American individualism and the gospel of self-help. Without the advantages of superior birth or sponsorship, he fought his own way to the top of the savage world of boxing. Although he was a special hero of working class, Irish-American males, his success in a sport that was becoming the ultimate symbolic test of masculinity won the admiration of many Victorians. "In 1892 I was reading aloud the news to my father," William Lyon Phelps, a professor at Yale reported. "My father was an orthodox Baptist minister. . . . I had never heard him mention a prize fight and did not suppose he knew anything on the subject, or cared anything about it. So when I came to the headline CORBETT DEFEATS SULLIVAN, I read that aloud and turned the page. My father leaned forward and said earnestly, 'Read it by rounds!' "[9] Sullivan remained a celebrity long after his loss to Corbett. He performed in numerous vaudeville acts and plays (including the role of Simon Legree in a traveling production of *Uncle Tom's Cabin*), and even gave temperance lectures.

[7]Quoted in Gorn, *The Manly Art*, p. 235.
[8]Quoted in Dale A. Somers, *The Rise of Sports in New Orleans, 1850–1900* (Baton Rouge, LA, 1972), p. 184.
[9]William Lyon Phelps, *Autobiography with Letters* (New York), p. 356.

Yet neither the popularity of Sullivan, the Marquis of Queensberry rules, nor the reforms instituted by the athletic clubs completely erased the traditional stigma associated with the prize ring. Even "lace-curtain Irish," the more successful Irish-Americans who sought acceptance into Victorian society, dissociated themselves from the ring. The sport remained illegal almost everywhere and respectable women did not attend prize fights until the 1920s. Without a national regulatory body or a rational system for determining champions, boxing was an unusually chaotic and disorderly sport. Champions invariably avoided challengers unless they could be assured of a large stake—"win or lose." Young fighters with dreams of reaching the top sought out "patsys" so they could leave their records unblemished. And the bottom line for any fight was the anticipated profits of promoters. "Carrying" an opponent, "taking a dive," and "fixing records"—these and other fradulent tactics were endemic to the fight game. Thus, despite the growing popularity of boxing among all social groups, the ambience of boxing remained working class and ethnic, and shrouded by the shady world of bookies, thugs, and racketeers.

THE VOLUNTARY ASSOCIATION

The formation of sport clubs by various social groups in the postbellum era was only one indication of the rage for voluntary associations. As early as the 1830s, voluntary associations became a striking feature of American society. Alexis de Tocqueville observed that "in no country in the world has the principle of association been more successfully used or applied to a greater multitude of objects than in America."[10] A contemporary of Tocqueville believed that since Americans had destroyed "classes, and corporate bodies of every kind, and come to simple direct individualism," the vacuum had been filled by the "production of voluntary associations to an immense extent."[11] Voluntary associations, or clubs, could chose members according to any criteria: common interests, sex, ethnicity, occupation, religion, status, or a combination thereof. Likeminded persons found in voluntary associations a milieu in which they could partly counteract the impersonality of the new society.

The voluntary association became one of several means by which Americans sought to replace the old village style of life with new subcommunities. As in voluntary societies, important criteria that determined membership in a subcommunity based on status could include: living in a particular neighborhood, marrying into a proper family, belonging to a particular religious denomination, having English origins, and attending specific educational institutions. Sports

[10] Alexis de Tocqueville, *Democracy in America*, 2 vols. (New York, 1951), II, 191. See Benjamin G. Rader, "The Quest for Subcommunities and the Rise of American Sport," *American Quarterly*, 29 (1977), 355–69.
[11] Quoted in Walter S. Glazer, "Participation and Power: Voluntary Associations and the Functional Organization of Cincinnati in 1840," *Historical Methods Newsletter*, 5 (1972), 153.

clubs could be important to groups seeking either to attain status exclusivity or to preserve an ethnic identity. Not only sports clubs, but neighborhoods, ethnic theaters, music societies, restaurants, saloons, and, above all, churches or synagogues, furnished the sinews of ethnic subcommunities.

ETHNIC SPORTS CLUBS

The need of immigrant groups to form separate ethnic communities depended upon a host of variables including their nationality, religious beliefs, language, and status. The majority of old-stock Americans were likely to discriminate least against immigrants who were most like themselves. Immigrants from England, Scotland, and Wales tended to assimilate more rapidly than those from other parts of Europe. The history of nineteenth- and early twentieth-century sport clubs reflected the process of acculturation by distinctive ethnic groups. The Scottish Caledonian clubs and the English cricket clubs, for example, functioned briefly as distinctive ethnic communities. But as Scottish and English immigration declined and they adopted the old-stock, largely Victorian-American culture, the need for ethnic communities subsided. The German Turner societies began as ethnic communities, and, as the members assimilated, sometimes became status communities.[12]

The Scottish Caledonian clubs may have been the most significant ethnic community in encouraging the growth of nineteenth-century American sport. Back in the mists of Scottish history, rural communities had held annual track and field games. During the 1850s, these games began to provide one of the bases for organizing Caledonian clubs in America. Eventually, well over one hundred clubs formed. Wherever a few Scots settled, they usually founded a Caledonian club. In 1887, for example, the *Scottish-American Journal* reported that "A Caledonian Club has been organized at Great Falls, Montana, with a membership of 37 enthusiastic Scots."[13] The clubs restricted membership to persons of Scottish birth or descent.

Although the evidence is not conclusive, it appears that the Caledonian clubs functioned as a major agency for the formation of a Scottish ethnic community in many American cities. The purpose of the clubs, as one of the founders of the Boston organization put it, was to perpetuate "the manners and customs, literature, the Highland costume and the athletic games of Scotland, as practiced by our forefathers."[14] Apart from sport, the clubs sponsored extensive social activities, such as dinners, dancing, and bagpipe playing. In short, the clubs provided a sense of community in a strange society.

---

[12]For an example of the transition of a Turner group from an ethnic to a status community, see Noel Iverson, *Germania, U.S.A.: Social Change in New Ulm, Minnesota* (Minneapolis, 1966).

[13]Quoted in Gerald Redmond, *The Caledonian Games in Nineteenth-Century America* (Rutherford, NJ: 1971), p. 45.

[14]Ibid., p. 39.

From the 1850s to the mid-1870s, the Caledonians were the single most important promoters of track and field in the country. Even old-stock Americans exhibited an enthusiasm for the annual games. Huge crowds, as many as 20,000 in New York City, turned out in the 1870s to view competition in footracing, tug o' war, hurdling, jumping, pole vaulting, throwing the hammer, and putting the shot. In 1886 the New York Caledonian Club even added a 220-yard dash for women, which resulted in the crowd breaking through the ropes in order to get a better view. The clubs early recognized the opportunities for financial gain. They opened competition to all athletes regardless of ethnicity or race, charged admission, and offered cash prizes to winners. The success of the Caledonians was also one of the stimuli for the formation of wealthy old-stock American athletic clubs (see Chapter 6). In the late nineteenth century, as Scottish immigration slackened and Scots assimilated into the host society, nearly all of the Caledonian clubs folded. By then the Scots no longer sensed a need for distinctive ethnic communities.

For a brief time, cricket clubs assisted English immigrants in establishing ethnic communities. By the 1840s, when a new influx of immigrants arrived in the United States, England was already in the midst of a sporting revolution. Cricket was popular in both the southern Downs and the industrial north of England. The skilled textile workers from the North brought the sport with them to the mills at Lawrence and Lowell, Massachusetts, and to the Manheim district of Philadelphia. Their version of cricket often included a rough-and-tumble style of play, strictly male companionship, and hard drinking. After the matches, the immigrant workingmen gathered at a favorite drinking establishment to recount matches of the past and swap stories of the homeland. In New York, Brooklyn, and Boston, English merchants and professional men founded formal cricket clubs. Their version of cricket was only somewhat more decorous. They usually wagered for side bets and hired professional players if they could afford it, but they might also interrupt matches for a dinner, and the matches might continue over two or three days. Both types of cricket helped preserve English traditions and customs in a new environment.[15]

In the 1850s, cricket rivaled American baseball as a team sport spectacle. The St. George Cricket Club of New York, which employed a professional cricketer from England as a trainer and was the premier club in the United States until the Civil War, attracted large crowds in the 1840s and 1850s to its matches with clubs from Montreal, Toronto, and Boston. New York newspapers regularly gave its matches more coverage than the city's baseball games. In 1859, over 24,000 attended a cricket match at the Elysian Fields in Hoboken between an all-star American team and a touring professional English eleven. Extra ferries had to be engaged to handle the crowds who crossed the river

---

[15]See Melvin L. Adelman, *A Sporting Time: New York City and the Rise of Modern Athletics, 1820–70* (Urbana: 1986); John A. Lester, ed., *A Century of Philadelphia Cricket* (Philadelphia, 1951); and George B. Kirsch, *The Creation of American Team Sports: Baseball and Cricket, 1838–72* (Urbana and Chicago, 1989).

from Manhattan. By 1860, there were ten clubs in New York and Brooklyn. Several pioneers of American baseball, such as Harry Wright and Henry Chadwick, came from the ranks of the English cricket clubs. For a decade or so after 1850, old-stock American clubs sometimes played both cricket and baseball. The Civil War dealt cricket in New York and Brooklyn a blow from which it never fully recovered.

In the last half of the nineteenth century, teams from the British Isles, Australia, and Canada regularly toured the United States, playing both the ethnic clubs and the powerful old-stock American clubs of Philadelphia. By 1887, there were at least fifty clubs scattered throughout the larger cities of the country. For a few years in the 1890s, clubs in Chicago, Detroit, Pittsburgh, New York, Philadelphia, Boston, and Baltimore played in the Inter-City Cricket League, an amateur circuit, and on the Pacific Coast clubs engaged in lively competition for the Harrison Championship Cup. But in the early twentieth century, as English immigration declined sharply and later generations assimilated into the host society, the English cricket clubs rapidly faded from the sporting scene.

Being predominately Catholic and maintaining a centuries-old animosity toward the English, Irish ethnics rarely assimilated as quickly or easily into the dominant American culture. From the 1850s on, Irish-Americans played a conspicuous role in the sporting fraternity, but after the Civil War they formed their own clubs for both the preservation of their Old World games and the playing of New World sports. A revival of Irish nationalism in the 1870s and 1880s stimulated a rebirth of such folk games as hurling and Gaelic football in both the Emerald Isle and the United States. Perhaps typical of cities containing substantial numbers of Irish was an announcement in the Boston *Pilot* in 1881: "A large number of the Irish people in Boston are becoming interested in the exhibitions of the games and pastimes of their ancestors."[16] In the 1880s and 1890s, at least five Irish athletic clubs in Boston regularly engaged in hurling, the national game of Ireland. With even more alacrity, Irish-Americans formed associations for playing baseball, boxing, wrestling, and track and field.

TURNER SOCIETIES

Unlike the Scottish Caledonian and the English cricket clubs, the *Turnverein*, or the Turner societies, had first been organized in their native land. In reaction to the rule of Napoleon, the power of the German aristocracy, and the disunity of the German states, Friederick Ludwig Jahn formed the first Turnverein in Berlin in 1811. From the start, the Turners had a strong ideological cast. By establishing universal education and a systematic program of gymnastics (the latter modeled after the ancient Greeks), Jahn hoped to create a united Germany ruled by the people. Young men of the middle class—petty officials, intellectuals, journalists,

---

[16]Quoted in Stephen Hardy, *How Boston Played: Sport, Recreation, and Community 1865–1915* (Boston, 1982), p. 138.

and students—flocked to Jahn's new society. The Revolution of 1848 brought disaster for the Turners in Germany; many of them emigrated to the United States.

The Turner immigrants faced a different challenge in America, for the Americans had already achieved several of the Turner goals. The United States had no hereditary aristocracy to combat, and a representative democracy was accepted as the ideal political form. Yet the Turners were utopian, free-thinking, and socialistic. They sought an organic community. American individualism ran counter to their deepest social instincts. They also arrived during the heyday of the Know-Nothing movement, a nativist movement of the 1850s. Though the nativists directed their energies primarily at the Catholic Church and Irish immigrants, the Turners bore the brunt of mob action in several American cities. Perhaps even more crucial in driving the Turners together was the fierce antagonism they experienced from the "church" Germans. The haughty anti-clericalism and superior cultural achievements of the Turners made it impossible for them to find refuge in the larger German ethnic communities. Consequently, the Turner societies formed distinctive subcommunities in many American cities, sharply separated from those Germans whose lives revolved around their churches.

Shortly after their arrival in the New World, the revolutionary émigrés of 1848 began to organize Turner societies. Friedrich Hecker, a hero of the revolution in Baden, erected a gymnasium in Cincinnati in 1849 to cultivate "rational training, both physical and intellectual." The Turner halls provided a complete social center with lectures, libraries, and usually a bar. Here the Turners tried to preserve the speech, songs, and customs of the Fatherland. They often formed separate militia companies. In 1851 the Turners held a national gymnastics festival in Philadelphia. This competitive event became an annual affair, with gymnasts from over 150 societies participating. After the Civil War, the Turners abandoned most of their radical political program and began to assimilate more rapidly into the host society. In 1881, by competing in a gymnastics festival held at Frankfurt on the Main, a group of Turners from the Normal School of the *Turnerbund* located at Milwaukee initiated irregular competition between Turner teams from the United States and Germany that continued until World War I. One of the striking features of the Chicago World's Fair of 1893 was a mass exercise performed by 4,000 German-American members of the national *Turnerbund*. In 1898, the United States Commissioner of Education declared that the introduction of school gymnastics in Chicago, Kansas City, Cleveland, Denver, Indianapolis, St. Louis, Milwaukee, Cincinnati, St. Paul, and San Francisco was due to the Turners and that "the directors of physical education [in these cities] are graduates of the Seminary or Normal School of the North American Turnerbund."[17] Moreover, modern Olympic gymnastics originated primarily from the Turner societies.

[17]Quoted in A. E. Zucker, ed., *The Forty-Eighters: Political Refugees of the German Revolution of 1848* (New York, 1950), p. 109. See also Riess, *City Games*, pp. 96–99.

Sports could both ease the transition of ethnic groups into a new society and aid them in protecting their identity. Nineteenth-century baseball illustrated the twin processes. Since baseball could be played quickly, and equipment requirements were minimal, any open space could serve as a playing area and it did not long remain an exclusive sport of old-stock Americans. Beginning in the 1850s, the Irish and the Germans took up the sport. In New Orleans, for example, the Germans founded the Schneiders, Laners, and Lanwehrs, and the Irish, the Fenian Baseball Club. Baseball invariably accompanied the ethnic picnics of the Germans, Irish, French, and later, Italians. As late as the 1920s, a French-Canadian faction in Woonsocket, Rhode Island, resorted to baseball as a means of preserving their community from the forces of assimilation.[18] Sports not only provided ethnics with shared experiences but they tended to blur status, ideological, and personal differences within ethnic communities.

Inadequate evidence makes it difficult to reach more than tentative conclusions about the black experience in nineteenth-century sport. Newspapers and sporting journals rarely reported the sporting activities of Afro-Americans. Until 1865, slavery obviously curtailed the athletic opportunities for blacks. In the antebellum era, planters sometimes promoted boxing bouts among their slaves and used them as crews for boating regattas. To the extent that they had equal leisure time and funds, free blacks in the urban areas probably were as active in sport as their white counterparts. In the New York City area, blacks sponsored occasional prize fights and scheduled a few professional pedestrian races. In New Orleans, where the largest aggregation of free blacks lived in the antebellum era, Afro-Americans formed two sport clubs—Bayou and LaVille—for the playing of raquette. Apparently borrowed from the Choctaw Indians, raquette was a team game resembling lacrosse. The Sunday matches between black clubs in the 1850s sometimes attracted as many as 4,000 spectators from all social ranks and both races. For a brief interval after the Civil War, a few interracial raquette contests were held, but interest in the game soon gave way to other sports.[19]

After the Civil War, many ex-slaves fled the plantations for the cities. Little is known of their athletic activities. But prize fighting within the black communities was common, a few black athletic clubs existed, and many black baseball teams were organized. Baseball was by far the most popular team sport of the urban blacks. In New Orleans, for example, several clubs scheduled a city-wide "Negro championship" series in the 1880s. As in other parts of the country, it was not unusual for black and white amateur or semiprofessional teams to play against one another. A newspaper account of a game played in 1887 at New Orleans, in which a black nine defeated a white club, noted: "The playing of the colored club was far above the average ball playing and elicited hearty and

[18]Richard Sorrel, "Sports and the Franco-Americans in Woonsocket, 1870–1930," *Rhode Island History*, 31 (1972), 112.

[19]Somers, *Rise of Sports*, pp. 71–72, 208–09. For a general treatment of blacks in nineteenth-century sports, see Arthur R. Ashe, Jr., *A Hard Road to Glory: A History of the African-American Athlete, 1619–1918* (New York, 1988).

generous applause from the large crowd in attendance, which was about evenly divided between white and colored."[20] From the scanty evidence available, it appears that the black athletic organizations served as agencies for promoting the formation of subcommunities of blacks.

ETHNICS AND BLACKS IN PROFESSIONAL SPORTS

Professional sports have long been regarded as the very symbol of democratic opportunity. Presumably, ethnic and racial minorities found in sport that only their athletic skills counted. Education, ethnicity, skin color, and parental status were irrelevant, for on the athletic field all men competed on an equal basis. For the athletically talented ethnic or black, professional sport purportedly offered an easier exit out of the ghetto than other possible careers. John K. Tener, president of baseball's National League and former governor of Pennsylvania, probably reflected the self-perception of professional sportsmen when he declared: "I tell you that baseball is the very watchword of democracy. There is no other sport or business or anything under heaven which exerts the leveling influence that baseball does. Neither the public school nor the church can approach it."[21]

For aspiring athletes of whatever social origin, professional baseball offered far more jobs than did the other sports combined. The rosters of major-league teams suggest that baseball did indeed measure men more by athletic talent than by ethnic origins. Contemporary observers often commented on the large number of German and Irish players in the major leagues. One expert estimated that about one-third of the major leaguers in the early 1890s were of Irish origins. There were "so many Irish in the game that some thought they had a special talent for ball playing. Fans liked to argue the relative merits of Irish as against those of German extraction."[22] Apparently well over half of the big-league ball players in the 1880s and 1890s were either of German or Irish origins. The hostility of middle- and upper-status old-stock American groups toward professional baseball as a career choice undoubtedly increased opportunities for ethnics.

The story of the black in professional baseball was another matter. As early as 1867, the National Association of Base Ball Players, composed of "amateur" athletes, specifically excluded black players and clubs from membership.[23] The professional association of the early 1870s did not formally ban blacks—at least one black played briefly in the association—but apparently did practice exclusion by gentleman's agreement. Informally, the National League, organized in 1876, enforced a "color ban" from its founding. In the 1880s, a few clubs in other professional leagues experimented with integrated teams. In 1883, Moses

---

[20]Quoted in Somers, *Rise of Sports*, p. 120.

[21] Quoted in Harold Seymour, *Baseball*, 2 vols. (New York, 1960, 1971), I, 83.

[22]Ibid., p. 334.

[23]See ibid., p. 42, for the official statement of the NABBP.

Fleetwood Walker, a former Michigan and Oberlin College student, signed with Toledo. The next year Toledo entered the American Association, then a major league, with Walker behind the plate. Later in the season, Weldy Walker, Moses' younger brother, played in six games with Toledo. Neither of the Walkers obtained a contract in 1885, but Moses Walker along with seven or eight other blacks continued to play on white minor-league teams.

The experiment with integrated professional baseball was brief. Racial antagonism intensified in the 1880s, and the white players deeply resented having to compete with blacks for playing positions. In 1887, Adrian C. "Cap" Anson, the player-manager of the Chicago White Sox, refused to allow his team to play an exhibition game with Newark until Moses Walker and another black were removed from the Newark lineup. In the same year, the St. Louis Browns' players successfully petitioned their owner to block a match with the Cuban Giants, a black professional team. (In an effort to escape discrimination, black players and teams sometimes tried to use the ploy of advertising themselves as Cubans.) Also in 1887, several of the best white players in the International League threatened to quit unless blacks were dropped from the circuit. According to the *Sporting News* in 1889 "race prejudice exists in professional baseball ranks to a marked degree, and the unfortunate son of Africa who makes his living as a member of a team of White professionals has a rocky road to travel."[24] Indeed, he did. Black players had to withstand withering ridicule from fellow players, their managers, and the white spectators. In the 1890s, total segregation became the rule, corresponding in time with the passage of a new array of Jim Crow laws in the South and the increased disenfranchisement of blacks by state legislatures. The "color ban" remained in the major leagues and their affiliates until 1945, when Jackie Robinson signed with the Montreal Royals, a minor-league club owned by the Brooklyn Dodgers.

Promoters, both black and white, filled the void caused by the exclusion of blacks from white teams by forming black barnstorming teams. Traveling throughout the nation, the barnstorming teams met all-comers, including major league barnstorming teams in the off-season. Although financially marginal operations, the teams provided several hundred blacks with incomes considerably above that of the average black worker.

Sometimes blacks found opportunities in professional sports other than baseball. A few became pedestrians and competed on both sides of the Atlantic Ocean, but after the 1870s, professional running nearly disappeared. Prior to the 1890s, many blacks served as jockeys. The bicycling rage of the last decade of the nineteenth century reflected the typical problems confronted by blacks in sport. Prior to 1890, when the cycle was expensive, the question of black membership in the amateur League of American Wheelmen (LAW), organized in 1880, was practically nonexistent. But in the early 1890s, the manufacturers perfected inexpensive "drop frame," or "safety" bicycles, which opened the sport to nearly all income groups. To protest black membership in the LAW, southern affiliates

---

[24]Quoted in Robert Peterson, *Only the Ball Was White* (Englewood Cliffs, NJ, 1970), p. 41.

in the early 1890s began to withdraw from the league. In response, the 1894 LAW convention adopted a "whites only" membership policy. "There is no question of our accepting the negro in preference to the white wheelman of the south," wrote a LAW official. "If it should be narrowed down to a question such as that, we should undoubtedly decide that we want our southern brothers in the league in preference to the negroes of the country."[25]

Only Marshall W. "Major" Taylor, a black man from Indianapolis, Indiana, succeeded in breaking the racial barrier in professional bicycle racing.[26] Hailed as the "Fastest Bicycle Rider in the World," Taylor, who won the national sprint championships in 1898, 1899, and 1900, broke many national and world records before retiring in 1910. From the beginning of his career as a "scorcher," as bicycle racers were dubbed, at the tender age of fourteen, Taylor experienced nearly every conceivable form of discrimination from white racers. Apart from frequent racial slurs, white riders often colluded in throwing him from his cycle or "boxing" him in, and, in at least one instance, he was physically attacked by a white rider after the completion of a match. Promoters prohibited Taylor from racing on all southern and several northern tracks. In 1897, fellow riders tried to exclude him from all "white" tracks, but the conspiracy collapsed, attributable largely to the influence of the bicycle manufacturers and racing promoters. Despite the hostility of the other scorchers toward Taylor, the bike makers and race promoters had a stake in keeping him on the tracks. For the black scorcher attracted larger crowds than any other single performer. Apart from Taylor, however, few other blacks competed in "white" events. Most of them raced only in an all-Negro league. In the early years of the twentieth century, the popularity of cycle racing rapidly declined, to be replaced in part by automobile racing.

Although opportunities in the prize ring did not extend equally to blacks, boxing was somewhat less discriminatory than other sports. If pitting a black against a white could be profitable, the sporting fraternity was not averse to promoting such a battle. In the 1890s George Dixon, a black who fought several interracial bouts, claimed both the bantam and featherweight championships. For a time both Joe Gans and Joe Walcott held titles in the lower weight divisions. Peter Jackson, winner of the Australian championship in 1886 and the leading black heavyweight in the 1880s and early 1890s, was not so fortunate. Sponsored by the (white) California Athletic Club in San Francisco, Jackson defeated several prominent white heavyweights in the United States. In 1891, the year before the Sullivan–Corbett bout for the championship, Jackson fought Corbett to a sixty-one round draw in San Francisco. The California Athletic Club offered a $20,000 purse for a Sullivan–Jackson match, but the champion declined.[27] The white successors to Sullivan also drew the "color line." A black did not get a shot at the

---

[25]Quoted in Somers, *Rise of Sports*, p. 223.

[26]See Marshall W. "Major" Taylor, *The Fastest Bicycle Rider in the World* (Battleboro, VT, 1972).

[27]*New York Clipper*, May 3, 1890. See David K. Wiggins, "Peter Jackson and the Elusive Heavyweight Championship: A Black Athlete's Struggle Against the Late Nineteenth Century Color Line," *Journal of Sport History*, 12 (1985), 143–68.

heavyweight title until 1908, when black challenger Jack Johnson defeated Tommy Burns.

Those outside of the mainstream of Victorian life represented one rich strand of nineteenth-century sporting life. Ethnics and blacks formed hundreds of athletic clubs for track and field, gymnastics, cricket, hurling, baseball, and a half dozen other kinds of games. Their clubs and games aided them in the formation of subcommunities. The subcommunities in turn helped to hold together the nineteenth-century social order. In addition, the "outsiders" were the major entrepreneurs as well as patrons of urban entertainment. Young, displaced males in the city, who might also be blacks or ethnics, frequently turned to sports to earn money or seek satisfactions missing from other parts of their lives.

5

THE RISE
OF THE
NATIONAL GAME

Baseball evolved by three main stages. First was the simple, informal folk game played mostly by boys. (Contrary to the myth propagated by Organized Baseball, General Abner Doubleday had nothing to do with the invention of baseball. See Chapter 9.) Second was the club-based fraternal game. In the 1840s and 1850s young men in several of the larger cities formalized the bat and ball games that had been played by boys for decades. They organized clubs, adopted written rules, and initially, placed a higher priority on playing for personal pleasure than on playing for spectators. Third, baseball became a commercial, spectator-centered sport. The formation of the National League in 1876 signalled the full arrival of baseball as a business enterprise.[1]

[1]For a contemporary but not always trustworthy account, see Albert Spalding, *America's National Game* (New York, 1911). Harold Seymour, *Baseball*, 2 vols. (New York, 1960, 1971) and David Quentin Voigt, *American Baseball*, 3 vols. (Norman, OK, 1966, 1970, University Park, PA, 1983) represent the first scholarly histories of the sport. Important revisions of the early history have been made by Melvin L. Adelman, *A Sporting Time: New York City and the Rise of Modern Athletics, 1820–70* (Urbana and Chicago, 1986); Stephen Freedman, "The Baseball Fad in Chicago: An Exploration of the Role of Sport in a Nineteenth Century City," *Journal of Sport History*, 5 (Summer 1978), 42–64; Warren J. Goldstein, " 'Playing for Keeps': A History of Baseball, 1857–1876," unpub. Ph.D. diss., Yale University, 1983; George B. Kirsch, *The Creation of American Team Sports: Baseball and Cricket, 1838–72* (Urbana and Chicago, 1989); Peter Levine, *A.G. Spalding and the Rise of Baseball: The Promise of American Sport* (New York, 1985); and Lee Lowenfish/Tony Lupien, *The Imperfect Diamond: The Story of Baseball's Reserve System and the Men Who Fought to Change It* (New York, 1980). For a controversial argument that the popularity of baseball arose from the desire of the players to replicate their work experience see Steven M. Gelber, " 'Their Hands Are All Out Playing:' Business and Amateur Baseball, 1845-1917," *Journal of Sport History*, 11 (Spring 1984), 5–27 and Gelber, " 'Working at Playing:' The Culture of the Work Place and the Rise of Baseball," *Journal of Social History*, 16 (June 1983), 3–20.

BASEBALL AS A CLUB-BASED FRATERNAL SPORT

It is unclear why a group of clerks, store keepers, professional men, brokers, and assorted "gentlemen" in New York City began playing what had formerly been a child's game. Perhaps it was simply an extension of their childhood experiences or of the social activities of the volunteer fire department to which they all belonged. At any rate, beginning in 1842, this group gathered regularly to play baseball at 27th Street and 4th Avenue in Manhattan. In 1845, Alexander Cartwright, a bank clerk, urged the young men to form a club and secure a permanent playing site. Once organized, the Knickerbocker Base Ball Club restricted membership to forty, charged annual dues of five dollars, and required members to attend "Play Days" every Monday and Thursday. Perhaps in an effort to obtain the endorsement of suspicious Victorians as well as to strengthen the fraternal bonds within the club, the Knickerbockers prescribed strict codes of dress and behavior. Members had to purchase like uniforms of blue woolen pantaloons, white flannel shirts, and straw hats. The club fined those members who disobeyed the captain, disputed an umpire's decision, or used profanity.

Apparently, in 1845, Alexander Cartwright, on behalf of the Knickerbockers, set down the first written rules for baseball. Until then, several versions of baseball, labeled variously as "base ball," and "town ball," all of which were probably derivatives of the English game of rounders, had competed for popularity. Cartwright stipulated that the infield be diamond-shaped with bases at each of four corners; he located the bases ninety feet from one another. Tagging a runner between bases replaced "soaking" or "plugging," a painful feature of rounders in which base runners could be retired by striking them with a thrown ball. In another departure from rounders, Cartwright limited the team at bat to only three outs. Fielders could obtain outs by catching the batted ball on the first bounce or in the air, by throwing the ball to first base ahead of the runner, or by tagging the runner between bases.

The New York Knickerbockers, the first club for which any written records survive, represented all of the essential elements of the rapidly growing baseball fraternity of the mid-nineteenth century. Unlike the larger sporting fraternity, the baseball fraternity's existence revolved mainly around organized clubs. Like other voluntary associations, the clubs drew up bylaws, elected officers, and held regular meetings. In the earliest days of the sport, one became a club member by invitation only. Consisting of enough members to comprise at least two teams, the clubs initially played intraclub rather than interclub games. A common interest in baseball, colorful uniforms similar to those of the volunteer fire departments of the era, and a large array of social activities strengthened the fraternal bonds of the ball players. Club members met throughout the year to share food, drink, and good cheer.

Rituals helped heal the divisions within the fraternity that arose from vigorous competition on the field of play. In a postgame ceremony, the winning team received the game ball as a prize; the ball was properly inscribed with the outcome and date of the contest. After interclub games, the home club usually provided the visitors with gala dinners. In 1858, for example, "the Excelsior Club was escorted to the Odd Fellows Hall, Hoboken, by the Knickerbocker Club, and entertained in splendid style. . . . Dodsworth's band was in attendance to liven the scene."[2] An extreme example of the effectiveness of the postgame ritual in promoting amity within the fraternity occurred in 1860. According to the *New York Clipper*, after having shared a keg of lager, the players were unable to recall the score of the game that they had played earlier in the day.[3]

Like the larger sporting fraternity, the baseball fraternity satisfied the needs of specific social groups. Apparently the membership of the Knickerbockers came almost entirely from the ranks of the rapidly growing white collar class, but soon the sport spread to the skilled and semiskilled blue collar workers. At the time of baseball's rapid "take-off" in popularity, the work experiences of both the clerks and the artisans were undergoing profound changes. At midcentury, both groups found less satisfaction in their respective workplaces. Frequently unmarried and perhaps living in boardinghouses, young clerks and artisans often sought excitement, opportunities to display their individual skills, and a sense of belonging in associational activities such as baseball clubs.

THE GROWTH OF BASEBALL

The fraternal potential of the sport, the exciting nature of the game itself, its capacity to feed upon neighborhood and urban rivalries, the experience of American boys playing in ball games, the brevity of the playing time (compared to cricket, baseball's major rival for popularity), and improved transportation (particularly railroads) and communication (telegraph and newspapers) all combined in intricate ways to ensure baseball's rapid growth. Any group of men who enjoyed a working schedule that left a few daylight hours free and had the wherewithal to rent playing space could form a club; boys often played informal matches in the streets. In 1858, the early clubs formed the National Association of Base Ball Players (NABBP), which assumed responsibility for rulemaking and attempted to preserve the fraternal character of the sport.

Special games and tours excited widespread interest in the game. In 1858, an "all-star" series between the best players from Brooklyn and the New York stars captured the attention of the entire city. As early as 1859, Massachusetts scheduled a state baseball championship at the Boston Agricultural Grounds. In 1860, the Brooklyn Excelsiors team toured towns in upstate New York, and then moved on by train to Philadelphia and Baltimore. According to a careful estimate of one scholar, when the Civil War erupted in 1861, there were "more than six hundred junior and senior clubs in more than one hundred cities. Probably more than twelve thousand [men and boys] engaged in regular

[2]Quoted in Seymour, *Baseball*, I, 21.
[3]Goldstein, " 'Playing for Keeps,' " p. 27.

AN EARLY BASEBALL GAME, CIRCA 1887
Although located in a pastoral setting, notice that this field sported a players'
bench, clearly marked base paths, and an outfield fence. Colorful uniforms and
outfield flags were a part of the sport's pageantry.

formal competition, while countless thousands more enjoyed more primitive forms of the sport."[4] The Civil War, far from impeding the growth of the sport, encouraged the introduction of baseball by veterans (especially the Union ones) to hamlets across the nation. Representation at the annual baseball convention grew from 62 clubs in six states in 1860 to 91 clubs in ten states at the war's conclusion in 1865.

As early as the mid-1850s, the baseball fraternity began to promote their sport as "the national game." Such a strategy fitted perfectly the mood of the 1850s. In the decade that spawned the nativist, anti-Catholic, Know Nothing political movement and the bitter sectional rivalries that culminated in the Civil War, yearnings for national unity spilled over into the sports arena. Few public events captured the public imagination more than American challenges to English supremacy in horseracing, yachting, and boxing. Comprised of old-stock Americans, many of the first baseball clubs openly avowed their nationalism by taking on such patriotic names as Young America, Columbia, Union, Eagle, American, National, and Liberty. As the English had their cricket and the Germans had their *Turnvereins, Porter's Spirit* declared in 1857 that the Americans should have "a game that could be termed a 'Native American Sport.' "[5] Baseball,

---

[4]Kirsch, "The Creation of American Team Sports," manuscript version, p. 120.
[5]*Porter's Spirit of the Times,* 1 (Jan. 31, 1857), 357.

its supporters agreed, filled the need; for it had evolved as a distinctive American sport and embodied more completely than any other sport the fast-paced nature of American life.

Baseball thrived on urban rivalries. Determining urban supremacy in terms of population growth, community leadership, or the quality of life might be difficult, but baseball games offered an unambiguous test of urban superiority in the form of a symbolic contest. A city's baseball team often rallied the citizens behind a common cause as nothing else short of a natural disaster could do. When the result of an 1875 match between the winning St. Louis Brown Stockings and the Chicago White Stockings "was announced, deep gloom settled upon the city," the *Chicago Times* reported. "Friends refused to recognize friends, lovers became estranged, and business was suspended. All Chicago went to a funeral, and the time, since then, has dragged wearily along, as though it were no object to live longer in the world."[6]

The press also helped to promote baseball. While the regular newspapers initially gave only cursory attention to the sport, such sporting sheets as the *New York Clipper* and *Porter's Spirit of the Times* not only reported the results of matches and other baseball news but even lent direct aid to young men interested in forming clubs. No single journalist gave the sport greater assistance than Henry Chadwick, the dean of baseball publicists and a longtime member of the NABBP's rules committee. Chadwick edited baseball's annual guidebook, which by the mid-1860s claimed to have a circulation of more than 65,000. The guidebooks enabled avid fans to keep abreast of the latest rules, franchises, and statistics, as well as other news of the diamond. Chadwick also invented the box score and batting averages, quantitative devices that enhanced the appeal of the sport.

To counter charges that the sport encouraged uninhibited behavior and general immorality, the baseball fraternity quickly developed a Victorian-like defense of the game. Unlike other sports, the defenders of baseball insisted, baseball encouraged manliness, or self-control, rather than boyishness, or uninhibited behavior. Consistent with this argument, widespread agitation arose within the fraternity in the mid-1860s for requiring fielders to catch the ball "on the fly" rather than on the first bounce for a putout. Defenders also claimed that, whether one be a fan or a player, participation in baseball improved one's health and furnished a much-needed respite from work. Play by boys, according to the *Brooklyn Eagle,* kept the youngsters "out of a great deal of mischief. . . . [Baseball] keeps them from hanging around [fire] engine houses, stables, and taverns." The game merited "the endorsement of every clergyman in the country," concluded Henry Chadwick, because it was a "remedy for the many evils resulting from the immoral associations [that] boys and young men of our cities are apt to become connected with."[7] Nonetheless such arguments by no means stilled Victorian suspicions of the fraternity and its game.

---

[6]Quoted in Gregg Lee Carter, "Baseball in Saint Louis, 1867–1875: An Historical Case Study of Civic Pride," *Missouri Historical Bulletin*, 31 (1975), 257.

[7]Quoted in Adelman, *A Sporting Time*, p. 173.

BASEBALL AS A COMMERCIAL ENTERPRISE

Although baseball as a fraternal, club-based sport never completely disappeared, commercial considerations transformed several essential features of the early game. By 1860, inviting the general public to attend games and charging admissions had become commonplace. At first, the clubs used the gate receipts simply to cover club expenses, but soon clubs and promoters of matches began to allocate a part of the proceeds to pay star players. As early as 1863, the *Brooklyn Eagle* reported that "ball matches have of late years got to be quite serious affairs, and some have even intimated that ballplaying has become quite a money making business, many finding it to pay well to play well."[8] Fraternal bonds weakened. By the mid-1860s the postgame rituals of awarding the game ball to the winning team and hosting a dinner for visitors had disappeared from the sport. Unlike the earliest days of the game, the "cranks" (fans) cheered wildly for their heroes, heckled umpires and opposing players, and sometimes rioted. Blue collar youth, often of Irish or German extraction, also took up the sport.

Furthermore, despite the loud protests of its promoters, in the 1860s and 1870s baseball became more closely identified in many quarters with the larger Victorian counterculture. Employers hesitated to employ clerks who played baseball. "The invariable question put to young men applying for situations in New York," according to the secretary of the Irvington, New Jersey, baseball club in 1867, "is, whether they are members of ball clubs. If they answer in the affirmative, they are told that their services will not be needed."[9] The Victorian press accused both professional and amateur players of consorting with gamblers and show people. In 1872, *The New York Times* described the typical player as a "worthless, dissipated gladiator; not much above the professional pugilist in morality and respectability." The players spent their off-seasons according to the *Times*, "in those quiet retreats connected with bars, and rat pits, where sporting men of the metropolis meet for social improvement and unpremeditated pugilism."[10]

Patrons of the Victorian underworld found in baseball a sport to satisfy the widespread hunger for gambling. In all the larger cities, pool rooms determined odds, kept records of bets, and assured payments—all for a commission. At some parks, gamblers openly hawked their odds. Justifiably, fans suspected that some games were fixed. New York gamblers, for example, controlled the Troy, New York, Haymakers, a team that enjoyed a notorious reputation for "hippodroming," or fixing games. In California, just as a fielder was about to catch a fly ball, the gamblers, who had placed wagers on the side at bat, would fire their six-shooters. On several occasions, bettors even mobbed playing fields

---

[8]Quoted in ibid, p. 151. On spectator behavior, see esp. George B. Kirsch, "Baseball Spectators, 1855–1870," *Baseball History* (Fall 1987), 4–20.

[9]Philadelphia *Sunday Mercury*, Aug. 26, 1866, as quoted in Kirsch, "The Creation of American Team Sports," manuscript version, p. 369.

[10]*New York Times*, March 8, 1872.

to prevent the completion of games in which they stood to lose money. "So common has betting become at baseball matches," complained a *Harper's Weekly* editor in 1867, "that the most respectable clubs in the country indulge in it to a highly culpable degree, and so common . . . the tricks by which games have been 'sold' for the benefit of the gamblers that the most respectable participants have been suspected of baseness."[11]

The formation of the Cincinnati Red Stockings in 1869 as the first avowedly all-professional team ended the pretense of baseball's pristine amateurism. Although the sport continued to provide fraternal functions for thousands of young men and boys, the step by the Cincinnati club manifestly placed it and its professional successors in the same arena with the theater and other forms of commercial show business. Led by Harry Wright, a former professional cricket player and a baseball player with the Knickerbockers, the Red Stockings recruited five eastern stars and swept through the 1869 season of 58 games without a loss and only one tie. Over 23,000 fans watched their six-game series in New York, the center of the baseball world. In Washington, D.C., President Ulysses S. Grant welcomed the western "Cinderella" team and complimented the members on their excellent playing. In September, the club crossed the United States on the newly completed transcontinental railroad to play a series of games in California. Altogether, the Red Stockings traveled 11,877 miles by rail, stage, and boat, and over 200,000 fans witnessed their games.

Despite the fantastic success of the team on the playing field, Wright experienced several headaches in managing the touring Red Stockings. Sometimes the gate receipts did not meet team expenses. For example, at Mansfield, Ohio, the club grossed only $50, and in Cleveland $81. The team arrived in Syracuse, New York, to find no opposition. At times they cut practices, missed trains, and drank far too much alcohol. Wright's pitcher, Asa Brainard, was a hypochondriac and eccentric. During one game, a wild rabbit ran across the infield in front of Brainard. He impulsively turned and hurled the ball at the frightened bunny. He missed, and the ball rolled into the crowd, allowing two rival runners to score. All was not lost, for the Red Stockings proceeded to win the game anyway.

The success of the Red Stockings encouraged the formation of the first all-professional league, the National Association of Professional Base Ball Players (NAPBBP) in 1871. The association (1871–1875) bore only a faint resemblance to modern professional sports leagues. It did assure that in the future professional baseball would dictate rule changes and the style of play. But the league welcomed the addition of any team that could muster a mere ten-dollar entry fee. Consequently, many teams located in smaller cities, joined but quickly dropped out of the NAPBBP. Teams scheduled their own matches; a team could qualify for the championship pennant by playing all other clubs at least five times during the season. To maximize profits, big-city clubs attempted to avoid playing more than the minimal number of games in the smaller towns. The players were free

---

[11]*Harper's Weekly*, Oct. 26, 1867.

to move from one club to another at the end of each season, and enjoyed salaries two or three times higher than the ordinary workingmen of the era.

Harry Wright's Boston Red Sox team dominated the new loop. After the 1870 season, Wright brought most of his Cincinnati team with him to Boston. Although narrowly losing the pennant to Philadelphia in 1871, the Red Sox then won the next four consecutive championships. George Wright, Harry's brother, was the club's superb fielding, hard-hitting shortstop. Young Albert Spalding was the most baffling pitcher in the league, and Roscoe Barnes was the perennial batting champion. In 1875 Boston had the top four hitters in the circuit and ran away with the league pennant, winning seventy-one games while losing only eight.

THE NATIONAL LEAGUE

In 1876 a few men, led by William A. Hulbert, president of the Chicago club, conspired to overthrow the national association and found a new professional league that would be profitable to investors. After secretly obtaining the support of the western clubs that resented the eastern domination of the NAPBBP, Hulbert called a meeting in February, 1876, with representatives of five eastern clubs. When assembled, as a dramatic gesture, Hulbert reportedly locked the hotel door and dropped the key into his pocket. After reviewing the weaknesses of the association, he proposed a new league, "The National League of Professional Base Ball Clubs." Charter members of the new league were Boston, Chicago, Cincinnati, Louisville, Hartford, St. Louis, Philadelphia, and New York. Significantly, the term "Clubs" had been substituted for "Players." The constitution of the new National League gave the owners complete control of the management, regulations, and the resolution of disputes. To appeal to Victorian sensibilities, the league forbade Sunday games and betting in ball parks. In time, the league assumed full responsibility for scheduling games, setting uniform game admission rates, and paying umpires.

The National League pioneered in developing a business structure that would become standard for all twentieth-century professional team sports. In economic terms, the league was a loosely organized cartel, an arrangement among the clubs designed to restrict competition among franchises for players. Although the founders did not initially have enough foresight to devise a reserve clause to bind players to one team for their entire playing careers, the league did forbid negotiations with players from another team while the season was in progress. In 1879 the owners secretly agreed to "reserve" five players, a policy later expanded to include virtually every player on a club's roster. Such a system prevented competitive bidding among the teams for the services of players. The National League also essentially prohibited the planting of more than one franchise in each city. Finally, the league established an entry monopoly. Two blackballs by existent franchises barred new applicants from the league. Thus in order for an aspiring baseball owner to obtain a league franchise, he either had to purchase an existing club, win the vote of the owners of existing clubs to add a franchise, or form a competing major league.

Yet the National League, like most arrangements based upon gentlemen's agreements, often failed to function as a genuine cartel. Ownership and management decisions of the individual franchises remained largely free of league authority; the league had only one employee, a secretary-treasurer. Ultimately, restrictive agreements could be enforced neither by the league nor the courts. Consequently, each club owner tended to place the economic interest of his franchise before that of the welfare of the league. As Albert Spalding, a shrewd observer of baseball history explained: "The [baseball] magnate must be a strong man among strong men, else other club owners in the league will combine in their own interests against him and his interests. . . . "[12]

For its first six years, William Hulbert did offer the National League strong, albeit sometimes questionable, leadership. He immediately cracked down on the loose player behavior that had blemished the integrity of professional baseball in the past. In 1877 he dramatically expelled four Louisville players for taking bribes from gamblers. Under Hulbert's direction, the league made other decisions that were more debatable. The charging of a uniform admission price of fifty cents when the daily wages of workingmen ranged from one to three dollars led opponents of the loop to describe it as a "rich man's" league. When both the Philadelphia and New York teams failed to take their final road tours of the 1876 season, Hulbert led the movement to expel them from the league, and he stubbornly refused to permit either city to field teams in the league while he was alive. Thus, until Hulbert's death in 1882, the league sacrificed potential revenue from the nation's two most populous cities. By 1878 only three of the original eight clubs remained in the league. When the Cincinnati club persisted in selling beer at its park and playing Sunday games, Hulbert forced them out of the league in 1880. Hulbert's highhanded and dictatorial methods may have kept the league intact and improved the image of professional baseball, but when he died, the league directors made certain that none of his successors obtained similar powers.

The expulsion of Cincinnati led to a direct challenge to the National League. In 1881 Cincinnati called together delegates from cities that had been excluded from the league to form the American Association of Base Ball Clubs, which was dubbed by critics as the "Beer Ball League" since four of the six directors of association clubs owned breweries. Charter franchises were located in Baltimore, Cincinnati, Louisville, Philadelphia, Pittsburgh, and St. Louis. By charging only a twenty-five cent admission fee, selling liquor at games, and playing on Sunday, the association hoped to profit from the strictures of the older league. The association openly invited league players to jump to the new circuit, and several did. The success of the association caused the leaderless National League to call for a strategic surrender. In 1882, the presidents of the two leagues plus the head of the Northwestern League (which operated in Michigan, Ohio,

---

[12]Seymour, *Baseball*, I, 206.

and Illinois) signed a tripartite National Agreement. At the heart of the agreement was the mutual recognition of reserved players and the establishment of exclusive territorial rights.

The booming prosperity of the 1880s resulted in whirling turnstiles at the parks of both the National League and the American Association. With the implementation of an informal post-season series between the two circuits, interest in professional baseball increased phenomenally. On the playing field, the Association clubs proved fully equal to the senior loop. The powerful St. Louis Browns, managed by young Charles Comiskey (later owner of the Chicago White Sox), won four consecutive Association pennants and two "World Series" from National League opponents. For the first time, most of the clubs made profits, but competition for player talent drove up salaries. To obtain an advantage over opponents, clubs in both leagues from time to time violated the spirit if not the letter of the National Agreement of 1882.

Association club owners, in particular, found cooperation difficult to achieve. Brooklyn and St. Louis fought each other regularly for both the pennant and the management of the circuit. When the Association chose a puppet of the St. Louis Browns as president in 1890, Brooklyn and Cincinnati resigned from the Association and joined the National League. To accommodate the two new clubs, the league conveniently ignored the National Agreement, indicating that it was prepared to resume an all-out war with the Association. The formation of the Players' League in 1890 added to the woes of the Association. Attendance dropped drastically. At the end of the 1891 season, the Association surrendered to the National League. The league then absorbed four Association clubs, making the National League a twelve-member loop, and bought out the four other clubs.

THE PLAYERS' REVOLT

The players posed yet another challenge to the National League. Employer-employee relations in professional baseball reflected the general industrial unrest of the 1880s and 1890s. With player salaries making up some two-thirds of the costs of owning a franchise, the owners devised ingenious methods of keeping their players' wages at a minimum. From its founding in 1876, the National League clubs had employed the dreaded "blacklist." Once a player had been dismissed by one club or the league for any reason, no other club could negotiate with him. In the mid-1880s, the club owners introduced a salary classification plan whereby they agreed on uniform salary limits.

The backbone of owner control of the players was the reserve clause in player contracts. In effect, the club that first signed a player had a lifetime option on that player's services. Negotiating individually, a player had only two weapons: either refuse to play until he was promised the salary he wanted or quit baseball. Neither alternative was attractive. For the player of ordinary ability, holding out would probably mean a loss of income for the playing time that he had cost the club, and most players could not find jobs outside baseball that paid equally well. The reserve clause also made it possible to buy and sell players. All of the strictures on the players depended on the mutual cooperation of club owners. When a particular club saw that the league rules failed to benefit its interest, they often successfully ignored them.

The player-control measures of the league and baseball's prosperity in the 1880s triggered a players' revolt. By the mid-1880s, the players probably earned an average of $1,750 annually, about three times the wages of an industrial worker, but the rising expectations of the players collided with the salary ceilings of the league. In 1885, John Montgomery Ward, who was a lawyer as well as a star player, founded the Brotherhood of Professional Base Ball Players. Initially, the secret organization was little more than a fraternal order. But when the league set a $2,500 ceiling on all players in 1887, the angry players demanded a strike. Ward advised caution. He presented the league with an ultimatum—abandon the salary ceiling system and stop selling players or face competition from a brotherhood league in 1890.

When the league ignored Ward's threat, he formed the Players' League. The players challenged the National League directly. They invaded seven of its cities with new franchises and lured most of its players away from the senior loop. The Players also obtained enough financial backing to ensure initial success. In a novel departure from the traditions of private enterprise, the players and investors assumed joint management of the new enterprise.

Albert Spalding, a former star player but now a sporting goods entrepreneur and a stockholder in the Chicago club, headed a war committee appointed by the National League to suppress the player uprising. Capitalizing upon the popular fears of the day, Spalding denounced the players as "hotheaded anarchists," who were bent on a "terrorism" that was characteristic of "revolutionary movements." While the newspapers happily printed Spalding's scorching statements, he had less success in prosecuting players for violating the reserve clause. The courts held that the contracts containing reserve clauses lacked equity, thereby permitting the players to jump to the new circuit with impunity. Efforts to bribe star players to stay in the loop were also less successful than the magnates had hoped. Spalding offered Mike "King" Kelly, a superstar, a "blank check" to remain in the league, but Kelly refused, saying "I can't go back on the boys."[13]

Nonetheless, the Players' League survived only one season. Competing on the same day in the same city for the same customers cost both leagues heavily. Both leagues also gave away free tickets. The richer owners in the National League could withstand such financial sacrifices more easily than could the Players' League investors. Although the Players' League attracted more fans and their financial losses had been less than the senior loop, some of their backers withdrew support and some players defected back to the National circuit. After one season, the experiment in cooperative-capitalistic baseball ended in failure.

---

[13]Spalding, *America's National Game*, p. 297.

LIFE ON THE DIAMOND

Most fans had little interest in the squabbles taking place in the executive suites; they were far more excited by the action on the diamond. To attract more fans, the league experimented with numerous rule changes. When the National League began in 1876, pitchers threw from below the hip at a distance of forty-five feet from home plate. While three strikes constituted an out, the hitter could call for a strike above or below the waist. Fouls did not count as strikes until 1901. Nine balls delivered outside the zone designated by the hitter gave him a free base on balls. Finally, in 1887, the batters lost their "high-low" privilege, and in 1889 the number of base on balls was reduced to four. In 1884, pitchers received the right to throw overhanded, but the pitching distance was gradually extended until it reached the modern figure of sixty feet, six inches in 1893. Since the turn of the century, baseball rules have essentially remained unchanged.

During the 1880s, managers developed most of the tactics familiar to the modern fan. Infielders played away from their respective bases, and catchers moved closer to the plate. Fielders learned to back each other up in case of wild throws or muffed balls. Unlike modern professional baseball, most of the fielders played several positions, even within a single season. Initially, players sporting gloves were subjected to pitiless ridicule from the fans, but in the 1880s, catchers began to don primitive masks and use mitts and in the 1890s, the other fielders began to use gloves. Overhanded pitching resulted in a wide assortment of new pitches but placed a greater stress on the pitcher's arm. By the end of the 1890s, most teams rotated at least three pitchers, though sometimes one pitcher would pitch several games in a row. Unless injured, the pitcher usually worked the entire nine innings.

The managers increasingly stressed offensive teamwork. Most batters swung freely in the 1880s, though a few were known as "place hitters." Sometimes a hitter bunted the ball, but such a move would likely draw the ire of the fans who considered it unmanly. From time to time, the league considered making the bunt illegal. A few clubs used the "hit-and-run" play in the 1880s, but it was not perfected nor regularly employed until the late 1890s. The psychological warfare of the players developed into a brutal art. By the 1890s ragging opponents was commonplace, a far cry from the early history of the game.

To the modern fan, the baseball park of the 1880s and 1890s would be both familiar and strange. Most of the parks were surrounded by wooden stands and a wooden fence. A roof protected some of the stands while the others were unprotected wooden seats of sun-bleached boards (hence the term bleachers). A crowd of 4,000 was considered large. As late as the early 1900s, clubs sometimes allowed patrons to park their carriages or automobiles in the outfield, though by this time middle- and upper-income groups could reach the park by fast trolleys. When the stands had been filled, spectators crowded around the infield and stood in the outfield. At a Baltimore–Boston game in 1897, over 25,000 fans appeared, far exceeding the park's capacity. The outfielders stood only a few feet behind the infielders, and any ball hit into the crowd was ruled an automatic double. (Incidentally, Boston triumphed by a score of 19–10.) Scorecards and concessions could be purchased at all parks, but the lack of a public address system or numbers on the players' uniforms challenged the fan's ingenuity in following the action. Often a brass band played during lulls in the action. Since the owners wanted to maximize profits, a fan could sometimes encounter his favorite player taking tickets at the gate.

Until the 1890s, the Chicago White Stockings, under the leadership of Adrian C. "Cap" Anson, dominated National League play. Anson, who stood six feet, two inches and weighed over 200 pounds, was for that era a veritable giant. He could play any position but finally settled on first base. As a hitter he won four league batting crowns and in twenty-two seasons failed to hit .300 only twice. Anson became the playing-manager of the Stockings in 1880, a position he retained for nineteen years. Under Anson's capable command from 1880 to 1886, Chicago won five pennants. Another player, Mike "King" Kelly, competed with Anson for the adoration of the Chicago fans. A colorful player both on and off the field, Kelly excelled at hitting and baserunning. "Slide, Kelly, Slide!" later became a hit song. Apart from baseball, Kelly also loved race horses and liquor. In 1887 Chicago shocked the baseball world by selling Kelly to the Boston Red Sox for the then-astronomical sum of $10,000.

"As Celtic as Mrs. Murphy's pig," Kelly inspired many legends. Most of them centered around his opportunism and trickery. It was Kelly who allegedly took advantage of a rule that permitted a substitute to enter the game at any time by simply notifying the umpire. In Boston, he leapt from the dugout bench shouting, "Kelly now catching," and caught a foul fly which the regular catcher could never have reached. On another occasion, as the sun began to set in the last of the 12th inning in Chicago, Kelly pulled an even more startling stunt. With two out and the bases full, Kelly, as the rightfielder, leapt into the twilight trying to catch a mighty drive that would win the game. As he came down, he held his glove high in the air and jauntily jogged to the dugout. The umpire yelled, "Out number three! Game called on account of darkness!" "Nice catch, Kell," his teammates exclaimed. "Not at all, at all," Kelly responded. " 'Twent a mile above my head."[14]

For youth with lower socioeconomic origins, baseball offered a glamorous career opportunity. Most of the 240 big-league players of the 1880s advanced from the unstable minor-league professional teams; others came from amateur teams or directly from the sandlots. Only a handful of players ever attended college, and only a few enjoyed professional careers outside of baseball. Most had short playing careers and when released became either blue-collar workers or workers employed in jobs provided by the Victorian underworld. An unusually large number of German and Irish names appeared on club rosters, suggesting that to these ethnic groups, major-league baseball may have provided a means

---

[14]As told and quoted in Tristram Potter Coffin, *The Old Ball Game in Folklore and Fiction* (New York, 1971), pp. 36–37.

MICHAEL J. "KING" KELLY (1857–1894)
A colorful player both on and off the field, in the 1880s, fans hailed Kelly as the "King of Baseball." In sixteen major league seasons, he compiled a .307 lifetime batting average, and in 1887 he was sold by the Chicago White Stockings to the Boston Red Stockings for the then-astonishing sum of $10,000.

of social mobility. Almost all of the big leaguers came from cities, particularly the large metropolitan areas of the Northeast. In 1897, only three of 168 National Leaguers were from as far south as Virginia, only seven came from the Far West, and over one-third of the players were born in either Massachusetts or Pennsylvania.

By and large the owners failed to impose Victorian codes of personal behavior on the players. Most of them were genial, fun-loving, big spenders. Albert Spalding, as manager of the White Sox, once hired a Pinkerton detective to follow his players. Seven of the players, the detective reported, spent almost every night going "up and down Clark Street [in Chicago] all over the tenderloin districts, through the whole roster of saloons and 'speakeasy' resorts." After Spalding had the report read to the team, King Kelly broke the long silence by saying: "I have to offer only one amendment. In that place where the detective reports me as taking a lemonade at 3 a.m. he's off. It was straight whiskey; I never drank a lemonade at that hour in my life."[15] Spalding fined each of the offenders $25 to cover the costs of hiring the Pinkerton man, but such actions failed to curb player misbehavior.

[15]Spalding, *America's National Game*, p. 184; See also Levine, *A.G. Spalding*, pp. 41–44.

Baseball promoted itself as a democratic sport, claiming to reach all social classes and ethnic groups. "The average American boy," wrote a reporter in 1888, "although he may be rather ignorant as to how delegates are elected to national [political party] conventions, the number of electoral votes apportioned to the different states of the Union, or the date of Lee's surrender, can call the names of eminent professional ball players offhand, or with equal ease give the principal events of Captain John Ward's history as pitcher and short-stop, and Adrian C. Anson's record from the date he left Philadelphia. . . . "[16] Yet, while lower-income groups may have been aware of the actions of the big leaguers, and played baseball themselves, it appears that few of them attended major-league games. The fifty-cent admission charge of the National League excluded many working-men, who rarely earned more than three dollars per day. Since games were played in the daylight hours, usually beginning at 3:30 or so in the afternoon, most workers could not attend weekday games. The starting time, on the other hand, was convenient for clerks, some skilled workers, and professional men. Most fans therefore probably came from the sporting fraternity, show people, gamblers, and those middle-income groups who were uninhibited by Victorian attitudes.

The American elite, the leading proponents of a player-centered ethos, tended to consider professional baseball a crude, ungentlemanly sport. As one of them wrote: "Our professional baseball, with its paid players and its thousands of smoking, and sometimes umpire-mobbing spectators, is doing more harm than good. The players are devoting their lives, instead of their spare time, to diversion instead of duty; and the spectators are wasting two or three hours of fresh air and sunshine looking at what they ought to be doing."[17] The sporting tastes of the most elite groups leaned toward actual participation or, if spectators, to watching club games or intercollegiate football matches. Henry Chadwick sarcastically described them as a "shoddy class of Anglomaniacs."[18] Nevertheless, the baseball magnates made special efforts to attract both "respectable" men and women. They believed women would improve crowd behavior. Early photographs suggest, however, that few women attended professional games.

For the committed fan, baseball had become something more than a simple diversion from daily routines. The game brought overwhelming feelings of exhilaration or depression. The last stanza of "Casey at the Bat" expressed the emotional power of baseball to the nineteenth-century fan.

> Oh! somewhere in this favored land
> the sun is shining bright;
> The band is playing somewhere,
> and somewhere children's hearts are light.
> And somewhere men are laughing,
> and somewhere children shout;

[16]Harry Palmer, "America's National Game," *Outing*, 12 (1888), 351.
[17]Price Collier, "Sports' Place in the Nation's Well Being," *Outing*, 32 (1898), 384–85.
[18]Quoted in Seymour, *Baseball*, I, 333.

But there is no joy in Mudville—
mighty Casey has Struck Out.

After the mighty Casey had struck out, Mudville no longer had room for joy, laughter, shouting children, brass bands, or bright sunshine. A kind of pall hung over the village. The baseball game had reenacted in a capsulized and symbolic form the "game of life."

'Tis the old game of life,
with its conquest and strife,
With its wonderful outings and innings;
Where the umpire of fate
forever doth wait
Giving gladness and sorrow for winning.[19]

---

[19]S. P. Richardson, "Base Ball," reprinted in Spalding, *America's National Game*, p. 457. For the full text of "Casey at the Bat," see ibid., pp. 540–51.

6

SPORTS AMONG THE WEALTHY

The first United States tennis championship tournament opened on August 31, 1881, at the posh Casino Club in Newport, Rhode Island. Less than fifty spectators, all wealthy vacationers who spent their summers in their magnificent stone "cottages," milled around the court. The gentlemen, decked out in white flannels, striped jackets, and straw bowlers, stood while the ladies, who wore ankle-length petticoats and carried parasols to protect their delicate skin from the sun, sat on folding chairs or camp stools. The players likewise sported white flannels, long-sleeved shirts, and neckties, though they exchanged their bowlers for striped caps when playing. They played by the rules established by the All-England Croquet and Lawn Tennis Club, Wimbledon, England, in 1877. Richard D. "Dicky" Sears, a slight, bespectacled lad of nineteen from a Boston Brahmin family, conquered a field of twenty-two players, all of whom came from rich families residing on the eastern coast of the United States.

A deep chasm separated the sporting world of the Newport summer crowd from the sporting universe of the lower, blue and white collar working classes. Only those in the highest social strata could watch or play in the tournament; the Casino Club was so exclusive that it had once turned away a president of the United States (Chester A. Arthur) for his inadequate social standing. The spectators paid no admission; they never cheered or gesticulated. Only polite, whispered conversation punctuated the progress of the match. To the Newport crowd, winning or losing was of no more importance than playing with proper grace, style, and etiquette. No one was paid to play. Following the match the players and spectators retired to the elegant Casino clubhouse where they could

LAWN TENNIS, 1887
In the nineteenth century, only the nation's wealthiest citizens played lawn
tennis. Notice that the women wore bustles and full-length dresses.

enjoy sumptuous food and drink. To most of the wealthy Newport residents, the
tournament represented a pleasant interlude in the summer social season.

Yet the significance of tennis and other sports played by the rich extended far beyond the obvious. In a society characterized by an exceptionally
fluid social structure, expensive sports provided one of the means by which the
wealthy, especially the parvenu, could distinguish their numbers from the
masses. The wealthy therefore tended to look upon sports requiring merely a
field and a ball with contempt; these were the diversions of ordinary people.
Instead, they lavished their attention on thoroughbred horse racing, yachting,
polo, track and field, cricket, tennis, and golf, games that might require much
time, costly facilities, elaborate equipment, and sometimes travel to far-away
places. Furthermore, for the rich, socially exclusive sports became an integral
part of a larger effort to construct elite subcommunities. Within these communities the elite could compete with one another without seriously jeopardizing
group unity.[1]

[1]For general treatment of elite sports in the post-Civil War era, see esp. E. Digby Baltzell,
Philadelphia Gentlemen: The Making of a National Upper Class (New York, 1958), Chap. 13;
Frances G. Courvares, *The Remaking of Pittsburgh: Class and Culture in an Industrial City,
1877–1919* (Albany, 1984), Chap. 7; Stephen Hardy, *How Boston Played: Sport, Recreation, and
Community, 1865–1915* (Boston, 1982), Chap. 7; Donald J. Mrozek, *Sport and the American
Mentality, 1880–1910* (Knoxville, 1983), Chap. 4; Benjamin G. Rader, "The Quest for Sub-
communities and the Rise of American Sport," *American Quarterly,* 29 (1977), 355–69; and
Dale A. Somers, *The Rise of Sports in New Orleans, 1850–1900* (Baton Rouge, LA, 1972).

WEALTHY NEW YORK SPORTSMEN

Of America's three largest cities in the nineteenth century, New York assumed the leadership of the world of elite sports. Since colonial times the city's high society had been more tolerant of conspicuous play than its counterparts in Philadelphia or Boston. In all three cities a residue of the colonial elite joined with new men in the late eighteenth and nineteenth centuries to exploit the vast new opportunities presented in foreign trade, real estate, banking, law, and politics. But unlike New York, the Boston and Philadelphia "mercantile-Federalist" elites founded virtual dynasties. Their descendants managed to perpetuate their inherited status; they continued to dominate the industrial, financial, and cultural activities of their respective cities. To this day, the Boston Brahmin and Philadelphia Main Line families retain a large share of the power, property, and prestige of their respective cities.

On the other hand, the rapid surge in population growth, commerce, railroad building, and the factory system in the latter half of the nineteenth century fractured the older New York elite. "Separate enclaves dominated trade, politics, culture, and fashion, although some common membership existed among these groups," concluded a historian of New York's upper class.[2] The absence of a clear-cut dynasty or social arbitrator in New York gave rise to the "beautiful people" in the post-Civil War era. The nouveau riche defied Victorian restraints. The "smart set," or "Four Hundred," as the press dubbed them, splurged their wealth on highly publicized activities available only to the super rich. Expensive sports furnished them with a vehicle of self-advertisement.

A classic example was James Gordon Bennett, Jr., the colorful and eccentric owner of the *New York Herald*.[3] Bennett's father, a recent Scottish immigrant who had built the *Herald* into the world's most profitable newspaper, had been a social outsider. The younger Bennett, however, used his father's vast fortune and sport as levers to lift himself into fashionable circles. In 1857, at the tender age of sixteen, he became a member of the New York Yacht Club. Nine years later, he captured the attention of the entire nation by winning the world's first transatlantic yacht race. The large purse of $60,000 won from side bets and the loss of six members of his crew who were swept overboard in a violent storm added immensely to Bennett's reputation for bravado. In the meantime he sponsored Henry Stanley's exotic search for David Livingstone who had been missing for several years in the African jungles. Both Europeans and Americans avidly followed Stanley's reports from the heart of Africa. His eventual success in locating Livingstone became the stuff of a monumental legend.

[2]Frederic Cople Jaher, "Style and Status: High Society in Late Nineteenth-Century New York," in Jaher, ed., *The Rich, the Well Born, and the Powerful: Elites and Upper Classes in History* (Urbana, 1973), p. 259. See also Jaher, *The Urban Establishment: Upper Strata in Boston, New York, Charleston, Chicago, and Los Angeles* (Urbana, 1982).

[3]See Donald Seitz, *The James Gordon Bennetts* (Indianapolis, 1928) and Richard O'Connor, *The Scandalous Mr. Bennett* (Garden City, NY, 1962).

Bennett had a direct influence on several sports. Beginning in 1873 he awarded cups and medals to collegiate track and field champions. While visiting England in 1875, he witnessed a game of polo played by English army officers. In 1876 he imported British mallets and balls and hired an English polo player to teach the game to his rich friends. Shortly thereafter Bennett and his wealthy friends formed the Westchester Polo Club in New York and took the sport to the Newport summer colony. Trying to stay current with the latest English sporting fashions, polo enthusiasts even provided their ponies with monogrammed linen sheets upon which to sleep. In 1886 Newport hosted the first international match with the Hurlingham Club of England. Bennett's assistance to the sport of lawn tennis had more bizarre origins. According to legend, in 1878 he secured for a British army officer a guest card to Newport's most exclusive club, the Reading Room. He then dared his friend to ride a horse up the steps of the club's front hall. The Englishman accepted the challenge and the Reading Room immediately revoked Bennett's guest privileges for instigating such a provocative act. Miffed, Bennett retaliated by building a lavish sports complex called the Casino a few blocks away. The Casino subsequently became the site for the first thirty-four national tennis championships.

By 1878 Bennett had departed from New York to live in Paris, an exile caused by a gross indiscretion. In mixed company he had relieved himself into a fireplace at his fiancée's New Year's Day party. His fiancée's family immediately broke the engagement; later her brother publicly attacked and humiliated Bennett, and eventually the two men fought a nonlethal duel. Bennett then left America, forever shunned by New York's Four Hundred. He seldom returned to the United States, but his *New York Herald* led the major dailies in reporting sporting news. Later in the century he contributed to the Olympic movement, and he promoted horse, auto, and air races. Bennett was one of the first of a long line of eccentric millionaires who promoted and popularized sport as a means of gaining self-attention.

THOROUGHBRED HORSE RACING

No sport served the needs of New York City's parvenu for conspicuous display more effectively than thoroughbred horse racing. Failing to obtain consistent patronage from the nation's wealthiest classes, wracked by the ricocheting business cycle, and confronted with persistent charges of gambling, chicanery, and commercialism, antebellum racing had never enjoyed sustained prosperity. But, during the 1860s, a small group of newly made millionaires decided to place horse racing on a fresh footing. By building new tracks, providing large stakes, reducing corruption, substituting the dash for long distance racing, and founding the New York Jockey Club as a central governing body, these men ushered horse racing into a new "golden age."

The main leader of the movement to transform the sport was New York City's Leonard W. Jerome, a man who had made a fortune selling short in the

Panic of 1857. Blessed with enormous energy, Jerome was by day a calculating investor on Wall Street and by night a dashing man-about-town. The handsome financier engaged in scandalous love affairs, patronized the theater and the opera, and threw dazzling parties. At one of his parties, the fountains spouted champagne and eau de cologne. Infatuated by singer Jennie Lind, the Swedish Nightingale, he named a daughter after her—the daughter who would one day make Jerome the grandfather of Winston Churchill. But as much as he loved beautiful women, Jerome's special and life-long passion was the turf.

In 1866, Jerome and his friends, William R. Travers and August Belmont, founded the American Jockey Club. Modeled after the socially exclusive New-market in England, the club purchased over 200 acres of land in Westchester County where it built Jerome Park. The new park was by far the most lavish course in the nation. Located high on a bluff overlooking the backstretch, the luxurious clubhouse contained a spacious dining room, overnight sleeping quarters, and facilities for trap shooting, skating, and later, polo. Initially, only club members could sit in the grandstands. "From this sacred spot the respectable public are tabooed," noted the *New York Clipper* sarcastically, "and none but the sweet scented and kid glove subscribers can enter."[4] Led by the ostentatious display of the New Yorkers, the parvenu across the nation began to make horse racing an integral part of upper crust social life. Other, less exclusive tracks—Monmouth Park (1870) in New Jersey, Pimlico (1870) in Baltimore, and Churchill Downs (1875) in Louisville—soon followed the construction of Jerome Park.

The golden age of horse racing entailed more than the opening of new tracks. To reverse the negative antebellum reputation of the turf, Jerome Park barred the sale of intoxicants, discouraged professional gamblers, and made a special effort to attract "the carriage trade." The wealth and social position of the club extended its influence far beyond the City. The New Yorkers led the movement to replace the old system of racing three- or four-mile heats with the modern dash system of racing; the dash placed more emphasis on speed rather than "bottom," or stamina, and permitted the running of several races the same day. Large, permanent stakes, such as the Travers and the Belmont, added excitement and lent greater stability to the turf. In 1894, fifty giants in industry and finance founded the Jockey Club; the club provided uniform, national rules, appointed officials, licensed jockeys, and set national racing dates. By then, racing had become a more thoroughgoing commercial enterprise. Although only the wealthy could own a stable of race horses or provide stakes for races, persons from all walks of life attended the races and wagered on the outcomes.

---

[4]Quoted in Allen Guttmann, *Sports Spectators* (New York, 1986), p. 99. On horse racing see esp. Melvin Adelman, *A Sporting Time: New York City and the Rise of Modern Athletics, 1820–70* (Urbana and Chicago, 1986), Chap. 4; William H. P. Robertson, *The History of Thoroughbred Racing in America* (Englewood Cliffs, NJ, 1964); and Somers, *The Rise of Sports in New Orleans,* Chap. 5.

ELITE SUBCOMMUNITIES

Individual millionaires such as Bennett and Jerome relished the excitement and attention generated by their role in sports. Other actual and would-be members of the elite projected a lower public profile; they simply tried to close their ranks to those whom they considered inferior. As nineteenth-century society became more egalitarian in principle and perhaps more chaotic in fact, withdrawal and exclusion was a strategy for the wealthy to demonstrate their "superior" achievements and family connections. In their homes, schools, private clubs, and summer resorts, they sought to cultivate a lifestyle that would exclude outsiders. The style usually included the pursuit of appropriate sports and a host of in-group behavioral nuances. Men and women of new wealth were especially avid in seeking membership in high status communities for themselves and their children. They sent their sons to the schools that catered only to the nation's wealthy. For example, Edward H. Harriman, the railroad tycoon who went to work at the age of fourteen, sent his sons to Groton and Yale, H.J. Heinz, another self-made millionaire, sent his son to Yale, and John D. Rockefeller's children attended Brown and Vassar.

Private clubs served as barometers of different levels of nineteenth century status communities. At the apex of the status pyramid in large cities were the metropolitan men's clubs, such as the Philadelphia (founded in 1835), the Union in New York (1836), the Century in New York (1847), and the Somerset in Boston (1851). Membership in these clubs came from old wealth; most members looked upon sport and conspicuous display with utter disdain. They rarely tolerated any activity more vigorous than napping in their easy chairs, smoking cigars, sipping brandy, reading newspapers, or quiet conversation. After the Civil War, the Union Leagues, centers of Republican respectability, and the University clubs, comprised of the graduates of the nation's most prestigious colleges, ranked slightly below the patrician metropolitan clubs. A variety of athletic, cricket (among old-stock Americans), and country clubs came next in the urban club hierarchy. Unlike the clubs above them, these clubs usually welcomed women as guests or as auxiliary members and they promoted a gay, physically active club life.

Fascination with, and efforts to imitate, the European upper classes, especially the English, was often a conspicuous component of elite community life in the United States. The nouveau riche frequently sent their children on European tours, married off their daughters to sons of the European nobility, and took up the latest European pastimes with alacrity. Prior to the 1850s, the English gentleman's leisure activities had consisted mostly of country weekend excursions, balls, riding to the hounds, perhaps a bit of cricket, horse racing, and abundant gambling and hard drinking. But in the middle decades of the nineteenth century, many of the upper class became avid sportsmen—forming hundreds of clubs for cricket, yachting, track and field, rowing, cycling, lawn tennis, and eventually golf. In most instances, the English sportsmen preceded the Americans by a decade or more in organizing their sports.

THE FORMATION OF ATHLETIC CLUBS

For a dozen years or so, New York City's first athletic club seemed little concerned with status. Inspired by the formation of the London Athletic Club in 1863, the first English amateur championship meet in 1866, and the athletic activities of the New York Caledonian Club, three well-to-do young athletes founded the New York Athletic Club (NYAC) in 1866. Apparently the founders simply wanted an opportunity to engage in track and field with men of similar social standing and congenial interests. (The existing world of track and field was dominated by professional athletes, gamblers, and "rowdies.") All three of the founders belonged to local boating clubs, and they induced several of their fellow rowers to join the NYAC. During inclement weather the athletes worked out in the back parlor of a private residence. On fair days they went to the Elysian Fields or some other open space for running, vaulting, and shot-putting. In 1868 the club incorporated with fourteen members and sponsored the first open amateur track and field meet. Having issued the New York Caledonian Club a special invitation, the meet was hailed as "an international match—America against Scotland."[5]

Soon other clubs—among them the Staten Island, American, Manhattan, Pastime, University, and Crescent clubs, all of New York—organized on the NYAC model. By 1879 Baltimore, Buffalo, Chicago, Detroit, and St. Louis had also established athletic clubs. The New York Athletic Club assumed the leadership role for the new clubs. In the 1870s the club expanded its activities by building the first cinder track in the country at Mott Haven, introducing the use of spiked shoes, and sponsoring the first national amateur championships in track and field (1876), swimming (1877), boxing (1878), and wrestling (1878). In 1878 the NYAC transferred the track and field championships to the newly organized National Association of Amateur Athletes of America. In addition to the individual sports, many of the clubs eventually sponsored football and basketball teams.

Beginning in 1882 the New York Athletic Club no longer functioned as a club devoted exclusively to athletics. In that year Alfred H. Curtis interested two of the city's wealthiest citizens, Herman Oelrichs and William R. Travers, in the club. Both Oelrichs and Travers were members of an exclusive status network supported by prestigious social clubs; they were also prominent in the Four Hundred. Oelrichs, described by a contemporary as a "social leader" of the city, belonged to the Union and New York Yacht clubs as well as eighteen other clubs. He was a leading patron of "gentleman's sports," being himself a capable swimmer, boxer, and polo player. Travers, a stockbroker, bon vivant, and raconteur, was also a member of the Union and the Yacht Club as well as twenty-four

---

[5]Frederick W. Janssen, *History of Amateur Athletics* (New York, 1885), p. 35. See also Bob Considine and Fred B. Jarvis, *The First Hundred Years: A Portrait of NYAC* (London, 1969) and Joe D. Willis and Richard G. Wettan, "Social Stratification in New York City Athletic Clubs, 1865–1915," *Journal of Sport History*, 3 (1976), 45–63.

other clubs. The decisions of Oelrichs and Travers to support the club drew into the "club's ranks the most prominent and successful men in New York City and vicinity."[6] By 1885 New York Athletic Club membership had grown to 1,500.

Obtaining membership in NYAC aided those seeking admission to even more socially exclusive clubs, such as the Union and the Knickerbocker. The NYAC carefully screened membership applicants, and required a written application with pertinent personal information and the signatures of the members proposing and seconding the nominee for membership. With this information the membership committee could place the applicant within the city's status hierarchy. The initiation fee of $100 and annual dues of $50 also helped weed out undesirables. Athletic clubs could impose other strictures. The University Athletic Club, for example, required that all applicants possess a college degree, preferably from an Ivy League school. In short, membership in the metropolitan athletic clubs became an important link in a web of associations that constituted an exclusive status community.

With Oelrichs and Travers at the helm, the club rapidly expanded its social activities. In 1885 it completed construction of an elegant five-story, Venetian-style clubhouse at a cost of $150,000, which contained a gymnasium, swimming pool, dining rooms, club rooms, a bowling alley, rifle range, billiard room, a superb wine cellar, and sleeping rooms. In 1888 the NYAC acquired a country home at Travers Island where it built a track, clubhouse, boat house, and clay tennis courts. Expanding the membership limit to 2,500 in 1892, the club constructed an even more lavish facility at the corner of 59th Street and 6th

THE NEW YORK ATHLETIC CLUB DINING ROOM, 1898
This photograph reveals the splendor of the socially exclusive New York Athletic Club.

[6]Malcolm W. Ford, "The New York Athletic Club," *Outing*, 33 (Dec. 1898), 251.

Avenue. Several of the other New York clubs attempted to emulate the opulence of the NYAC. Each club established an elaborate social calendar, and most of them sponsored activities for women. "Wine, women, and song," according to the historians of the NYAC, "became more than a catch phrase—they were woven into the texture of NYAC activities."[7] Perhaps the ultimate in social snobbery by the clubs was the practice of allowing spectators at some athletic events by invitation only.

The 1880s and early 1890s marked the heyday of the athletic club. In 1887 an observer reported: "Athletic clubs are now springing into existence in the United States in such profusion as to baffle the effort to enumerate them. Scarce a city can be found having a population of more than 30,000 inhabitants, in which there is not at least one club of this class."[8] While the clubs in smaller cities enjoyed far less commodious facilities than the metropolitan clubs, they were usually made up of the community's wealthiest citizens. In most cases they also sponsored annual track and field competition, although their athletes rarely competed successfully with the larger clubs.

Clubs in Boston, New Orleans, Chicago, and San Francisco rivaled the New York clubs in terms of facilities and membership. In 1893 the Chicago Club, for example, built a nine-story clubhouse costing nearly one million dollars, a structure more costly than any of the New York clubs. Sometimes the clubs sponsored exotic and extravagant shows. In 1895 the Olympic Club in San Francisco put together a detailed reconstruction of Greek and Roman games, complete with a Caesar, courtiers, senators, gladiators, and vestal virgins. Over 4,000 persons attended the event, which cost $2.50 per seat.[9] But the 1890s also brought severe financial problems to many of the clubs. Some had overbuilt and the economic depression of that decade brought about their collapse. After the 1890s the metropolitan athletic club movement never fully recovered, but the early twentieth century witnessed the formation of many less pretentious, smaller clubs whose energies were devoted primarily to sport rather than social exclusion.

THE EMERGENCE OF AMATEURISM

Ironically, as the metropolitan athletic clubs became more effective as agencies for the establishment of status communities, their sporting activities became less player-centered. The active athletes in all of the clubs witnessed a steady diminution in their power. Increasingly, responsibilities for staging and management of athletics shifted from the active players to the social element. (The social element consisted of those club members who were more concerned with the fate

---

[7]Considine and Jarvis, *The First Hundred Years*, p. 43.

[8]Henry Hall, ed., *The Tribune Book of Open-Air Sports* (New York, 1888), p. 332.

[9]John W. Hipwell, "The Chicago Athletic Club," *Outing*, 33 (Nov. 1898), 145–52; Arthur Inkersley, "Graeco-Roman Games in California," ibid, 25 (Feb. 1895), 409–16.

of the club as a whole rather than sport per se.) Thus the wider social interests of the clubs began to supersede the interests of the players; the social element tended to view the active players as simply representatives of the clubs. To the social element, sport was primarily a means of enhancing the prestige of the club, not something to be pursued for its own sake. While continuing to espouse a player-centered pristine amateurism, the clubs, in fact, began to engage in intense rivalries with one another, charge gate receipts, and even extend thinly disguised subsidies to star athletes.[10]

The evolution of amateurism reflected the subtle, conflicting forces at work within the sporting world of the insiders. Initially, the clubs seemed unconcerned about insisting upon an amateur–professional distinction. In the early days, many of the club members competed for bets of several hundred dollars. An athlete might run in a match for a $500 side bet one week and compete in his club's closed games a week later for a medal. Threatened with the possibility of an invasion by "professional" athletes and athletes with "inferior" social credentials—working class, ethnics, and blacks—the clubs gradually placed strictures on participants at their meets. For their fall games in 1876, NYAC defined an amateur as "any person who has never competed in an open competition for public or admission money, or with professionals for a prize . . . nor has at any period of his life taught or assisted in the pursuit of athletic exercises as a means of livelihood."[11] The National Association of Amateur Athletes of America, commonly called the N4A, formed in 1879 by the most exclusive clubs (mostly from metropolitan New York), essentially copied the NYAC definition. At least one athletic club member regretted the exclusion of the less privileged. Frederick Janssen wrote: "The youths who participate in health-giving competitions, as a rule, cannot afford the expense of membership in the so-called Athletic Clubs, and they retire in favor of the wealthy young man whose sole claim to athletic distinction is his connection with a 'high-toned' club."[12]

The more typical opinion was that of Caspar W. Whitney, the dignified sports editor of *Harper's Weekly*. "And what drivelling talk is all this that prates of ignoring the poor 'laborer,' " wrote Whitney, " . . . and wants to drag him into *our* sport, putting him under restrictions with which he has no sympathy, and paying him for the time he may lose from his trade! What sporting 'Coxeyism'* is this that has neither rhyme nor reason to warrant it serious consideration by intelligent mankind?"[13] If the clubs permitted open professionalism, as Whitney recognized, they could no longer serve as effective agencies of status communi-

*In 1894 Jacob Coxey, a self-appointed "General," led an army of a few hundred unemployed men to Washington to support a roads bill that was supposed to put people back to work. The army was quickly dispersed and the leaders arrested on a technicality. But the incident alarmed conservatives everywhere.

[10]Janssen, *History of Amateur Athletics*, p. 103; Considine and Jarvis, *The First Hundred Years*, pp. 18–20.
[11]*Spirit of the Times*, Sept. 2, 1876.
[12]Janssen, *History of Amateur Athletics*, p. 103.
[13]Caspar W. Whitney, *A Sporting Pilgrimage* (New York, 1895), p. 208.

ties. In short, the clubs had an important vested interest in discrimination. William B. "Father Bill" Curtis, a founder of the NYAC, asserted in 1886 that while the amateur-professional distinction discriminated against lower income groups "the practical point is that under existing laws there has grown up a system of clubs and associations whose best interests, pecuniary and social, would partially or wholly lose their value were the amateur fence to be taken down or even materially lowered. So that, in advocating any racial change, one must fight—not abstract right or wrong—but these interests."[14]

Nonetheless, the amateur code was less restrictive in practice than it was in principle. The American amateur code, unlike its English counterpart, rested neither upon a body of established customs or the sponsorship of an inherited aristocracy. In England centuries of tradition and the perquisites of old wealth had prescribed behavior appropriate to a gentleman and a sportsman. To win at all costs, in particular to exert oneself unduly to obtain victory, was bad form. Work and play were distinctive spheres of gentlemanly activity; no gentleman could claim such a status if he made his living from sport. In contrast to the English upper strata, members of the American athletic clubs were often men of new wealth. They usually brought with them the acquisitive values of the marketplace. While paying lip service to the concepts of "fair play" and ama-teurism, defeating one's rivals by any means within the rules was perfectly consistent with their experiences in the world of commerce and industry. Thus the major metropolitan athletic clubs engaged in intense rivalries to field the strongest bevy of athletes possible and in many cases extended subsidies to the most outstanding athletes. A superior athlete, unless he were black, a recent immigrant, or too crude in social demeanor, could expect little difficulty in finding a club that would grant him membership and perhaps other valuable perquisites as well.

Lawrence E. "Lon" Myers, "the world's greatest runner," is an example of the gap between principle and practice.[15] Born in Richmond, Virginia, of Jewish ancestry, Myers had moved with his family to New York where his father had become a successful businessman. Plagued by sickness as a youth, Myers had been urged by a physician to take up athletics. For most of his amateur career, extending from 1878 to 1885, he ran for the Manhattan Athletic Club. His appearance—he stood a mere five feet, seven and three-quarters inches and weighed only 114 pounds—belied his speed. As an amateur, he won fifteen American championships plus several English and Canadian titles. At one time or another he held every American record in all distances from fifty yards to the one-mile run. When he died in 1899, he still held records in five distances. As late as 1929, fifty years after Myers had been in his prime, his time in the quarter mile was superior to that of the winner of the American National Champion-ships. Myers dominated his era as no runner had done before or since.

---

[14]Quoted in *Outing*, 6 (May 1886), 251.
[15]Joe D. Willis and Richard G. Wettan, "L.E. Myers, 'World's Greatest Runner,' " *Journal of Sport History*, 1 (1975), 93–111.

In 1884 charges surfaced that Myers had violated the N4A amateur code. He had, according to a newspaper reporter, received monies for directing the construction of the Manhattan Athletic Club's new grounds, for serving as secretary of the club, and for editing a portion of a sporting sheet. It was also alleged that Myers sold some of his medals. Without denying the validity of the charges, the executive committee of the N4A formally upheld Myers' amateur standing. In the next year the Manhattan Club even scheduled a benefit in his behalf which netted for the athlete some $4,000. Shortly thereafter, Myers became an announced professional, but the N4A continued to founder due to problems that rose out of similar behavior by other athletes.

Rivalry between the clubs for athletic supremacy, especially between the NYAC and the Manhattan Club, and disputes over the amateur standing of athletes resulted in the demise of the N4A. Amidst bitter charges and counter-charges, the NYAC withdrew from the association in 1886 and led a group of clubs in forming the Amateur Athletic Union (AAU) in 1888. By prohibiting any athlete from participating in AAU games who had competed in games governed by the Association, the AAU succeeded by the summer of 1889 in destroying the N4A. But formation of the AAU did not eliminate conflicts between clubs or eligibility controversies. By offering more generous expense and traveling allowances and superior facilities to athletes, the larger clubs continued to "steal" the better athletes from the smaller clubs. Since the larger clubs controlled the Board of Governors of the AAU, the smaller clubs had no recourse in solving their grievances. Likewise the affiliates of the AAU, especially the colleges, resented the power of the AAU. In the first two decades of the twentieth century, the AAU, the colleges, the American Olympic Committee, and other athletic organizations engaged in a running battle for control of amateur sports. Since each organization had an important stake in the athletes or the activities sponsored by the others, there was no simple solution to the conflicts.[16]

Despite a history of controversy, social discrimination, and blatant hypocrisy, the athletic clubs and the AAU played a significant role in the promotion of track and field in the United States. Prior to 1900 the clubs produced most of the outstanding performers in running, jumping, pole vaulting, and shot-putting. At a celebrated international meet in 1895, the Americans swept to victory in every event. Bernard J. Wefers equalled the world record in the 100-yard dash at nine and four-fifths seconds and broke the 220-yard mark with a run of twenty-one and one-fifth seconds.[17] The clubs also assisted in the development of collegiate track and field. Beginning in the 1870s the collegians gained valuable experience by competing in club meets and most of the early

[16]Richard G. Wettan and Joe D. Willis, "Effect of New York Athletic Clubs on American Amateur Athletic Governance, 1870–1915," *Research Quarterly*, 47 (1976), 499–505; Eric Danhoff, "The Struggle for Control of Amateur Track and Field in the United States," *Canadian Journal of History of Sport and Physical Education*, 6 (1975), 43–85; Robert Korsgaard, "A History of the Amateur Athletic Union in the United States," Ed.D. Project, Teachers College, Columbia University, 1952.

[17]"International Track and Field Contests of 1895," *Outing*, 26 (Sept. 1895), 454–61.

intercollegiate meets were held on the superior grounds of the athletic clubs. In the first two decades of the twentieth century, the exclusive clubs continued to sponsor major amateur meets. (Until the 1970s, the NYAC's annual indoor meet was the single most prestigious winter track and field event.) But increasingly, a larger share of the athletes of championship caliber came from the colleges, the YMCAs, and ethnic clubs like the Irish-American Athletic Club of New York.

CRICKET CLUBS AND COUNTRY CLUBS

Those aspiring for social exclusivity used sports other than track and field as a means of building status communities. In Philadelphia but not in other American cities, old-stock Americans became enthusiastic cricketeers. The popularity of cricket among Philadelphia's elite sprang partly from chance. In the 1840s a group of young Philadelphians residing in the Manheim region became acquainted with cricket from the English textile workers employed at the nearby Wakefield Mills. William Wister, one of the youngsters, played a pivotal role in teaching and organizing the sport on the Manheim estates. In the 1850s three clubs were organized; one, the Young America Cricket Club, explicitly excluded from membership anyone who was foreign-born. By so doing, the club helped dissociate itself from the "steak and ale" style of cricket played among the English workingmen. Yet in the 1850s no clear distinction had yet evolved between amateur and professional cricketeers nor had the clubs yet constructed fancy clubhouses and playing fields. The main purpose of the clubs was simply to provide a means by which wealthy young men of similar social origins could play cricket. But even in the 1850s the sport's major sponsors in Philadelphia came from families of high social standing. Without their support, cricket in Philadelphia would probably have followed the path of cricket in other cities and remained primarily a sport of English immigrants.[18]

After the Civil War, each club built elaborate clubhouses and acquired spacious grounds. All five of the major clubs were located in the most socially prestigious neighborhoods of Philadelphia. By the 1890s, within a ten-mile radius of Philadelphia, there were four beautifully kept, sumptuous grounds with lavish clubhouses; London, by comparison, had only two grounds of equal stature. Membership in the five "first class" clubs ranged from 500 to 1,300 persons. In 1874 a team picked from the Philadelphia clubs accepted an invitation to play a series of matches at Halifax, Nova Scotia, with British and Canadian elevens for an international prize. After the Philadelphia eleven won the cup, it became the object of intense competition among the major clubs of the city. By 1891, Philadelphia teams had played touring professional and amateur teams from the British Isles at least seven times, Australian clubs twice, and Canadian teams on

---

[18]Adelman, *A Sporting Time*, Chap. 5; Baltzell, *Philadelphia Gentlemen*, pp. 358–61; George B. Kirsch, *The Creation of American Team Sports: Baseball and Cricket, 1838–72* (Urbana and Chicago, 1989); John A. Lester, ed., *A Century of Philadelphia Cricket* (Philadelphia, 1951).

numerous occasions. In both 1884 and 1889 the "Gentlemen of Philadelphia" visited England. They acquitted themselves well, winning four, losing three, and drawing five matches against top-flight English competition.

The cricket clubs became integral parts of upper class status communities within Philadelphia's suburbs. Not only the expense of membership but the time required to play cricket automatically excluded the ordinary workingman. As the "national game" of England, cricket also appealed to status-conscious Americans who were intrigued with emulating the habits of English sportsmen. The clubs assumed a wide array of social functions similar to the metropolitan athletic clubs. The report of the Board of Governors of the Germantown Cricket Club in 1891 reveals the social character of the typical first-class club:

> That the grounds are socially a success is now an undisputed fact, and too much credit cannot be given to the Ladies' Committee. . . . Ladies' teas have been served every Tuesday; Thursday has been made music day, and Saturday match day, so that the entire week has been made attractive, and the attendance consequently large."[19]

The Germantown club enjoyed a new clubhouse, designed by the distinguished New York architectural firm of McKim, Mead, and White. Like the other clubs, it also sponsored an elaborate program of cricket for juniors. Club leaders believed that playing cricket inculcated the young with gentlemanly values.

While the Philadelphia cricket clubs continued to thrive in the twentieth century, cricket as a sport declined rapidly. As the clubs became agencies of social exclusion, cricket tended to be only a by-product of the clubs' main function. Other diversions such as lawn tennis, golf, and swimming could serve the club membership equally well. Since tennis required less space and could be played much more quickly than cricket, it became, in time, the rage of the cricket clubs. Two members of the Merion Club, William Jackson Clothier and Richard Norris Williams, were United States doubles champions in 1906, 1914, and 1916. And William "Big Bill" Tilden, the country's greatest player in the 1920s, learned his tennis on the courts of the Germantown Cricket Club. By the 1920s the cricket clubs could hardly be distinguished from any other super-wealthy metropolitan country or golf club.

The metropolitan athletic and cricket clubs were forerunners of the great country club movement that has flourished since the 1920s. The country club was, in effect, a substitute for the English country home of the aristocracy or monied gentry. "It is a banding together for the purpose of making available to the group facilities which previously had been the privilege of the wealthy aristocrat," declared the official historians of the original Country Club at Brookline, Massachusetts.[20] While in England the upper strata of society usually lived in the country and belonged to clubs in the cities, rich Americans normally resided in the cities and sought an approximation of the English country home with its

[19]Quoted in Lester, ed., *A Century*, p. 313.
[20]Fredric H. Curtiss and John Heard, *The Country Club, 1882–1932* (Brookline, MA, 1932), p. 4.

aristocratic privileges of servants and exclusive outdoor sports. The main activities of the early clubs centered on hunting, fishing, horseback riding, and other activities which in England were reserved to those able to afford country estates.

The first "Country Club," founded in 1882, was far more exclusive than later imitators. "For many years after 1882 Boston had that of which it was very proud—its Society," wrote the country club historians. "Everybody was either in it or out of it; and those who were in it were proud of the fact and guarded its boundaries jealously. They played with each other, not with others; they competed with each other, not with others; above all, they married each other only, and so their children carried on the good (?)* tradition."[21] The Brookline Country Club was one of the primary agencies for preserving the exclusiveness of Boston "Society." In the twentieth century, the country club became a haven for those seeking to establish status communities in the smaller cities and the suburbs of metropolises. Some ethnic groups—Jews, for example—established country clubs, but most clubs were composed of status-conscious, old-stock Americans.

The country clubs and the summer resorts of the rich eased the process by which the wealthy shed their Victorian suspicions of play-for-play's-sake. At these private retreats, the rich could release inhibitions with far less fear of exposure than in public places. In sharp contrast to those Victorians who insisted that play could be justified only when it aided in doing one's proper work, the upper strata frankly favored play for its inutility, in short, simply for the pleasures it afforded the participants. The Grafton Country Club of Worcester, Massachusetts, for instance, even adopted as its motto, "Each to His Pleasure," a direct contradiction of the Victorian work ethic.[22] Club social life everywhere inclined toward greater personal freedom for the enjoyment of sensual pleasures.

Such a milieu also expanded the opportunities for upper-class women to engage in sports. Apart from having more discretionary income than women in the lower classes, women in the families of the "idle rich" escaped much of the confinement implied in the popular Victorian notions of a separate women's sphere and a cult of domesticity. Personal servants relieved them of a vast range of duties associated with household management and childcare. Wealthy women were thus free to exhibit family wealth by cultivating lives of conspicuous leisure and consumption. They dressed according to the latest fashions, hosted and attended expensive parties, and spent their summers in either American or European resorts. Although initially most women engaged only in the social life of the elite clubs, wealth, social prominence, and the privacy of the clubs helped shield would-be women athletes from charges of being unfeminine.

Even before 1890, a few wealthy women inched their way toward a more active sporting life. They took up archery, croquet, tennis, and golf; all of which

---

*The question mark in parentheses appears in the original quotation and suggests that the official historians of the first country club either had some doubts about the merits of the traditions of the Boston "Society," or were attempting to be humorous.

[21]Ibid., p. 139.

[22]Quoted in Roy Rosenzwieg, *Eight Hours For What We Will: Workers and Leisure in an Industrial City, 1870–1920* (New York, 1983), p. 140.

were individual rather than team sports, undemanding in terms of strength, and conducive to graceful physical movement. As early as 1877 women in Staten Island, New York, formed their own athletic club under the umbrella of the men's Staten Island Cricket and Base Ball Club. The new sport of lawn tennis was apparently responsible for the founding of the Ladies' Club. Two years earlier, Mary Outerbridge, who had watched English army officers play tennis in Bermuda, convinced her brother to lay out a court at the Staten Island club. Wives and daughters of the club members soon took up the game with alacrity; the club sponsored the earliest women's tournaments, although the first women's national tennis championship took place in 1887 at the Philadelphia Cricket Club. Within a decade, the Ladies' Club had grown to over 200 members. Similar circles of sporting women emerged in the other major northeastern cities.[23]

Nonetheless, the joys of competition in elite women's sports were often subordinated to courtship rituals. Physically undemanding sports offered the sexes opportunities to mingle and flirt unchaperoned in non-threatening settings. When at play, the women usually wore regular, full-length dresses, including tight-laced corsets that emphasized full bosoms and fleshy hips. Play entailed the utmost discretion; for example, a woman did not dare place the mallet between her legs to execute a more effective croquet shot, or if playing tennis, smash overheads or run swiftly about the court. Both women's archery and tennis, *Godey's Lady's Book* concluded in the mid-1880s, remained "tame diversions."[24] Major departures from such decorums awaited the post-1890 era.

[23]See esp. Cindy L. Himes, "The Female Athlete in American Society, 1860–1940," unpub. Ph.D. diss., Univ. of Pennsylvania, 1984, Chap. 1; and Mrozek, *Sport and American Mentality*, Chap. 5.
[24]Quoted in Lois Banner, *American Beauty* (New York, 1983), p. 141.

7

THE RISE
OF INTERCOLLEGIATE
SPORTS

A jerky little train loaded with students steamed out of Princeton, New Jersey, early on the morning of November 6, 1869. Upon arrival at the sleepy town of New Brunswick, New Jersey, the students from Princeton received a warm welcome from the youngsters of the College of Rutgers. During the rest of the morning, the Princeton lads strolled about the town with their hosts; a few played billiards at a local parlor. That afternoon at three o'clock perhaps two hundred spectators gathered on the Rutgers Common. The milling fans did not have to purchase tickets; there were no seats for comfort nor refreshments to satisfy hunger or thirst. Before play commenced, the students burst forth with a few college songs as the nation's first intercollegiate "football" contest got underway. Twenty-five young men lined up on the Common for each side. Rutgers soon demonstrated its superiority at "dribbling"—kicking the ball along the ground with short strokes—and won the game by six goals to four. (To a modern football fan, the game they played could more aptly be described as soccer.) That evening the Rutgers players treated their visitors to a festive supper and the guests joined their hosts in song and good humor.

Few of those present at the historic occasion of the nation's first intercollegiate football match dreamed that colleges would soon become major centers of sport. Nor did they dream that sports would contribute to the creation of a new social form, the college community. Invariably small, parochial, and mostly sectarian, the pre-Civil War colleges had been largely peripheral to the mainstream of American life. But after the war, the number of colleges and universities (as the institutions that included graduate work and professional schools came to be known) more than doubled and their enroll-ments tripled. Students countered the heterogeneous character of the new institutions by making extracurricular activities central to their college experi-ences. One of their activities, intercollegiate sports, soon exhibited a remark-able capacity to generate communal loyalties both within and outside the campus walls.[1]

THE FIRST INTERCOLLEGIATE SPORT

Even before 1869, rowing, or crew, the first intercollegiate sport, revealed that it had some potential for evoking enthusiasm beyond that of the participating athletes. Rowing probably owed its beginnings to the experiences of students in private clubs and to the publicity surrounding the intermittent English matches between Oxford and Cambridge that began at Henley in 1829. By 1844 students had formed small, informal clubs at both Harvard and Yale. Although initially the Harvard Club used its boats mostly to transport its members across the inlet to Boston drinking establishments, the club also competed for cash prizes against noncollegiate clubs in local Boston regattas.

Exciting and colorful, the first intercollegiate match in 1852 lacked the seriousness of later regattas. By offering to pay all expenses, a small New England railroad persuaded Harvard and Yale crews to race on Lake Winnipesaukee as one of several festivities to promote the area as a summer resort. An estimated 1,000 spectators witnessed the contest, including General Franklin Pierce, the soon-to-be elected president of the nation. Harvard won the race, but neither crew had hired a coach or trainer or otherwise prepared systematically for the contest. In fact, the Harvard crew, according to one report, had "only rowed a few times for fear of blistering their hands." After the race was over, the crews and other students "passed a very pleasant week at the Lake, and returned together to Concord, New Hampshire, where, amid much good feeling and many fraternal adieus, they finally separated."[2]

In the meantime, the widely publicized exploits of English boys kindled an interest in sports among American collegians. In particular, Thomas Hughes' phenomenally popular novel, *Tom Brown's School Days* (1857), which in the United States alone sold more than 225,000 copies in its first year of publication, excited American students. The muscular Christian perspective of Hughes and his vivid descriptions of sporting life at Rugby, according to a Harvard student in 1857, resulted in a "multitude from every class . . . playing at base[ball] or

[1]Ronald A. Smith, *Sports and Freedom: The Rise of Big-Time College Athletics* (New York, 1988) and Patrick Bryant Miller, "Athletes in Academe: College Sports and American Culture, 1850–1920," unpub. Ph.D. diss., Univ. of California, Berkeley, 1987, are the best treatments of the rise of college sports.

[2]Quoted in John A. Blanchard, ed., *The H Book of Harvard Athletics, 1852–1922* (Cambridge, MA, 1923), pp. 26, 24.

cricket, in a manner that would excite the admiration, even if it shocked the taste, of Tom Brown and his fellows at Rugby."[3]

Reports the next year from England of the Oxford–Cambridge crew race aroused American collegians to action. To the chagrin of the American students, the correspondents who covered that race seized the opportunity to laud the English students for their physical prowess while expressing their dismay at "the entire disregard for exercise among Americans." Angered by these reports, the editor of Harvard's student magazine wrote: "What say we, Yale, Dartmouth, Brown, Columbia, Harvard, shall we introduce a new institution in America."[4] Student representatives from four colleges responded by forming the College Union Regatta Association in 1858. The association sponsored successful races in 1859 and 1860 on Lake Quinsigamond. As many as 20,000 spectators may have watched each regatta.

The race of Harvard against Oxford in 1869 on the Thames River in England, the race that "will be henceforth ever immortal in Anglo-American annals," as the London *Times* declared, indicated both the increasing public attention given to rowing and the seriousness with which the collegians approached the contests. The Harvard crew practiced a full month before the Oxford race but lost. The newspapers speculated that the loss might have been due to their "soft diet" of too much milk and fruit rather than beef and ale, the hardy diet of the Oxford crew. The Harvard–Oxford race stimulated collegians to form a new rowing association of northeastern colleges in 1870. As many as sixteen colleges competed in the regattas of the Rowing Association of American Colleges.

The "democratization" of college rowing eventually resulted in the withdrawal of Harvard and Yale from the association. In the mid-1870s both schools suffered from humiliating defeats at the hands of smaller, less prestigious institutions. The victory of the "bucolics" over the "intellectuals," wrote a Harvard student after the Massachusetts Agricultural College defeated Harvard for the championship in 1871, "was a bitter pill for us to swallow."[5] After a smashing Cornell victory in 1875, both Harvard and Yale pulled out of the association; thereafter, for the remainder of the century, they proceeded to row almost exclusively against one another. Rowers representing the nation's two most patrician schools snubbed the other northeastern collegians and refused as well to join an intercollegiate rowing association formed by the students of seven colleges in 1883.

In the 1870s and 1880s the emotional stake that students had in winning regattas increased. The clubs went all out to win. They hired professional trainers and coaches (sometimes from England) to prepare them for the major regattas. Training was Spartan: crews maintained a strict diet (consisting mainly of meat)

[3]"Mens Sana," *Harvard Magazine*, 4 (1858), 201.
[4]"Editor's Table," ibid, 178.
[5]Quoted in Guy M. Lewis, "America's First Intercollegiate Sport: The Regattas from 1852 to 1875," *Research Quarterly*, 38 (1967), 643.

and rowed three to five miles before breakfast and about four miles in the afternoon. The crews gave up "their pleasure: they resigned their very will to the control of others," a contemporary wrote, all for "twenty thrilling minutes of the race." The regattas likewise became an important date on the social calendars of alumni and the fashionable set of the Northeast. "The moneyed aristocracy which assembles yearly at Saratoga," *Outing* reported of the 1875 regatta, "gilded the grand stand and the shore of the lake, outshown in turn by the kaleidoscopic ribbons of the intent, excited, uproarious mob which represented the thirteen colleges."[6] Newspapers frequently carried more than a page of "special dispatches" plus extended discussions of the social leaders who graced the regattas by their presence. Even in the 1880s and 1890s, when football began to supplant rowing in popularity, crews continued to evoke strong loyalties at several northeastern colleges.

OTHER EARLY INTERCOLLEGIATE SPORTS

From the first, intercollegiate baseball indicated the tendencies of collegians to transform informal games into serious contests and the capacity of sport to form allegiances among the students far more powerful than anything experienced in the college's academic programs. In the first recorded intercollegiate contest in 1859 Amherst subdued Williams by a lopsided score of 73–32. Unlike Williams, Amherst had trained carefully for the contest. According to a Williams professor, Amherst took "the game from the region of sport and carried it into the region of exact and laborious discipline."[7] When the Amherst students learned of the win, they rang the chapel bell, lit a huge bonfire, and set off fireworks. The Civil War temporarily set back baseball, but in the war's wake college clubs (unlike the early crew and football clubs that were restricted to the Northeast) formed in all parts of the nation.

Until the 1880s, the Harvard Base Ball Club, organized in 1862, fielded the strongest college nine in the country. For a seven-year span they did not lose a single intercollegiate game. In the summer of 1870, the team took an extended road trip through the West, playing all the major amateur and professional nines in the nation. They won 44 of 54 matches, and even frightened Harry Wright's powerful Cincinnati Red Stockings. In the words of a contemporary: "The game was remarkably close, the Harvards outplaying their opponents at bat and in the field; but at a critical moment in the last inning, professional training showed its superiority over amateur excitability, and the Red Stockings won by 20 to 17."[8]

Throughout the nineteenth century, baseball remained the most widely played sport on college campuses. The better teams sometimes tested their talents

---

[6]J.R.W. Hitchcock, "The Harvard–Yale Races, *Outing*, 6 (1885), 403, 393.

[7]Quoted in Smith, *Sports and Freedom*, p. 55.

[8]J. Mott Hallowell, "American College Athletics: I. Harvard University," *Outing*, 13 (1889), 241.

with some success against major league professional teams. In 1879, in an effort to draw a sharp line between professional and amateur players, the northeastern clubs formed an association, but provided neither for a regular schedule of games nor for the naming of a champion team. The unstable association folded in 1887. Baseball confronted other problems. In the fall it had to contend with the growing popularity of football, in the spring with inclement weather, and in the summer with the hostility of college authorities to team tours. During the summers, college players (usually under assumed names) sometimes joined professional teams. For almost a century, college officials tried without much success to prevent students' playing for pay.

Intercollegiate track and field, destined to rival crew and baseball as a popular spring and summer sport during the last quarter of the century, had origins in annual college field days. Probably influenced by the examples of the Scottish-American Caledonian games and the Oxford–Cambridge competition first scheduled in 1864, American students began in the 1860s to devote a special day to contests in running, jumping, and throwing. In 1874, Amherst even included a "fat man race" as part of their field day; later in the century Nebraska students awarded winners of the 100-yard dash a copy of Dante's *Inferno*. But the field days had a far more serious side. At Princeton, for example, the games came under the direction of the university's gymnasium director, George Goldie, who was himself a preeminent Caledonian athlete. Nearly everywhere the collegians used the field days to generate interest in intercollegiate track and field.

Formal intercollegiate track and field began as an offshoot of crew. In 1873 James Gordon Bennett, Jr. of the *New York Herald* offered a silver challenge cup valued at $500 for a two-mile race as part of the Saratoga intercollegiate regatta. Only three men, one each from Amherst, Cornell, and McGill College of Canada, competed in the first meet. The next year an expanded program included a 100-yard dash, 120-yard high hurdles, one- and three-mile runs, and a seven-mile walk. That most of the contestants had rowed for their varsity crews the previous day indicates the desultory character of the meet. By 1876, the collegians and their sponsors became more serious; that year they organized the Intercollegiate Association of Amateur Athletics of America (IC4A). The IC4A decided to make the rather "costly prizes" awarded to the winner of each event of equal value and switched its annual games to the grounds of the New York Athletic Club at Mott Haven. Between 1880 and 1897 either Harvard or Yale won all of the IC4A meets.

Until the 1880s, track and field training varied widely. In the northeastern colleges, an aspiring sprinter or walker might hire a professional trainer. As the professional coaches vied with one another for the services of college athletes, unseemly disputes arose that were not "in keeping with the spirit of the gentleman's sport."[9] In 1882 Harvard hired J.G. Lathrop as a general trainer and supervisor of track and prohibited any association of the collegians with

---

[9]Samuel Crowther and Arthur Ruhl, *Rowing and Track Athletes* (New York, 1905), pp. 275–76.

professional coaches, reforms that represented one of the earliest instances of college administrators assuming the control and management of athletics.

THE MAKING OF COLLEGE FOOTBALL

College students used the first football games, the medieval interclass matches, as initiation rites for incoming freshmen. As with most rites of passage, the game entailed the degradation of the initiates as a precondition for their acceptance into the group. Beginning in 1827, sophomores at Harvard subjected freshmen to a violent game on the first Monday of the school term. As early as 1840, Yale also took up the practice. Invariably, these melees resulted in black eyes, bloodied noses, sprained limbs, and shredded clothes. "The result of it all is," according to a Brown periodical, "that one class is *beaten* collectively, each class individually. It affords talk for the winter; and the bruised limbs, black eyes and cracked heads are carefully treasured by the Freshmen as spoils of the battlefield to be du(al)ly handed down to the incoming class the following year."[10] Postgame drinking, singing of songs, and the cheering of the classes signified acceptance of the freshmen by upperclassmen and the deepening of fraternal bonds among all the participating students. Since the rites were intrinsically disorderly and often caused serious injuries, college authorities frowned on them. By 1860 the interclass matches had been abolished at both Harvard and Yale.

As with crew and track, England exercised an important early influence on intercollegiate football. Apparently, *Tom Brown's School Days* inspired students at the New England academies to take up football in the 1860s. In the 1870s students began to form clubs in the northeastern colleges. All of the clubs except Harvard played under some version of the London Football Association rules (essentially soccer). A series of games at Cambridge, Massachusetts, between clubs from McGill University of Montreal, Canada, and Harvard in 1874, represented a turning point in the history of the sport. In the first game, the two schools engaged in a contest peculiar to Harvard that combined features of both association football and rugby. The next day, the clubs met under the Rugby Union rules favored by McGill. After struggling to a scoreless tie, the Harvard athletes became immediate converts to rugby, a game that allowed the players to carry the ball and engage in more direct physical contact.

Within only a few years the other northeastern colleges adopted the "Harvard" or "rugby" game. In 1876, student delegates from Princeton, Columbia, Yale, and Harvard founded the Intercollegiate Football Association and adopted rules closely resembling those of the Rugby Union. Initially the association counted touchdowns as only one point and kicked goals as four. (A modern

---

[10]Blanchard, *The H Book*, p. 328. Apart from Smith, *Sports and Freedom*, and Miller, "Athletes in Academe," see also Parke H. Davis, *Football: The American Intercollegiate Game* (New York, 1912); Alexander M. Weyand, *American Football: Its History and Development* (New York, 1926); and Guy Maxton Lewis, "The American Intercollegiate Football Spectacle, 1869–1917," unpub. Ph.D. diss., Univ. of Maryland, 1965, for the rise of college football.

observer would be especially surprised by the "drop kick"—this entailed the kicker dropping the ball and, as it bounced up, kicking it through the goal. As the ball became more oblong in shape [at first, the teams played with a large round ball] and the points for touchdowns increased, the drop kick disappeared from football.) The delegates to the 1876 convention set up a schedule and decided to hold a championship game at the end of the season, a decision that encouraged teams to emphasize winning.

For the remainder of the century, no single person exceeded Walter C. Camp, the "Father of American Football," in shaping the modern college game. A member of the Yale squad from 1875 to 1882, Camp acquired a taste for outdoor sports while attending a prep school adjacent to the Yale campus. At Yale, he played baseball, crew, track, lawn tennis, and football. After obtaining a bachelor's degree in 1880 he continued at Yale as a medical student and football player for two more years, eventually withdrawing from medical school because he could not tolerate the sight of blood. While employed as an executive with a local watch manufacturing firm, Camp continued an active involvement in the game until his death in 1925.

Camp's recommendations for rule changes transformed the American game into a sport distinct from both English football (soccer) and rugby. He believed that the rugby game could be improved by reducing the element of chance and providing for sustained offensive action. Play in rugby started with a scrum: The ball was set down in the midst of a huddle of opposing players. The players then tried to drive the ball free with their feet so that a "back" could pick it up or kick it toward the opponent's goal line. Several minutes could transpire before the ball squirted out of the struggling mass of players. Once a back had been downed with the ball, the players formed a new scrum.

In 1880 Camp obtained approval from the association rules committee for a revolutionary way of putting the ball into play. The new rule provided for a line of scrimmage. Unless the ball was fumbled or kicked to the opposing side, the offensive team could repeatedly begin play at the line of scrimmage without interference of the defensive team. Unfortunately, Camp failed to make any provision for the offensive team to surrender the ball when they were unable to move it forward. Consequently, much to the disgust of the fans and the players alike, the Yale–Princeton game of 1881 turned into a fiasco. Princeton repeatedly lost yardage while retaining possession of the ball for the entire first half; Yale employed the same strategy in the second half. The next year, Camp came forward with an ingenious solution to this problem. The offensive team had to give up the ball if it was unable to gain five yards in three attempts. This rule change led to the placement of lines across the field at five yard intervals, hence, the origin of the term "gridiron." The adoption of the scrimmage line and the down-yardage system marked fundamental departures from rugby.

The new rules widened opportunities for the invention of new tactics and strategies as well. Soon teams began to employ offensive signals, though the use of offensive huddles did not become a standard practice until the 1910s. At first, quarterbacks used sentences in which one word or another might be omitted, but by 1885 combinations of words and numerical signals began to supersede prior systems. In the 1880s the offensive line and backs typically lined up far apart, forcing the defense to do likewise. Although prohibited from throwing the ball across the line of scrimmage, teams frequently threw long, sideline passes. Prior to 1888, the game featured wide-open offensive action with sideline passes, open field running, and frequent kicking.

In 1888, the adoption of Camp's recommendation that tackling be permitted below the waist replaced wide-open, improvisational play with carefully designed plays emphasizing mass and momentum. Already officials had been allowing offensive players to run between the ball carrier and potential tacklers, a violation of rugby rules. As early as 1884 Pennsylvania had initiated their offensive action with the famous "V Trick," in which players formed a V with their arms encircling the players ahead of them. Formed some ten yards behind the ball, the V moved forward, enclosing the ball carrier within the V. Breaking this fearsome formation required defensive men without protective gear to hurl themselves directly in front of the V or to try crashing its flanks. The low tackle encouraged a host of other power plays. Although teams moving forward en masse became illegal in 1895, tight formations (in which teams tried to squeeze out the five yards necessary for a first down by brute physical power) remained commonplace throughout the first decade of the next century.

Apart from the ingenuity of Walter Camp, the evolution of college football rules owed much to the absence of a well-defined and accepted genteel tradition among American collegians. Because English college students had been reared as "gentlemen," they acquiesced to a large set of understood conventions in their sports. Countless situations in rugby, for example, were not governed by explicit rules. But when American collegians took up rugby, they quickly exploited the undefined areas to the benefit of their team. Thus rule-writing necessarily became a preoccupation of American collegians. Rules had to be adopted for every ambiguous situation. And often the new rule resulted in unforeseen possibilities for a team to violate the spirit of the game to its advantage so that yet another rule had to be written. Thus American football has been a continuously evolving sport.

Camp also played an important role in undermining student control of football. In the early years of the sport, the students themselves organized the clubs, scheduled the contests, managed the finances (such as they were), and determined the rules of the games. Student-elected team captains determined who would play and what player deployment and the team's training regimen would be. Football captains soon occupied one of the most prestigious positions on campus. According to President Francis A. Walker of Massachusetts Institute of Technology, the captains replaced those students renowned for "speech-making, debating, or fine writing" as campus heroes.

Nonetheless, in the 1880s students began to invite alumni to campus to assist in the preparation of the team for key games. Since the "graduate coaches" appeared irregularly and received no salaries, they wielded far less influence over the clubs than does today's full-time professional coach. About 1885 Camp became a regular advisor to Yale captains and coaches; from 1888 to 1906 he was the unpaid "advisory coach" and supervisor of Eli athletics. Because of his job at the watch manufacturing firm, Camp could rarely attend practices, but his wife, Alice, observed the players in action and carefully noted their progress. Then, in the evenings Camp advised the team leaders. In addition to central direction, Camp provided Yale's program with continuity. Such was Camp's stature as an authority on the game that for two decades or so he was the unofficial advisor of dozens of other football programs across the country.

Everywhere, schools tried to emulate the Yale program, but without complete success. The record established by Yale from 1872 through 1909 has never been equalled. In those years Yale elevens recorded 324 victories, 17 losses, and 18 ties. From 1883 to 1898, Yale produced nine undefeated teams and from the final game of the 1890 season to the ninth game of 1893 the Elis scored 1,265 points to none for its opponents. Yale so dominated archrival Harvard that "Harvard felt a certain loss of manhood in not winning a single football game with Yale in the eighties and only two in the nineties," reported the school's historian.[11] Among the prominent Yale athletes were Amos Alonzo Stagg, the future renowned coach of the University of Chicago team, W. W. "Pudge" Heffelfinger, who revolutionized line play, and Lee "Bum" McClung, who scored 500 points in four seasons. Perhaps Frederic W. Remington, who became a famous illustrator, best typified the spirit of Yale. In preparation for the Harvard game of 1878, he took his football jacket to a local slaughterhouse where he dipped it in blood to "make it more businesslike."

Walter Camp not only guided rule changes and developed the Yale system but was football's most successful promoter. The early clubs had financed their games by student subscriptions, but Camp, as the treasurer of the Yale Field Association, recognized the potential for making football a profitable sport. He urged that the major matches be scheduled in New York City rather than on the

YALE FOOTBALL TEAM OF 1879
Walter Camp, shown here holding the ball, was the main architect of the uniquely American game. He was responsible for most of the earliest departures from English rugby and soccer. Compare the size of the neck and shoulders of the Yale team members with the members of a modern football squad.

[11]Samuel Eliot Morison, *Three Centuries of Harvard, 1636–1936* (Cambridge, MA, 1936), p. 410.

college's home field. Camp flooded the newspapers and periodicals with feature stories of games, summaries of seasons, inside knowledge of football fundamentals, and trivia. Altogether, he wrote twenty books on sports—boys' novels, histories, and coaching manuals. In 1889 he devised an ingenious promotional gimmick—the creation of a fictional "All-America" football team. Each year until 1924 Camp personally determined the composition of a hypothetical team of the nation's best players. In due course, football fans everywhere waited anxiously to see if their local heroes would be immortalized by Camp in his All-America team.

By the 1890s, intercollegiate football in the Northeast had taken on many of the characteristics of a full-blown commercial sport. Initially, college-wide student-run athletic associations had assessed students' dues and embarked upon drives to finance the teams, but by the 1890s gate receipts had become the predominant source of funds. Although the athletic associations did not pay players a formal salary, they often provided star players with such benefits as free tuition and room and board. Generating adequate revenues often depended upon a winning record or beating an archrival. To win, teams had to approach football more rationally and systematically. Amos A. Stagg and Henry L. Williams entitled their 1893 treatise on coaching, *A Scientific and Practical Treatise on American Football for Schools and Colleges.* Winning, the two coaches argued, required careful planning, organization, and specialization—in short, "system" and "order."

THE INVENTION OF PAGEANTRY

Led by the students, college sport enthusiasts invented an exceptionally rich set of symbols and rituals to accompany their games. As had the nineteenth-century militia units, voluntary fire departments, and baseball teams, the students adopted special colors that distinguished their enterprise from others. As early as 1854 Yale rowers donned blue flannel. Apparently crimson was first identified with Harvard when the crew purchased China red bandanas to distinguish themselves from the Irish green of other rowers participating in a Boston regatta. Georgetown's blue and grey arose from the divided loyalties of students during the Civil War. Rochester students rejected goldenrod yellow, the recommendation of an alumni committee, because of its association with the women's suffrage movement. Whatever the origins or associations of school colors, in due course they became powerful symbols of a school's identity.

Mascots and nicknames offered more room for innovation. Sometimes students called their teams by the name of their institution's founder. Thus Yale became the Elis and Williams College became the Ephs, an abbreviation of the first name of their founder, Ephraim Williams. Nicknames could evoke humorous images. For a time Washington College teams were known as the Shoo Flies and the University of Nebraska as the Bugeaters. After Yale students paid the princely sum of $300 for a prize English bulldog as a mascot, their teams became known as both the Bulldogs and the Elis. When Texas students discovered that

Bevo, their first longhorn mascot, had been branded with the score of the Texas A&M victory of 1915, they unceremoniously slaughtered and ate the steer.

College yells and songs typically belittled opponents. Illinois students chanted at their chief rival, Chicago:

> Tell all those Standard Oil Tanks
> Old Rockefeller's pride and joy
> Just how the boys in Old Chicago
> Got a jolt from Illinois.[12]

Dating from the 1890s, a Yale song (not printed in the college's official songbook) suggested the rape of "Fair Harvard."

> Though Harvard has blue stocking girls
> Yale has blue stocking men
> We've done Fair Harvard up before
> We'll do her up again.[13]

Even in the nineteenth century, those who were more squeamish complained that martial yells such as "Kill him" and "Smash him" were unseemly.

By the 1890s, the annual Thanksgiving Day games represented a special holiday for the college community at large. "Thanksgiving Day is no longer a solemn festival to God for mercies given," declared the *New York Herald* in 1893. "It is a holiday granted by the State and the Nation to see a game of football."[14] By the mid-1890s, according to the estimate of a leading historian of college sport, some 120,000 athletes, belonging to colleges, athletic clubs, and high schools, played in some 5,000 Thanksgiving Day football games. Colorful pageantry invariably accompanied these games.

THANKSGIVING DAY GAME, NEW YORK CITY
Few occasions equaled the glamor of a Thanksgiving Day game between Yale and Princeton, held in New York City in the 1890s. Here, Yale supporters wear greatcoats and carry banners as they prepare to make their way by coach up Fifth Avenue on the morning of the game.

[12]Quoted in Miller, "Athletes in Academe," p. 198. For the paragraphs on football's pageantry, I am deeply indebted to Miller.

[13]Ibid., p. 201.

[14]As quoted in Smith, *Sports and Freedom*, p. 181. For the estimates that follow in this paragraph, see also ibid.

For sheer theatrics, few spectacles anywhere exceeded the Thanksgiving Day game waged in New York City between the nation's two top colleges. On Wednesday, an advance contingent of collegians arrived in the city. By evening, "the sidewalks of Broadway flashed with blue and orange ribbons and the buildings along the way resounded with the impact of many and diverse college cheers." By ten o'clock the next morning a parade of horsedrawn coaches, "a feature that was second only to the game itself," slowly made its way through the heart of the city to Manhattan Field. Bright banners featuring the school colors hung from many residences and hotels along the way. The sight of each brought forth "salvos of cheers from the collegians whose colors were displayed."[15]

Festivities continued on the field. From atop their coaches, the rich ate their lunches and drank champagne. During the game the fans were regaled with vivid displays of school colors, vociferous school cheers led by "yell captains," and boisterous songs. After the game, the great crowd, perhaps as many as 40,000, boarded the coaches or the elevated train for the return trip downtown. Happy parties crowded every restaurant for a bacchanalian Thanksgiving Day feast. During the evening many of the celebrants attended the theaters where they more often than not interrupted performances with raucous displays of school spirit.

By the 1890s colleges were already playing what later became known as "The Big Game." No other game on a team's schedule was as significant as the Big Game with a traditional rival. The success of an entire season hinged on winning the contest; a team could win all its other games, but a loss in the Big Game signified failure. The Big Game sometimes entailed the winning or losing of a trophy. Stanford and California struggled to win the Axe, Minnesota and Michigan for possession of the Little Brown Jug, and Purdue and Indiana for ownership of the Old Oaken Bucket. Enterprising undergraduates periodically devised ingenious schemes to steal trophies from their rightful owners.

Success or failure in the Big Game was sometimes interpreted as a reflection of the fundamental character of the participating colleges. For example, Yale partisans claimed that the more democratic spirit at New Haven accounted for their dominance over Harvard. Frank Merriwell, the fictional Yale hero, explained that at Harvard "a man's worth does not carry him so far as in Yale or Princeton. Here a man is accepted for just what he proves himself to be; there, he is accepted for what he has the reputation of being. Aristocracy cuts a mighty small figure at Yale, but in Harvard the bloods are the ones who play ball, row, and so forth."[16] Although in fact the students at both colleges came predominantly from the upper strata, the fathers of Yale's collegians were more likely to represent new wealth than the fathers of Harvard's students. Furthermore, until at least the twentieth century, Harvard students exhibited a certain disdain toward

---

[15]Davis, *Football*, pp. 103-4.

[16]Burt L. Standish, pseud. [Gilbert Patten], *Frank Merriwell's Loyalty* (New York, 1904), p. 29. See the interpretations of Allen L. Sack, "Yale 29–Harvard 4: The Professionalization of College Football," *Quest*, 19 (1973), 24–34; George Santayana, *The Middle Span* (New York, 1945); and Edwin H. Cady, *The Big Game: College Sports and American Life* (Knoxville, TN, 1978).

Yale's sporting "excesses." Philosopher George Santayana perceptively described Harvard's spirit as that of ancient Athens and Yale's as that of ancient Sparta.

THE MAKING OF COLLEGE COMMUNITIES

The excitement of football and its accompanying fanfare were vital ingredients in the creation of compelling communal experiences. That football was a physically aggressive sport also accounted for much of its appeal. The upper and middle class football fans normally reined in aggressive and extreme emotions; Victorian sensibility required decorum and circumspection. Yet at the football games, athletes, students, and fans all seemed to relish the physical collisions, the brandishing of fists, the pushing and shoving, the broken limbs, and the bruised and bloodied bodies characteristic of the games. Only the nineteenth-century prize fighting ring offered an equivalent display of brute physicality. While proper Victorians endangered their reputations when they patronized a prize fight, college football permitted them to express primeval feelings in a respectable and controlled setting.

College football's iconography added to the intensity of the experience. Carefully orchestrated pageantry gave spectators the sense that they were actually participating alongside the athletes on the field of play. Fans enthusiastically cheered the successes of their favorites and audibly groaned if the team failed. Rituals and symbols not only deepened the experience of sports, they also defined in sharp relief college identities. Nothing else about the colleges, certainly not their academic programs, equalled the power of sports and its accompanying fanfare in nurturing distinct identities. To this day, nothing distinguishes college from professional sports better than its special colors, cheers, mascots, nicknames, and pre- and postgame rituals.

The games bonded students of diverse backgrounds into a larger college community. Neither the honing of intellectual skills nor the acquisition of a body of new knowledge excited much interest among most postbellum students. The sons and daughters of the new rich frequently sought degrees as a means of achieving social positions commensurate with their family's wealth. A college degree, particularly from an Ivy League school, was perceived as a passport to polite society or as a requisite to membership in a high status community. By the 1890s, families of middling status came to believe that a college experience was valuable in nurturing the personality traits essential for success in the world of corporations. Corporate managers, who replaced individual business leaders by the late nineteenth century, looked to college campuses for men with social poise. Whether motivated by status or hopes of becoming corporate managers, such students viewed higher education as a social rather than an intellectual or spiritual investment.

Confronted with the absence of common purpose in the academic side of college life, a more impersonal academic setting, and the apparent need to make their college years more worthwhile as social experiences, the new students made extracurricular activities the center of college life. The number of literary societies, debate clubs, Greek letter societies, and college athletic associations burgeoned. The first sports clubs were usually composed of students who shared an interest in sport, but sometimes they were socially exclusive as well. Any freshman who wanted to join the Yale Navy in 1862, for example, had to pay an entry fee of ten dollars and be elected to membership by upper classmen. But as the rowing and football fevers mounted in the 1870s, the students began to organize college-wide athletic associations. Everyone was invited if not pressured to join; in the early years student subscriptions paid most of the expenses required to sustain intercollegiate sports.

Student involvement in sports transformed the spirit of nineteenth century college campuses. Student newspapers became major proponents of sport, editorially condemning "slackers," those who failed to attend games or display adequate enthusiasm. "School spirit," expressed in terms of loyalty to the football team, was often a precondition for acceptance by one's peers. The average man at Oxford or Cambridge, Caspar Whitney reported in 1895, evinced only a "lukewarm" interest in the football team's prospects "compared with the spirit with which a Harvard, Yale, or Princeton undergraduate will discuss his eleven, and grow eloquent over the brilliant rushes of the half-back, or sorrowfully deprecate the slowness with which an end rusher gets down the field under a kick."[17]

College presidents and faculties quickly recognized football's sway over the undergraduates. Student riots, rebellions, hazings, and drunkenness declined with the advent of football at Yale, according to professor of mathematics Eugene L. Richards in 1885, for football had created a common bond among the students. Football cultivated "a sense of friendship among the students—not fellowship in mischief, but fellowship in pluck and manliness, in generous admiration of their mates."[18] Students might be divided by social background, personal values, and lack of a common curriculum, but football, in the words of President Arthur T. Hadley of Yale, took "hold of the emotions of the student body in such a way as to make class distinctions relatively unimportant," and make "the students get together in the old-fashioned democratic way."[19] In effect, football promoted a college community of cheerleaders rather than scholars. College authorities welcomed the change, for football assisted them in making the peer group a major force in orderly student behavior.

Administrators also quickly concluded that football offered other tangible benefits to the colleges. They seized on the sport to draw attention to their colleges and recruit students. Unlike England, where only Oxford and Cambridge competed for eminence, literally dozens of American colleges scrambled

---

[17]Caspar Whitney, *A Sporting Pilgrimage*, (New York, 1895), p. 90.

[18]Eugene L. Richards, "Athletic Sports at Yale," *Outing*, 6 (1885), 453.

[19]Arthur Twining Hadley, "Wealth and Democracy in American Colleges," *Harper's Monthly* 93 (1906), 452.

for public acclaim. Since what constituted preeminence in higher education was ill-defined, college authorities tended to equate success with bigness and public recognition. They soon found that football was far more effective in attracting public attention than an institution's reputation for either scholarship or inspired teaching.

Consciously or unconsciously, administrators recognized that the rugged character of football might counter the traditional image of college men as effeminate. Until late in the nineteenth century, the popular media depicted college men as shriveled-up, dyspeptic, cowering scholars bent only upon the cultivation of useless intellectuality or ineffectual spirituality. Football, on the other hand, projected the archetypical college man as a rugged, fearless athlete who could hold his own in the brutish world outside the walls of academe. Although many college presidents and faculties long remained skeptical about the alleged benefits of intercollegiate sports, even the older, more prestigious institutions of the Northeast turned to football to recruit students. As early as 1878 President James McCosh of Princeton wrote an alumnus in Kentucky: "You will confer a great favor on us if you will get . . . the college noticed in the Louisville papers. . . . We must persevere in our efforts to get students from your region. . . . Mr. Brand Ballard has won us [a] great reputation as captain of the football team which has beaten both Harvard and Yale."[20] Football seemed an even more potent weapon in the battle for students among the land-grant institutions and numerous sectarian colleges of the West. Upon securing Princeton's Hector R. Cowan as "coach" in 1895, University of Kansas president Frank Snow was ecstatic. "I repeat, this is an immense thing at U. K. and will tend to develop the green eyes rapidly of other Kansas institutions."[21] Faculty, students, and the townspeople of Lawrence enthusiastically joined in raising the money necessary to pay Cowan's salary.

Upon assuming the presidency of John D. Rockefeller's newly endowed University of Chicago in 1892, William Rainey Harper set out to publicize the new university by establishing a winning football team. Harper hired Amos Alonzo Stagg, a famed Yale player, as coach, making Stagg the first coach with professorial rank in the country. Harper gave Stagg unambiguous instructions. "I want you to develop teams which we can send around the country and knock out all the [other] colleges," he explained to the new coach. "We will give them [the players] a palace car and a vacation too."[22] Stagg responded with enthusiasm. "If Chicago University places a team in the field it must *be a winning team* or one which will bring honor to the university."[23] According to Stagg, during the halftime of a game in which Chicago trailed Wisconsin 12–0, Harper delivered an impassioned plea to the Chicago players. "Boys, Mr. Rockefeller has just

[20]Quoted in Frederick Rudolph, *The American College and University: A History* (New York), p. 385.

[21]Quoted in Lewis, "The American Intercollegiate Football Spectacle," pp. 158–59.

[22]Ibid., p. 141.

[23]Stagg to Harper, March 18, 1892, as quoted in Kooman Boycheff, "Intercollegiate Athletics and Physical Education at the University of Chicago, 1892–1952," unpub. Ph.D. diss., Univ. of Michigan, 1954, p. 19.

announced a gift of $3,000,000 to the University," the President declared. "He believed that the University is to be great. The way you played in the first half leads me to wonder whether we really have the spirit of greatness. . . . I wish you would make up your minds to win this game and show that we have it."[24] Chicago players responded in the second half by winning 22–12.

College authorities also found that football developed an alumni loyalty that was far more profound than fond memories of chapels, classrooms, pranks, or professors. "You do not remember whether Thorpwright was valedictorian or not," wrote a young college alumnus in 1890, "but you can never forget that glorious run of his in the football game." The alumni continued to identify with the football team long after their official connection with the college had been severed. The lament of a Bowdoin alumnus in 1903 could be heard in countless variations from alumni everywhere. Referring to a 16–0 defeat of Bowdoin by the University of Maine, he declared: "In my day the University of Maine was a standing joke. . . . We got licked to-day because we hadn't the stock—the stock sir . . . Old Bowdoin must fling open her gates and get some—some stock sir."[25]

In the closing years of the century football encouraged the growth of an alumni subculture. Alumni in cities remote from their college campuses organized chapters, sponsored elaborate homecoming events, and printed bulletins listing the achievements of their classmates and the latest exploits of the football team. "The feeling of solidarity and loyalty in the student body that intercollegiate contests develop is a good thing," ex-President William Howard Taft explained in 1915, "it outlasts every contest, and it continues in the heart and soul of every graduate as long as he lives."[26] College authorities tried to convert the alumni's enthusiasm into generous contributions. But the alumni demanded a price; they wanted a winning football team and, sometimes a substantial voice in the management of the school's football program. By the turn of the century, alumni in many places were recruiting athletes, raising money for sports, and assisting in the administration of college athletics.

College football, whether it was in a small college town like Ames, Iowa, or the metropolis of New York City, especially attracted social climbers. Alumni or not, by becoming football devotees they could identify with a college. Increasingly, identification with a college was essential to those who wanted to be in upper-status communities. As early as the mid-1880s, the wealthy social aspirants in New York City went to great lengths to display conspicuously their allegiance to a college. After Yale's defeat in 1889, the New York *Herald* reported, "Mr. Cornelius Vanderbilt [who had never attended a college] and his son William went back to the big house on Fifth Avenue and sadly removed the Yale flag that had floated so bravely all day."[27] Thereafter, at each of the Thanksgiv-

[24]Amos A. Stagg and Wesley W. Sterit, *Touchdown!* (New York, 1927), p. 203.

[25]Quoted in Rudolph, *The American College*, p. 383.

[26]William Howard Taft, "College Athletics," *Proceedings of the Tenth Annual Convention of the National Collegiate Athletic Association* (1915), p. 67.

[27]Quoted in Lewis, "The American Intercollegiate Football Spectacle," p. 92.

ing Day battles the Vanderbilts and Whitneys hung blue and white Yale banners between their mansions across Fifth Avenue. Other wealthy families—the Sloanes, the Alexanders, and the Scribners—displayed the colors of Old Nassau (Princeton) with equal pride.

Aspirants to the inner social circle of New York City and elsewhere basked in the attention given to them by the newspapers. Reporters always provided their readers with detailed lists and accounts of the fashionable set who attended the games. The *New York Herald,* referring to those present at the Yale–Princeton game of 1892, reported that "Mrs. William C. Whitney had a conspicuous box, trimmed profusely in Yale colors and beautifully decorated with a bevy of young girls." In another box, "His Luminous Magnificence the Sun was patted pleasantly on the back by Mrs. Elliott Shepard when she stepped into the Shepard-Vanderbilt box and remarked, 'what a perfect day; what glorious sunshine.' And, indeed, the sun reciprocated thankfully to the compliment and smiled full and bright in her lovely face."[28] Little wonder that Richard Harding Davis concluded in 1893 that "the sporting character of the event has been overwhelmed by the social interest . . . which has . . . made it more of a spectacle than an athletic contest."[29]

Mirroring the larger culture's conceptions of proper gender roles, athletics had meanings quite different for female students. The institutions that first introduced intercollegiate sports were all northeastern men's colleges. But as women's colleges and coeducational state universities grew in numbers and size, the defenders of female education were confronted with the argument that the rigors of intellectual activity were damaging to the health of young women, especially to the proper growth of their reproductive systems. Educators responded that a properly regulated exercise program could prevent such damage. Consequently, physical training became an integral part of the curriculum for women, and consisted mainly of exercises designed to improve the female reproductive system. Educators concluded that vigorous sport could not accomplish this aim.

Although women rowed, hiked, rode horseback, and ice-skated on college campuses before the 1890s, they rarely engaged in competitive physical activities.[30] Instead women remained on the sidelines of men's intercollegiate sports. Until the advent of college football, women had usually been forbidden by the dictates of Victorian decency from attending the more disreputable sporting spectacles. Football was different. The annual fall horse show and the Thanksgiving Day contest in New York launched the city's winter social season; debutante balls and banquets soon followed. The antics, cheering, and enthusiasm of the younger ladies at football games led G. Stanley Hall, the psychologist-president of Clark University in 1900, to conclude that "while the human

[28]Ibid., pp. 119–20.

[29]Richard Harding Davis, "Thanksgiving Day and Football in New York," *Harper's Weekly,* 37 (Dec. 9, 1893), 1170).

[30]See esp. Cindy L. Himes, "The Female Athlete in American Society," unpub. Ph.D. diss., Univ. of Pennsylvania, 1984, Chap. 2.

female does not as in the case of many animal species look on complacently and reward the victor with her [sexual] favor, military prowess has a strange fascination for the weaker sex, perhaps ultimately and biologically because it demonstrates the power to protect and defend."[31] Only an academic could have put the matter so delicately.

Unlike educational institutions elsewhere in the western world, in the latter half of the nineteenth century sport became an integral part of American college life. Students provided the impetus for staging the games as well as for the invention of an elaborate pageantry to accompany them. Eventually, college varsity sports excluded all but a few of the undergraduates from actual participation and oriented higher education away from intellectual pursuits toward commercial entertainment. Nevertheless, they were instrumental in defining college identities and in binding students, faculties, administrators, alumni, and social climbers into a single college community.

[31]Quoted in Rudolph, *The American College*, p. 393.

8

THE ASCENDANCY
OF
ORGANIZED SPORTS, 1890–1950

In the annual Thanksgiving Day championship football game of 1893, Princeton defeated mighty Yale 6–0. In the jubilant dressing room after the game, a Princeton coach held up his arm for silence. "Boys, I want you to sing the doxology," the coach solemnly said. Outside, fellow students cheered and yelled. Imploring their heroes to emerge so they could be lauded, the students banged their fists on the doors and windows. Inside, the men, their naked bodies matted with blood, sweat, and mud, sang the doxology "as sincerely as they ever did in their lives." In the meantime, not far away in the Yale dressing room, the losing men sobbed "like hysterical school-girls."[1]

Such scenes reflected the growing importance of sports. Indeed, in the 1890–1950 era organized sports were no longer peripheral spectacles, occasional oddities, or activities freighted with meaning only for certain workingmen, ethnics, blacks, or members of the nation's upper strata. "Ball matches, football games, tennis tournaments, bicycle races, [and] regattas, have become part of our national life," concluded a writer in *Harper's Weekly* in 1895, "and are watched with eagerness and discussed with enthusiasm and understanding by all manner of people, from the day-laborer to the millionaire."[2] In the new era, organized sports achieved an institutional permanency and prominence in American life in some ways equal to that of business, politics, ethnicity, race, or religion. This

[1] Richard Harding Davis, "The Thanksgiving-Day Game," *Harper's Weekly*, 37 (Dec. 9, 1893), 1171.
[2] Henry Smith Williams, "The Educational Value and Health-Giving Value of Athletics," ibid, 39 (Feb. 16, 1895), 165.

chapter explores the salient, underlying conditions that undergirded the ascendancy of organized sports.

THE MEDIA AND SPORTS

New forms of communication and transportation, such as radio, movies, television, automobiles, and eventually air travel, joined steady improvements in newspapers, special sporting sheets, telegraph, the telephone, steamships, and railways to continue the conquest of time and space begun in the nineteenth century. Throughout the 1890–1950 era, the sports page of the daily newspaper and the broadcasting of sports on radio especially encouraged public interest in sports.

The modern sports page began to take shape in the 1890s, but did not become a standard feature in all major daily newspapers until the 1920s. In that decade the percentage of total newspaper space allocated to sports was more than double what it had been three decades earlier. Even the *New York Times* gave front-page coverage to major prize fights and the World Series. With the exception of two columns on page one, the *Times* devoted the entire first thirteen pages of its issue of July 3, 1921, to the Dempsey–Carpentier heavyweight championship fight. Rather than having to confront the turmoil and unpredictability of front page news, many Americans (especially men) turned first to the sports page where they found clear-cut triumphs and defeats, continuity, and orderliness. Regardless of natural disasters, revolutions, murder, rape, or economic crises, the games went on. "You pulled off the double play the same way for the Richmond County Juniors, the Auks or the White Sox," wrote Tom Wicker, a *New York Times* columnist, about baseball. "Baseball was a common denominator . . . it was the same one day as the next, in one town as another."[3]

The twentieth century brought to the fore a new generation of writers specializing in sports. Some converted the sporting experience into poetry; only poetry, they believed, could reduce the wonder of sports to human comprehension. Grantland Rice, the dean of early twentieth-century sportswriters, had a gift for writing verse a cut above the popular commercial jingles of the day. Youngsters memorized his lines and coaches used them to inspire their teams. His most famous: "When the one Great Scorer comes to write against your name, he marks—not whether you won or lost—but how you played the game." After Knute Rockne's 1924 Notre Dame team defeated powerful Army, Rice composed the best known opening lines in sportswriting history: "Outlined against a blue-grey October sky, the Four Horsemen rode again. In dramatic lore they

[3]Quoted in Benjamin G. Rader, *In Its Own Image: How Television Has Transformed Sports* (New York, 1984), p. 13. A 1930s survey revealed that 80 percent of all men read at least portions of the sports page regularly. See James Howard Slusser, "The Sports Page in American Life in the Nineteen-Twenties," unpub. M.A. thesis, Univ. of California, Berkeley, 1952, p. 4. For content analyses that demonstrate the increased coverage of sport compared to other news, see Robert S. Lynd and Helen Merrell Lynd, *Middletown: A Study in Modern American Culture* (New York, 1929), p. 473 and Howard J. Savage, et al., *American College Athletics* (New York, 1929), pp. 267–72.

are known as Famine, Pestilence, Destruction, and Death. These are only aliases. Their real names are Stuhldreher, Miller, Crowley, and Layden."[4] Sportswriters frequently dispensed on-the-spot immortality to athletes. Even the racehorse Man O' War was immortal; he was dubbed the "horse of eternity."

Despite Rice's continuing popularity, by the 1920s his form of sportswriting had begun to wane. Rather than writing poetry or stringing together quotations from participants (often a characteristic of sports reporting in the age of television), Paul Gallico, Frank Graham, Damon Runyan, Ring Lardner, Westbrook Pegler, Heywood Broun, and Arch Ward (among others) saw their task to be the construction of an interesting and interpretive story of what had happened or was likely to happen. The best of them could weave a story as terse and tight as the strands of a steel cable. Apart from presenting a coherent narrative, they employed powerful, often onomatopoetic verbs, colorful figures of speech, and alliterative nicknames. Nicknames came in a virtual flood: The Galloping Ghost (Red Grange), The Fordham Flash (Frankie Frisch), The Sultan of Swat (Babe Ruth). They also delighted in using all three names of people involved in sports, such as Grover Cleveland Alexander, Kenesaw Mountain Landis, or George Herman Ruth, thereby conferring upon them a kind of tongue-in-cheek grandeur.

As in earlier times, newspapers continued to promote sports. For example, the famous Golden Gloves boxing program got underway in the mid-1920s with the aid of Captain Joseph Medill Patterson, copublisher of the *Chicago Tribune* and later publisher of the New York tabloid, *The Daily News*. In 1928, led by Patterson and the sports staff of the two newspapers, the Golden Gloves became a national tournament. By 1955, some 25,000 youngsters tried to fight their way through the regionals to become one of eight finalists. Arch Ward, longtime sports editor of the *Chicago Tribune* was especially important as a promoter; he invented both the annual All-Star Baseball Game (1933) and the College All-Star Football Game (1934). At the local level, newspapers frequently sponsored athletic teams and a wide variety of sporting events.

Radio began to have an impact on sport in the 1920s but did not reach the apogee of its influence until the 1940s and 1950s. Initially, radio aired only the more spectacular events rather than regularly scheduled contests. As early as 1923 an estimated two million fans listened to the broadcast of the Louis Firpo–Jess Willard heavyweight fight. The *New York Times* deemed the twenty-three station network established to carry the 1926 World Series to be such a pioneering venture that it printed the entire narrative of the broadcasts in its sports section. Until upstaged by television in the 1950s, the radio broadcasts of the World Series were an annual rite. As early as 1934, the three major networks of the day paid $100,000 for the privilege of carrying the series. Broadcasts of regular season big league games did not become universal, however, until the 1940s. When the number of local AM radio stations doubled between 1945 and 1950, the quantity of big league games aired on radio ballooned astronomically. Apart from the

---

[4]*New York Herald Tribune*, Oct. 19, 1924.

sometimes far-flung regional networks associated with each club, nearly 500 stations scattered across the nation carried Mutual Broadcasting Company's "Game of the Day."

Radio executives soon discovered that sports fans liked announcers who were something more than disembodied voices objectively and dispassionately describing the action. The fans wanted announcers capable of becoming celebrities in their own right. Graham McNamee became the first star of the new medium. As the chief announcer of the National Broadcasting Company in the 1920s, McNamee enjoyed a remarkable capacity for using his voice to convey the gamut of emotions. Hailed as "The World's Most Popular Announcer," McNamee covered the World Series, prize fights, major college football games, national political conventions, and important live news developments.

For many decades, millions of Americans found in the radio coverage of sports both an escape from the humdrum of everyday life and an entry into the wonderland of the imagination. "Radio—mysterious, disembodied, vivid as a dream—screamed for a fantasy response," wrote Bil Gilbert about his experiences listening to the games of the Detroit Tigers while a youngster in the 1930s. Even when not listening to the games, Gilbert imitated the Detroit broadcaster's voice as he described to himself his own tossing of a ball on the roof or throwing stones at a target. In his private world, where Gilbert always had his beloved Tigers crush rivals, he never suffered from the humiliation of defeat. To Gilbert and millions like him, the introduction of television in the 1940s and 1950s, destroyed the magic. "Thereafter baseball was never again serious," Gilbert concluded.[5]

THE CONSUMER CULTURE

The entrenchment of organized sports in American life probably owed more to the emergence of modern consumer culture than it did to the sports media. By the 1890s the nation's economy had begun to shift from one organized around production to one organized around mass consumption and leisure. In the industrial revolution's first phase, the main catalyst for rapid economic expansion had been the growing demand for "producer goods," those made for other producers rather than for individual consumers. A classic example in the nineteenth century was the steel industry, which had grown up primarily to meet the demands of the nation's burgeoning railway network. Although producer goods remained important to the nation's prosperity in the twentieth century, by the 1920s the manufacture for, and sales of goods to, millions of individuals had become the hallmark of a new phase of the industrial revolution.

By then, industrial technology had transformed the United States into a consumers' paradise. The automobile, the most prized of all the new consumer goods, emancipated millions of Americans from a network restricted to home,

[5]Quoted in Rader, *In Its Own Image*, p. 28. On radio sports, see also Curt Smith, *Voices of the Game* (South Bend, IN, 1987).

neighborhood, and workplace. Electricity revolutionized the home; by 1940, four out of five Americans could, if they had the financial means, plug in electric lamps, washing machines, vacuum cleaners, refrigerators, toasters, and radios. The Great Depression of the 1930s and World War II temporarily set back the national buying spree, but in the postwar era, plastics, aluminum, and transistors became the staples of a new round of consumption. The consumer cornucopia extended to commercial leisure. As early as 1909, the A.G. Spalding and Brothers catalog contained more than 200 pages of advertisements for sporting goods and exercise devices. Overall, the first half of the twentieth century witnessed a twelvefold increase in recreation expenditures.

The changing nature of work, rising real incomes (adjusted for changes in prices), a shorter work week, and paid vacations abetted the development of consumer culture. Although workers were subject to cycles of unemployment, wage earnings in manufacturing nearly quadrupled between the Civil War and 1929. The Great Depression set back worker gains, but earnings rebounded in the 1940s. At the same time, the average work week for those engaged in manufacturing followed a descending curve from 60 hours in 1890 to 47 in 1920 and 40 at mid-twentieth century. A week's paid vacation first became the norm for white collar workers in the 1920s and then for blue collar laborers in the 1940s. As income and leisure time both increased and the factories and bureaucracies gnawed away at job satisfaction, consumption became the centerpiece of more and more lives.

Newspapers, mass circulation magazines, movies, and radio encouraged this change. The media bombarded the public with new models of "the good life" that had been only furtively glimpsed by earlier generations. To encourage buying, salesmen and advertisers unrelentingly assaulted the older virtues of thrift and prudence. They urged consumers to "buy now, pay later," to "live for the moment." "Life is meant to live and enjoy as you go along. . . . ," insisted Bruce Barton, a leading apostle of the consumer culture in the 1920s. "If self-denial is necessary I'll practice some of it when I'm old and not try to do all of it now."[6] The suggestions or implications of advertisers and the media that consumption aided in the solution to such personal problems as loneliness, weariness, absence of sexual gratification, and meaninglessness in the workplace won increasing favor.

Although consumer culture by no means obliterated traditional values or behaviors, it spawned an alternative set of powerful dreams and expectations. Growing numbers of Americans were no longer so concerned with work, thrift, or self-restraint; they were more concerned with obtaining the immediate pleasures

---

[6]Quoted in Richard Wightman Fox and T.J. Jackson Lears, eds., *The Culture of Consumption: Critical Essays in American History, 1880–1980* (New York, 1983), p. 32. Apart from the essays in Fox and Lears, see a summary of the ballooning literature on the consumer culture found in the introduction and notes pertaining thereto in Daniel Horowitz, *The Morality of Spending: Attitudes toward the Consumer Society in America, 1875–1940* (Baltimore, 1985) For an important book published since Horowitz, see Kathy Peiss, *Cheap Amusements: Working Women and Leisure in Turn-of-the-Century New York* (Philadelphia, 1986).

arising from devotion to fun, play, sensual experiences, and less inhibited behavior generally. Consistent with the new attitudes, states and municipalities across the nation relaxed legal restrictions on amusements. Many states repealed or neglected to enforce their Sabbatarian laws. New York City, for example, finally obtained legal approval of Sunday baseball in 1919, though Philadelphia and Pittsburgh did not succumb until 1934. In the 1920s several states dropped their bans on such low sports as prize fighting. But these changes came not without conflicts. Many tried to preserve traditional virtues, and even those who embraced consumption values experienced agonizing doubts. In their personal lives, they often tried the difficult if not impossible task of accommodating the older values conducive to production with the newer ones that encouraged consumption.

ISLANDS OF PLEASURE

Islands of pleasure flourished in the consumer culture. Some were holdovers from the nineteenth century. Blue collar voluntary associations declined in importance and workingmen's theaters disappeared altogether, but urban workers continued in the twentieth century to gather on street corners and in saloons, billiard halls, bowling alleys, and other "low" spots of entertainment. In the first two decades of the twentieth century, the ethnic saloon reached its heyday in popularity. In Chicago, for example, a survey revealed that on an average day the number of saloon customers equalled over half of the city's population. But Prohibition in the 1920s, a depressed economy in the 30s, and the growing privatization of leisure in the post-World War II era all contributed to a decline in the importance of the saloon as a special workingmen's oasis.

As in the past, saloon keepers offered patrons opportunities for direct participation in sport and a place to discuss and wager on sports. In 1909, for example, over half of Chicago's 7,600 saloons contained at least one billiard table. Despite persistent criticism by "respectable" people and competition from multifarious rivals in entertainment, even in the post-World War II era saloons continued to furnish countless men with opportunities for sport and places to nurture an all-male subculture.[7]

At the other end of the social spectrum, the wealthy continued to enjoy their own islands of pleasure. In the last half of the nineteenth century, the rich

[7]See Steven A. Riess, *City Games: The Evolution of American Urban Society and the Rise of Sports* (Urbana and Chicago, 1989), pp. 72–81; Jon M. Kingsdale, "The 'Poor Man's Club': Social Functions of the Urban Working-Class Saloon," *American Quarterly*, 25 (1973), 472–88. For the persistence of the saloon into the 1960s and 1970s, see E.E. LeMasters, "Social Life in a Working-Class Tavern," *Urban Life and Culture*, 2 (1973), 27–52. For the persistence of the importance of ethnicity to sport see Riess, *City Games*, Chap. 3, and Gary Ross Mormino, "The Playing Fields of St. Louis: Italian Immigrants and Sports, 1925–1941," *Journal of Sport History*, 9 (1982), 5–19.

had established posh yacht, athletic, cricket, and country clubs as well as special compounds in cool summer places like Newport, Rhode Island, or in warm winter spots like Pinehurst, North Carolina. The summer and winter playgrounds of the super rich often displayed private mansions with an army of servants year-round, golf courses, tennis courts, and handsome clubhouses. Each of the larger cities also had clubs reserved for only the wealthiest residents.

A notch or two below the super wealthy, active business and professional men in cities and towns across the nation formed and joined country clubs. In the 1920s the country club came of age in the United States. Membership in a country club became a salient badge of distinction, obligatory for anyone striving for higher status in large and small communities. Wealthier clubs erected large, Mediterranean-style clubhouses, sometimes valued at more than a million dollars, while at the other extreme, avid golfers in small towns sometimes built clubhouses of unadorned pine at a cost of only a few hundred dollars. Regardless of the cost of their clubs, in their isolated playgrounds the nation's upper strata partook of hedonistic pleasures that had been earlier frowned upon. The lifestyle of the materially successful eased the transition of many Americans from a production to a consumption ethic.[8]

Although traditional places of pleasure of both the upper and lower classes persisted into the twentieth century, new islands of commercial leisure in which all classes and both sexes mingled grew in popularity. Beginning in the last quarter of the nineteenth century and continuing into the twentieth century, dance halls, amusement parks, vaudeville, and, above all, movie houses furnished millions of urbanites with intense experiences not found in the workplace or the home. Around the turn of the century, amusement parks proliferated; every large city had one or more parks, which usually included bathing facilities, vaudeville theaters, dance halls, band pavilions, circus acts, and mechanical contrivances such as Ferris Wheels, all located in exotic settings. "Coney Island has a code of conduct which is all her own," Guy Carryl wrote in 1901.[9] Indeed, while at the amusement parks patrons suspended Victorian proprieties. Unlike the prevalent gender-segregated leisure of the nineteenth century, the younger members of both sexes and all classes came together at the amusement parks where they laughed merrily, talked loudly, embraced one another openly, and cavorted. The itinerant carnivals and circuses furnished similar entertainment to millions in the smaller towns and in the countryside.

But the popularity of amusement parks, carnivals, and circuses paled beside that of the movies. By the 1920s over 50 million people a week went to the movies, a figure equivalent to half of the nation's population. Even the hardships of the 1930s failed to curb movie-going; movie attendance continued to climb

---

[8]See Jesse Frederick Steiner, *Americans at Play: Recent Trends in Recreation and Leisure Time Activities* (New York, 1933) and citations in Chap. 6. For a comprehensive examination of upper-class leisure in the suburb of Westchester, New York, in the 1930s, see George A. Lundberg, et. al., *Leisure: A Suburban Study* (New York, 1934).

[9]Quoted in John F. Kasson, *Amusing the Millions: Coney Island at the Turn of the Century* (New York, 1978), p. 41.

until the nation entered the age of television in the 1950s. Awe-inspiring classical architecture and uniformed ushers lent the movie houses an aura of respectability, but, as in the amusement parks, the classes and sexes came together indiscriminately. The films presented models of consumption rather than production, treating moviegoers to a picture of a leisured class that enjoyed sumptuous homes, lovely clothes, sleek cars, and personal servants.

In the meantime, reformers sought to construct completely respectable islands of leisure. This process included the use of public school buildings and playgrounds, church and Young Men's Christian Association gymnasiums, municipal auditoriums and playing fields, and especially city parks. As early as the 1840s, reformers visualized parks as retreats in which urban residents could escape the ills of the cities and be rejuvenated by the powers of nature. In 1856 New York City acquired land in Manhattan that, under the direction of Frederick Law Olmstead, became Central Park; other larger cities soon followed the lead of New York. In the 1890s a new, more successful movement called for the creation of a system of smaller parks in neighborhoods rather than one large, centrally located park. By 1920 nearly every city in the nation had a network of parks and a parks commission. Municipal expenditures on parks continued to mount in the 1920s; in the depressed 1930s the federal government became the main funding agency for city parks.

Although reformers provided the initiative for the city parks movement, the history of parks invariably reflected struggles between groups with conflicting interests and values. In the nineteenth century, Protestant upper-class reformers sought to construct romantic parks that were in sharp contrast to life in the streets while ethnics and workingmen sought to open parks to vigorous games and even commercial amusements. In the twentieth century, reformers insisted that parks should be carefully managed by professionals. "The mere presence of open spaces is not enough, leisure itself is not enough," concluded a study of the municipal park movement.[10] Park administrators should nurture the social and cultural development of the parkgoers by organizing dramatic and musical performances, providing nature classes, and supervising recreational activities. Actual park use usually resulted from delicate compromises worked out between park reformers and park users. By mid-twentieth century, parks reflected efforts to maintain sylvan oases alongside busy ballfields, basketball courts, and swimming pools.

Business and industrial concerns began to establish recreation programs for workers. In the nineteenth century, most businessmen had either paid little attention to the spare time activities of their employees or condemned them when they interfered with worker efficiency. George M. Pullman, the manufacturer of luxury railroad cars, was something of an exception.[11] Beginning in the 1880s, he

---

[10]Paul Boyer, *Urban Masses and Moral Order in America, 1820–1920* (Cambridge, MA, 1978), p. 240.
[11]Wilma J. Pesavento, "Sport and Recreation in the Pullman Experiment, 1880–1900," *Journal of Sport History*, 9 (1982), 38–62.

tried to encourage worker loyalty and productivity by building a model town on the outskirts of Chicago. The town included worker housing, shops, a theater, a library, schools, parks, and a recreation program. The failure of the Pullman experiment to avoid a violent strike in 1894 led many industrialists to conclude that "welfare capitalism" was useless in preventing labor conflict.

Nevertheless, efforts by management in the 1920s to reverse union gains of the World War I era gave new life to welfare capitalism. Apart from such traditional union-busting techniques as blacklists, yellow dog contracts, injunctions, espionage, and violence, employers sought to prevent unionization by forming company unions, distributing chatty newspapers, inviting employees to make suggestions for improvements in the firm's operation, and forming company recreation programs. "Industrial amateur athletics organized on a business-like basis will promote plant morale quicker than any other single method," waxed an executive of a corporation in 1927.[12] Often companies, YMCA's, YWCA's, and city governments cooperated closely in providing facilities and supervision for organized sports programs. Industrial sports suffered setbacks during the Great Depression, but, despite the unionization of basic industries, bounded back strongly during the war years of the 1940s.

THE STRENUOUS LIFE

A growing enthusiasm for organized sports by the nation's intellectual leadership accompanied the emergence of the consumer culture. In the antebellum era, only a small band of muscular Christians had had the temerity to suggest that individual and national strength required as much attention to physical fitness as it did to work or to the cultivation of spirituality. But by the 1890s calls for the strenuous life had become a virtual chorus; by then, certain members of the old Eastern elite joined with a rising corps of experts on the human body in insisting that properly regulated sports and other physically vigorous activities were essential to the nation's well-being. In the twentieth century, more and more Americans agreed; they attributed to sports a potential utility equal to, or sometimes even larger than, that which had been traditionally assigned to religion, the home, or the school.[13]

A belief that the nation, or at the least the nation's upper class, was suffering from a massive malaise of the spirit kindled the interest in physical

---

[12]U.S. Bureau of Labor Statistics, "Outdoor Recreation for Industrial Employees," *Monthly Labor Review*, 24 (1927), 8.

[13]For this section, see esp. Donald J. Mrozek, *Sport and the American Mentality, 1880–1920* (Knoxville, 1983); James C. Whorton, *Crusaders for Fitness: The History of American Health Reformers* (Princeton, 1982); Elliot J. Gorn, *The Manly Art: Bare-Knuckle Prize Fighting in America* (Ithaca, 1986), pp. 185–206; George M. Fredrickson, *The Inner Civil War: Northern Intellectuals and the Crisis of the Union* (New York, 1965), Chap. 11; Harvey Green, *Fit for America: Health, Fitness, and American Society* (New York, 1988), Chap. 9; and Gerald F. Roberts, "The Strenuous Life; The Cult of Manliness in the Era of Theodore Roosevelt," unpub. Ph.D. diss., Michigan State University, 1970.

strenuosity. Perhaps disturbed personally by religious skepticism and by growing suspicions of a decline in the public esteem that they had once been accorded,
the apostles of the strenuous life concluded that the vitality of the nation depended upon the generation of higher purposes than simply making or spending
money. "No amount of commercial prosperity can supply the lack of the heroic
virtues" found in modern life, wrote Theodore Roosevelt.[14] Likewise, too many
of the old elite had withdrawn from an active involvement in the world to a
"cloistered life" of ease and sloth; there, they had become "effeminized." Ancient
Rome had fallen, declared Alfred T. Mahan, "when the strong masculine impulse
which first created it had degenerated into . . . worship of comfort, wealth, and
general softness."[15] In short, modern man was "over-civilized." Intrigued by
Darwinian analogies depicting human society as a jungle in which only the fittest
(often conceived unconsciously as the physically fittest) survived, the elite worried that human races possessing greater animal virility would crush the "Anglo-
Saxon race."

Without a Civil War or a frontier to provide opportunities for the expression of heroism or nobility of character, the elite manifested its activism in an
aggressive nationalism, an intense interest in untamed nature, and an enthusiasm
for organized sports. No one expressed the genteel ideology of "dangerous sport"
more fully than Francis A. Walker, a Civil War veteran who had become the
president of Yale. In an address to the Phi Beta Kappa at Harvard in 1893, he
declared that the Civil War had fortunately produced "a vast change in popular
sentiments and ideals," showing that the "strength of will, firmness of purpose,
resolution to endure, and capacity for action" expressed in the war was far nobler
than the soft intellectuality and sentimentalism prevalent in the antebellum era.
He went on to say, "The competitive contests of our colleges" offered the best
hope of preserving "something akin to patriotism and public spirit," which
counteracted "the selfish, individualistic tendencies of the age." Sports not only
instilled idealism in the youth, Walker added, but they toughened the "cultivated
classes" for leadership roles.[16]

No one exemplified in practice the strenuous life more fully than
Theodore Roosevelt. From a genteel family, being something of an intellectual
and unable to participate with enthusiasm in the sordid business of making
money, Roosevelt rejected a life of ease for one of political and physical combat.
He sought to embody the heroic virtues found in the soldier, the cowboy, and
the prize fighter. Perhaps compensating for his puniness as a youth, he began
at the age of fourteen to take boxing lessons (even in his forties, while occupy-
ing the White House, he continued to spar) and he worked out regularly with
dumbbells and horizontal bars. In his twenties, he left the safe confines of the
East for the hazardous life of a cowboy in the Dakotas where he relished the

---

[14]Theodore Roosevelt, *American Ideals and Other Essays* (New York, 1897), p. 11.

[15]Alfred T. Mahan, *The Interest of America in Sea Power, Present and Future* (Boston, 1903), p. 121.

[16]Quoted in Fredrickson, *The Inner Civil War*, 223–24.

THEODORE "TEDDY" ROOSEVELT (1858–1919)
This picture of Teddy Roosevelt on the front cover of the September 1904 issue of *Physical Culture* magazine illustrated the compatibility between the President's "strenuous life" ideology and that of huckster and muscleman Bernarr Macfadden, the publisher of *Physical Culture*.

opportunity to help in the capture of a band of cattle rustlers. Upon the outbreak of the Spanish–American War in 1898, he created and lead a cavalry unit of cowboys and college boys that won national acclaim for bravado. Succeeding to the Presidency upon the assassination of William McKinley in 1901, Roosevelt enthralled the nation with his vigor. He preached to and bullied opponents both at home and abroad. "In life, as in a football game," he advised the nation's boys, "the principle to follow is: Hit the line hard, don't foul, and don't shirk, but hit the line hard!"[17]

Experts on the human body gave support to the turn-of-the century campaign for the strenuous life. In fact, the patricians probably drew some of their ideas from the professional physical educators. Roosevelt, Walker, and dozens of others passed through Dudley A. Sargent's famous physical fitness program (1879–1919) at Harvard. Sargent agreed that violent sports allowed young men to replicate the courage and hardiness that their fathers had experienced in Civil War combat. But, unlike the old elite, Sargent advocated exercises and the playing of sports primarily as a means of achieving general fitness rather than more esoteric social goals. Indeed, not all young men should play football; each person should engage in those sports and exercises that contributed to their all-around fitness.

[17]Theodore Roosevelt, "What We Can Expect of the American Boy," *St. Nicholas*, 27 (1900), 574.

The ideology of strenuosity penetrated deeply into American life. During the first half of the century, it shaped a large body of juvenile literature and was a core ingredient in programs designed to manage the spare time activities of adolescent boys. (See Chapter 13). The rising profession of physical education employed it effectively to convince reluctant school boards and state legislatures across the nation to require physical training in the schools. That strenuosity, especially as expressed in organized sports, built personal character and improved fitness became a truism. Not even those with an evangelical Protestant temperament challenged the tenets of the strenuous life; after World War II, evangelicals openly used sports as a means of recruiting converts. Acceptance of the ideology also eased guilt feelings arising from the abandonment of the work ethic. After all, disciples of the strenuous life worked hard, even if only at their play.

IDEALS OF WOMANHOOD

Prevalent assumptions about the proper role of females and their basic nature worked against the acceptance of the strenuous life for women. Even though millions of women performed back-breaking chores such as farm labor, factory work, cleaning, and child-rearing, most Americans accepted the age-old notion that women were by nature more delicate than men. This premise was reinforced by the changes in nineteenth-century economy. The rapid decline of the household as an economic unit contributed to the popularity of a "separate women's sphere." Success in this separate sphere required women to cultivate restraint, compassion, piety, and delicacy rather than aggressiveness, competitiveness, masterfulness, and robustness. To the extent that this ideal of success for women was accepted, it deprived women of one of the most important popular arguments used by men to rationalize participation in sports.[18]

Neither did the social interpreters of Darwin lend support to women's athleticism. They assumed that males and females had acquired distinct instincts and propensities over the course of human evolution. Of utmost importance to survival for males had been an adeptness in fighting, hunting, and running—activities recapitulated in the games of boys. Those females, on the other hand, who had become most adept in caring for the home were more likely to survive and produce offspring. "So it is clear," wrote organized play leader Luther Gulick in 1920, "that athletics have never been either a test or a large factor in the survival

---

[18]For a flat rejection of the strenuous life for females, see Henry Van Dyke, "The Strenuous Life for Girls," *Harper's Bazaar*, 36 (1902), 575–78. See also Linda K. Kerber, "Separate Spheres, Female Worlds, Womans' Place: The Rhetoric of Women's History," *Journal of American History*, 75 (1988), 9–39 and Stephanie L. Twin, "Women and Sport," in Donald Spivey, ed., *Sport in America* (Westport, CT, 1985), 193–218. For historiography, see Nancy L. Struna, "Beyond Mapping Experience: The Need for Understanding in the History of American Sporting Women," *Journal of Sport History*, 11 (1984), 120–33.

of women; athletics do not test womanliness as they test manliness." Another Darwinist, psychologist G. Stanley Hall, opined that a woman "performs her best service in her true role of sympathetic spectator rather than as a fellow player."[19]

Many physicians and health authorities added practical objections to strenuous play. They worried that robust play would damage or inhibit the maturation of female reproductive organs. They therefore urged young women to shepherd their energies and engage in only mild, carefully regulated exercises. Believing that the menstrual period was an illness, they concluded that strenuous sport during menstruation could lead to a displaced uterus and a reduction in childbearing capacities. Even as late as 1953, the Amateur Athletic Union, in a study of the effects of athletics upon women, quoted a woman physician as saying that competition during menstruation might adversely affect the capacity of the athlete to be "a normal mother."[20]

Nonetheless, the persistence of these powerful strictures failed to curb a general trend after 1890 toward a greater freedom of physical expression for women. Rural, working-class, recently arrived ethnic, and wealthy women had never been as circumscribed in their roles as were middle-class Victorian women. By the late nineteenth century, women in the middle income ranks also began to break out of the confines of a rigidly defined special sphere. The widely-heralded "new woman" of the 1890–1930 era sought an advanced education, often remained single, sometimes entered a profession or engaged in full-time social work, and supported women's suffrage.

The bicycling rage of the 1890s afforded one of the first widely publicized tests of the limits of female physical expression. Welcoming the freedom of movement afforded by the cycle, thousands of women of the middle and upper classes took to "the wheel." They boldly rode astride the vehicle and donned shorter, more comfortable skirts. Most physicians, both male and female, welcomed the potential of mild exercise and the more practical forms of dress introduced by the bicycle but worried that cycling might lure young women away from the home and its duties, lead them to remote spots alone with men where they might succumb to seduction, or stimulate the genitals resulting in equally unimaginable horrors. Although the cyclists conjured up images of autonomous women emancipated from Victorian inhibitions, freer forms of female dress seemed to be the most enduring legacy of the cycling fad.[21]

Changing ideals of physical beauty affected the sporting experiences of both sexes, albeit in distinct ways. Male ideals tended to encourage strenuous play and exercises. The wrestler and weightlifter, Eugene Sandow, who had been

---

[19]Luther Halsey Gulick, *A Philosophy of Play* (New York, 1920), p. 92; G. Stanley Hall, *Adolescence*, 2 vols. (New York, 1904), I, p. 207.

[20]*A.A.U. Study of Effect of Athletic Competition on Girls and Women* (New York, 1953), p. 8. See also Patricia Vertinsky, "Exercise, Physical Capability, and the Eternally Wounded Woman in Late Nineteenth Century North America," *Journal of Sport History*, 14 (1987), 7–27.

[21]See esp. Cindy L. Himes, "The Female Athlete in American Society, 1860–1940," unpub. Ph.D. diss., Univ. of Pennsylvania, 1984, pp. 117–21; Whorton, *Crusaders for Fitness*, pp. 321–30.

THE BICYCLING CRAZE OF THE 1890s
This advertisement for Crawford bicycles suggested greater physical freedom for women and opportunities for the sexes to mingle without chaperones, both of which were daring departures from Victorian constraints.

introduced to the American public at the Chicago World's Fair in 1893 by Florenz Ziegfeld, popularized body-building and the Greco-Roman muscular form among men. Rudolph Aaronson, the producer of the burlesque shows of the voluptuous Lillian Russell, humorously noted that one could quickly calm the sexual aggressiveness of college men by merely telling them that they looked like Sandow. Although by no means the only model of male beauty, the Greco-Roman form enjoyed wide popularity among men in the twentieth century. In the 1920s and 1930s Johnny Weismuller, an Olympic swimming medalist, displayed his seminude muscular body dozens of times as Tarzan in the movies, and for three decades (beginning in the 1930s), Charles Atlas, a man of enormous muscles, sold countless mail-order courses to men and boys who wanted to achieve a similar body shape.

The Gibson girl, who dominated standards of female beauty between 1895 and World War I, provided a more ambiguous model for would-be sportswomen. Although possessing an aristocratic air, the Gibson girl's popularity cut across age, class, and regional lines. Witty, sophisticated, and at ease on the golf course, the tennis court, or on horseback, she expanded the acceptable boundaries of physical freedom for women. Living embodiments of the Gibson girl could be found among certain women in the upper strata. Eleonora Sears, as the winner of four national women's doubles championships in tennis, a mixed doubles championship, and a national women's squash championship, pressed well beyond the behavior expected of the typical Gibson girl. Her women's "firsts" included swimming four and one-half miles between Bailey's Beach and

First Beach at Newport, automobile racing, and airplane flying. When in 1912 she wore pants, rode astride her horse, and requested permission to participate in a polo practice with men, the men not only rebuffed her but the Burlingame Mother's Club censured her behavior as "immodest and wholly unbecoming a woman."[22]

The negative reaction to Sears in 1912 reflected the limitations of the Gibson girl ideal. The Gibson girl, as a contemporary accurately put it, possessed "a wholesome athletic air that does not smack too much of athletics."[23] The relationship between the female athlete and romance (ultimately including marriage) always lurked in the background of the Gibson archetype. "Even today, when athletics are fast opening to women, when tennis and golf and the rest are possible to them," explained Charlotte Perkins Gilman in 1898, "the two sexes are far from even in chances to play." Unlike male sports, women in their sports were "forced to court 'attentions,' when not really desirous of anything but amusement."[24]

Nor did the flapper, the prevailing model of female beauty from about 1915 until the 1930s, usher in a women's revolution in sports. The flapper broke far more sharply than the Gibson girl with Victorian notions of proper dress and behavior. She bobbed her hair short, smoked and drank in public, mingled freely with men, danced the fast steps of the Charleston, abandoned corsets, shortened skirts, and wore fewer underclothes. The quantity of cloth in a typical woman's outfit shrank from nineteen and a half yards in 1913 to seven yards in 1925. And the popular Kellerman bathing suit of the 1920s completely bared legs and arms while clinging closely to the natural shape of the body.

Yet the energy, bravado, and physical freedom of the flapper signalled more precisely the advent of the modern beauty culture rather than a new era of women's sports. While Helen Wills, the queen of women's tennis, and Gertrude Ederle, the first woman to swim the English Channel, became celebrities in the 1920s, the typical American woman reserved her greatest admiration for Hollywood actresses. Most women devoted far more energy to competition in the beauty arena than on the playing fields. Actresses, beauty contestants, and fashion models established beauty standards for all women. Although in the 1930s and 40s the flapper gave way to new models of female beauty found in the more sophisticated and imperious movie queens, the beauty culture continued to influence profoundly the behavior of American women. Not only did it circumscribe the potential of women as athletes, but those women who did venture onto the playing field found themselves publicly measured against the prevailing standards of feminine beauty and behavior.

[22]Phyllis Hollander, *100 Greatest Women in Sports* (New York, 1976), p. 59. Also see Joanna Davenport, "Eleonora Randolph Sears," in Barbara Sicherman, et. al., eds. *Notable American Women: The Modern Period* (Cambridge, MA, 1980), p. 638.

[23]Quoted in Lois W. Banner, *American Beauty* (New York, 1983), p. 157. This discussion of female beauty follows closely that of Banner, but see also Valerie Steele, *Fashion and Eroticism: Ideals of Feminine Beauty from the Victorian Age to the Jazz Age* (New York, 1985).

[24]Charlotte Perkins Gilman, *Women and Economics* (Boston, 1898), pp. 308–09.

AN AGE OF RACIAL SEGREGATION

Race, like gender, also limited the sporting opportunities of many Americans.[25] Blacks soon discovered that the end of slavery and the new amendments added to the Constitution during Reconstruction failed to end racial prejudice or discrimination. In due time blacks in the South even lost the effective right to vote and hold public office. Disfranchisement, terror, and segregation laws all worked to keep blacks "in their places." By the 1890s, "Jim Crow" policies, the common expression for the systematic segregation of Afro-Americans, legally separated whites and blacks in ball parks, beaches, churches, trains, toilets, schools, and even water fountains. A series of decisions by the United States Supreme Court gave official sanction to segregation; in *Plessy* v. *Ferguson* (1896) the Court ruled that "separate but equal" public facilities were consistent with the Fourteenth Amendment. This opinion held sway for the next fifty-eight years.

Legal segregation was only one of the manifestations of deeply embedded racism in the 1890–1950 era. Vicious racial stereotyping in the popular media depicted blacks as irresponsible and dangerous savages. For example, D. W. Griffith's epic film, *Birth of a Nation* (1915), explicitly played upon white sexual fears; white audiences everywhere cheered a famous scene in which the Ku Klux Klan saved southern white womanhood from the ravages of black sexual lust. The application of Darwinian ideas to the evolution of races added a supposedly scientific note to the belief in racial superiority. Racists argued that peoples with the highest material cultures, namely whites, had succeeded best in the racial "struggle for survival," whites were thus a genetically superior race. Such views remained part of the conventional wisdom of white social scientists as late as the 1940s and 1950s.

Racial segregation and racism extended to sport as well, albeit not uniformly or consistently. In the mid-1880s, whites rejected a short-lived experiment in racially integrated professional baseball. Although black and white professional teams played one another in exhibition matches, racially integrated professional baseball did not return until 1946 when Jackie Robinson joined the Montreal farm club of the Brooklyn Dodgers. Throughout the 1890–1950 era a tiny number of blacks (probably less than one percent of the total players) played on racially integrated college football teams in the North; likewise a somewhat larger number engaged in track and field competition on behalf of northern colleges. During the 1920s a few blacks played in the National Football League before being unofficially banned in the 1930s. Blacks and whites rarely competed against one another in the elite sports of tennis and golf.

Of the major sports, blacks achieved something approaching equal opportunity only in the individual, unregulated, and countercultural sport of prize fighting. In the late nineteenth century, the sporting fraternity had not been

[25]For historiography, see David K. Wiggins, "From Plantation to Playing Field: Historical Writings on the Black Athlete in American Sport," *Research Quarterly*, 57 (1986), 101–16, and for Afro-American performances in this era, Arthur R. Ashe, Jr., *A Hard Road to Glory*, vols. 1 & 2 (New York, 1988).

adverse to pitting a black against a white when it promised to be profitable. From 1908 to 1915 it was a black, Jack Johnson, who held the world heavyweight crown, but the succeeding white heavyweight champions avoided black fighters until 1937 when Joe Louis won the title. On the other hand, below the championship levels black-versus-white fights were not uncommon. In fact, promoters frequently played on racial and ethnic antagonisms to generate interest in matches. Nonetheless, fears that too many blacks in boxing or that blacks with unpopular personalities might endanger potential profits circumscribed black opportunities in the sport.

In addition to discrimination and prejudice, the failure of blacks to share fully in the fruits of the consumer society in the 1890–1950 era sharply reduced the potentialities of black sports. By and large, blacks simply had far less income than whites. Prior to World War I, nearly nine out of ten blacks toiled as farm laborers or tenant farmers in the southern countryside. Although the number of blacks employed in northern manufacturing had doubled by 1930, they received lower wages than white counterparts. The vast majority of blacks occupied the lower rungs of the occupational ladder; in Chicago in 1920, for example, only a tenth of the black males worked at skilled jobs compared to over one-quarter of the whites. Even as late as 1950 the median family income for blacks was about half of that for whites.

Nonetheless, the "Great Migration" of blacks to northern cities in the twentieth century provided a precondition for the growth of a separate world of black sports. The increased demand for workers in World War I triggered a massive movement of blacks to northern cities—about two million in the 1910s, one million in the 1920s, 400,000 in the 1930s, and another million in the early 1940s. Excluded by income and color from living where they pleased, the migrants crowded into ghettos. Despite high rates of poverty, disease, crime, and marital discord, the ghettos had some community structures. A sense of community arose in part from the services provided by black professionals, newspapers, small businesses, and even racketeers. Black voluntary associations, such as churches, lodges, and athletic clubs, also lent stability to the ghetto communities. (For a discussion of baseball in black communities, see Chapter 10.)

In the 1890–1950 era sport achieved an entrenched prominence in American life similar to other important institutions. As it had in the past, sport continued to provide certain groups with satisfactions missing in other parts of their lives. It also continued to provide groups and places with a special sense of community and identity. Moreover, in the new era, the growing popularity of consumer values along with the ideology of the strenuous life swept away much of the traditional suspicion of sport. But not all groups shared equally in the fruits of the new era. In particular, those with inadequate incomes as well as women and blacks found their opportunities both to participate in sport and to consume commercial sport were sharply circumscribed or nonexistent.

9
THE AGE
OF SPORTS HEROES

The 1890–1950 era, especially the decade of the 1920s, teemed with sport heroes. "Never before, or since, have so many transcendent performers arisen contemporaneously in almost every field of competitive athletics as graced the 1920s," concluded veteran sports reporters Allison Danzig and Peter Brandwein in 1948.[1] Each sport had its magic name: George Herman "Babe" Ruth in baseball, William Harrison "Jack" Dempsey in boxing, Harold "Red" Grange in football, Robert T. "Bobby" Jones in golf, William T. "Big Bill" Tilden in tennis. And many others (including such female athletes as Suzanne Lenglen and Gertrude Ederle) stood close to the magic circle.

Why sport idols? The public acclaim accorded star athletes sprang from something more than performance, though indeed their athletic feats were often phenomenal. The same skill and shrewd promotion that successfully hawked automobiles, breakfast foods, and lipstick also sold athletes to the public. Behind

---

[1]Danzig and Brandwein, eds., *Sport's Golden Age: A Close-Up of the Fabulous Twenties* (New York, 1948), xi. Most efforts to explain the American need for heroes in modern times see them as fulfilling cherished American ideals or myths. See esp. Leo Lowenthal in *Literature, Popular Culture and Society* (Englewood Cliffs, NJ, 1961), pp. 109–40; Lary May, *Screening Out the Past: The Birth of Mass Culture and the Motion Picture Industry* (New York, 1980); Leverett T. Smith, Jr., *The American Dream and the National Game* (Bowling Green, OH, 1975); Tristram Potter Coffin, *The Old Ball Game: Baseball in Folklore and Fiction* (New York, 1971), Chap. 4; John W. Ward, "The Meaning of Lindbergh's Flight," in Joseph J. Kwait and Mary C. Turpie, eds., *Studies in American Culture* (Minneapolis, MN, 1960); Roderick W. Nash, *The Nervous Generation: American Thought, 1917–1930* (Chicago, 1970), pp. 126–37. For women athletic heroes, see esp. Cindy L. Himes, "The Female Athlete in American Society, 1860–1940," unpub. Ph.D. diss., University of Pennsylvania, 1984, Chap. 5.

the sport heroes stood professional pitch men: George "Tex" Rickard, Jack "Doc" Kearns, Charles C. "Cash and Carry" Pyle, and Christy Walsh, to name a few. Then there were the journalists and radio broadcasters prone to hyperbole such as Grantland Rice and Graham McNamee. They created images of athletes which often overshadowed the athlete's actual achievements. Yet the public idolization of athletes went even deeper than the skillful ballyhooing of the promoters and journalistic flights of fancy. Ultimately, the emergence of a dazzling galaxy of sport idols was a creation of the American public itself. The athletes as public heroes serve a compensatory cultural function. They assisted the public in compensating for the passing of the traditional dream of success, the erosion of Victorian values, and feelings of individual powerlessness. As the society became more complicated and systematized and as success had to be won increasingly in bureaucracies, the need for heroes who leaped to fame and fortune outside the rules of the system grew. No longer were the heroes lone businessmen or statesmen, but the "stars" of movies, television, and sports.

In the new age of mass consumption and burgeoning bureaucracies, a popular culture of compensation flourished. The media helped create defense mechanisms for the helpless individual that rested upon a complex set of images, fantasies, and myths. Some were comic: Charlie Chaplin in the movies was the carefree little tramp who eluded cops, bullies, and pompous officials; even the machine could not bring him to heel. Some were dashing and romantic: Douglas Fairbanks slashed his way through hordes of swift-sworded villains. Some were tough: The classic western hero, brave and handsome, killed bad men and Indians, thus dramatically serving the forces of "good" while saving white America from the "savages." The popular culture of compensation also projected images of heroes vaulting to the top. In nineteenth-century drama and fiction, the hero won the hand of the rich man's daughter through his virtuous character; Rudolph Valentino won her through his irresistible physical charm. Even the kings of organized crime, who themselves enjoyed something of a celebrity status in the 1920s, furnished forceful images of power and success.

Above all, fantasies and images of power and instant success flourished in the world of sport. In sport—or so it seemed—one could still catapult to fame and fortune without the benefits of years of arduous training or acquiescence to the demanding requirements of bureaucracies. Unlike most vocations, sheer natural ability coupled with a firm commitment to sport for its own sake could propel the athlete to the top. Determining the level of success of a doctor, lawyer, or business manager might be difficult, but achievement in the world of sport was unambiguous. It could be precisely measured in home runs, knockouts, touchdowns, victories, and even in salaries. Those standing on the assembly lines and those sitting at their desks in the bureaucracies found the most satisfaction in the athletic hero who presented an image of all-conquering power. Thus they preferred the towering home runs of Babe Ruth to the "scientific" style of base hits, base stealing, sacrifices, and hit-and-run plays personified by Ty Cobb; they preferred the smashing knockout blows of Jack Dempsey to the "scientific" boxing skills displayed by Gene Tunney. Perhaps it was little wonder that boys now dreamed of becoming athletic heroes rather than captains of industry, and girls dreamed of Hollywood stardom rather than the hearth.

BABE RUTH

No modern athletic hero exceeded Babe Ruth's capacity to project multiple images of brute power, the natural, uninhibited man, and the fulfillment of the American success dream. Ruth was living proof that the lone individual could still rise from mean, vulgar beginnings to fame and fortune, to a position of public recognition equalled by few men in American history. With nothing but his bat, Ruth revolutionized the National Game of baseball. His mighty home runs represented a dramatic finality, a total clearing of the bases with one mighty swat. Everything about Ruth was extraordinary—his size, strength, coordination, his appetite for the things of the flesh, and even his salary. He transcended the world of ordinary mortals, and yet he was the most mortal of men. He loved playing baseball, swearing, playing practical jokes, eating, drinking, and having sex. Despite his gross crudities, wrote Billy Evans, a big-league umpire, "Ruth is a big, likeable kid. He has been well named, Babe. Ruth has never grown up and probably never will. Success on the ball field has in no way changed him. Everybody likes him. You just can't help it."[2]

GEORGE HERMAN "BABE" RUTH, JR. (1895–1948)
The peerless compensatory hero of the 1920s, Ruth may have been the most celebrated athlete in American history. This photograph reveals a somber, younger Ruth, before he became conspicuously overweight.

[2]As quoted in Smith, *The American Dream*, p. 207.

Ruth saw himself as a prime example of the classic American success story. "The greatest thing about this country," he said in his ghostwritten autobiography, "is the wonderful fact that it doesn't matter which side of the tracks you were born on, or whether you're homeless or homely or friendless. The chance is still there. I know."[3] Ruth encouraged the legend that he had been an orphaned child. While the story had no basis in fact, his early years were indeed grim. His saloon-keeping father and sickly mother had no time for the boy; he received little or no parental affection. By his own admission, he became a "bad kid," who smoked, chewed tobacco, and engaged in petty thievery. At the age of seven, his parents sent him to the St. Mary's Industrial Home for Boys, an institution in Baltimore run by the Xaverian Order for orphans, young indigents, and delinquents. Except for brief interludes at home, Ruth spent the next twelve years at St. Mary's. There, as a teenager, he won a reputation for his baseball prowess and in 1914 signed a professional contract with the Baltimore Orioles of the International League. In the same year the Boston Red Sox purchased him as a left-handed pitcher.[4]

Ruth never had to struggle for success in baseball. For him, both pitching and hitting were natural talents rather than acquired skills. Converted from a top pitching star to an outfielder, Ruth surprised the world of baseball in 1919 by hitting twenty-nine home runs, two more than the existing major-league record that had been set in a crackerbox ball park in 1884. He followed in 1920 as a member of the New York Yankees with a stunning total of fifty-four four baggers, which was a larger number than any entire team (except the Yankees) in the major leagues compiled. For Ruth, this was only the beginning. From 1918 through 1934 he led the American League in homers twelve times with an average of more than forty a season; from 1926 through 1931 he averaged slightly more than fifty home runs per season. For every 11.7 times at bat he hit a round tripper. In addition, Ruth hit for an exceptionally high average. His lifetime mark of .342 has been equalled by few players in baseball history.

The public responded to Ruth's feats with overwhelming enthusiasm. Before Ruth, the Yankees' best annual attendance had been 600,000, but with him, the team drew more than a million each year. Everywhere in the league, the fans poured out to the ball parks to see the Yankees play, apparently caring little whether the home team won or lost, only hoping to witness the Babe hammer a pitch out of the park. Even Ruth's mighty swings that failed to connect brought forth a chorus of awed "Ooooooohs," as the audience realized the enormous power that had gone to waste and the narrow escape that the pitcher had

[3]Babe Ruth and Bob Considine, *The Babe Ruth Story*, (New York, 1969), p. 9.
[4]Tom Meany, Martin Weldon, Claire Ruth with Bill Slocum, Lee Allen, Daniel M. Daniel, and Waite Hoyt wrote early biographies of Ruth. Four recent books are superior in most respects: Ken Sobel, *Babe Ruth and the American Dream* (New York, 1974); Kal Wagenheim, *Babe Ruth* (New York, 1974); Robert W. Creamer, *Babe* (New York, 1974); and Marshall Smelser, *The Life That Ruth Built* (New York, 1975). But perhaps the best analyses of Ruth are found in Smith, *The American Dream*, and Harold Seymour, *Baseball: The Golden Age* (New York, 1971).

temporarily enjoyed. Each day, millions of Americans turned to the sports page of their newspaper to see if Ruth had hit another homer. Indeed, the response may have been unique in the annals of American sport. "In times past," Paul Gallico, a sportswriter, reflected, "we had been interested in and excited by prize fighters and baseball players, but we had never been so individually involved or joined in such a mass outpouring of affection as we did for Ruth." To players and fans alike, Ruth was a pioneer exploring "the uncharted wilderness of sport. There was something almost of the supernatural and the miraculous connected with him too," continued Gallico.[5] "I am not so certain now that Ruth is human," added Cleveland catcher, Chet Thomas. "At least he does things you couldn't expect a mere batter with two arms and legs to do. I can't explain him. Nobody can explain him. He just exists."[6]

The Ruthian image of home-run blasts ran counter to the increasingly dominant world of bureaucracies, scientific management, and "organization men." Ruth was the antithesis of science and rationality. Whereas Ty Cobb relied upon "brains rather than brawn," upon, as he put it, the "hit-and-run, the steal and double-steal, the bunt in all its varieties, the squeeze, the ball hit to the opposite field and the ball punched through openings in the defense for a single," Ruth, on the other hand, swung for the fences.[7] Ruth, according to sportswriter F.C. Lane in 1921, "throws science itself to the wind and hews out a rough path for himself by the sheer weight of his own unequalled talents."[8] Ruth seemed to embody the public preference for a compensatory hero with mere brute strength rather than one who exercised intelligence. Ruth played baseball instinctively; he seemed to need no practice or special training. He loved the game for its own sake. "With him the game *is* the thing. He loves baseball; loves just to play it," asserted a sportswriter.[9] No ulterior motives seemed to tarnish his pure love of the game.

The Ruthian image also ran counter to Victorian rules. Ruth's appetite for the things of the flesh was legendary. He drank heroic quantities of bootleg liquor; his hotel suite was always well stocked with beer and whiskey. People watched him eat with awe; he sometimes ate as many as eighteen eggs for breakfast and washed them down with seven or eight bottles of soda pop. Ruth was not only the "Sultan of Swat," he was a sultan of the bedroom. In each town on the spring training tours and in each big-league city, Ruth always found a bevy of willing female followers. His escapades were so well known that a sportswriter wrote a parody of them. "I wonder where my Babe Ruth is tonight? He grabbed his hat and coat and ducked from sight. I wonder where he will be at half past three? . . . I know he's with a dame. I wonder what's her

---

[5]Paul Gallico, *The Golden People* (Garden City, NY, 1965), pp. 36–37.

[6]As quoted in Smith, *The American Dream*, p. 198.

[7]Ty Cobb with Al Stump, *My Life in Baseball—The True Record* (Garden City, NY, 1961), p. 280.

[8]As quoted in Smith, *The American Dream*, p. 190.

[9]Ibid., p. 205.

name?"[10] Ruth probably did not know her name, for he had a notorious reputation for being unable to remember the names of even his closest friends. In the 1920s, to those many Americans who were rejecting what they called "Puritanism," Ruth could be identified as a fellow rebel. Marshall Smelser has written that Ruth "met an elemental need of the crowd. Every hero must have his human flaw which he shares with his followers. In Ruth it was hedonism, as exaggerated in folklore and fable."[11]

Ruth's propensity for immediate gratification had its more endearing side. He won a deserved reputation for loving children. Everywhere he went, children flocked to him, simply to see the great Bambino and perhaps to touch his uniform and obtain his autograph. Ruth enthusiastically welcomed their attention. He regularly visited children in hospitals. A legend that has some basis in fact added immeasurably to Ruth's popularity. In its simplest version, Ruth visited a young boy who was dying in a hospital. He promised the lad that he would hit a home run for him that afternoon. He did, which so inspired the boy with the will to live that he miraculously recovered. The public also adored Ruth for his crude egalitarianism. He deferred to no one. Introduced, for instance, to President Calvin Coolidge, he responded: "Hi, Pres. How are you?" According to one story, possibly apocryphal, while Ruth was holding out for a higher salary in 1930, someone pointed out to him that a depression existed and that he was asking for more money than President Herbert Hoover earned. "What the hell has Hoover got to do with it?" Ruth demanded. "Besides, I had a better year than he did."[12]

Ruth's huge earnings added to his heroic stature. From the time Ruth set his first home run record in 1919, he was besieged by commercial opportunities outside of baseball. Since the early days of the game, star players had supplemented their salaries by product endorsements, vaudeville acts, and personal appearances, but no player had the opportunities that became available to Ruth. In the winter of 1921, Christy Walsh, a sports cartoonist turned ghost writer, convinced Ruth to permit him to handle the demand by newspapers for Ruth's "personal analysis" of each home run that he hit. For fifteen years Walsh employed a stable of ghost writers, among them Ford Frick, future commissioner of baseball, to write pieces allegedly by Ruth for newspapers and magazines. Ruth "covered" every World Series from 1921 through 1936. Eventually Walsh's syndicate provided ghost-writing services for a large number of athletes and public celebrities.[13]

Walsh became the first modern athletic business agent. Beginning in 1921, he handled nearly all of Ruth's nonbaseball commercial ventures. In 1921 he signed Ruth to a vaudeville tour, the first of several, which called for Ruth to receive $3,000 per week for twenty weeks, a record-shattering sum for a vaude-

---

[10]Quoted in Seymour, *Baseball*, p. 431.
[11]Marshall M. Smelser, "The Babe on Balance," *American Scholar*, 44 (1975), 299.
[12]As quoted in Seymour, *Baseball*, p. 428.
[13]See Christy Walsh, *Adios to Ghosts!* (New York, 1937).

ville performer. He also managed Ruth's many barnstorming baseball tours in the off-seasons. He assembled a list of all the commercial products with which his client could be associated and set out to convince the manufacturers of the benefits to be gained by Ruth's endorsements. In time, Ruth promoted, among other products, hunting and fishing equipment, modish men's wear, alligator shoes, baseball gear, and sporty automobiles. In Boston he might trumpet the virtues of Packards, in New York Cadillacs, and in St. Louis Reos. He received between $250 and $10,000 for appearing at banquets, grand openings, smokers, boxing and wrestling matches, and celebrity golf tournaments. When the purchasing power and the low income tax of that era are taken into account, Ruth's earnings were phenomenal. His total baseball income ranged between $1.25 million and $1.5 million, his nonbaseball earnings between $1 million and $2 million, for a total in the neighborhood of $3 million. Although Ruth was a hopeless spendthrift, Christy Walsh convinced him to put some of his income into untouchable annuities. Thus he survived the stock market crash in 1929 with enough money to retire comfortably in 1935.

Of America's legendary heroes, Ruth is the country's preeminent athletic hero. Even in an age that takes a special delight in smashing false idols, Ruth remains the demigod of sports. His astonishing success reassured those who feared that America had become a society in which the traditional conditions conducive to success no longer existed. He transcended the world of sport to establish an undefinable benchmark for outstanding performances in all fields of human endeavor. The media has heralded Willie Sutton as "the Babe Ruth of bank robbers," Chuck Stearns as "the Babe Ruth of water skiing," Jimmy Connors as "the Babe Ruth of tennis," and Franco Corelli as "the Babe Ruth of operatic tenors"—the list goes on. Americans resented anyone who threatened to tarnish Ruth's heroic stature. When Henry Aaron approached Ruth's career record of 714 home runs, he said, "I can't recall a day this year or last when I did not hear the name of Babe Ruth."[14] Roger Maris, when he broke Ruth's mark of sixty home runs in one season in 1961, found himself the victim of a steady stream of abuse from fans, sportswriters, and people in the streets. They repeatedly noted that Ruth had compiled sixty home runs in a 154-game season while Maris had only fifty-nine after 154 games. After the 1961 season, Maris quickly sank into obscurity, but the legend of Babe Ruth lived on. Long after the 1920s, Ruth remained peerless among compensatory heroes.

RED GRANGE

Pitch-men and journalists also found in the football player Red Grange an almost perfect subject for elevation to the status of a compensatory hero. Like Ruth, Grange projected an image of swift, decisive, all-conquering power. Rather than methodically grinding down the opposition with power plays, Grange's forté

[14]Creamer, *Babe*, p. 16.

was the sudden and total breakthrough, the punt return, the kickoff return, or the long run from scrimmage that climaxed in a touchdown. By exhibiting his phenomenal talent for open field running in a game against Michigan in 1924, Grange stunned the football world. Before the game, Fielding H. Yost, the veteran mentor of many powerful Michigan elevens, assured everyone that the Illinois redhead could be stopped. With 67,000 fans present at the opening of Illinois' new stadium, Grange responded by scoring four touchdowns in the first twelve minutes of the game. He took the opening kickoff for a 95-yard touchdown run; he then had touchdown runs of 67, 56, and 45 yards from the line of scrimmage. Modern technology accentuated the dramatic quality of Grange's feats. While few Americans were able to see Grange perform in the flesh, millions saw him in the newsreels of thousands of theaters. The image of Grange, speeded up on the flickering screen, was almost eerie, as it darted, slashed, cut away from would-be tacklers, and crossed the goal line one, two, three, or even five times within a few seconds. Little wonder that Grantland Rice hailed Grange as the "Galloping Ghost of the Gridiron."

Grange's career seemed to confirm traditional virtues and the survival of the dream of the self-made man. Like Ruth, he began life under adverse circumstances. One of five children, he was born in the small rustic town of Forksville, Pennsylvania, where his father supported the family by working in local lumber camps. His mother died when Grange was but five years old. Yet as a youth, he, unlike Babe Ruth, practiced all the Victorian virtues that seemed to be fast disappearing in the United States of the twentieth century. He neither drank nor smoked. He was modest, softspoken, and hard-working; in both his high school and college years he toted ice to Wheaton, Illinois, residents. These character traits, according to Grange in his ghostwritten autobiography, paid dividends. Athletics "was my whole life and I put everything I had into it," he wrote. "The future took care of itself. When the breaks came I was ready for them." Confirming the legendary dream of American success, he wrote: "Any boy can realize his dreams if he's willing to work and make sacrifices along the way."[15]

Grange, of course, exaggerated. He owed his success to more than hard work and impeccable personal habits. He enjoyed marvelous natural talents for quickness afoot and the ability to change directions while carrying a football. In high school he was the Illinois sprints and hurdles champion. As a high school football player at Wheaton he created something of a sensation by scoring seventy-two touchdowns in three seasons of play. Contacted by the alumni of several midwestern colleges who wanted to bring his talents to their campuses, Grange finally resolved to attend the University of Illinois. Robert "Zup" Zuppke, the Illinois head coach, recognized in Grange a potential football immortal. In the spring practice of 1923, he designed a powerful single

---

[15]Red Grange as told to Ira Morton, *The Red Grange Story* (New York, 1953), p. 178. On Grange, see also John Underwood, "Was He the Greatest of All Time?" *Sports Illustrated*, 63 (Sept. 4, 1985), 114–35.

EARL "RED" GRANGE AS THE "ICE MAN"
This publicity photograph of the nation's best known football player of the
1920s suggests how heroes might satisfy conflicting values. On the one hand,
part of the Grange legend arose from publicizing his hard-working life as a
youth delivering ice to residents in Wheaton, Illinois. In this sense, he fit
perfectly the formula of a self-made man. On the other hand, the photo with
Grange accompanied by beautiful women suggests that he embodied the new
consumer ethic as well.

wing formation with Grange running at tailback. "I got a great break at
Illinois," Grange later confessed. " . . . I ended up making most of the team's
touchdowns and getting all the publicity, because Coach Bob Zuppke let me
carry the ball 90 percent of the time. In most of the games I carried the ball thirty
or forty times."[16]

Bare statistics give only a partial indication of Grange's outstanding
collegiate performance. In three seasons he scored thirty-one touchdowns,
gained 3,637 yards on the ground (including kickoff and punt returns), and
passed for an additional 653 yards. He accounted for an average of 214 yards
for each of the college games in which he appeared. By the close of the 1925
season Grange was, according to the *New York Times,* "the most famous, the most
talked of, and written about, the most photographed and most picturesque
player the game has ever produced."[17]

As did other athletic heroes of the 1920s, Grange capitalized financially
upon his celebrity status. Shortly before he began his final season at Illinois, he
was approached by Charles C. "Cash and Carry" (or "Cold Cash") Pyle, a
small-time theater operator who was shortly to become a sports impresario with
few peers. According to Grange's recollection, Pyle simply said: "How would

[16]Grange, *The Red Grange Story,* pp. 174–75.
[17]*New York Times,* Nov. 22, 1925.

you like to make one hundred thousand dollars, or maybe even a million?"[18] Grange promptly replied in the affirmative. Pyle then negotiated a secret deal with George Halas and Ed Sternamen, the co-owners of the Chicago Bears, a professional football team in the fledgling National Football League. At the end of the college season, Grange was to play the remaining league games of the Bears and then he and the Bears would embark on a national exhibition tour to be staged by Pyle.

The decision of Grange to join the professional ranks touched off a national debate. By abandoning his studies in the middle of his senior year, Grange flaunted the myth of the college athlete as a gentleman-amateur who played merely for the fun of the game or the glory of his school. Furthermore, professional football in the 1920s was associated with the working class and recent ethnic groups; it was held in low esteem by the middle and upper classes. Initially, sympathetic newsmen depicted Grange as an "innocent, decent, trusting chap," who was the "victim of a kind of conspiracy of get-rich-quick promoters who did not care how far they went in prostituting him to their ends."[19] But Grange was hardly an innocent victim. He acknowledged, "I'm out to get the money, and I don't care who knows it . . . my advice to everybody is to get to the gate while the getting's good."[20] He did promise his admirers that he would someday finish his senior year of college, a promise he never kept.

Pyle's plan succeeded beyond expectations. Five days after Grange's final game with Illinois, he played with the Bears at Wrigley Field in Chicago on Thanksgiving Day, 1925. The publicity barrage accompanying Grange's departure from Illinois helped to attract 35,000 fans, to that date the largest crowd ever to attend a professional game. (The Bears considered 5,000 to be a good draw in Chicago.) The Bears, with Red Grange obliged to play at least half of each game, then played a grueling schedule of ten games in seventeen days. Everywhere they went—St. Louis, Philadelphia, New York twice, Boston, Providence, Washington, and Pittsburgh—they broke professional football attendance records. After taking an eight-day rest in Chicago, Grange and the Bears embarked upon Pyle's 7,000-mile, thirty-five day, fourteen-game barnstorming tour of the South and West. In matches against "pick-up" teams of mostly former collegians, Pyle insisted upon a $25,000 guarantee from local promoters. Newspapers and press syndicates assigned their most distinguished sportswriters to accompany Grange. Westbrook Pegler, Damon Runyan, and Ford Frick, among others, reported daily every facet of Grange's behavior both on and off the field of play. Never had such a tour by an athletic team attracted so much publicity nor been so financially rewarding. Ironically, the Galloping Ghost's perfor-

[18]Grange, *The Red Grange Story*, p. 91. On Pyle see *New York Times*, Feb. 4, 1939; Hugh Leamy, "Net Profits," *Collier's*, 78 (Oct. 2, 1926), 9, 32; Myron Cope, "The Game That Was," *Sports Illustrated*, 31 (Oct. 13, 1969), 93–96, 102–03.

[19]"Football History as Made by the Illinois Ice Man," *Literary Digest*, 87 (Dec. 26, 1925), 30.

[20]As quoted in John B. Kennedy, "The Saddest Young Man in America," *Collier's*, 77 (Jan. 16, 1926), 15.

mance, perhaps because of a nagging injury, was far less spectacular than it had been as a collegian.

In the meantime, Pyle lined up commercial endorsements for Grange. Within the first ten days after Grange had signed a contract with Pyle, they received 187 phone calls, sixty telegrams, and thirty-nine personal visits from advertising men. Grange endorsed sweaters, shoes, caps, a Red Grange football doll, and soft drinks. The "Red Grange Chocolates," according to Pyle, sold six million bars in thirty days. In New York, Grange signed a movie contract, and Pyle flashed a $300,000 check to amazed reporters. Although the press headlined the event, Grange later admitted that it was "one of Pyle's wild publicity stunts."[21] Grange was actually to receive $5,000 a week while working on the film. Pyle recognized that large sums of money were important in establishing the heroic status of his clients. Altogether in the first year of their partnership Pyle and Grange split about $250,000 as their share of gate receipts and income from endorsements and promotions.

Emboldened by his spectacular financial success with Grange in the winter of 1925–1926, Pyle expanded his promotional horizons. He first demanded that he and Grange be granted one-third ownership of the Bears. When Halas and Sternamen refused, he attempted to place a second NFL team in New York, only to be blocked by the owner of the New York Giants. He then formed a new professional loop, the American Football League, with Grange and himself as co-owners of the New York Yankees. Because of Grange, the Yankees drew large crowds, but the other teams in the league lost money. After the 1926 season, the new league collapsed. Pyle, with Grange and the financial losses suffered by NFL teams during the 1926 season as leverage, forced the NFL to admit the Yankees as a "road team" for the 1927 season. A permanent knee injury suffered by Grange in the third game of the 1927 season brought financial ruin to the Yankees. Grange and Pyle amicably severed their partnership. Pyle went on to other forms of sport promotion—professional tennis tours and two long-distance walking contests from San Francisco to New York ("Bunion Derbies"). Grange returned to the Bears as a superb defensive back and above-average straight-ahead running back. He played his last game in 1935 and, in the 1940s and 1950s, became a successful radio and television sportscaster.

JACK JOHNSON

Prize fighting champions, perhaps more than heroes from any other sport, evoked intense feelings about gender, ethnicity, race, and social class. Amidst the great changes in nineteenth-century life, many men had turned to boxers for behavioral cues that would clearly distinguish men from women. And prize fighters often served as heroes of the working class and recently arrived ethnic

---

[21]"Football History," 29–34.

groups. In the 1890–1950 era blacks also found in boxers a source of self-worth and inspiration. Few if any blacks were as well-known or had infused blacks with greater pride than Jack Johnson, the heavyweight champion between 1908 and 1915.[22]

Johnson got a shot at the championship under unusual circumstances. Prior champions had drawn the "color line," refusing to meet black challengers. But Johnson persisted; he literally pursued Tommy Burns, the reigning champion, around the world, issuing challenges as he went. Money finally changed Burns's mind. Hugh McIntosh, a wealthy Australian businessman, guaranteed to Burns $30,000 win or lose, a purse far larger than for any previous prize fight, to fight the black challenger. Johnson was to receive only $5,000. John L. Sullivan probably expressed the typical response of American whites to the decision of Burns. "Shame on the money-mad champion! Shame on the man who upsets good American precedents because there are Dollars, Dollars, Dollars in it."[23] In 1908, in far-off Sydney, Australia, Johnson easily battered Burns into submission.

Almost at once, ex-champions, fight promoters, and newspapermen launched a hunt for a "Great White Hope" to retake the crown from Johnson. As Johnson disposed of several second-rate white contenders, the demand grew for James J. Jeffries, a popular former heavyweight champion, to come out of retirement and rid boxing of the "black menace." Finally, in 1910, Jeffries agreed to battle Johnson at Reno, Nevada. Jeffries himself interpreted the fight in racial terms. "That portion of the white race that has been looking for me to defend its athletic superiority may feel assured," he said, "that I am fit to do my very best."[24] Jeffries's very best was not enough, for Johnson knocked him out in the fifteenth round. Johnson's victory ignited black celebrations across the country, but so much happiness was premature. In violent racial confrontations at least eight persons lost their lives.

The victories of Jack Johnson stunned white America. For to both white and black, Johnson's ascension to the heavyweight throne possessed incalculable symbolic significance. In the most primeval of American sports, the ultimate metaphor of masculine conflict, the best of the black men had defeated the best of the white men. Newspaper columnist Max Balthazer wrote of the prospective Jeffries–Johnson fight: "Can the huge white man [Jeffries] . . . beat down the wonderful black and restore to the Caucasians the crown of elemental greatness as measured by strength of blow, power of heart and being, and, withal, that

[22]Johnson has inspired a large body of literature. See esp. the biographies by Finis Farr, *Black Champion* (New York, 1964); Al-Tony Gilmore, *Bad Nigger! The National Impact of Jack Johnson* (Port Washington, NY, 1975); and Randy Roberts, *Papa Jack: Jack Johnson and the Era of White Hopes* (New York, 1983). But note also Fredric Cople Jaher, "White America Views Jack Johnson, Joe Louis, and Muhammad Ali," in Donald Spivey, ed., *Sport in America* (Westport, CT, 1985), 145–92, and Lawrence W. Levine, *Black Culture and Black Consciousness: Afro-American Folk Thought from Slavery to Freedom* (New York, 1977), pp. 430–33.
[23]Quoted in Gilmore, *Bad Nigger!* p. 27.
[24]Quoted in Farr, *Black Champion*, p. 107.

THE PURSE FOR THE
JOHNSON-JEFFRIES BOUT, 1910
Tex Rickard (far left) and Jack
Johnson examine the purse for the
heavyweight championship bout
between Johnson and James J.
Jeffries. Rickard, who was to
become the leading boxing
impressario in the nation, acted as
both promoter and referee for the
bout. The public response to the fight
reflected the tense race relations of
the era.

cunning or keenness that denotes mental as well as physical superiority?"[25] To both races the fight could signify or suggest racial equality or even black superiority; above all, to whites, it might suggest a potential threat to the status quo in American race relations. While Johnson personally ignored organized efforts for greater racial justice in America, his feats might inspire blacks to mount formidable challenges to white supremacy. To many whites, Johnson represented an enormous threat to the entire superstructure of racial segregation.

Never had a heavyweight champion been more controversial than Johnson. In an age in which racial animosity had reached a fever pitch, he exacerbated deep-set white fears. In the ring, while smiling broadly, he badgered, taunted, and jeered his white opponents. He was a big spender who loved the high life—flashy dress, champagne, night clubs, fast cars, and women of questionable character. To most whites and some blacks he was the embodiment of the "uppity Nigger." He defied age-old racial customs; he married three white women and had sexual liaisons with many others. By openly flaunting this taboo, Johnson intensified white sexual anxieties. Deeply embedded in black-white mythology was a gnawing suspicion of black sexual superiority and the silent fear that white females fantasized about sexual relations with black men. Speaking at the annual governors' conference in 1912, the governor of South Carolina described Johnson as a "black brute." "If we can not protect our white women from black fiends, where is our vaunted civilization?" he asked rhetorically.[26]

Johnson's enemies struck back. Local and state governments barred the showing of the Johnson–Jeffries fight films in American theaters; in 1912 Congress cooperated by prohibiting the transportation in interstate commerce of all

[25]Quoted in Randy Roberts, "Jack Dempsey: An American Hero in the 1920s," *Journal of Popular Culture* 8 (1974), 412.
[26]Quoted in Gilmore, *Bad Nigger!* p. 107.

moving pictures of boxing matches. Johnson himself became the victim of legal attacks. In 1912, the mother of one of Johnson's consorts charged him with abducting her daughter across state lines for immoral purposes, which, if true, would have constituted a federal crime under the Mann Act of 1910. But the young woman in question refused to substantiate her mother's accusation, and Johnson was acquitted. In the meantime, a federal grand jury returned another charge against Johnson for violating the Mann Act. Belle Shreiber, formerly a prostitute at the fancy Everleigh Club (reputedly the nation's finest brothel) in Chicago, confessed that she had been paid by Johnson to engage in "immoral" and "unnatural" acts during the pair's travels about the country. In 1913 a Chicago jury found Johnson guilty, and the judge sentenced him to jail for one year and a day. During the stay of execution to appeal the decision, Johnson jumped bail and fled the country, first to Canada and then to Europe.

Johnson's flamboyant career then careened toward a climax. While the search continued in the United States for a "Great White Hope," in Europe the champion met a few nondescript challengers, and performed in vaudeville while his financial sources dwindled away. Finally in 1915, a year after World War I erupted in Europe, he met Jess Willard in Havana, Cuba. Willard knocked Johnson out in the 26th round. Johnson was thirty-seven years old and had inadequately trained for the bout; he later claimed that he threw the match in return for $50,000 and an exemption from his prison sentence. A famous photograph of Johnson on the canvas during the knockout lends some credence to his claim, for the champion appears to have raised his glove over his face to shield his eyes from the blinding Havana sun. However, boxing authorities present at the fight and Johnson's most recent biographer have concluded that Johnson was indeed the victim of a genuine knockout.[27]

In any case, American officials refused to rescind the sentence. In 1920, he returned to the United States and served his time at Fort Leavenworth prison. Afterwards, he performed in vaudeville, gave temperance lectures, appeared in a few fights, and engaged in sparring exhibitions until 1945, when he was sixty-eight years old. The next year Johnson died from injuries suffered in an automobile accident, thus ending perhaps the most dramatic and symbolically significant athletic career in the annals of American sport.

THE GOLDEN AGE OF BOXING

The need for compensatory heroes, the ballyhooing of Tex Rickard and Jack Kearns, and the ascension of Jack Dempsey to the heavyweight championship of the world helped make the 1920s the "Golden Age" of American boxing.[28] Never

[27]See esp. Roberts, *Papa Jack*, Chap. 12.
[28]See esp. James B. Dawson, "Boxing," in Danzig and Brandwein, eds., *Sport's Golden Age*, pp. 38–85; Paul Gallico, *Farewell to Sport* (New York, 1938); Randy Roberts, *Jack Dempsey: The Manassa Mauler*, (Baton Rouge, LA, 1979); and Jeffrey T. Sammons, *Beyond the Ring: The Role of Boxing in American Society* (Urbana, IL, 1988), Chaps. 3 & 4.

before or since has boxing achieved such a high plateau of popularity. In the prewar years gate receipts from a single bout never exceeded $300,000; in the 1920s, Rickard promoted five consecutive million-dollar gates. Fans paid over $2 million to see the second Dempsey–Tunney fight. In terms of purchasing power, these sums were far larger than any modern gates. Over 100,000 fans witnessed each of the Dempsey–Tunney fights—again, figures unequalled in the annals of the boxing history. Day after day the major newspapers placed boxing items on the front page. They detailed both the private and public lives of the pugilists.

World War I helped soften the traditional animosity toward prize fighting. During the war, the army used boxing as part of the training of doughboys. After the war, often at the instigation of the American Legion, state after state dropped legal barriers to prize fighting. Boxing acquired a new level of respectability. The old days of clandestine fights on barges, in the backrooms of saloons, or in isolated rural spots gave way to fights held in glittering arenas and in huge stadiums. No longer were fights patronized exclusively by the slummers, roughnecks, ethnics, workingmen, and the "sporting set"; even "high society," "proper" women, and middle-income groups went to see the fights. Celebrities from all fields of American life turned the heavyweight championship fights into big "social events." The ordinary people may have come as much to see the celebrities as the fight itself.

No one in the 1920s sensed the possibilities of exploiting the public hunger for heroes better than Tex Rickard.[29] Rickard was aptly dubbed variously as the "King of the Ballyhoo," "King of Sport Promoters," and "Phineas T. Barnum" of the twentieth century. Long before the 1920s, he revealed a propensity for taking high risks and a talent for promotion. As a youth in the 1890s he had left a dusty cowtown in Texas for the Yukon-Klondike gold fields. While in Alaska, he reputedly won and lost several fortunes as a professional gambler, gold speculator, saloon owner, and barroom fight promoter. Rickard catapulted to the national level when he staged the famous Johnson–Jeffries fight in 1910 in Reno.

For the next five years, Rickard pursued multiple careers as a gambling house proprietor, rancher in Paraguay, and fight promoter. In 1916 his name again appeared in the sports headlines. He promoted a "no-decision" bout between the heavyweight champion Jess Willard, who had beaten Jack Johnson in 1915, and Frank Moran in New York. Earning a $30,000 stake from the fight, he promptly doubled it by betting on Woodrow Wilson to win the 1916 presidential election.[30] Having established a tacit priority for the promotion of future Willard fights, he was in a position to launch the Golden Age of American boxing. He needed only a new boxing hero to replace the uncharismatic Willard. Jack Dempsey, an unknown western fighter, was soon to fill that need.

[29]In addition to works cited in note 28, see Jack Koefoed, "The Master of the Ballyhoo," *North American Review*, 227 (1929), 282–86; Charles Samuels, *The Magnificent Rube: The Life and Times of Tex Rickard* (New York, 1957); Mrs. "Tex" Rickard with Arch Oboler, *Everything Happened to Him* (New York, 1936).

[30]Rickard, *Everything Happened to Him*, p. 261.

On the face of it, Dempsey was an unlikely prospect for a popular hero. True, his social origins were modest; he was born into a poor, itinerant Irish-American family at Manassa, Colorado. But until Jack Kearns became his manager in 1917, Dempsey had been little more than a saloon brawler, fighting in western tank towns for a hundred dollars or less per bout. Dempsey's reputation as a great slugger rested as much on myth as fact. He had been the victim of a knockout in 1917, and he had lost a decision in 1918. His career knockout percentage of .613 was unexceptional, well below that of Floyd Patterson and Primo Carnera, for instance, and only slightly above that of Tommy Burns, who is considered the worst of all heavyweight champions by ring historians. As champion, Dempsey defended his title only six times in seven years and met only two genuinely formidable foes. As a potential hero, Dempsey suffered from an even more serious liability. Having not served in the armed forces in World War I, the federal government in 1920 charged him with being a "slacker." Although acquitted on the grounds that he had provided financial support to his wife and mother, the issue clouded Dempsey's heroic image.[31]

Dempsey acquired the reputation of being "Jack the Giant-Killer" largely through the hokum of Jack Kearns and Tex Rickard. Dempsey had the good fortune of meeting Jess Willard, the "Pottawatomie Giant," in a championship bout staged by Rickard at Toledo, Ohio, in 1919. Willard towered over Dempsey. He stood six feet and six inches tall and weighed 245 pounds, while Dempsey was six feet and one inch tall and weighed 191 pounds. Dempsey floored the massive Willard five times in the first round; at the end of the third round, Willard, his face swollen twice its normal size, bloody and bewildered, conceded defeat. The image of Dempsey as a giant-killer caught on at once. Publicity stunts, such as having Dempsey's sparring partners wear inflated chest protectors and catcher's masks, reinforced the image. The public accepted the mistaken notion that Dempsey was a little man. As Dempsey told it: "Jack Kearns' ballyhoo that made me 'Jack the Giant-Killer' was partially responsible. Various pictures that were published of my different fights, too, added to the misconception. Repeatedly they showed me fighting against men who were inches taller than I and many pounds heavier."[32]

The Dempsey–Willard fight launched Rickard's career as the nation's premier sports impresario. In 1920 the New York legislature legalized prize fighting and set up a state athletic commission to supervise it. Two weeks after the law was passed, Rickard, with the aid of John Ringling of circus fame as a silent partner, obtained the financial backing to lease Madison Square Garden. Under his astute management, the Garden, which had been something of a white elephant to prior managers, became a highly profitable enterprise. Rickard offered a variety of attractions unequalled by any other palace of entertainment in the world. Boxing, wrestling, circuses, horse shows, six-day bicycle races,

---

[31]Roberts, "Jack Dempsey," 413.
[32]Jack Dempsey, *Round by Round: An Autobiography* (New York, 1940), p. 176.

rodeos, professional hockey—these and many other activities became regular fare on the Garden's schedule.

Rickard juggled conflicting interests with the same skill and daring that he had perfected as a professional gambler. He courted newspaper reporters with frequent "leaks," free cigars, liberal quantities of liquor, and special seating privileges. He always reserved a number of free seats for the minions of the Tammany Hall political machine. Simultaneously, he won the support of New York's superrich. In 1921 at the invitation of Anne Morgan, philanthropic sister of J. Pierpont Morgan, he held a benefit fight in the Garden to kick off a fundraising drive for war-torn France. Such clever gestures assisted Rickard in marshaling the funds for the Carpentier–Dempsey fight in 1921 and for the construction of a new $5 million Madison Square Garden in 1926.[33]

Rickard exhibited the full arsenal of his promotional skills in the Dempsey–Georges Carpentier fight of 1921. Because of political hostility at the State Capitol in Albany, Rickard transferred the fight to Jersey City, where he had a huge wooden stadium built. As Dempsey later confessed, Rickard "dug up" Carpentier, the light heavyweight champion of Europe, and set out to convince the public that the fragile Frenchman was a serious contender for the crown. Rickard explained to Dempsey and Kearns how he planned to ballyhoo the bout. It would be a "foreign foe" versus an American; a war hero—Carpentier had twice been decorated for valor in World War I—versus a "slacker," the "rapier" of the skilled fencer versus the "broadsword" of the peasant; the civilized man versus the "abysmal brute." "That's you, Jack," the elated Rickard reputedly exclaimed.[34] The contrast in images was almost perfect. Ike Dorgan, Rickard's assistant, nicknamed Carpentier the "Orchid Man," set up his training camp on Long Island amidst the "social crowd," refused to allow reporters to watch Carpentier spar, and touted the Frenchman's attractiveness to women. According to Dorgan and the press, Carpentier was handsome, debonair, a "boulevardier," who danced beautifully and sang French chansonnettes.[35]

As Rickard had hoped, the nation took sides. The American Legion passed a resolution condemning Dempsey for his lack of military service in World War I; the Veterans of Foreign Wars retaliated by siding with the champ. In general, the "lowbrows," workingmen and ethnics, favored Dempsey. The "highbrows," especially the nation's literati, supported Carpentier. Even George Bernard Shaw, the distinguished British playwright, enlisted his vast literary talents in Carpentier's behalf. As a financial event, the fight was an unprecedented success. Over 80,000 fans paid $1,789,238 to see the fight. Present were the "Who's Who of the social, financial, and entertainment world."[36] As an athletic

[33]See esp. Dawson, "Boxing," pp. 38–85, and Zander Hollander, ed., *Madison Square Garden* (New York, 1973).

[34]Jack Dempsey with Charles J. McGuirk, "The Golden Gates," *Saturday Evening Post*, 207 (Oct. 20, 1934), 11.

[35]See esp. Gallico, *A Farewell to Sport*, p. 95.

[36]Jack "Doc" Kearns with Oscar Fraley, *The Million Dollar Gate* (New York, 1966), pp. 147–48.

contest, the bout was a farce. Dempsey had little difficulty in knocking Carpentier out in the fourth round. Nonetheless, everyone seemed satisfied. Even the dignified *New York Times* announced the results of the fight in front-page head-lines. Few Americans were left untouched by the spectacle at Boyle's Thirty Acres.

Rickard used similar tactics in promoting his next bonanza—Dempsey's fight with Louis Angel Firpo at the Polo Grounds in New York in 1923. Firpo, formerly a bottle washer for a Buenos Aires pharmacy, had come to the United States looking for easy money. Rickard corralled for Firpo a "proper assortment of weak-chinned or canary-hearted boxers . . . to pole-ax into unconscious-ness."[37] Firpo, a big, awkward man, soon won appellations by the press as the "Argentine Giant" and the "Wild Bull of the Pampas." Rickard hoped to convince the public that the bout would be "two cave men fightin' with tooth and claw."[38] The actual fight conformed to the ballyhoo much better than anyone expected. In less than four minutes of action, Firpo went down to the canvas ten times Dempsey twice. After the seventh knockdown of Firpo in the first round, Firpo arose and shot a right to Dempsey's jaw that sent the champion sprawling through the ropes. (George Bellows memorialized the event with his renowned painting, *Dempsey–Firpo*.) Reporters hoisted Dempsey back into the ring and the champ finished the round on unsteady legs. But in the next round, Dempsey, swinging both fists wildly, crushed Firpo for a knockout. The exciting battle produced boxing's second million-dollar gate. Most Americans might be the victims of forces beyond their control, wrote Bruce Bliven in the *New Republic*, but within the confines of the boxing ring both Firpo and Dempsey had decided "their own fates."[39] No sport in the 1920s exceeded boxing's capacity to furnish Americans with compensatory heroes.

In the succeeding three years in which Dempsey failed to defend his title, Rickard often stated that a "million-dollar fight" could be staged only once every two years. Rickard himself was busy with the management of the new Garden. Perhaps more importantly, Dempsey enjoyed living the life of a celebrity. Earning perhaps as much as $500,000 annually from endorsements, movie contracts, and vaudeville performances, he was in no hurry to return to the ring. Personal problems also intruded. Dempsey broke with Jack Kearns, his long-time man-ager, and Kearns proceeded to harass the champion with legal suits. Finally, Dempsey's wife, Estelle, did not want him to return to the ring.

But the primary reason for Dempsey's absence from the ring may have been Harry Wills, the "Brown Panther" from New Orleans, who was clamoring for a crack at the championship. In every respect except race, Wills was a qualified challenger. The story of his inability to get a match with Dempsey is obscured in intrigue. On several occasions the New York Athletic Commission, which was appointed by the governor, ordered Dempsey to fight Wills. Apparently these

---

[37]Koefoed, "The Master of the Ballyhoo," 295.
[38]Dempsey, "The Golden Gates," 75.
[39]As quoted in Roberts, *Jack Dempsey*, p. 181.

actions were designed to please the black voters of New York City. But according to Rickard, each time he agreed to give Wills a title shot, he received a word from high political figures in Albany that the match would be blocked. Rickard claimed that the politicians in New Jersey likewise opposed the match. Nonetheless, if there is a single culprit in the controversy, it seemed to be Rickard. He showed no interest in staging the fight outside of New York or New Jersey, and he was probably the only person who could have raised a purse adequate for the bout. Apart from possibly being racist himself, Rickard may have feared a loss by Dempsey, a consequent reduction in the gates of future fights, and violent racial incidents similar to the outbreaks that had accompanied Johnson's defeat of Jeffries in 1910.[40]

At any rate, Rickard safely sidetracked Wills and eventually found a new challenger for Dempsey, Gene Tunney, who "was almost universally regarded as a second-rater" by boxing aficionados. The insistence of the New York Athletic Commission upon a Dempsey–Wills match forced Rickard to hold the bout elsewhere. He chose Philadelphia's Susquecentennial Stadium and scheduled the fight for September 23, 1926. The buildup followed Rickard's familiar formula. In the "Battle of the Century" it was the dark, savage-visaged, mauling Dempsey versus the smooth, "scientific" boxer Tunney. To the surprise of nearly all of the 120,757 fans present and several million radio listeners, Tunney defeated Dempsey in the ten-round match on points. While scoring repeatedly on solid but nonlethal blows, Tunney simply avoided Dempsey's famed rushes. The fight was reminiscent of James J. Corbett's upset of John L. Sullivan in 1892. The gate exceeded $1.75 million and Dempsey collected $711,268 for one night's work.

Soon there was a demand for a return bout. Rickard achieved the pinnacle of his promotional career with the second "Fight of the Century" between Tunney and Dempsey in 1927. Over 104,000 customers paid $2,658,660 to witness the event at Soldier Field in Chicago, both records that still stand today. Spectators on the outer perimeter of the stadium sat as far as 200 yards from the ring, making the boxers almost undiscernible. An estimated fifty million Americans heard Graham McNamee's broadcast from one of seventy-three stations connected to the NBC radio network. For the first six rounds, the fight seemed to be a replay of the Philadelphia bout. Then in the seventh round, Dempsey landed a series of blows that crumpled Tunney to the mat. As the referee began to count, he waved Dempsey to a neutral corner of the ring. Dempsey ignored the motion, an action that may have cost him the heavyweight crown. By the time the referee convinced Dempsey to retire to a neutral corner, several seconds had expired. The referee than began the count anew, reaching nine before Tunney came to his feet. Although the referee's action conformed to the Illinois boxing codes, the legendary "long count" furnished a source of endless debate among fight fans. Tunney survived the seventh round and outboxed Dempsey in the final three rounds to win a unanimous decision. In defeat, Dempsey's popularity soared higher than when he had held the championship.

[40]See the conflicting treatments of Roberts, *Jack Dempsey*, and Sammons, *Beyond the Ring*.

The contrast in the popularity of Dempsey and Tunney reflects the type of hero sought by the American public. The image of Dempsey as the mauler who relied upon quick, physical solutions was far more satisfying to the public than Tunney's exhibition of complex, defensive finesse. Millions of Americans who worked in large corporations, bureaucracies, and on assembly lines dreamed of equally direct and decisive answers to their countless frustrations. In addition, Dempsey seemed more human than Tunney, who projected an image of snobbery and intellectuality. He married a socialite, had lectured to a class at Yale on Shakespeare, and was a personal friend of the writer Thorton Wilder. He remained aloof from ordinary people and was disdainful of reporters and the camaraderie of the "hangers-on" in the fight game. Americans wanted their heroes to be "average" in all respects except their specialty. Leo Lowenthal has written: "It is some comfort for the little man who has become expelled from the Horatio Alger dream, who despairs of penetrating the thicket of grand strategy in politics and business, to see his heroes as a lot of guys who like or dislike highballs, cigarettes, tomato juice, golf, and social gatherings—just like himself."[41] The "little man" could find confirmation of his own pleasures and discomforts by participating in those of Dempsey.

Dempsey's defeat by Tunney signalled the end of the Golden Age of American boxing. The public did not respond to the new heavyweight king; in 1928 Rickard lost some $400,000 in promoting the Tunney–Tom Henney bout. After the fight, Tunney retired from the ring, leaving the heavyweight scene in chaos. Then, in 1929, Rickard, while launching an elimination series to determine a new champion, suddenly died from an attack of appendicitis. Rickard's funeral revealed that the promoter was in his own right a public celebrity. Over 15,000 persons filed past his ornate, $15,000 bronze casket in the main arena of Madison Square Garden. The next day, 9,000 attended his funeral. No new impresario replaced Rickard. The age of athletic heroes seemed to be over. "After 1930 our stream of super-champions ran dry, replaced by a turgid brook," wrote John R. Tunis in 1934. "The champions were now just ordinary mortals, good players but nothing more."[42] Perhaps super athletic champions simply could not arise in a decade suffering from acute economic want.

---

[41]Lowenthal, *Literature*, p. 135.

[42]John R. Tunis, "Changing Trends in Sport," *Harper's Monthly Magazine*, 170 (Dec. 1934), 78.

10
THE SUPREMACY
OF BASEBALL

Until the 1950s no other team or individual sport seriously challenged baseball's supremacy as "the National Pastime." Wars and economic downturns only temporarily set back steady gains in attendance at all levels of the game. Despite the often unrestrained behavior by players (and sometimes by managers and owners as well), the sport gained in acceptability among all social groups. Even the president of the nation extended his support; in 1910 William Howard Taft established the precedent of the president opening each season by throwing out the first ball. Baseball stars were sometimes better known than the president of the United States; only Hollywood actors and actresses successfully competed with them for celebrity status. Minor league professional baseball also grew, from thirteen leagues in 1903 to fifty-one circuits at mid-century. Every city, town, and village of any consequence had one or more amateur, semiprofessional, or professional teams. Boys everywhere grew up reading baseball fiction, learning the rudiments of the game, and dreaming of one day becoming diamond heroes themselves.[1]

[1]For general treatments see Steven A. Riess, *Touching Base: Professional Baseball and American Culture in the Progressive Era* (Westport, CT, 1980); Harold Seymour, *Baseball*, 2 vols. (New York, 1960, 1971); David Quentin Voigt, *American Baseball*, 3 vols. (Norman, OK, 1966, 1970 and University Park, PA, 1983); Lee Lowenfish/Tony Lupien, *The Imperfect Diamond: The Story of Baseball's Reserve System and the Men Who Fought to Change It* (New York, 1980); Bill James, *The Bill James Historical Baseball Abstract* (New York, 1988).

THE MAGNETISM OF THE NATIONAL PASTIME

Baseball's supremacy sprang from attractions tangible and intangible. As in the past, teams helped to bind communities and neighborhoods together, heroes sprang from the ranks of the players, and the game itself, with its rich history and body of statistics, provided a source of continuity and stability in a society wracked by change and uncertainty. No other sport, it seemed to contemporary observers, quite captured the essence of the nation's character as much as baseball. Such a contention was beyond argument, declared Albert Spalding, former player and sporting goods entrepreneur in 1911. It was like saying that "two plus two equal four."[2]

Appropriate to its embodiment of the nation's character, the custodians of the National Game nurtured a legend that baseball was solely of American origins. The myth that Abner Doubleday invented baseball at Cooperstown, New York, in the summer of 1839 took official form in 1907 with the report of a special commission of men of "high repute and undoubted knowledge of Base Ball." The commission engaged in no first-hand research, but did send out letters of inquiry to old-timers who had been associated with organized teams in the antebellum era. (Later scholars discredited the work of the commission. See Chapter 5.) The commission's conclusions, as Albert Spalding so effectively put it, helped free baseball "from the trammels of English traditions, customs, conventionalities."[3] In 1939 the major leagues celebrated the "centennial" of baseball with impressive ceremonies at Cooperstown. There they dedicated a Hall of Fame, presented a pageant showing Doubleday's alleged contribution to the sport, and staged an all-star game. The United States government joined the festivities by issuing a commemorative stamp, marking 1839 as the date of the birth of the "National Game."

The Doubleday-Cooperstown myth helped give baseball a quasireligious status. As Muslims have their Mecca and Christians have their Jerusalem or Bethlehem, baseball followers have their Cooperstown. Each year, thousands of Americans make the "pilgrimage" to the "shrine" at Cooperstown, the site of the Hall of Fame and Museum. There they can see statues and pictures of their former heroes and observe the "relics" used by them—old, discolored bats, balls, and uniforms. They can visit the "hallowed ground" of Doubleday Field, where the young Doubleday "immaculately conceived" the game. Cooperstown is rich in religious terminology: "shrine," "pantheon," "sanctuary," and "relics." Each year, sportswriters dutifully select great players of the past for "enshrinement," after which they become "immortals."[4]

The pre-1950 ballparks themselves had rustic qualities, thus reminding the fans of the nation's simpler agrarian past. For the urban spectator, surrounded by noise, dirt, and squalor, entering a major-league ball field could be an exhila-

---

[2]Albert Spalding, *America's National Game* (New York, 1911), p. 4.
[3]Ibid.
[4]For these parallels I am especially indebted to Seymour, *Baseball*, I, 4.

rating experience. Suddenly he was transported into another world, one characterized by vistas of green grass and clean, white boundaries. The owners gave their edifices pastoral-sounding names: Ebbets Field, Sportsman Park, the Polo Grounds. Such nomenclature remained popular until 1923, when Yankee Stadium was built. Parks built since then have more urban names: Shea Stadium, Astrodome, Superdome. Perhaps the change from rustic names to urban names reflected the growing urbanization of the country. Whatever they were called, the massive baseball parks, built of concrete and steel, bore mute testimony to the values Americans placed upon baseball. To the fans, they were more than simply a place for commercial amusement; the park was a civic monument representing the entire community.[5]

Baseball was allegedly a vehicle for promoting social integration, for building social solidarity through support of local teams, and for the assimilation of new immigrants. As Morgan Bulkeley, one-time president of the National League put it, "There is nothing which will help quicker and better amalgamate the foreign born, and those born of foreign parents in this country, than to give them a little good bringing up in the good old-fashioned game of Base Ball." Baseball would help prevent revolutionary conspiracies. "They don't have things of that kind on the other side of the ocean," declared Bulkeley, "and many spend their hours fussing around in conspiring and hatching up plots when they should be out in the open improving their lungs."[6] Yet, in fact, Organized Baseball excluded blacks, and the newer immigrants from southern and eastern Europe apparently found no greater opportunities for advancement in baseball than they did in other professions.[7]

Among the most tangible attractions of baseball was the annual World Series. Beginning in 1903 the pennant winners of the two leagues agreed to play a nine-game "World Championship" series. No postseason games were played in 1904, but in 1905 the World Series became a permanent feature of big-league baseball. The series furnished an exciting conclusion to the regular season; the entire nation soon became absorbed in the outcome. Fans congregated in the city streets to watch the play-by-play progress of the series as reported on the boards posted in front of newspaper offices. Reportedly, the series sometimes even delayed the proceedings of the United States Supreme Court. In the 1920s fans began to listen to the series on radio.

The sheer drama of baseball was yet another attraction. Baseball had a cast of well-defined heroes and villains, familiar plots, comedy, and the unexpected. Since most of the fans had played the sport as youths and watched many contests, they understood the intricacies of the plot–the purpose of bunting, the hit-and-run play, a deliberate base on balls, the removal of a struggling pitcher,

[5]See Steven A. Riess, "Baseball Myths, Baseball Realities and the Social Functions of Baseball in the Progressive Era," *Stadion*, 3 (1980), 273–311.

[6]Quoted in Seymour, *Baseball*, II, 4.

[7]Riess, "Baseball Myths," 292–309; Riess, "Race and Ethnicity in American Baseball, 1900–1919," *Journal of Ethnic Studies*, 4 (1977), 39–55.

and the appropriate place for the insertion of a pinch-hitter. Baseball was a rational sport, one in which means were specifically related to ends. Even though one could never predict when a ground ball might strike a pebble and bounce over a fielder's outstretched glove, "baseball, year by year, [has] grown more scientific, more of a thing of accepted rules [of tactics], or set routine," wrote F. C. Lane, a baseball reporter. "This slow evolution of the sport displayed itself in batting, in the form of the bunt, the place hit and various other manifestations of skill."[8]

Like the melodrama, baseball seemed unusually well suited to present a marvelous set of type characters. "You know, there were a lot of characters in baseball back then," recalled Samuel "Wahoo Sam" Crawford in the 1960s. "Real individualists. Not conformists, like most ball players—and most people—are today."[9] The fans noticed and adored the special physical traits and idiosyncratic behavior of the players. Their colorful nicknames—Bugs, Babe, Rube, Wahoo Sam, Mugsy, Chief, Muddy, Kid, Hod, Dummy, Dutch, Stuffy, Gabby, and Hooks, to list only a few—suggested baseball's capacity to produce stock characters. And, of course, the umpire served as the chief villain.

The players seemed to take a special delight in spicing the game with comedy and the unexpected. Perhaps none equalled the feat of Herman "Germany" Schaefer. He stole first base! With the score tied in a late inning, Schaefer was on first base and Davy Jones on third. Schaefer gave the sign for a double steal and broke for second. The catcher, fearing that Jones would steal home if he threw the ball, simply held it. In the words of Jones:

> So now we had men on second and third. Well, on the next pitch Schaefer yelled, 'Let's try it again!' And with a bloodcurdling shout he took off like a wild Indian *back to first base*, and dove in headfirst in a cloud of dust. . . .
> But nothing happened. Nothing at all. Everybody just stood there and watched Schaefer, with their mouths open, not knowing what the devil was going on. Me, too. Even if the catcher *had* thrown to first, I was too stunned to move. . . . But the catcher didn't throw. He just stared! . . .
> So there we were, back where we started, with Schaefer on first and me on third. And on the next pitch darned if he didn't let out another war whoop and take off *again* for second base. By this time the Cleveland catcher evidently had enough, because he finally threw to second to get Schaefer, and when he did I took off for home and *both* of us were safe.[10]

Equally zany behavior was common off the field. Reportedly, Rube Waddell, a superb pitcher, accomplished all of the following feats in a single year:

> He began that year sleeping in a firehouse at Camden, New Jersey, and ended it tending bar in a saloon in Wheeling, West Virginia. In between those events he won twenty-two games for the Philadelphia Athletics, played left end for the

[8]Quoted in Leverett T. Smith, Jr., *The American Dream and the National Game* (Bowling Green, OH, 1975), p. 190.

[9]Lawrence S. Ritter, *The Glory of Their Time: The Story of the Early Days of Baseball Told by the Men Who Played It* (New York, 1966), p. 49.

[10]Ibid, pp. 44–45.

Business Men's Rugby Football Club of Grand Rapids, Michigan, toured the
nation in a melodrama called *The Stain of Guilt*, courted, married, and became
separated from May Wynne Skinner of Lynn, Massachusetts, saved a woman from
drowning, accidentally shot a friend through the hand, and was bitten by a lion.[11]

This account fails to mention Waddell's drinking binges. *Sporting News* called
him "the leading sousepaw" in baseball.

ORGANIZED BASEBALL'S QUEST FOR ORDER

The owners of professional baseball struggled to establish a modicum of order
within their ranks. On the one hand, they wanted to permit individual franchise
holders freedom to operate their ball clubs as they saw fit. Yet, if all or most of
the franchises were to prosper, collusive agreements and a tightly constructed
economic cartel seemed essential. Consequently, the major league owners sought
to devise means to avoid direct competition among franchises for players, to
prevent the formation of rival big leagues, to restrict the total number of big-
league teams, and to bring the minor leagues under big-league control. The
resulting entity that became known as Organized Baseball was a large, unwieldy
cartel, that was only partly and sporadically effective.

Baseball's quest for order in the pre-1920 era began inauspiciously.
Despite the collapse of both the Player's League in 1890 and the American
Association in 1891, the decade of the 1890s was a grim one for the National
League. Burdened by the debts accumulated from the brotherhood war and the
purchase costs of four American Association clubs, the league faced a general
economic depression, public disillusionment due to the brotherhood war, and
growing competition from other forms of entertainment. Moreover, the new
twelve-team loop was a disaster. Teams with poor records, such as the Louisville
and St. Louis franchises, which between them occupied last place for five of the
eight years that the circuit existed, attracted few fans at home or on the road, and
the New York Giants, who were vital to the success of the league, failed to field
a strong team. Because of vicious infighting, the barons of baseball were unable
to agree to reduce the size of the circuit or set up the league into two six-team
divisions. Either action might have generated more fan interest and profits.
Finally, in 1899, the league returned to eight clubs. The new circuit, composed of
Boston, Brooklyn, Chicago, Cincinnati, New York, Philadelphia, Pittsburgh, and
St. Louis, would remain intact until 1953, when the Boston Braves moved to
Milwaukee.

But the woes of the National League were not over. The return of
prosperity at the turn of the century, the elimination of the four weak franchises,
and the conflicts within the league's counsels encouraged a challenge by a
formidable rival—the American League led by the indomitable Byron Bancroft

---

[11]Quoted in Seymour, *Baseball*, II, 105–106.

"Ban" Johnson. When the National League dropped the four franchises and returned to an eight-team loop, Johnson, as president of the Western League (a minor league), convinced his followers to plant franchises in the abandoned cities. In 1901 he claimed major-league status for the western circuit, renamed the loop the American League, formed plans to invade New York, and began to raid National League player rosters. With Johnson in firm control of the American League franchises and the National League owners divided, the senior loop finally sued for peace.

The peace settlement, known as the National Agreement of 1903, became the centerpiece of professional baseball. The leagues agreed to recognize each other's reserve clauses and established a three-man National Commission to govern all of Organized Baseball. Composed of the presidents of the two leagues and a third member chosen by them, the National Commission served primarily as a judicial body to resolve disputes between the leagues and controversies involving the minor leagues. In the National League, the owners retained nearly absolute power to manage their franchises as they saw fit; in the American League, Ban Johnson ruled with a firm hand until the 1920s. The 1903 agreement also recognized the territorial monopolies of minor-league teams, granted them reserve rights in players, and set up a system by which the major leagues could draft players from the minors.

In the pre-1920 era, the club owners confronted two major challenges to the 1903 agreement: the appearance of a new players' union and another contender for big-league status. The reserve clause allowed the owners to limit salaries to less than the players would have received on the open market. As attendance and club profits rose rapidly in the early years of the century, player salaries slowly drifted upwards. Better players sometimes effectively "held out," refusing to play until they obtained higher pay. Probably as many as ten superstars received salaries of $10,000 or more by 1910, but players with ordinary talents might earn as little as $1,900 for a season of play. When a third major circuit, the Federal League, threatened the cartel between 1912 and 1915, the salaries of superior players jumped markedly. Ty Cobb's salary, for example, leaped from $9,000 in 1910 to $20,000 in 1915. Nonetheless, some owners refused to capitulate to the external pressure. Connie Mack, the owner-manager of the 1914 champion Philadelphia Athletics, sold or released all of his high-priced stars. With the demise of the Federal League at the end of the 1915 season, the magnates held the line on salaries until after World War I.

Salary conflict, capricious owner actions, and several other grievances led to the formation of a new players' union, the Base Ball Players' Fraternity, in 1912. Organized by David Fultz, an attorney and a former big-league player, the fraternity grew to 700 members (including minor leaguers). After instituting a number of lawsuits against various clubs for contract violations, the players presented the National Commission in 1913 with seventeen demands, most of which concerned the standardization of contracts, player releases, and severance payments. Faced with the Federal League war, the commission reluctantly granted a few minimal concessions, including the right of big-league veterans of ten years to negotiate with any club they pleased. Except for the last provision, the fraternity made no effort to challenge the reserve clause nor the right of the clubs to sell players. For several years, the union filed lawsuits in behalf of both major- and minor-league players, but the collapse of the Federal League in 1915 and the lack of adequate player support weakened the bargaining position of the fraternity. Not until the post-World War II era would the players again mount an organized movement against the owners.

The owners worried more about the Federal League. In 1914, James A. "Long Jim" Gilmore, a Chicago iron manufacturer, aligned wealthy men in Chicago, New York, and St. Louis to reorganize the old Federal League into a circuit claiming major-league status. The Federals offered established major-league stars high salaries to jump to the new league. The major-league owners responded as they had during the Player's League war of 1890; they blacklisted players who had abandoned the majors, obtained court injunctions, and raised the salaries of their players.

Even though high salaries and low attendance plagued the Federal League in both 1914 and 1915, the major league owners panicked and settled for an expensive peace. In effect, the magnates sabotaged the new loop by bribing the wealthiest Federal League owners. For example, Albert Sinclair, who later gained notoriety in the Teapot Dome scandal, received permission to buy a controlling interest in the Chicago Cubs at a bargain price. In addition, Sinclair received a regular payment of $10,000 for ten years from the major leagues. On the other hand, those owners of Federal League clubs that were not in direct competition with the majors received nothing except the revenues from player sales. The settlement may have cost the major leagues as much as $5 million, tarnished the owners' image, and brought disaster to many minor-league clubs.

THE "DEAD BALL" ERA

In terms of the delicate balance between offense and defense, during the three decades preceding 1920 superb pitching held the limelight. The pitchers gained a decided advantage when the National League in 1901 and the American League in 1903 decided to call foul balls strikes. Strikeouts immediately increased and batting averages fell. Until 1910 the pitchers worked with a rubber-centered ball which had less resiliency than the modern cork-centered baseball. The umpires used only a few new balls per game; consequently, a ball might become soft, lopsided, and stained with dirt, grass, or tobacco juice before it was thrown out of play. A variety of legal "trick" pitches added to the repertoire of several hurlers. Especially difficult to hit was the spit ball. By applying saliva to the fingers, the pitcher could remove the natural spin from the ball, causing it to behave much like a knuckle ball, dipping and breaking sharply in unpredictable ways as it approached the plate.

While a few pitchers had successful careers built on the spitball, most of the best hurlers relied on fast balls and curves. Cy Young, Grover Cleveland Alexander, "Smoky Joe" Wood, Joe "Iron Man" McGinnity, Christy Mathewson, and Walter Johnson—the pitching heroes of the era—all threw blazing fastballs. Walter Johnson, who pitched for the lowly Washington Senators from 1907 to 1927, was perhaps the greatest pitcher of all times. He won 414 games for a team that usually resided in the league's second division; he struck out 3,497 batters and pitched 113 shutouts during his career, both marks that no other hurler has approached. His strikeout record is all the more remarkable considering that the hitters in the dead ball era carefully guarded the plate rather than swinging freely. For ten years in a row Johnson won twenty or more games. In one incredible pitching span he shut out the Yankees three times in four days, then after three days' rest won two more consecutive games, for a total of five wins in nine days.

Given the superiority of the pitchers, managers tried to perfect the "scientific" or "inside" baseball strategy made famous by the Boston Beaneaters and the Baltimore Orioles in the 1890s. Most of the hitters choked the bat, trying simply to meet the ball squarely so that it could be driven through the infield or bunted. Managers often fined free swingers. Of the few home runs hit prior to 1910, almost all were inside the park. Since the outfielders of that day played very shallow, inside-the-park homers occurred more frequently than today. The bunt was another favorite weapon of the managers, being used to obtain hits, to cause errors, and to sacrifice runners into scoring position. The dead ball could be bunted much more effectively than the modern cork-centered ball. Manager Joe McCloskey of the St. Louis Cardinals once required his hitters to bunt seventeen consecutive times. The strategy produced the two runs needed to win the game. With the introduction of the cork-centered ball in 1910, batting averages ascended to especially high levels in the 1920s, but the managers continued long afterwards to employ the "scientific" strategy.

John J. McGraw, the colorful, controversial, and longtime manager of the New York Giants, was a master of the nuances of dead ball strategy. After nine years of play with the famed Baltimore Orioles in the 1890s, McGraw came to New York to take the helm of the Giants in 1902, a post he held for the next thirty years. He led the Giants to ten National League pennants and four "world championships." Like most of the managers of the era, McGraw concentrated upon the acquisition of good pitchers. Other than such pitchers as McGinnity, Mathewson, and Rube Marquard, the Giants had no outstanding stars, but they always had speed, aggressiveness, and the peerless McGraw.

Perfectly suited to New York City—the nation's center of commerce, high finance, show business, and ethnic diversity—McGraw attracted headlines both on and off the field. The epitome of martinet managers of the day, he exercised harsh discipline over the players with scathing verbal reprimands or stiff fines. Over and over again he drilled them in the game's fundamentals: covering bases, place hitting, bunting, sliding, and base running. He brawled with players, fans, umpires, and league officials. Fans in other National League cities liked nothing better than to see his hated Giants defeated. McGraw took advantage of the excitement offered by New York City away from the diamond. He liked the theater, horse racing, gambling, parties, and highballs. All of these things, plus his Irish charm, endeared him to New Yorkers.

Had it not been for Tyrus "Ty" Raymond Cobb, long-time star of the Detroit Tigers, the pre-1920 era would probably be remembered only for its pitching heroes. In a career that spanned twenty-four seasons (1905–1928), Cobb had the highest lifetime batting average (.367) and won the league batting championship the most seasons (12)—he won the title nine times in succession—of any player in baseball history. Statistics, of course, fail to do Cobb full justice. He had no peer as a master of the dead ball tactics. With his spread-handed grip he would bunt if the infield played deep; if the infield tightened up, he would slash the ball through the holes or over the fielders' heads. His dazzling speed and recklessness on the base paths terrorized opponents.

Ty Cobb personified, in an exaggerated form, the rugged individualism of the nineteenth century. Lacking the exceptional physical attributes of a Babe Ruth, Cobb relentlessly drove himself to excel. To Cobb, baseball was a form of warfare. "When I played ball," Cobb wrote in his autobiography in 1961, "I didn't play for fun. . . . It's no pink tea, and mollycoddles had better stay out. It's a contest and everything that implies, a struggle for supremacy, a survival of the fittest."[12] Given such a view, Cobb ignored the old amateur traditions of the sport.

STARS OF THE DEAD BALL ERA
During the first two decades of the twentieth century, Walter Johnson, a pitcher for the Washington Senators (on the left), and Ty Cobb, an outfielder for the Detroit Tigers (on the right), were perhaps the two most outstanding stars in baseball. Universally disliked by fellow players, in this publicity photograph Cobb appears uncharacteristically amiable.

[12]Ty Cobb and Al Stump, *My Life in Baseball: The True Record* (Garden City, NY, 1961), p. 280. See also Charles C. Alexander, *Ty Cobb* (New York, 1984).

Since the 1880s, players had engaged in brawling but usually within a framework of understood conventions that involved mostly verbal warfare but rarely slugging. Cobb used every weapon at his disposal—his spikes, fists, bat, and his tongue—all in an effort to intimidate and defeat his opponents. The other players and the fans soon recognized that Cobb was serious, that he was a man driven by internal demons that even left his sanity in question.

Instances of Cobb's aggressive behavior off the field were equally legion. Throughout the league he verbally challenged and sometimes fought taunting fans· in one case he leaped into the stands and struck a fan who happened to be physically handicapped. In 1914 Cobb's wife got into an argument with a butcher over twenty cents' worth of spoiled fish. Believing that his wife had been insulted, Cobb went to the butcher's shop, pulled out the revolver that he always carried, and demanded that the butcher telephone his wife to apologize. The butcher, naturally, complied, but the butcher's young assistant appeared and dared Cobb to resolve the issue without the pistol. Cobb was quite willing to accommodate and proceeded to beat the boy insensate; the boy's life may have been saved only by the quick arrival of the police. Cobb was particularly brutal to blacks; on at least two occasions he struck black women. At the Pontchartrain Hotel in Detroit he allegedly kicked a black chambermaid in the stomach and knocked her down the steps because she had objected to being called a "nigger." Repeated warnings, fines, and suspensions by Ban Johnson, president of the American League, failed to curb Cobb's violent temper.

Cobb never became a popular hero in the mold of a Babe Ruth or even a Cap Anson. Almost everybody thoroughly disliked him, including his own teammates. He evoked fear and respect, but never affection; he never had a close, personal friend among the big-league players or managers. He ate alone, roomed alone, and for years at a time did not speak to certain of his teammates. The depth of the feeling against Cobb by fellow players was demonstrated clearly in 1910 when Cobb appeared to have won the American League batting championship. In the final doubleheader of the season Napoleon Lajoie, the leading contender for the title, made eight hits in eight times at bat. Six of the hits came from bunts toward third base, which the notoriously slow-footed Lajoie had somehow beaten out. It soon became clear that the St. Louis Browns had deliberately tried to deny Cobb the crown by "giving" Lajoie free access to first base. (Incidentally, the strategy failed, for Cobb was able to retain the title by a single percentage point.) Fans everywhere came out to see the rampaging Cobb, partly in awe of his ability, but also in hopes of seeing him stymied by the local club or of witnessing a brawl in which Cobb would be the principal victim.

Cobb's ugly behavior and intense drive apparently arose from a combination of circumstances. Born of a proud family in Georgia that had once owned slaves, Cobb was inordinately defensive of his origins and the South. Teammates discovered this sensitivity. As a rookie he became the natural butt of unmerciful hazing. Teammates broke his bats, nailed his uniform to the clubhouse wall, hid his clothes, locked him in bathrooms, and tried to get him into a fight with the biggest man on the club. Cobb responded violently, eventually intimidating the rest of the players. Likewise, fans enjoyed ragging the superstar. At every league park except Detroit fans threw a steady barrage of verbal insults at Cobb. Sometimes Cobb had to be escorted from the park by the police. Perhaps it is little wonder that Cobb believed he was the target of a conspiracy.

Cobb was also obsessed with the bizarre circumstances of his father's death. He explained in his autobiography that "I did it for my father, who was an exalted man. They killed him when he was still young. But I knew he was watching me and I never let him down." The mysterious "they" referred to by Cobb was his own mother. Cobb's father had suspected his wife of unfaithfulness and had gone to her bedroom window to investigate. Apparently mistaking him for an intruder, she had killed him with a shotgun. The tragic incident occurred just as Cobb was entering the big leagues. "I had to fight all my life to survive," Cobb later wrote. "They were all against me . . . but I beat the bastards and left them in the ditch."[13] As Cobb grew older, the symptoms of insanity grew more pronounced. He talked frequently of a vague conspiracy to take away his life. When he died in 1961, only three people from Organized Baseball attended his funeral. Never had a more successful, a more violent, and a more maladjusted personality passed through the annals of American sport.

THE AGE OF KENESAW MOUNTAIN LANDIS

In September of 1920 a shocking revelation rocked the country: the 1919 World Series had been fixed. The worst team scandal in the history of American sport, soon labeled the "Black Sox Scandal," crowded the "Red Scare" and every other major story off the front pages of the nation's newspapers. Americans were incredulous. According to baseball legend, a small boy approached "Shoeless Joe" Jackson, one of the alleged conspirators and a star outfielder with the Chicago White Sox. "Say it ain't so, Joe," begged the lad as tears welled from his eyes. "I'm afraid it is, son," Jackson responded. The hurt cut deeply. Boston newsboys condemned the "murderous blow" to the National Pastime by the "Benedict Arnolds of baseball." In Joliet, Illinois, an angry fan charged Buck Herzog with being "one of those crooked Chicago ball players." A fight erupted, and Herzog was stabbed, even though he was a member of the Chicago Cubs rather than the White Sox. Sensitive Nelson Algren, then a lad on Chicago's South Side, became disillusioned. "Everybody's out for The Buck," he later concluded, "even the big leaguers." A character in F. Scott Fitzgerald's *The Great Gatsby* reflected; "It never occurred to me that one man could start to play with the faith of fifty million people. . . . "[14]

Although the disbelief and dismay that accompanied the Black Sox Scandal of 1919 proved that baseball had finally won wide-scale public acceptability, in retrospect the scandal should not have been so surprising. Wagering

[13]Quotations in Seymour, *Baseball*, II, 111.
[14]Quotations in ibid, 278.

on games had been commonplace since the middle of the nineteenth century. Baseball pools existed in all the big-league cities. Purchasing a pool ticket for as little as ten cents, a person could win cash for correctly picking which team would win the most games, score the most runs, and so forth, in a given week. By publishing odds on games and providing weekly totals of wins, hits, and runs, the newspapers cooperated with pool managers. While pools mounted to thousands of dollars weekly, these sums probably paled in comparison to the wagering handled by professional gamblers.

Moreover, owners, managers, and players had close ties with a subculture of commercial entertainment that existed outside of old-stock, Protestant, middle-class respectability. A disproportionate percentage of the baseball owners, as was true of entrepreneurs in other sectors of the commercial entertainment industry, came from recent ethnic stock. Their business and social lives often revolved around urban political machines, gamblers, saloons, and show people.[15] Managers and players likewise spent much of their spare time at the race tracks, theaters, and saloons where they consorted with publicly known gamblers. Most big-league players, including even Ty Cobb who was of old-stock, Protestant origins, did not hesitate to wager upon themselves or their teams. Yet the National Commission, fearing adverse publicity and perhaps the loss of valuable property in the form of the players, attempted to cover up all reports connecting baseball with gambling and game-fixing. Had it not been for an enterprising reporter, Hugh Fullerton, the 1919 Black Sox scandal might have remained a mere rumor.

Later evidence revealed that eight Chicago players had taken money from gamblers to fix the 1919 World Series. Apparently to protect his investment in the accused players, Charles A. Comiskey, owner of the White Sox, initially tried to contain the rumors of a fix. But eventually seven of the eight admitted to a grand jury they had received sums varying from $5,000 to $10,000—figures that exceeded the annual salaries of most of the accused—to throw the series to Cincinnati. Somehow, however, the grand jury records disappeared before the trial. (Later at a trial in which Joe Jackson sued Comiskey for back pay, the player confessions "mysteriously" reappeared—in the possession of Comiskey's attorney!)

At the trial held in 1921, all of the players repudiated their earlier confessions, leaving the testimony of Bill Maharg, a professional gambler, as the only substantial evidence against them. After a few hours of deliberation, the jury acquitted all the players plus two gamblers. The spectators in the courtroom roared their approval, and the jurymen and players retired to the local restaurant to celebrate. But the joy of the players was short-lived, for Judge Kenesaw Mountain Landis, the newly appointed Commissioner of Baseball, banished them from Organized Baseball for life. The players had become the scapegoats of a big-league effort to project a new moral image.

While the scandal of 1919 was a major reason for the reorganization of major-league baseball, discontent with the National Commission and the power

---

[15]For the involvement of baseball in machine politics, see Riess, *Touching Base*, Chaps. 3 & 4.

of Ban Johnson, imperious president of the American League, had been building for several years. Baseball attendance had failed to grow in the 1910s and rumors of fixed games were rife. The Commission had become almost impotent, and Johnson had, over the years, incurred the wrath of several powerful owners.

The new National Agreement of 1921 gave sweeping powers to a single man to head all of Organized Baseball. The owners extended to the Commissioner the power to investigate anything "suspected" of being "detrimental to the best interests of the national game." If he determined that leagues, club owners, or players had taken actions harmful to the sport, he was given the authority to suspend, fine, or banish guilty parties. In their eagerness to improve the image of baseball and bring a semblance of order to the game, the owners even agreed to waive their rights to take disputes between themselves or with the Commissioner to the civil courts. The Agreement of 1921 established the model for the governmental structures of professional football and basketball in the post-World War II era. By establishing a "czar" to censor movies in 1922, the movie industry also followed the example of baseball.

In the wake of the Black Sox scandal, "Czar" Landis brought to baseball what Calvin Coolidge would shortly bring to national politics after the revelation of the Teapot Dome scandal. Both men projected an image of staunch integrity, a "puritanism" in the midst of the excess of the 1920s. With a flair for the theatrical that he had revealed as a federal judge, Landis promised an "untiring effort" to rid baseball of gamblers and gambling. "If I catch any crook in baseball," Landis pledged, "the rest of his life is going to be a hot one."[16] His very appearance instilled confidence in his fearless rectitude. Unlike the pudgy, well-fed magnates, Landis was thin, almost emaciated. With a craggy face topped by long, shaggy, unkempt hair, he looked like Andrew Jackson, one of his heroes. Like Jackson, Landis had a gift for using his imposing appearance and his controlled temper to dominate those who confronted him.

Landis wasted little time in trying to alter the image of Organized Baseball. He arbitrarily banished more than a dozen players from the game for life. Even the owners did not escape his vigilance. He ordered Charles A. Stoneham, owner of the New York Giants, and John J. McGraw, Giant manager, to divest themselves of their stock in race tracks located in Cuba and New York. Yet during a reign which lasted until 1944, Landis treated the questionable actions of the owners far more gingerly than those of the players. He rarely interfered with trades between clubs or in their internal affairs. Despite his personal opposition to the "farm system," he took only limited steps to curb its growth. His power over the magnates was far from complete, for if he antagonized enough owners, he jeopardized his position. Nonetheless, upon the death of Landis in 1944, the barons of baseball quickly reduced the power of the commissioner's office. By comparison, Landis's successors were merely "ceremonial" commissioners.

[16]Quoted in Seymour, *Baseball*, II, 323. See also Norman Rosenberg, "Here Comes the Judge! The Origins of Baseball's Commissioner System and American Legal Culture," *Journal of Popular Culture*, 20 (Spring 1987), 129–46.

JUDGE KENESAW MOUNTAIN LANDIS (1866–1944)
Commissioner of Baseball (1920–1944), this photograph reflects
Landis's reputation for rectitude and toughness. In the wake of
the Black Sox scandal of 1919, Landis helped improve the
National Games's image of integrity.

While Landis gave baseball a new image of integrity, the United States
Supreme Court furnished its legal salvation. All of the Federal League clubs of
the 1913–1915 era except Baltimore had dropped their antitrust suits against the
major leagues. Having received no remuneration from the 1916 peace settlement,
Baltimore continued its court action. Justice Oliver Wendell Holmes, Jr., speaking
for a unanimous court in 1922, declared that professional baseball games did not
constitute a "trade or commerce in the commonly-accepted use of the words." In
a rather tortuous definition of terms, Holmes reasoned that the "personal effort"
of ball players was "not related to production" and therefore could not be
involved in commerce. Nor was interstate movement essential to their activity,
for the movement of ball players across state lines was simply "incidental" to
their playing ball. Whatever the merits of the legal justification of professional
baseball's exemption from the antitrust laws, the decision provided a legal
umbrella for the agreements upon which the professional baseball cartel rested.

At the same time that baseball sought to establish an image of moral
purity and received a new legal foundation from the Supreme Court, it took steps
to make the game more interesting to the spectator. By introducing the "jack
rabbit" baseball, using more balls per game, and outlawing the spit ball, the
magnates of baseball reduced the effectiveness of the pitchers and enhanced that
of the hitters. In 1910, Organized Baseball replaced the rubber-centered ball with
a more resilient, cork-centered ball. Gradually, ball manufacturers introduced
other modifications to the ball: tighter-wound yarn, reduction of the protrusions
of the seams, and thinner leather for the cover. In 1920, the rules committee also

banned all pitches that involved the application of foreign substances to the ball. However, existing big-league spitball pitchers were exempted from the ban.

These changes produced astonishing results. The "dead ball" era ended, and the "live ball" era began. Batting averages, scoring, and home run totals soared. By 1925 the combined batting averages of the major leagues was forty-five points higher than it had been in 1915. Only four hitters in the first two decades of the century had hit .400 or better; eight batters achieved this distinction in the twenties. By 1930, major-league teams averaged scoring three and a half more runs per game than in 1915. But the most remarkable development of all was the quantity of home runs. Major-league totals quadrupled from 384 homers in 1915 to 1,565 in 1930. Once owners became convinced of the popularity of the "Big Bang" style of play, they sometimes moved their fences closer to home plate to produce even more four baggers. The players, observing the large salaries of sluggers such as Babe Ruth, began to use lighter bats, grip the bat at the end of the handle, and take a full swing with a complete followthrough. Aficionados of the old style of play, which featured tight pitching duels, bunts, sacrifices, hit-and-run plays, and steals—"scientific" or "inside" baseball—regarded the Big Bang style as a capitulation to new fans ignorant of the finer traditions and nuances of the sport.

DISPARITIES IN COMPETITION

Presumably equalizing the conditions of the competition among teams would also increase fan interest. If more teams had a viable shot at winning the pennant, no single team would dominate the championships over the years and pennant races would be closely fought. Overall attendance should also be higher. The major leagues had long argued that the reserve clause in player contracts and the draft prevented the domination of the pennant races by a few of the wealthier franchises. Without the right to reserve players, professional baseball argued, wealthier clubs could offer higher salaries to players on other teams and eventually corner the market on the best player talent. In theory, the draft gave each club equal access to new player talent; it negated the potential advantages of superior wealth. But the historical record of baseball made a mockery of both of these arguments.[17]

From the beginning of the century, the clubs located in the largest cities enjoyed better records than those in smaller cities (see Figures 10–1 and 10–2). From 1900 to 1952 (when the Boston Braves moved to Milwaukee), the New York Giants, Brooklyn Dodgers, and Chicago Cubs, representative of the two largest metropolitan areas in the National League, won thirty of fifty-two pennants. After 1925, the "Rickey effect" (Branch Rickey's farm system at St.Louis) reduced the close correlation between city size and playing strength. Yet Philadelphia, Boston, and Cincinnati, which ranked fifth, sixth, and seventh in average popu-

---

[17]See esp. Lance E. Davis, "Self-Regulation in Baseball, 1909–1971," in Roger Noll, ed., *Government and the Sports Business* (Washington, DC, 1974), pp. 349–86.

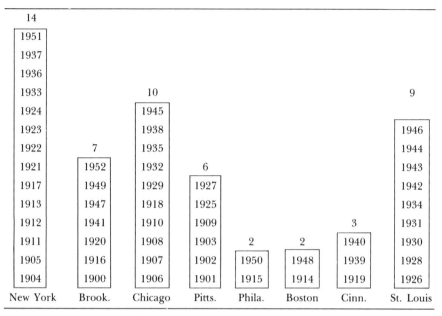

Figure 10–1 Disparity of competition as shown by pennants won in order of average population rank[a], National League, 1900-1952

[a]Based on average population during the period, adjusted for number of baseball teams in the metropolitan area.
Source: Adapted from Roger G. Noll, ed., *Government and the Sports Business* (Washington, D.C.: Brookings Institution, 1974), p. 46.

lation when adjusted to the number of teams in the metropolitan area, won only seven pennants between them. Until the purchase of the New York Yankees by new owners in 1915, the size of the market area bore little relationship to team success in the American League. But after the Yankees acquired Babe Ruth in 1920, they proceeded to win twenty of the next thirty-two flags. Through 1980, the combined franchises in New York, Chicago, and Los Angeles won over half of the total flags of the two leagues.

The main cause for the success of the teams in the biggest cities was quite simple. The disparities in population between metropolitan areas produced substantial inequalities in attendance and therefore in incomes. Since the nineteenth century, the owners had tried to offset market size by giving 50 percent of the base admission price to visiting teams. But any revenues collected from seats that exceeded the base price, such as box and reserve seats, went to the home club. As more of the higher-priced seats were added to the stadiums in the twentieth century, the percentage of total gate receipts of the visiting teams declined. In 1892 the visiting teams received about 40 percent of the total revenue, by 1929 their share had declined to 21 percent, and by 1950 to only 14 percent. This disparity of incomes benefited those franchises located in large market areas, giving them additional bargaining strength within the major league cartel and additional revenue for the purchase of superior players from other major or minor league clubs.

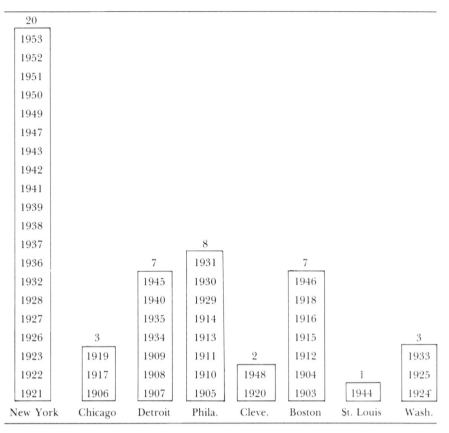

Figure 10–2 Disparity of competition as shown by pennants won in order of average population rank[a], American League, 1903–1953

[a]Based on average population during the period, adjusted for the number of baseball teams in the metropolitan area.
Source: Adapted from Roger G. Noll, ed., *Government and the Sports Business* (Washington, D.C.: Brookings Institution, 1974), p. 46.

The history of the New York dynasty vividly reveals the importance of the market area served by the club and the advantages of wealthy, freespending owners. Before Jacob Ruppert, Jr., a rich brewer, and Tillinghast Huston, a prosperous engineer, purchased the Yankees in 1915, the club had had a mediocre record. The club's performance slowly improved as the owners purchased player talent from the minor-league clubs and other big-league clubs. The big Yankee breakthrough came between 1919 and 1923 when the Boston Red Sox virtually became their farm club. Harry Frazee, a Broadway producer and owner of the Red Sox, always seemed short of money. To obtain liquid capital to finance his Broadway shows, he began to dismantle the powerful Red Sox in 1919. (The Red Sox had won pennants in 1915, 1916, and 1918.) That year, he sold star pitcher Carl Mays to the Yankees for $40,000; the next year he unloaded Babe Ruth to the Yankees for $125,000 (plus a $300,000 loan), a sum twice as high as had ever previously been paid for a player. By 1923, eleven of the twenty-four-man Yankee roster had formerly played with Boston. The hapless Red Sox sank to the American League cellar in 1922, where they remained for eight of the next nine seasons.

Superior financial resources permitted the Yankees to dominate the American League championships. Over the next forty-five years, the Yankees lost the flag only fourteen times. A star player was worth more to the owners of the New York franchise than he was to an owner of a club in a smaller city; thus, franchises in low-drawing areas typically sold good players to the Yankees. The incentive for selling was often a matter of survival. The Washington Senators, Philadelphia Athletics, and St. Louis Browns repeatedly unloaded star players to the richer clubs. According to economist James Quirk, from 1920 to 1950, while the Yankees spent $1.6 million for talent, the St. Louis Browns sold a platoon of players for some $2.5 million. Had the Browns not sold these players, they would have lost $1.5 million in revenue.[18]

One franchise, the St. Louis Cardinals, under the direction of their brilliant general manager Branch Rickey, devised an ingenious method of avoiding expensive player purchases and offsetting some of the advantages enjoyed by the clubs in the larger market areas. Rickey's solution was the farm system. When Rickey joined the Cardinals in 1917, the franchise was poverty-stricken. Rickey slowly but methodically purchased direct ownership of minor-league clubs; by 1940 the Cardinal system contained thirty-two clubs and 700 players. The Rickey system produced remarkable results. The Cardinals won nine league championships between 1926 and 1946 and took second place six times. Despite having lower attendance marks than four other National League franchises in this era, the Cardinals had larger profits than any other league club. Their profits came mostly from player sales. While not purchasing a single player between 1919 and 1945, the Cardinals, in one year alone, had sixty-five players who were products of their farm system on the rosters of other big-league clubs. Owners of the other clubs resisted the ownership of minor-league clubs, believing that the costs exceeded the benefits. But as the success of the Rickey system became evident, they too began to emulate St. Louis.

Despite the establishment of a commissioner's office, the introduction of the Big Bang style of play, and ostensible efforts to equalize competition on the playing field, evidence suggests that in the 1920s professional baseball declined in popularity in comparison to other forms of leisure activity. True, in the 1920s professional baseball (including the minor leagues) attracted more fans than any other single sport, and millions followed the game in the newspapers. But the total attendance failed to keep pace with the growth of the population. In the eleven cities which hosted major-league teams, the population climbed 20.5 percent in the twenties while attendance at ball games grew by only 11.5 percent.

[18]Ray Kennedy and Nancy Williamson, "Money: The Monster Threatening Sports," *Sports Illustrated*, 49 (July, 1978), 80.

The same trend appears to be valid for the minor leagues; the total number of professional leagues remained under the figures attained in the pre-World War I era. By contrast, attendance at motion picture theaters in the 1925–1930 era was 75 percent greater than during the preceding five-year period. While an estimated twenty million fans attended all professional baseball games in 1930, approximately 90 million patrons attended the movies each week.[19]

Professional baseball suffered heavily from the Great Depression and World War II. Attendance did not fully recover until 1946; it then enjoyed a temporary boom until 1949 when it entered another "famine era." There were great players aplenty in the thirties and forties—Hank Greenburg, Ted Williams, Joe DiMaggio, and Stan Musial, to name a few—but none had the magic of Babe Ruth. The introduction of night baseball in the late 1930s failed to produce immediate increases in attendance. Only a few clubs prospered. The "have-not" franchises promoted a profit-sharing scheme, but it was voted down by the wealthier clubs. "I found out a long time ago that there is no charity in baseball," Jacob Ruppert, owner of the Yankees, explained, "and that every club owner must make his own fight for existence."[20] The magnates did take effective action in reducing player salaries. Salaries had risen from an average of about $5,000 in 1923 to about $7,000 in 1933; by 1936 the average had fallen to $4,500. Wide disparities existed between franchises. The payroll of the Yankees, for instance, was almost five times that of the lowly St. Louis Browns.

In the face of the great economic crisis of the 1930s, professional baseball experimented with new ways to recoup lost fan support. Beginning in 1933 the major leagues scheduled an annual All-Star game between the best players of each league. Larry MacPhail, general manager of the Cincinnati Reds, daringly departed from some of the staid traditions of baseball. At Cincinnati, MacPhail introduced night baseball (1935), red uniforms, cigarette girls in satin pants, and usherettes. Such innovations led a sportswriter to predict that, when MacPhail arrived in Brooklyn in 1937, fans would be treated to the spectacle of a "merry-go-round in center field of Flatbush." MacPhail's promotional gimmicks, however, paled beside those of Bill Veeck, who, in the post-World War II era, once employed a midget as a pinch hitter.

MacPhail, more than any other single person, broke down big-league resistance to radio broadcasts of games. Although in the 1920s the Chicago Cubs had permitted all of the club's games to be broadcast and the club had experienced a sharp increase in attendance, most clubs feared that radio broadcasts would reduce attendance. In 1934 the Yankees, Giants, and Dodgers, all

---

[19]Jesse Frederick Steiner, *Americans at Play: Recent Trends in Recreation and Leisure Time Activities* (New York, 1933), pp. 84, 86, 109–10; John R. Tunis, "Changing Trends in Sports," *Harper's Monthly Magazine*, 70 (Dec. 1934), 80. There is also evidence that participation in amateur and semiprofessional baseball declined in the 1920s. See Alexander J. Young, Jr., "The Rejuvenation of Major League Baseball in the Twenties," *Canadian Journal of History of Sport and Physical Education*, 3 (1972), 24.

[20]Quoted in Voigt, *American Baseball*, II, 251.

located in New York, even signed a formal ban on the broadcasts of their games. But as radio stations and networks discovered that they could sell commercials during the broadcasts (and thus pay clubs for broadcast privileges) resistance weakened. When MacPhail came to Brooklyn as general manager he refused to renew the ban on baseball broadcasts in New York; he sold the rights to Dodger games for $70,000. Consequently, the Yankees and Giants felt compelled to permit the broadcasts of their games as well. Increased income from radio, especially in the larger market areas, offset some of the loss of gate receipts. By 1950 each club averaged $210,000 from broadcast rights.[21]

BLACK BASEBALL

Given the abysmally low incomes of the vast majority of blacks, the ghettos supported a surprisingly rich sporting life. As in white neighborhoods prior to the 1950s, baseball was by far the most popular sport. Every ghetto featured several black semiprofessional or professional teams. Sometimes local industries sponsored teams, but often blacks themselves organized and managed the teams. At the higher levels of play, black gamblers, especially those in the numbers racket, formed clubs. In Pittsburgh during the 1930s Gus Greenlee, that city's numbers king, poured massive amounts of money into his professional baseball team. Likewise black gamblers bankrolled teams in (among other cities) Newark, New York, Philadelphia, Baltimore, and Nashville.[22]

Grounded in the patronage furnished by the ghettos of the larger cities, several black professional baseball leagues rose and fell. In 1920, Rube Foster, a star pitcher and manager of the Chicago American Giants, formed the Negro National League comprised of teams in Detroit, Indianapolis, Kansas City, St. Louis, and two teams in Chicago, but the Great Depression temporarily killed the league in 1931. In 1933, the league re-formed, and four years later, became the Negro American League. The Negro leagues achieved their greatest prosperity in the 1940s when all-star games filled major league parks to capacity and teams frequently attracted as many as 5,000 (nearly all black) fans to regular season weekend contests. The success of the black teams in off-season exhibition games with white teams indicated that many of the players were of major league caliber, but for most white fans, such black superstars as Leroy "Satchel" Page and Josh Gibson toiled in total obscurity. The gradual integration of white baseball after 1945 eventually spelled the end of the black leagues.

[21]Richard C. Crepeau, *Baseball: America's Diamond Mind, 1919–1941* (Orlando, FL, 1980), pp. 112–13; Benjamin G. Rader, *In Its Own Image: How Television Has Transformed Sports* (New York, 1984), pp. 25–26.

[22]See esp. Robert Patterson, *Only the Ball Was White* (Englewood Cliffs, NJ, 1970); Donn Rogosin, *Invisible Men: Life in Baseball's Negro Leagues* (New York, 1973); Jules Tygiel, *Baseball's Great Experiment: Jackie Robinson and His Legacy* (New York, 1983), Chap. 2; and Rob Ruck, *Sandlot Seasons: Sport in Black Pittsburgh* (Urbana, 1987).

The Negro leagues were never as central to black baseball as the major leagues were to white baseball. Of some 200 games played by each black team in a season, only a third were league games. Ghetto residents simply did not have enough discretionary income to support talented black leagues. Thus, to survive, the black teams had to engage in barnstorming. While traveling throughout the United States, Central America, and the Caribbean, they played other black professional teams, local semipro teams (both black and white), and ad hoc major league barnstorming teams. The game played by barnstorming teams was skillful, but showmanship was also an essential ingredient of black baseball. Although successful in catching fans' interest, the stunts and comedy of the black teams reinforced the negative stereotypes of blacks held by white fans.

11

INTERCOLLEGIATE FOOTBALL SPECTACLES

No football team exceeded the "Fighting Irish" of Notre Dame in attaining a national following and fervent fan support. Beginning in the 1920s, Catholics everywhere, even those who had never been near a college (dubbed by sportswriters as "the subway alumni") and regardless of ethnic origins, became rabid fans of the Irish. When Notre Dame met Army in their annual tilt in New York, the passions of the city's large ethnic population reached a fever pitch. "New York was never before, or since, so sweetly gay and electric as when Rock [Knute Rockne] brought his boys to town," Paul Gallico wrote. "The city was wild with excitement."[1] As a minority within a predominately Protestant culture, the nation's Roman Catholic population found a source of identity and pride in the successes of the Fighting Irish.

Apart from evoking the support of a burgeoning college community of students, alumni, professors, and townspeople, college teams elsewhere also generated symbols that transcended the colleges themselves. Citizens in states without conspicuously significant history, great civic monuments, or remarkable physical scenery often formed strong emotional bonds to their state university football teams. Likewise, contests between teams located in the South and the North, the East and the West, and so on, evoked regional loyalties. The World Wars supplied ready-made cheering sections for the two service academies. Those who had worn khakis in the wars supported Army; bell-bottoms made one

[1]Paul Gallico, *The Golden People* (New York, 1965), p. 142.

a Navy rooter. In time, the annual Army–Navy game generated far more national interest than the classic Yale–Harvard contests.[2]

Yet the popularity of intercollegiate football in the 1890–1950 era rested on more than an intrinsic power to engender fierce loyalty. To hold fans' interest, the custodians of the sport experimented with rule-changes; these included the adoption of the all-important forward pass in 1906. To win games, the coaches devised innovative formations and plays; these included Knute Rockne's famed Notre Dame Box in the 1920s and Clark Shaughnessy's revolutionary T formation in the 1940s. In order to still criticism of the sport's departures from amateur traditions, to reduce unseemly squabbling among the colleges, and to establish equal conditions of competition among the football powers, the colleges formed associations including regional conferences and the National Collegiate Athletic Association (NCAA).

THE CRITICAL ERA

The two decades preceding 1910 marked the most critical era in intercollegiate football's history. While the sport was being institutionalized within the confines of colleges, the defenders of football confronted both a national crusade to abolish or reform the sport and grave obstacles in developing orderly relationships among the teams. Heated controversies arose over the appearance of the professional coach and the eligibility, recruitment, and subsidization of players. Above all, deaths and injuries suffered as a result of playing the game touched off a great national debate about the merits of the sport.

Much of the controversy revolved around the gap between principle and practice. Officially, those associated with the college community asserted that the game ought to be an athlete-centered affair that adhered to the conventions of upper class English sport. The athletes should play for personal enjoyment and their love for the college rather than for pay, and the game should never become so serious that it resulted in behavior unsuitable for gentlemen. Apart from the weight of custom, the ideal of pristine amateurism had its practical uses as well. Not only did amateurism encourage patrons of the sport to believe, or sense, that the spirit of the college game differed from comparable professional sporting spectacles, but problems that might have arisen between the colleges as "employers" and the athletes as "employees" could be more easily avoided.

[2]No adequate treatment of the intercollegiate football spectacle exists for the entire 1890–1950 era, but for scholarly studies of the 1890–1920 era see Ronald A. Smith, *Sports and Freedom: The Rise of Big-Time College Athletics* (New York, 1988); Patrick Bryant Miller, "Athletes in Academe: College Sports and American Culture, 1850–1920," unpub. Ph.D. diss., University of California, Berkeley, 1987; and Guy Maxton Lewis, "The American Intercollegiate Football Spectacle, 1869–1917," unpub. Ph.D. diss., University of Maryland, 1964.

Unlike English college sports, informal sanctions were utterly ineffective in controlling American college athletics. With most college students coming from the upper social strata, English college sports inherited class traditions that established effective behavioral boundaries. But in the United States many colleges competed for both eminence and students, and, even though nearly all of the students came from families with high incomes, they possessed few established customs to curtail a winning-at-all-costs approach to sports. Indeed, they brought to the gridiron the values of the marketplace. "The spirit of American youth, as of the American man, is to win, to 'get there,' by fair means or foul," observed a *Nation* writer in 1890, "and the lack of moral scruple which pervades the struggles of the business world meets with temptations equally irresistible in the miniature contests of the football field."[3]

One temptation was to use the best athletes available, regardless of their status as students. As early as the 1860s and 70s, northeastern colleges had hired professional rowers to become members of their crews. But before football became a serious campus activity, few objected to allowing anyone connected with the college to play the sport. As late as 1900 in some parts of the South and West townspeople and younger faculty members sometimes joined the teams as players. In the 1898 championship game, Virginia accused North Carolina of employing two professional stars but raised no questions as to the eligibility of Professor Edward V. Howell, who scored the winning touchdown for the North Carolina eleven. Some students "grew old" while playing football. After having played four years while pursuing a baccalaureate degree, they might continue to play while enrolled in professional or graduate programs. This practice resulted in intense controversies for years among the northeastern colleges before finally being resolved in the first decade of the twentieth century.

Obtaining and retaining players tempted athletic associations to extend to superior athletes special favors or outright subsidies. In 1900 Pennsylvania State College apparently became the first school to officially offer scholarships of tuition, room, and board to athletes. More commonly, the associations extended sub rosa aid to the players. Each fall in the 1890s so-called "tramp" athletes offered their services to the highest bidder. With some exaggeration, Caspar W. Whitney claimed in 1895 that in the Middle and Far West "men are bought and sold like cattle to play this autumn on 'strictly amateur' elevens."[4] At best, the tramps maintained only the vaguest of pretenses of being bona fide students; sometimes they played on the teams of more than one school during the same fall season.

Professionalism existed in the prestigious colleges of the Northeast as well. In 1905, *McClure's* magazine reported that James J. Hogan, the renowned captain of the Yale team, lived in a style befitting a prince. He enjoyed free tuition, a free suite in the swank Vanderbilt Hall, a $100 scholarship, a ten-day vacation to Cuba paid for by the Yale Athletic Association, a monopoly on the sale of

[3]"The Future of Football," *Nation*, 51 (Nov. 20, 1890), 395. See also Allen L. Sack, "Yale 29–Harvard 4: The Professionalization of College Football," *Quest*, 19 (1973), 24–34.
[4]*Literary Digest* 12 (Nov. 30, 1895), 128.

scorecards at games, and the exclusive commission for handling the products of the American Tobacco Company on the Yale campus. Apparently, the students took Hogan's good fortunes in stride, for they affectionately spoke of smoking "Hogan's cigarettes."[5]

Compared to the post-World War II era of jet air travel when professional full-time coaches acted also as recruiters, recruitment methods before 1920 were primitive. Nonetheless, promising players were sought out, usually in haphazard ways, by students, alumni, captains, and coaches. The elite northeastern colleges recruited mostly from the exclusive preparatory schools; thus Harvard's rosters abounded with the names of old-stock, patrician New England families. But in the 1890s, as football became more serious, Irish and German names began to appear in the lineups of northeastern colleges. In 1892 and 1893 Walter Camp even named William H. Lewis, a black player from Harvard, to his "All-America" team. State colleges sought players more frequently from their general student bodies or the public high schools.

The employment of a professional coach was yet another way to enhance the prospects of winning. Since the 1860s, crew, track and field, and baseball players had from time to time hired professional coaches, but they did not become commonplace in football until the 1890s. Early in the twentieth century, even Harvard, which had attempted more than most other schools to imitate the English system of athletics, resorted to a full-time professional coach. Embarrassed by the team's abysmal record against Yale, in 1905 the Harvard Athletic Committee offered Bill Reid a $7,000 package, which at that time was nearly twice the average salary for a Harvard professor. Reid promptly set out to bring order and rationality to the Harvard program. He carefully monitored the academic performance of his players, organized winter workouts using weights and wrestling, kept a card file on all 4,000 Harvard students as potential recruits, and scheduled weaker teams early in the season so that the Crimson could "lick [its] opponents in increasing strength as the season progressed and as [the] team developed."[6] The stress of coaching nearly destroyed Reid; his weight fell and, in order to obtain sleep, he turned to drink and drugs. Even though he lost only three games in two years, he viewed his coaching stint "as a failure." Two of his three losses had been to archrival Yale.

The arrival of the professional coach altered the experiences of the players. "Players like to win," observed a former Yale player in 1904, "but head coaches and especially paid coaches, had to win."[7] To win, the coaches drove their players relentlessly; they subjected them to countless repetition of the same plays, verbal harangues, and strict diets. "What has become of the natural, spontaneous joy of the contest?" asked Owen Johnson through a fictional character early in the century. "Instead you have the most perfectly organized

---

[5]Henry Beach Needham, "The College Athlete," *McClure's Magazine*, 25 (1905), 115–28, 260–73.

[6]Quoted in Smith, *Sports and Freedom*, p. 160.

[7]Quoted in ibid., p. 147.

business systems for achieving the required result—success. Football is driving slavish work."[8] The players hated the practices but loved the adoration heaped upon them on Saturday afternoons. No doubt Yale athletes also enjoyed their training table, which featured a choice of beefsteak or mutton for dinner, washed down with ample quantities of milk, ale, or sherry.

THE FORMATION OF CONFERENCES

Providing for uniformity in eligibility, recruitment, subsidization, and the employment of professional coaches was a formidable task. Reluctant to abandon the illusion that college football was an amateur affair, the custodians of football failed to organize an economic cartel strong enough to impose and enforce uniform rules or equalize the conditions of competition. Thus each school was free to govern its sports as it saw fit.

Internally, the colleges by 1900 had instituted three main types of self-control: student control with little or no external interference from faculty but often a strong alumni influence (as at Yale and Princeton); joint faculty/alumni/student control (as at Harvard); faculty control with various groups, including professional coaches, exercising a major influence (as at most of the colleges in the Midwest and the South). Since the self-imposed controls frequently failed to ensure harmony within the college ranks, colleges could resort to another method; they could simply refuse to play those schools that blatantly ignored the conventions of amateur sports. Such an informal regulatory system checked some of the excesses of college football programs.

Externally, the colleges increasingly turned to the formation of athletic conferences as a means of regulating sports. Students had formed the first intercollegiate association in 1858 when Harvard, Yale, Brown, and Trinity organized the College Rowing Association. Eventually the students also formed associations in baseball, football, and track and field. Beginning in 1895 with the organization of the Intercollegiate Conference of Faculty Representatives, later known as the Western Conference, and even later as the Big Ten, which was initially composed of the large midwestern universities of Chicago, Illinois, Purdue, Michigan, Minnesota, and Northwestern, college presidents took the initiative in attempting to bring a higher degree of order to intercollegiate athletic relations. From its founding, the conference conceived of itself as the "anchor of amateur athletics in America." The conference pioneered in the establishment of rules of eligibility, prohibition of subsidies to student athletes, and the faculty supervision of athletes—measures subsequently copied by other conferences. The Conference of Faculty Representatives had one major weakness: it left enforcement in the hands of faculty committees of the member institutions.

Faculty athletic committees by no means guaranteed that a college's sports program would adhere to strictly amateur principles. Edward S. Jordan,

[8]Quoted in Brooks Mather Kelley, *Yale: A History* (New Haven, 1974), p. 298.

after an examination of college football in 1905, flatly asserted that "faculty control is a myth."[9] In the first two decades of the twentieth century at the typical college, the faculty, regardless of its stated powers, shared the actual supervision of sports with coaches, presidents, trustees, and the alumni. Any of these groups might thwart faculty control. Moreover, for the most part, the faculties were just as interested in the success of the football team as any other group. Frequently, presidents handpicked sympathetic faculty members to sit on athletic committees and to represent the university at conference meetings, and even when a committee member had a firm commitment to player-centered ideals, he faced the problem of familiarizing himself with the intricacies of the institution's athletic programs while fulfilling his regular obligations. Finally, for a faculty representative to challenge prevailing athletic practices usually meant subjecting himself to exceptionally hostile reactions from football fans both inside and outside of the college.

An instance involving the University of Michigan and its football coach, Fielding H. "Hurry Up" Yost, illustrates the problems of faculty control. Before coming to Michigan, Yost had won a reputation for his recruiting talents. He liked experienced players. The star of his undefeated Kansas team of 1899, for example, had played five years at the University of West Virginia and one year as a professional before joining the Jayhawk squad. A Kansas "purity" campaign resulted in Yost's ouster after the 1899 season. Then Yost went to Stanford. David Starr Jordan, the president of Stanford, later related the following story:

> A young fellow came in from the mines who wanted to study mining engineering—a tremendously big and strong fellow. He was admitted because of certain symptoms of earnestness he showed—admitted as a special student. . . . [He] failed in his studies, and was dropped. Yost carried him to Michigan, where he has become the center of the strong team which is the pride of Michigan University; and this man, who was not able to pass any examinations [while at Stanford]. . . has been playing some ten or fifteen games a year at Michigan. . . . All of us who have ever had a Yost or any Yost-like man about are not to be counted as sinless.[10]

Yost recruited other players for Michigan besides the "tremendously big and strong fellow" from the mines. When he came to Michigan in 1901, he brought with him several experienced western players, including Willie Heston, a college graduate of San Jose State who was later to be named to many all-time, all-American teams. Heston, as a law student, played four seasons with the Wolverines, finally retiring after seven years in the college ranks. The enthusiastic alumni of Michigan cooperated fully with Yost in recruiting, keeping the

[9]Edward S. Jordan, "Buying Football Victories," *Colliers*, 36 (Nov. 18, 1905), 23. See also Howard J. Savage, et. al., *American College Athletics* (New York, 1929), pp. 100–01 and Lewis, "The American Intercollegiate Football Spectacle," p. 197.

[10]*School Review*, 11 (1903), 344. See also Wilfred B. Shaw, "Michigan and the Conference: A Ten Year Argument Over the University's Athletic Relations," *Michigan Alumnus*, 54 (1947), 34–48.

football players eligible, and providing subsidies to the star athletes, all of which violated the spirit of Western Conference rules. The results were phenomenal. From 1901 through the 1905 season Michigan lost only one contest. "The words 'Yost' and 'Michigan' were synonymous," concluded one historian of the university. "The newspapers regarded the whole institution as the backdrop for the football squad."[11]

A new set of conference rules in 1906, adopted in response to the national football crisis and apparently as a means of curbing the abuses of Michigan, threatened to emasculate Yost's high-powered program. (Ironically, President James G. Angell of Michigan was a major proponent of change.) First, the conference restricted the eligibility of the players to three years, which, since the rule was retroactive, would have excluded several of Yost's top performers. Second, the conference limited competition to undergraduates, which would have prevented one of Yost's favorite ploys, the use of experienced students in professional or graduate schools at key positions. Third, the conference required that coaches be regular members of the staff with a salary commensurate with their professorial rank. Yost was not a regular member of the staff and was paid more than any professor on the Michigan campus.

The Michigan faculty quickly approved the rule changes, but the students and alumni protested bitterly. They believed that the conference rules had been designed specifically to curtail the success of the Michigan team. The university regents responded by abolishing the faculty committee responsible for athletics and substituting a new Board of Athletic Control, a body solely responsible to the regents. Since games with Michigan produced lucrative revenues, the other Western Conference schools relented on most of the rule changes, but they refused to sustain the action of the Michigan regents in totally denying the principle of faculty control. With neither side willing to concede on this issue, Michigan withdrew from the conference in 1908.

Michigan's experience outside the Western Conference and its subsequent readmission in 1917 reflected the power and influence of the commercial interests in football. After dropping out of the conference, Michigan had difficulty scheduling games with major opponents. Receipts from football and the prestige of the team declined sharply. In 1917 Professor Ralph W. Aigler, an ardent Michigan football enthusiast, explored ways by which the university might be readmitted to the Western Conference. After visiting most of the conference schools, Aigler reported that what constituted faculty control varied widely from one university to the next. Michigan should be able to meet conference rules, he suggested, by giving the Faculty Senate veto power over the actions of the regents' Board of Athletic Control. The regents acquiesced. Recognizing the potential revenue growth that would accompany Michigan's readmission to the conference, the other schools quickly welcomed the Wolverines (complete with Yost as head coach) back into the fold.

[11]Quoted in Lewis, "The American Intercollegiate Football Spectacle," p. 211.

BRUTALITY AND THE REVOLUTION OF 1906

The commercialization, the seriousness, and disputes over eligibility and recruitment did not arouse as much public controversy as the issue of brutality. Since the 1880s, football had periodically been the subject of public outcries against its violent character. Deliberate slugging and kicking, both representing abrupt departures from the gentlemanly traditions of English rugby, plus the widespread use of mass plays in the 1890s intensified public criticism. In 1897 the state legislature of Georgia, after the death of a player in a college game in that state, even abolished football, but the governor vetoed the measure. Criticism of football reached a peak in 1905 and 1906, when muckraking journals, such as *McClure's, Collier's,* and *Outlook,* published a series of scathing exposés, revealing in shocking detail the absence of gentlemanly behavior and the "insidious" role of money in the sport. In order to ensure victories, according to the journals, teams often tried to "knock out" key opposing players early in the game.

In 1905 President Theodore Roosevelt decided to intervene in the controversy. The President had long been obsessed with physical fitness; he feared above all else that boys born into luxury would be effeminate. Football was a healthy antidote, teaching "pluck, endurance, and physical address." Roosevelt had a special interest in the Harvard eleven. His son was a member of the squad, and the President often sent the team letters of encouragement. Endicott Peabody, the distinguished headmaster of Groton School, was the immediate stimulus for Roosevelt's action. The masters of the elite prep schools along the East Coast were concerned that their boys tended to emulate the improper behavior of the college players. Peabody urged the President to "get the coaches of Harvard and Yale and Princeton together, and persuade them to undertake to teach men to play football honestly."[12]

Roosevelt agreed, but he had no intention of opening the conference to a full-fledged debate on the merits of college football. He invited only selected coaches, faculty, and alumni from the Big Three—Harvard, Yale, and Princeton—to attend the conference. His expressed hope was "to get them to come to a gentlemen's agreement not to have mucker play." Those who wanted a more open style of play and those who wanted to eliminate or reduce the commercial dimensions of the sport found themselves excluded from the conference. Walter Camp of Yale, leader of the forces demanding essentially the status quo in college football, immediately took charge. The delegates submitted to the President a mild statement promising to eliminate unnecessary "roughness, holding, and

---

[12]Ibid., 223–24. See also Smith, *Sports and Freedom,* Chap. 14; John Hammond Moore, "Football's Ugly Decades, 1893–1913," *Smithsonian Journal of History,* 2 (1967), 49–68; Roberta Park, "From Football to Rugby—and Back, 1906–1919: The University of California-Stanford Response to the Football Crisis of 1905," *Journal of Sport History,* 11 (1984), 15–40; and the official history of the NCAA, Jack Falla, *NCAA: The Voice of College Sports* (Mission, KS, 1981).

foul play." The President, satisfied with the resolution, urged its immediate release to the press.*

The White House football conference failed to still the critics of the sport. While *The New York Times* hailed Roosevelt's accomplishment as a feat equal to his success in mediating the Russo-Japanese War, President Charles W. Eliot of Harvard noted that those who drafted the resolution were the very persons most responsible for the abuses. And play in the 1905 season continued to be as brutal as ever. The *Chicago Tribune* dramatically reported that eighteen college and secondary students had lost their lives and 159 men had been injured in the 1905 season. The issue of brutality helped coalesce the forces demanding reform.

Several colleges took drastic action. Columbia and the Massachusetts Institute of Technology abolished the sport; Stanford and California substituted rugby for football. The Western Conference limited schools to five games, outlawed training tables, and restricted competition to undergraduates. Even Harvard, Yale, and Princeton banned freshmen and graduate students from varsity play. The final blow came late in the 1905 season when Harold P. Moore, a Union College player, died in a game with New York University. Henry B. McCracken, the chancellor of New York University, promptly called for a conference of college presidents representing schools on New York University's schedule. McCracken recognized that fundamental changes in football would not come from Walter Camp's rules committee. "I would not intrust the reformation of the game to the present Rules Committee," he flatly asserted.[13]

At this point, the proponents of a more open style of play seized upon the reform impulse in an effort to make football an even more exciting sport for spectators. The world of college football had for some time been split into two warring factions. One wanted to retain the sport as it existed and the other sought rule changes that would encourage more offensive action. Walter Camp's Intercollegiate Rules Committee, a self-constituted body representing a select group of northeastern schools plus the University of Chicago, staunchly defended the status quo. They conceded only the need to reduce foul play and brutality. The midwestern faction, led mostly by professional coaches whose tenure depended upon the financial returns from football, advocated radical rule changes that would increase the appeal of the sport to spectators. They wanted a game that featured long runs, more scoring, and the greater likelihood of upsets. Only the desire to schedule interregional contests had prevented a complete rupture with the Intercollegiate Rules Committee prior to 1906.

The representatives of the thirteen colleges that attended McCracken's conference on December 8, 1905, in New York did not even debate the possibility of abolishing the sport. Instead, they called for a national college convention and the formation of a new rules committee. Delegates from sixty-two colleges,

---

*There is a legend that Roosevelt threatened to abolish college football by executive order. Apart from the dubious constitutionality of such an action, there is no contemporary documentation that Roosevelt made such a threat. Moreover, such a threat would have been inconsistent with the President's numerous statements praising college football.

[13]Quoted in Lewis, "The American Intercollegiate Football Spectacle," p. 234.

representing all sections of the country, save the West Coast and the member colleges of Walter Camp's Rules Committee, met in New York on December 28, 1905. The convention quickly organized the Intercollegiate Athletic Association (IAA) with Captain Palmer E. Pierce of West Point as chairman and appointed its own rules committee. In 1910 the IAA became the National Collegiate Athletic Association (NCAA). The delegates gave no legislative or executive powers to the IAA, but did allow it to formulate standards of conduct for member colleges and the various conferences. Until the post-World War II era, the most important function of the NCAA was the creation of rules committees for college sports rather than regulation of the institution's athletic behavior.

The IAA convention still had to contend with Walter Camp. Creating a separate rules committee would not only offend the most powerful figure in college football, but might prevent the scheduling of interregional games. After a "stormy" nine-hour session, the convention agreed to explore the possibility of an amalgamated rules committee. With the urging of Roosevelt, delegates from Harvard and Navy finally broke ranks with the Intercollegiate Rules Committee. On January 12, 1906, the two rules committees held separate sessions in New York. After an exchange of notes, Camp's committee reluctantly acquiesced to a joint committee in which each group had equal representation. The joint arrangement continued until 1915, when Yale finally joined the NCAA.

In 1906, the new rules committee adopted a series of changes that it hoped would give the offense more freedom of action and reduce brutality. Rather than three attempts to gain five yards for a first down, the new rule provided for three downs to make ten yards. Supposedly, the additional yardage required for a first down would encourage teams to abandon the fashionable mass plays designed for short yardage gains. The committee also approved the forward pass, but placed severe restrictions on its use. The ball had to pass over the line of scrimmage five yards or more to the right or left of where it had been put into play, and an incomplete pass resulted in an automatic fifteen-yard penalty. With such strictures, only a foolish coach would make more than an occasional use of the pass. Whatever the consequences of these rule changes, the "Revolution of 1906," as it has been hailed, represented a ringing victory for those promoting football as a spectator-centered sport rather than those concerned with the preservation of the player-centered ideals of the sport. The midwestern coaches had taken a major step in making college football a bigger and more attractive spectacle.

The rule changes of 1906, however, failed to lead to an open game of wide end runs and numerous forward passes. The ten-yard rule and the limited utility of the pass led teams to engage in an even more conservative style of play. Most teams did not even bother to mount sustained offensive drives in their half of the field, but often kicked on first downs hoping for a mistake by the opposition. Play remained as brutal as ever; in 1909 thirty players (eight of them college men) lost their lives. The 1910 rules committee took more drastic action; it abolished interlocking interference and required at least seven offensive men on the line of scrimmage. (Nonetheless, between 1906 and 1946 over 500 athletes died from football injuries.) Over Camp's opposition, the committee liberalized the forward pass, allowing the ball to cross the line of scrimmage at any point. Two years later, the offense was given four downs to make ten yards, and the value of a touchdown was increased from five to six points.

The cumulative rule changes brought the "modern" game of football into existence. Slowly, the coaches, particularly in the West, began to exploit the potential of the forward pass. In 1913, when Notre Dame came East to play Army, the astonishing passes of Gus Dorais to Knute Rockne resulted in a stunning upset victory for the Irish. Later in the season the cadets profited from the disaster by using the "Western" passing game to defeat archrival Navy. After the 1913 season, coaches everywhere began to experiment with the forward pass. The custodians of college football had finally created an immensely exciting sport and had even brought a degree of order to the ranks of the college game.

THE GROWING POPULARITY OF INTERCOLLEGIATE FOOTBALL

In the 1920s and 1930s attendance at college football games grew at a much faster pace than the population. Between 1921 and 1930, attendance at all college games doubled and gate receipts tripled. Football's relative popularity shifted decidedly from the East to the Middle and Far West. Most of the crowds flocked to the games of only a few institutions; of the nearly 400 colleges playing football in 1930, forty of them drew about 60 percent of all of the fans. College football also weathered the Great Depression of the 1930s far better than professional baseball. In the early 1930s, attendance fell and several colleges dropped the sport, but estimates in 1937 placed total fandom at twenty million, a figure twice as high as that of 1930. Apparently college football attracted income groups that withstood the rigors of the Depression more successfully than did baseball fans.[14]

College football continued to take steps to increase the interest of spectators in the sport. In the 1920s, the colleges went on a stadium-building binge. Huge stadiums of concrete and steel reared above the landscape from Columbus, Ohio, to Los Angeles, California. Only one college field had a seating capacity of 70,000 in 1920; seven had in excess of that capacity in 1930. (By comparison, only two major-league baseball parks could seat 70,000 fans in 1930.)[15] The colleges also expanded their ballyhoo; they set up publicity bureaus to hawk the prowess of their teams, potential All-American players, and the wisdom of their head coaches. The colleges scheduled more intersectional and postseason games with teams they hoped would increase their "drawing power." The 1924 Notre Dame team traveled over 10,500 miles to play teams like Army, Princeton, Georgia Tech, Nebraska, and Stanford. Notre Dame was exceptional for its peripatetic ways, but all major colleges attempted to schedule at least one big intersectional game per season.

[14]See Jesse Frederick Steiner, *Americans at Play: Recent Trends in Recreation and Leisure Time Activities* (New York, 1933), 86–94; *New York Times*, Dec. 26, 1937.
[15]Steiner, *Americans at Play*, p. 91.

CONSTRUCTING A STADIUM OF STEEL AND CONCRETE, 1921
Both old and new technology were brought to the construction of this new
football stadium at the University of Nebraska. As monuments to the veterans
of World War I, the new stadia of the 1920s—most of which were called
"Memorial Stadium"—often identified college football with national patriotism.

The colleges tried to offer the fan a more exciting style of play. Like for baseball, the rulemakers attempted to shift the balance of strength from the defense to the offense. In 1927 the colleges moved the goal post ten yards in back of the goal line, thereby reducing the likelihood of field goals and encouraging efforts to score touchdowns. While the forward pass had been legalized in 1906, it had been surrounded by so many restrictions and potential penalties that teams rarely attempted to employ it. Gradually the rules were liberalized, though the last major restriction—the requirement that a forward pass must be made from at least five yards behind the scrimmage line—was not deleted until 1945. In 1912 the rulemakers reduced the circumference of the ball from 27 inches to 23 inches and in 1934 to 21 1/2 inches. The 1912 rule change encouraged the use of the spiral pass which could be thrown more accurately and longer distances.[16] In the twenties the pass-run option helped open up the game for more offensive action; it also enabled coaches to design more effective running formations. Speed, agility, and skill partly replaced sheer brawn as requirements for team success.

For students of the sport, college football offered a fascinating if somewhat bewildering variety of offensive formations and plays. Until 1940 most coaches employed some variation of the single wing, double wing, or Notre Dame box. All of these formations featured direct "hikes" from the center to the ball carrier (or passer) who stood several yards behind the line of scrimmage. The other backs (including the quarterback) blocked for the running back.

[16]John McCallum and Charles H. Pearson, *College Football U.S.A., 1869–1971* (New York, 1971), pp. 246–50.

Unlike the earlier mass formations which concentrated the attack somewhere near the center of the line, these three formations usually involved the ball carrier sweeping outside the tackles or ends. When successful, the plays could result in long gains. "There are no longer any distinctive systems in football," wrote Fielding H. Yost on the eve of the 1940 season. "Nobody sees a balanced line any more except at Notre Dame, and even some Rockne-trained coaches are getting away from it. There is only one formation that's any good and it's the single wing."[17] That very year, however, Clark Shaughnessey at Stanford introduced the "modern" T formation which rapidly replaced the single wing in popularity. All of the formations since then, be it the split T, pro set, power I, wishbone, or veer, essentially represent variations of the T.[18]

In baseball, heroes usually sprang from the ranks of the players, but in intercollegiate football the head coaches often won public renown. While football coaches like Amos Alonzo Stagg of the University of Chicago created virtual dynasties, players appeared on the field of play only three or four years and then sank into obscurity. In football, perhaps more than any other sport, coaches were the key to success or failure. To win consistently, teams with even superior talent required expert coaching. A slight change in the angle of a block, for instance, might spell the difference between victory or defeat. Under the leadership of a head coach, a staff of experts at the "big-time" football schools instructed linemen, ends, and backs in the intricacies of their positions. Some colleges used scouts, or "spies," a practice still frowned upon by many observers as being morally suspect, to observe the games of future opponents. On the basis of information gathered by the scouts plus an intimate knowledge of his own personnel, the coach carefully designed a preplanned strategy for accomplishing victory. Coaches tried to field teams that functioned like a precision, well-coordinated machine, with interchangeable parts and actions honed to the coach's design. Few private business firms could claim a more rational system for achieving their goals. Paradoxically, while bigtime college football achieved a remarkable degree of rationalization in the 1920s and 1930s, curious remnants of the player-centered era remained. For example, coaches could not "legally" transmit signals from the sidelines or send substitutes into the game with plays. The custodians of college football were reluctant to drop all pretenses of player-centeredness in the sport.

Coaches who succeeded won handsome rewards. Almost all college head coaches received a higher salary than the professors, and in some cases their salaries equalled or surpassed the college president's. According to a nationwide study made in 1929 by the Carnegie Commission, full professors averaged a salary of $5,158 annually, whereas head football coaches received an

[17]Quoted in Ron Fimrite, "A Melding of Men All Suited to a T," *Sports Illustrated*, 47 (Sept. 5, 1977), 92.
[18]Some dispute surrounds the invention of modern T formation. See George Halas with Gwen Morgan and Arthur Veysey, *Halas by Halas* (New York, 1979), pp. 136–45, 199–200.

average annual salary of $6,107. On the other hand, a losing head coach could expect a short tenure. The median tenure of all head coaches, according to the Carnegie study, was only three years.[19]

In the 1920 to 1950 era, such coaches as Knute Rockne of Notre Dame, Glenn S. "Pop" Warner of Pittsburgh, Stanford, and Temple, Robert Zuppke of Illinois, and Dana X. Bible of Texas A & M, Nebraska, and Texas won popular followings that often exceeded that of their star players. Rockne outdistanced all rivals in capturing the public imagination. Born in Norway, Rockne as a boy had immigrated with his family to Chicago. At the age of twenty-two, he "went down to South Bend with a suitcase and $1,000 feeling the strangeness of being a lone Norse-Protestant invader of a Catholic stronghold."[20] (Later Rockne converted to Catholicism.) At Notre Dame he compiled an outstanding academic record and won a certain fame as a pass receiver. After graduation, he remained at Notre Dame as a chemistry assistant and assistant football coach. In 1918, at the age of thirty, he landed the head coaching job at Notre Dame.

Rockne's fame stemmed from both his success on the field and his colorful personality. Sending his team against the best elevens from coast to coast, in thirteen years of coaching he compiled an enviable record of 105 victories, twelve defeats, and five ties. His team enjoyed five unbeaten and untied seasons. Rockne was as much a master of psychology as he was of football strategy. Both the players and the press loved him for his quick wit, humor, sarcasm, and ability to evoke pathos. While trailing Army by a touchdown in 1928, Rockne allegedly made the most memorable half-time speech in football history. He told of George Gipp, famed Notre Dame halfback, who had tragically died from pneumonia at the end of the 1920 season. Gipp instructed Rockne on his death bed: "When things are wrong and the breaks are beating the boys, tell them to go in there with all they've got and win one just for the Gipper."[21] In the second half, the Irish responded with two touchdowns, to win 12–6. In 1940 Warner Brothers retold the story in the popular film *Knute Rockne—All American*, in which Pat O'Brien played Rockne and Ronald Reagan played the Gipper. Rockne could be caustically hilarious. He reputedly told linemen: "The only qualification for a lineman is to be big and dumb." Then turning to the backs, he said: "To be a back, you only have to be dumb." He was always quotable, gregarious, and willing to hoist a few drinks with the sports writers. He won such acclaim that he had to hire a personal agent to answer his mail and handle his commercial endorsements. When Rockne died in a plane crash in 1931 he had allegedly just signed as sales promotion manager for Studebaker and had been offered $50,000 to play the coach in RKO's *Good News* movie.

[19]Savage, et. al., *American College Athletics*, pp. 171–72.

[20]Quoted in Edwin Pope, *Football's Greatest Coaches* (Atlanta, GA, 1955), p. 195.

[21]Ibid, pp. 189, 200. There are several versions of the Gipp story. See esp. "Scorecard," *Sports Illustrated*, 54 (Jan. 12, 1981), 7.

KNUTE "ROCK" ROCKNE (1888–1931)
First as a player, then as a coach, Rockne made Notre Dame synonymous with intercollegiate football. Catholic ethnics everywhere in the nation identified with Rockne's powerful teams of the 1920s.

CONTINUING INTERCOLLEGIATE CONTROVERSIES

Regardless of the skills of coaches, fielding winning teams consistently required the recruitment of high-quality athletes. As the 1920s began, many colleges recruited only in a haphazard fashion if at all. Even at such football powers as Notre Dame, perhaps half or more of the varsity squad obtained their positions simply by trying out for the team. Moreover, the open recruitment of football players violated the amateur code to which, in principle, the colleges universally adhered. Nonetheless, as the pressures to win became more intense, the temptation to recruit and even subsidize players became harder to resist. According to the Carnegie study of 1929, almost every major football power had intensive, highly organized recruiting systems. The colleges sent out thousands of letters to prospective athletes, invited some of them to campus for visits, and promised the better ones some sort of subsidy. However, unlike the post-1950 era, coaches did not travel about the country visiting high school athletes. To convince the player to attend their school rather than another, they relied mostly upon the college's alumni, the reputation of the college in football, and visits by the athlete to the college campus.

The intercollegiate programs employed ingenious and sometimes devious methods to subsidize athletes. Athletic departments offered a wide variety of job opportunities to the "needy" athletes; they might nominally work within the department dispensing towels, giving rubdowns, supervising intramural athletics, or pushing a broom. Athletes often obtained off-campus jobs; for example, in the 1930s, the Ohio State University track star Jesse Owens had a job operating an elevator in the State Capitol building in Columbus. Some colleges, especially those in the South and Southwest, avoided hypocrisy simply by granting direct "athletic scholarships." In a stunning understatement the Carnegie Commission report concluded: "Apparently the ethical bearing of intercollegiate football contests and their scholastic aspects are of secondary importance to the winning of victories and financial success."[22]

The commercialization, professionalization, and hypocrisy endemic to big-time college football, all signifying the ascendancy of the fan, evoked a running debate throughout the interwar years. One school of critics naively called for the voluntary compliance of the football schools to amateur principles. Consistent with this position, the NCAA relied entirely upon moral persuasion to discipline its membership. In contrast to the NCAA, the Western Athletic Conference (Big Ten), known for its self-proclaimed adherence to the amateur code, enjoyed the power to expel offending schools from the Conference. In 1922 the Conference, following the example of major-league baseball, created the position of Commissioner of Athletics, a post held by Major John L. Griffith until 1944. Yet Griffith's powers, unlike Landis's, were mostly nominal. Despite patent evidence of repeated violations of conference rules, the Big Ten did not bar a single member school from playing football in the 1920–1950 era.[23] After documenting a convincing case for the impossibility of devising a workable, voluntary system of compliance, the Carnegie Report of 1929 illogically called for college presidents and faculties to lead a crusade for institutional self-restraint.

College presidents and faculties were in a weak position to obtain compliance with traditional amateurism, even when they wanted to. So long as a football program avoided unseemly squabbles or public disclosures of blatant departures from amateurism, the public remained largely indifferent. Many people had a large emotional stake in the teams as well. Apart from the capacity of teams to cement together larger college communities and provide heroes for Americans to identify with, the colleges had a growing financial investment in football. By the 1930s many of them owed large sums of money for athletic plants and depended on the revenue from football for the support of other varsity sports. Henry S. Pritchett, who wrote the preface to the Carnegie Report of 1929 ought to have remembered what he had written in 1911. "Party politics," he then wrote, "have also played their part in the state institutions in the dismissal of men, notably of presidents who have stood . . . against the popular cry for . . . winning athletic teams."[24] As Blair Cherry, the head football coach at the

[22]Savage, et. al, *American College Athletics*, p. 298. The Carnegie survey, which took three and a half years to complete, was based on visits to and the accumulation of data from 130 colleges and secondary schools. It aroused a temporary national furor and remains the most thorough inquiry even conducted of intercollegiate athletics.

[23]See ibid, p. 229; Howard Roberts, *The Big Nine: The Story of Football in the Western Conference* (New York, 1948); Adryn Lowell Sponberg, "The Evolution of Athletic Subsidization in the Intercollegiate Conference of Faculty Representatives (Big Ten)," unpub. Ph.D. diss, University of Michigan, 1968. For the Big Eight Conference, see "What Football Players Are Earning This Fall," *Literary Digest*, 107 (Nov. 15, 1930), 28.

[24]Henry S. Pritchett, "Progress of State Universities," *Annual Report of the Carnegie Foundation for the Advancement of Teaching*, 6 (1911), p. 108.

University of Texas, bluntly put it: "In the final analysis the public, not the colleges, runs college football."[25]

A second school of critics recognized the power of those who had an enormous emotional or economic investment in intercollegiate football. But to them, football represented a serious misplacement of values and they demanded its complete abolition. Robert Maynard Hutchins, appointed president of the University of Chicago in 1929, led this school of critics. Hutchins rejected two major premises of American educational thought: the notion that education ought to be character-building and the pragmatic notion that truths were proximate and to be found through the interaction of speculation and experience. Instead Hutchins believed in a transcendental world of ultimate truths; the sole function of the university should be the development of the intellect for the perception of these higher truths. He thus rejected one of the principal, time-honored arguments for football, its alleged character-building function. To Hutchins, corruption was inevitable and unavoidable in big-time football. In 1939 he persuaded the trustees of the University of Chicago to abolish the sport.[26] This dramatic and highly publicized move had, however, little impact on the other colleges. Only those schools suffering from disastrous financial losses from football followed Chicago's example.

[25]Quoted in Harry T. Paxton, ed., *Sport U.S.A.: The Best From the Saturday Evening Post* (New York, 1961), p. 405.

[26]See Kooman Boycheff, "Intercollegiate Athletics and Physical Education at the University of Chicago, 1892–1952," unpub. Ph.D. diss., University of Michigan, 1954; John M. Hutchins, "Gate Receipts and Glory," *Saturday Evening Post*, 211 (Dec. 3, 1938), 23; Hal A. Lawson and Alan G. Ingham, "Conflicting Ideologies Concerning the University and Intercollegiate Athletics: Harper and Hutchins at Chicago, 1892–1940," *Journal of Sport History*, 7 (1980), 37–67.

12

THE CLUB SPORTS
GO PUBLIC

On September 16, 1926, the domination of William T. "Big Bill" Tilden over the world of tennis came to an end. During the quarterfinals of the national championships at the West Side Tennis Club, Forest Hills, New York, Tilden's six-year reign crumpled before the attack of a Frenchman, Henri Cochet, in five sets at 6–8, 6–1, 6–3, 1–6, 8–6. The spectators repeatedly broke into wild cheers in the final set. Trailing at 1–4, Tilden appeared to be on the verge of one of his patented comebacks. As he served with smashing force and volleyed crisply at the net, the crowd roared with applause at each of Tilden's winning shots. He pulled even at 4–4. "The champion, it was agreed, was still the champion of old, capable of lifting his game in an emergency to unassailable heights," according to one reporter. Both men held service for three games to give Tilden a 6–5 lead. Then the debacle came. Tilden won only four points in the last three games, conceding the final set 8–6. "Tilden, the invincible, whose magic with a racquet confounded the greatest players of the world and made America supreme in tennis, at last . . . relinquished his scepter."[1]

In the forty-five years separating Richard Sears's victory at the Newport Casino Club in the first national championship tournament and Cochet's dramatic upset of Tilden, tennis experienced a remarkable transformation. In the first instance, a small cadre of wealthy summer vacationers had casually followed the action. In 1926, over 7,000 gathered in the steel and concrete stadium of the West Side Tennis Club to watch each stroke, and newspapers all over the

---

[1] Allison Danzig and Peter Brandwein, eds., *The Greatest Sport Stories from The New York Times* (New York, 1951), pp. 256, 255.

world reported the upset in blazing headlines. The quality of play had improved sharply. The players at Newport had relied upon soft, looping shots; the serve had functioned merely to put the ball into play. Both Tilden and Cochet could hit smashing serves at over ninety miles an hour; from either the forehand or backhand side, they could hit deep, hard drives or they might hit deft drop shots. For Sears, tennis had been an avocation, but for Tilden and Cochet (although both were technically amateurs) tennis was a full-time endeavor. They played or practiced nearly every day. Tennis was an international sport that featured both men's and women's competitions. Top-flight players might travel to Italy, France, Germany, England, and Australia to play in tournaments. In short, tennis, like the other elite club sports of track and field and golf, went public. The spectators rather than the clubs became the ultimate determinants of the character of the sport.

TENNIS GOES PUBLIC

Before the 1920s, tennis showed few signs of going public. From the outset of its history, the sport had been associated with the English upper classes and rich Americans who played on their estates or in their exclusive clubs. In 1873, Major John Wingfield, an avid player of the ancient game of court tennis, popularized a game of lawn tennis in England. Soon thereafter the Marylebone Cricket Club in England and the All England Croquet Club at Wimbledon took up the game. Wimbledon held the first of its famous tournaments in 1877. Controversy surrounds the issue of when and who first introduced the game in the United States, but apparently two courts—in Staten Island, New York, and Nahant, Massachusetts—were built in 1874. The posh Newport Casino Club became the home of the United States Lawn Tennis Association (USLTA) in 1881 and served as the site of the first national tennis championships.

Association with elite clubs, women players, and the absence of brute physicality in the game were both blessings and handicaps. At the turn of the century even the term "lawn tennis" evoked images of prissy dudes in white flannels, pitter-pattering a ball across a net at Newport, Bar Harbor, or Seabright with lady friends. When several Harvard men "deserted" rowing for tennis in 1878, a *Harvard Crimson* editorial writer heaped scorn upon them. "Is it not a pity that serious athletics should be set aside by able-bodied men for a game that is at best intended for a seaside pastime?" he asked. "The game is well enough for lazy or *weak* men, but men who have rowed or taken part in a nobler sport should blush to be seen playing Lawn Tennis."[2] Paul Gallico recalled that during his childhood in New York in the early twentieth century "it was worth your life to be caught anywhere east of Lexington Avenue carrying a tennis racquet under

[2]Quoted in United States Lawn Tennis Association, *Official Encyclopedia of Tennis* (New York, 1972), p. 10. General histories of tennis include Will Grimsley, *Tennis* (Englewood Cliffs, NJ, 1971) and Angela Lumpkin, *Women's Tennis* (Troy, NY, 1981).

your arm." Invariably a player would be greeted by boys who hooted in falsetto voices: "Deuce, darling," or "Forty-love, dear."[3] Despite such verbal abuse, a few brave men played the sport, perhaps partly because of its popularity among the upper classes of England. By 1895, 106 clubs belonged to the USLTA. Then, primarily because of the sudden popularity of golf in the elite clubs, membership in the association fell sharply, not returning to the 1895 level until ten years later.

The early twentieth century witnessed harbingers of a new era of tennis. One was an increase in international competition. As early as the 1880s, Englishmen had invaded the Newport tournament and Americans had reciprocated by competing at Wimbledon; such visits became common in the first two decades of the twentieth century. In 1900, a wealthy Harvard player, Dwight F. Davis, encouraged national rivalries by establishing the International Lawn Tennis Challenge Cup (Davis Cup). In the pre-World War I era, teams from the United States, England, and later Australia and New Zealand competed annually for the cup. Until the 1960s, the Davis Cup was one of the most coveted prizes in international competition. In 1909, Maurice McLaughlin, a flashing redhead from San Francisco, brought a new brand of tennis to Newport. His power and speed, learned on the fast, hard-surfaced courts of California, excited an interest never before felt in the East.[4] Finally, the transfer of the national championships in 1915 from Newport to the West Side Tennis Club at Forest Hills, a section of Queens in New York City, reflected the determination of the USLTA to attract a larger audience. In 1923 the West Side Tennis Club built the first modern tennis facility in the United States, which seated 14,000 spectators.

The turning point for tennis as a public spectacle came in the 1920s with the appearance of two outstanding players: Big Bill Tilden and Suzanne Lenglen.[5] The victory of Lenglen in the women's singles at Wimbledon in 1919 and Tilden's triumph in men's singles at Forest Hills in 1920 marked the beginning of an age in which tennis players could become public celebrities. Both Lenglen and Tilden combined superb athletic performances with colorful personalities. Between 1919 and 1926, Lenglen took six titles at Wimbledon, while Tilden won the same number at Forest Hills. Tilden, a tall, gaunt egotist, shared the limelight of men's tennis with no one. Lenglen, glamorous and equally controversial, held sway just as imperiously over women's tennis.

High-caliber play combined with a tempestuous personality contributed to Lenglen's celebrity status. For Lenglen, tennis had never been a dainty, social sport. She was probably the first player in tennis history to be systematically groomed for championship play. Born to a well-to-do family, her early potential for the game was recognized by her father and he decided to make her a champion. At the age of fourteen she won the French Hard Courts championship

[3]Paul Gallico, *The Golden People* (Garden City, NY, 1965), p. 64.

[4]Lewis R. Freeman, "Why California Tennis Players Win," *Outing*, 65 (1914), 22–31.

[5]For Lenglen and Tilden see esp. Allison Danzig and Peter Brandwein, eds. *Sport's Golden Age: A Close-up of the Fabulous Twenties* (New York, 1948), pp. 208–27; Frank Deford, *Big Bill Tilden: The Triumphs and the Tragedies* (New York, 1975); Larry Englemann, *The Goddess and the American Girl: The Story of Suzanne Lenglen and Helen Wills* (New York, 1988).

and in 1919 made her debut at Wimbledon, the world center of tennis. In winning the championship, she completely captivated English fans, including King George V and Queen Mary. No previous woman player had been so uninhibited. "I just throw dignity to the winds," she reportedly said, "and think of nothing but the game."[6] She had sex appeal. Though lacking in facial beauty, she had a figure that could have adorned the stage. She wore daring, low-cut, one-piece dresses with hemlines slightly below the knees permitting an occasional glimpse of her thighs. To tennis fans, accustomed to seeing women players bounded by corseted waists, long-sleeved blouses, and skirts with padded petticoats, Lenglen's attire was daringly risqué.

Lenglen's most famous and most publicized match was her meeting with Helen Wills at Cannes in 1926. In the finals at Forest Hills in 1923, the sixteen-year-old Wills had routed Molla Mallery, the reigning American champion. "Little Miss Poker Face," as Wills was dubbed by the sportswriters, went on to win six more singles titles at Forest Hills and eight British championships at Wimbledon. Americans rallied behind her as the new women's champion of the world. Although no title of consequence was at stake at Cannes, the match created more excitement than any tennis contest until Billie Jean King played Bobby Riggs in 1973. Seats for the contest sold out far in advance; from all over France and England enthusiasts came to see the "women's tennis match of the century." Hundreds perched on neighboring house tops and in the trees near the court. The atmosphere resembled that of a heavyweight championship fight more than the finals of a staid tennis tournament. Lenglen won in a close, rugged contest 6–3, 8–6, and the French hailed her as the "Jeanne d'Arc of tennis." That was the only match in which the two queens of tennis met. Lenglen left the amateur ranks in 1926 to become a professional player, and Wills dominated amateur play into the early 1930s.

Unlike Lenglen, Bill Tilden was slow to develop into a championship player. From a once socially prominent Philadelphia family whose status had slipped downward, Tilden learned his tennis at the Germantown Cricket Club. Remarkably, even for his day, he did not become a master of the sport until he was twenty-seven years old. After defeat in the finals of the national championships in 1919, he spent the next winter correcting a weak backhand. The next year he stormed back to win the first of seven national championships; he shared the doubles title five times at Forest Hills, won Wimbledon singles crowns three times, and won seventeen Davis Cup matches while losing only five.

Sportswriters did not have to resort to hyperbole to make Tilden an interesting personality. To Tilden, the tennis court was a dramatic stage and he was the leading actor. He loved the theater and performed the lead in several shows, including one Broadway production. If attention at a tournament wandered from him, he brought it back by subtly allowing himself to teeter on the brink of defeat. He then made what appeared to be an incredible comeback. On

[6]Quoted in "Decidedly Unconquerable is Mlle. Lenglen, Tennis Champion," *Literary Digest,* 62 (Sept. 13, 1919), 80.

the court he could be arrogant and irritating. Linesmen who made "bad" calls received menacing glares, and Tilden might deliberately "throw" the next point to show his utter contempt. To the American public, Tilden was the colossal, all-male American giant, who single-handedly held off the tennis invaders from Europe.

Throughout his career, Tilden feuded with the American tennis authorities. While promoting tennis as a spectator sport, the USLTA persisted in trying to preserve the amateur image of the game; it adamantly refused to permit players to profit directly from the sport. As early as 1924 the USLTA tried to prevent Tilden from earning money from his ventures into tennis journalism. He earned as much as $25,000 annually from books, syndicated newspaper pieces, and articles for magazines. The controversy reached a climax in 1928 when the USLTA suspended Tilden from Davis Cup play. News of the banishment even drove the 1928 presidential election, the assassination of Mexico's president-elect, and a search for aviators lost in the Arctic off the front pages of the nation's newspapers. Even the phlegmatic president, Calvin Coolidge, demanded an explanation. The decision threatened to destroy public interest in the Davis Cup challenge round scheduled for Paris. After infuriated French officials complained through diplomatic channels, the USLTA backed down. Nonetheless, two years later Tilden turned professional.

Tilden's conflicts with the USLTA reflected the dilemmas confronting a socially exclusive, amateur sport that had gone public. In its early days, tennis had flourished among the wealthy. But even before the 1920s, upwardly mobile men of new wealth, the "social climbers," had turned to tennis as a vehicle for entering the upper echelons of elite social circles. By the 1920s, when tennis began to attract big box office receipts, these men controlled the USLTA, the regional associations, and many of the tennis clubs. To retain the image of tennis as a high-status sport, the social climbers were adamant in defending a rigorous definition of amateurism.[7]

Yet, for tennis to be successful as a spectator sport, the athletes had to reach professional standards of play. They had to become full-time athletes devoting themselves to long hours of practice and frequent play in tournaments. Thus, unless the players were wealthy, they were forced to circumvent the amateur rules. Moreover, local clubs and their members could gain prestige by sponsoring the development of star players. Consequently, a promising boy or girl, even if from families of modest financial circumstances, could find himself or herself sponsored by a club or a patron. The player's expenses for instruction and appearance in tournaments would be paid fully by someone else. Such a system, according to Sumner Hardy, president of the California Lawn Tennis Association, "made bums out of the boys."[8] At a tender age their lives centered around little else but tennis. Hypocrisy was another inevitable byproduct. While

[7]See Gallico, *The Golden People*, pp. 124–27; Paul Gallico, *Farewell to Sport* (New York, 1938), pp. 149–150; John R. Tunis, *$port$: Heroics and Hysterics* (New York, 1928), pp. 44–75.
[8]Quoted in Tunis, *$port$*, p. 165.

tournament authorities paid the traveling expenses of players (the more promi-nent the player, the higher the allowance granted), they refused to offer cash prizes or schedule open tournaments in which both amateurs and professionals could compete. To have done so would have jeopardized the social functions performed by the sport for the social climbers.

Because powerful amateur associations controlled the major tourna-ments of the world and the press generally took a dim view of professional tennis, only a few players could equal their earnings as amateurs. In 1926 Charles C. "Cash and Carry" Pyle, Red Grange's business manager, attempted to eliminate "shamateurism" in tennis by organizing a pro tour. He hoped to force the amateur associations to open their tournaments to pros and award cash prizes. He signed Suzanne Lenglen, Mary K. Browne, and Vincent Richards (but not Tilden) to a tour of the United States and Canada.[9] Apparently Pyle profited from the venture, but when Lenglen demanded a larger share of future gates, he abandoned the promotion of professional tennis. In the early 1930s only Tilden, though in his forties and no longer the world's premier player, could command a large enough audience to make pro exhibitions profitable. For pro tours to succeed, they required continual infusions of new talent, in other words, recent winners of major amateur tournaments who had received large quantities of free publicity. Such a system meant that only a few professional players could earn a decent living from tennis. Pro tennis had to wait for the advent of television and open tournaments in the 1960s before it became a success.

GOLF GOES PUBLIC

The history of golf going public both paralleled and departed from that of tennis. Both sports had origins in socially exclusive clubs. Historians of golf credit Joseph M. Fox, a member of Philadelphia's Merion Cricket Club, and John Reid, a transplanted Scot and an executive of an iron works in Yonkers, New York, with introducing modern golf into the United States. In 1887 Reid organized the first modern golf club, the St. Andrews Club, named after the historic club in Scotland. In the early 1890s, golf caught the fancy of super-rich tycoons in New York, Boston, Philadelphia, and Chicago. In 1891, William K. Vanderbilt brought over Willie Dunn, famed Scottish golfer, to build the first professionally designed links, the Shinnecock Hills course, located at Southampton, Long Island, where many wealthy New Yorkers had summer homes. The Shinnecock Hills Golf Club hired Stanford White, the noted architect, to design an opulent clubhouse. The clubhouse and course became models for wealthy men interested in forming clubs elsewhere. By 1900 rich golfers could follow the seasons. When the winter winds began to blow, they left their courses at Newport, Brookline, Yonkers, Long Island, and Chicago for sumptuous resorts built for them in Florida,

[9]See Hugh Leamy, "Net Profits," *Colliers*, 78 (Oct. 2, 1926), 9, 32; "Girding for the War Against Professional Tennis," *Literary Digest*, 92 (March 19, 1927), 72–78.

Georgia, and North Carolina. In 1894 both the St. Andrews Club and the Newport Golf Club scheduled national tournaments. With but few exceptions, a reporter concluded in 1898, golf "is a sport restricted to the richer classes of the country."[10]

Social exclusivity and the time and money required to play the game led most Americans initially to ignore or scorn the sport. Popular hostility to golf in the first decade of the twentieth century impelled Theodore Roosevelt to warn William Howard Taft of the political dangers of playing the game. "It would seem incredible that anyone would care one way or the other about your playing golf, but I have received literally hundreds of letters from the West protesting it." He further cautioned: "I myself play tennis, but that game is a little more familiar; besides you never saw a photograph of me playing tennis. I am careful about that; photographs on horseback, yes; tennis, no. And golf is fatal."[11] Ignoring Roosevelt's warnings, Taft became the nation's first golf-playing president.

Like tennis, golf developed lively international competition. Long before 1920 golfers participated on both sides of the Atlantic. In 1922 George H. Walker presented a cup for biennial competition between amateur teams representing the United States and Great Britain, and in 1927 Samuel Ryder did the same for professional teams. As in tennis, both sexes competed in golf, though the best-known women golfers, Alexa Stirling and Glenna Collett, never achieved the celebrity status of a Suzanne Lenglen or a Helen Wills nor the public recognition of such male golfers as Walter Hagen, Gene Sarazan, or Bobby Jones. Yet while the two sports had these important similarities, they evolved in significantly different ways.

Golf went public without the controversy that characterized the emergence of tennis as a public spectacle. Unlike tennis, which had developed almost simultaneously in both Great Britain and the United States in the late nineteenth century, golf was already a well-established sport in Scotland when it invaded American shores. Thus the American clubs tended to imitate Scottish customs. In the British Isles the unoccupied links of land (hence the term "links" to describe golf courses) that bordered or stretched into the sea furnished natural hazards. Having no equivalent physical features along the Atlantic seaboard, American clubs had to build inland courses. To approximate the hazards found in the British Isles, they constructed artificial bunkers, sandtraps, small lakes, and planted trees along the fairways. From the earliest days of the sport in the United States, the clubs hired professional Scottish or English golfers to teach their members the finer arts of the game and followed the British custom of holding open tournaments. Both amateur and professional golfers could compete in open tournaments. Finally, the absence of gate receipts at golf tournaments until the

[10]H. L. Fitz Patrick, "Golf and the American Girl," *Outing,* 32 (Dec. 1898), 294–95. For the diffusion of golf in the 1890s, see a series of articles in *Outing,* 34 (May–Aug. 1899), 260–68, 354–65, 443–57. General histories of golf include Herbert Warren Wind, *The Story of American Golf,* 3rd rev. ed. (New York, 1975); H. B. Martin, *Fifty Years of American Golf* (New York, 1936); Will Grimsley, *Golf: Its History, People, and Events* (Englewood Cliffs, NJ, 1966); Herb Graffis, *The PGA: The Official History of the Professional Golfer's Association of America* (New York, 1975).

[11]As quoted in Harold Seymour, *Baseball,* 2 vols (New York, 1971), I, pp. 45–46.

1920s discouraged the adoption of the tennis practice of extending traveling expenses to amateur players.

Golf enjoyed a larger fan constituency than tennis. Abetted by the rapid growth of country clubs in the 1920s, golf spread (as one wag put it) from the upper "Four Hundred" to the upper "Four Million." Apart from being a conspicuous status mechanism, golf furnished an escape from the confinement and annoying details of downtown offices. On the course, according to the promoters of the sport, businessmen found a pastoral retreat in which they could soothe overwrought nerves. The golf course also became a substitute for the office and the conference room; there businessmen laid the groundwork for future transactions or confirmed old agreements. Sometimes golf seemed only a pretext for convivial gatherings at the "nineteenth hole," the clubhouse bar.

As early as 1913 golf exhibited potential as a public spectacle. Prior to that date a gallery of 200 was considered unusual for a national tournament, but in 1913 a crowd of more than 3,000 watched Francis Ouimet, a twenty-year-old amateur golfer, upset Britain's two leading professional golfers in a playoff in the United States Open tournament. Earlier, whenever overseas stars had consented to play in American meets, they had nearly always emerged victorious. Only one American, Walter J. Travis, had ever won a major European championship. In 1913 Harry Vardon, winner of six British open titles and often hailed as the world's greatest golfer, and Edward "Ted" Ray, reigning British Open crown holder, embarked upon an exhibition tour of the United States. Attracting record crowds wherever they went, they interrupted their tour in mid-September to play in the American Open at The Country Club in Brookline, Massachusetts.

An almost unknown golfer, Francis Ouimet, a former caddy at The Country Club and the son of a French-Canadian father and an Irish-American mother surprised everyone by tying the British aces at the end of regulation play. The next day, on a rain-soaked course, Ouimet won the playoffs, trouncing Vardon by five strokes and Ray by seven strokes. Newspapers across the country gave Ouimet's victory headline coverage. Overnight, Ouimet was an American hero. "Here was a person all of America, not just golfing America, could understand—the boy from 'the wrong side' of the street, the ex-caddie, the kind who worked during his summer vacations from high school—America's idea of the American hero."[12] Ouimet was golf's version of the Horatio Alger success story, even though he never again captured an American Open title.

One participant in the Brookline tournament, Walter C. Hagen, was largely responsible for making professional golf a respectable occupation. The first golf pros, mostly transplanted Scotsmen and Englishmen, had been jacks-of-all-trades. They designed the early courses, kept the grounds, made and repaired the hickory-shafted golf clubs, trained and managed caddies, and gave instructions to novices. Little or none of their earnings came from tournament winnings, product endorsements, or paid exhibitions. While wealthy club mem-

---

[12]Wind, *The Story of American Golf*, p. 85. See also Stephen Hardy, *How Boston Played: Sport, Recreation, and Community, 1865–1915* (Boston, 1982), pp. 179–85.

bers sometimes joined the club pro in friendly games, they viewed him as simply another employee and therefore as a social inferior. In open tournaments the clubs barred the pros from the locker rooms and other clubhouse amenities. As late as 1930, the official programs of the United States Open prefixed the names of amateurs with "Mr." while deleting this distinction from the names of professionals.[13]

Hagen helped erase social discrimination in golf. Being a former caddy from a family of modest means did not deter the irrepressible Hagen. He treated kings, industrial tycoons, and caddies all alike. Because of his prowess as a golfer, his pleasing personality, his sartorial elegance, and his impeccable manners, he broke down social barriers in both the United States and Europe. Apparently Hagen unintentionally touched off the "Midlothian Incident" of 1914 at the United States Open held at the Midlothian Country Club in suburban Chicago. Hagen, then a brash, young, but personable professional who feigned ignorance of clubhouse social conventions, simply made himself at home in the Midlothian locker room and clubhouse. While no one knows whether words were exchanged or threats were issued, the country club finally acquiesced, constituting what has been described as a "social revolution in American golf." When Hagen arrived at Deal to play in the 1920 British Open, he learned that the clubhouse was off limits to pros—again because they were not regarded as gentlemen. Much to the chagrin of the stuffy British golf officials, Hagen ordered his big, black limousine parked at the front door of the clubhouse and proceeded to use it as a dressing

WALTER HAGEN, HERO OF GOLF
Walter Hagen, the first professional hero of golf, sipped from one of the many gold cups that he won during his thirty-year career. Hagen also seemed to embody the new consumer ethic that had become so conspicuous by the 1920s.

[13]"What a 'Czar' Means to Golf Pros," *Literary Digest*, 105 (May 10, 1930), 68.

room. The same year, Hagen and the British Open champion, George Duncan, threatened to boycott the French Open unless the social restrictions against the pros were removed. The French, confronted with the possible collapse of their tournament, yielded. The British soon followed the American and French custom of extending equal amenities to both professionals and amateurs.

Hagen was the first golfer to make the full-time playing of golf a profitable enterprise. Before the late 1930s, professionals could earn only a few dollars in prize money; they earned their living by serving as club pros. Yet the prize money gradually increased. In 1916 Tom McNamara, a salesman in the golf department of Wanamaker's, sold the idea of the Professional Golfer's Association (PGA) to millionaire Rodman Wanamaker. Wanamaker initially donated a total prize of $2,500; the winner of the annual PGA tournament received $500. During World War I, the American Red Cross sponsored a benefit tour to which it charged admissions to spectators. In 1921 the United States Open copied this practice and soon other golf meets followed suit. Swelling gate receipts permitted the major tournaments to increase their meager purses. In the early 1920s a professional tour of sorts developed in the South. Wealthy golf enthusiasts, often with real estate promotion as a primary motive, began to sponsor professional tournaments in resort areas. Yet no golfer could earn a decent living on tournament winnings alone.

Hagen relied upon tours and product endorsements rather than tournaments for his earnings. Combining a colorful personality with the fact that for nearly fifteen years he seldom was without a national title made Hagen the most sought-after exhibition golfer in the country. Hagen employed Robert "Bob" Harlow, a veteran Associated Press correspondent, as his business manager. (Harlow, hailed as the "founder of professional golf as it is today," later served many years as the tournament manager of the PGA.) Harlow capitalized upon Hagen's popularity by lining up endorsements for golf equipment and arranging elaborate tours that took Hagen from the largest cities to golf's remotest outposts. Except for tournament interruptions, from late spring to early fall Hagen gave exhibitions five days a week and during the winter months he played on the "winter circuit" from Florida to California. Harlow "ticketed" the galleries at one dollar a person for weekdays and two dollars for weekends. During the twenties Hagen probably earned between $30,000 and $50,000 annually.

GOLF'S HERO: BOBBY JONES

While Hagen wooed thousands of golfers to his exhibitions, only the amateur Bobby Jones became a truly national, even international, golfing celebrity. Jones was born into a wealthy Atlanta, Georgia, family. In 1916, when Jones was but fourteen, he competed in the United States Amateur at the Merion Cricket Club in Philadelphia. He managed to qualify and swept through his first two challengers before succumbing to the defending champion in the third round. Despite defeat, Jones was the sensation of the tournament, hailed by sportswriters as the "kid wonder" and the "child prodigy" of golf. For several years, the high expectations generated at Merion went unfulfilled, but in 1923, when he was apparently on the verge of retiring from competitive golf, he won his first major tournament, the U.S. Open. From 1923 to 1930, he was the king of world golfers, both professional and amateur. He collected thirteen national titles—five United States Amateurs, four United States Opens, three British Opens, and one British Amateur. In the last nine years of his career he competed in twelve national championships and finished first or second in eleven of them, a feat Jones considered to be greater than his winning of the Grand Slam in 1930. He climaxed his short golfing career with the Grand Slam—the American Open and Amateur and the British Open and Amateur, a feat not duplicated since. After the Grand Slam in 1930, when he was at the very peak of his game at the age of twenty-eight, Jones announced his retirement.

The American public adored Bobby Jones. Every time he returned from victories in Europe, he received the welcome of a conquering hero—a ticker-tape parade down Broadway to New York's City Hall to receive the keys of the city from Mayor Jimmy Walker. Public excitement knew no bounds when Jones won the last leg of his Grand Slam, the American Amateur at the Merion Cricket Club in 1930. A vast throng, estimated at 18,000, made a great human fringe around the greens and packed the fairways, following Jones from hole to hole. "Today's match was far more of a spectacle than it was a contest," declared William D. Richardson of *The New York Times*. "It was merely an exhibition on Jones' part, a parade to victory."[14] Women reached out to touch him and little boys sat on their fathers' shoulders to catch a glimpse of their fabulous hero.

The conservative image of Jones stood in sharp contrast to that of the hedonistic Hagen. Golfing commentators referred repeatedly to Jones' game as "mechanical" while Hagen played with an unorthodox flair. Jones seemed to embody traditional Victorian virtues. At the same time that he competed in golf tournaments, he attended college, obtained a law degree, was admitted to the bar, and began the practice of law. Paul Gallico, after reviewing all of the major sports heroes of the 1920s, asserted that Jones was "the greatest gentleman of them all."[15] Above all, the public loved the fact that Jones, as an amateur, had defeated the best of the professional golfers and taken the measure of the European champions. By a large strain on the imagination, weekend "duffers" could identify Jones as one of their own crowd. He, like they, held down a regular job and presumably played the sport for the sheer fun of the game.

That the image of Jones sometimes failed to correspond with the facts did not bother his admirers. Upon retirement from tournament competition, Jones, like the pro golfers, attempted to capitalize upon his reputation. With his "Boswell" and longtime traveling companion, O.B. Keeler, Jones did a weekly half-hour radio show recreating the highlights of his career. He made two series of instructional films for Warner Brothers, reputedly for a profit of $180,000, and

[14]Danzig and Brandwein, eds., *The Greatest Sport Stories*, p. 342.
[15]Gallico, *The Golden People*, p. 268.

lent his name to a Spalding line of golfing equipment. He furnished the initiative and much of the design for a magnificent new golf course at Augusta, Georgia, the Augusta National. In 1934 the Augusta course became the home of the Masters tournament, an invitation-only affair consisting of the world's top golfers. In due time, the Masters became one of four major recognized tournaments in the world. As a leisure-time golfer, Jones occasionally played in the Masters (even as late as 1948) and other meets, but never again won a major tournament.

The retirement of Jones, the Great Depression of the 1930s, and World War II set back the American enthusiasm for golf. Without Jones as a drawing card or the emergence of a new golfing celebrity of equal stature, major amateur tournaments were fortunate if gate receipts equalled expenses. Almost a third of the country clubs folded; several became privately owned, daily fee or municipally owned courses. The Public Works Administration and the Works Progress Administration of the New Deal built about 200 courses. Of about 5,200 courses in 1941, some 2,000 were either municipal or privately owned, daily fee courses. In the 1930s, the "Age of the Amateur" also passed. After the victory of Jones in 1930, only one amateur (in 1933) ever again won the U.S. Open.

Finally, the 1930s introduced the "Age of Steel" and concerted assaults on pars. The average winning score for the U.S. Open in the 1930s dropped six strokes below that of the 1920s. Experts attributed the better scores to high-pressured balls, replacement of hickory shafts with steel, the use of more specialized and more perfectly matched clubs, and the "New Look" of the nation's golf courses. In the 1930s, many clubs filled in traps, thinned the roughs, cropped the grass shorter on the fairways, and softened the greens by watering them more copiously.[16] The 1940s brought forward a new breed of professional precisionists—Ben Hogan, Byron Nelson, and Sam Snead, for instance—but not until the advent of television and Arnold Palmer in the 1960s did golf again achieve the public attention it had received in 1930.

TRACK AND FIELD

Before 1890 the fan had been a potent force in track and field. As early as the 1840s and 50s, professional pedestrianism had gained a considerable following, and it continued to enjoy some support in the early years of the twentieth century. The Scottish Caledonian clubs had also welcomed fans to their meets; they had charged admissions to spectators and awarded cash prizes to winning athletes. Initially, spectatorship was an issue that divided the sporting world of the social elites. The fashionable clubs had sought to use a sport as an agency for building status communities. Status ascription might be strengthened by restricting competition to amateur athletes and spectators to club members and invited guests. On the other hand, the clubs might enhance their status by building a reputation for holding outstanding meets and fielding superior athletes. Eventually this

---

[16]Wind, *The Story of American Golf*, p. 268–70.

view prevailed. The clubs went public; they opened their gates to the public at large and became the nation's premier promoters of track and field. In the twentieth century, the athletic clubs and their parent body, the Amateur Athletic Union (AAU), continued to stage some of the most eminent meets in the nation.

The elite athletic clubs encountered increasing competition from other organizations in the nurture of superior athletes and the sponsorship of track and field meets. Foremost of these competitors were the high schools and colleges. Northeastern colleges organized the Intercollegiate Association of Amateur Athletes of America (commonly known as the IC4A) in 1876 to supervise running events that had been held at Saratoga, New York, since 1873. In 1876, the IC4A began to conduct annual, full-scale track meets. Until the NCAA staged its first championships in 1921, the IC4A was the nation's most prestigious collegiate track meet. After 1921 it remained an important event for eastern schools.

The University of Pennsylvania Relays, which began in 1895, introduced a colorful athletic carnival that combined intercollegiate and interscholastic track. At the Penn Relays of 1925 more than 3,000 athletes representing more than 500 colleges and secondary schools competed before 70,000 fans in the finals. The Penn Relays spawned imitators across the country, perhaps the most notable being the Drake University Relays at Des Moines, Iowa. Early in the twentieth century, several other groups joined the athletic clubs, the AAU, and the colleges in the promotion of track and field. In New York City the Millrose Games, the Knights of Columbus Games, and the Wanamaker Mile, among others, added to the opportunities available to spectator and athlete alike.

For more than half a century havoc reigned in the governance of track and field. Promotional groups and regulatory bodies competed for hegemony; the main power struggle involved the NCAA and the AAU. As the colleges furnished ever larger numbers of the nation's top-flight athletes, they increasingly resented the senior organization's (the AAU) authority to determine the eligibility of amateur athletes, its collections of fees for meets that it did not sponsor, the control that it attempted to exercise over international competition, and the AAU's domination of the American Olympic Committee. Sometimes only ad hoc compromises allowed the United States to field a team at the Olympic Games.[17] Only in 1978, and then only after an act of Congress, did the warfare between the AAU and the NCAA finally end. (See Chap. 17.)

All too often the athletes were the victims of both the power struggle between the AAU and the NCAA and of a hypocritical amateur code. While in principle amateur athletes could receive no financial remuneration from their feats, promoters could win both glory and profits from staging meets. Anxious to attract star athletes to their meets, unscrupulous promoters secretly "overpaid" expense allowances and apparently sometimes made direct payments to the athletes. As in the case of tennis and golf, to be a champion in track and field

---

[17]See Arnold William Flath, *A History of Relations between the National Collegiate Athletic Association and the Amateur Athletic Union of the United States* (Champaign, IL, Stipes, 1964); Jack Falla, *NCAA: The Voice of College Sports* (Mission, KS, 1981), Chap. 5.

required training and frequent competition. Unless the athlete was independently wealthy, he had to supplement his income in some fashion. The temptation to benefit financially from one's athletic skills was difficult to resist. Furthermore, according to world champion sprinter, Charles W. Paddock, who repeatedly warred with the AAU, the promoters often placed the athletes in an impossible position. On the one hand, they would extend to the young, inexperienced athletes "extra expenses." On the other, whenever the athlete protested any matter, he then could be threatened with exposure and suspension.[18] "Shamateurism" continued to plague the world of track and field after World War II.

THE REVIVED OLYMPIC GAMES

In due time, the revived Olympic Games became the world's premier track and field spectacle.[19] According to the official ideology of the Olympic movement, the Games were held solely for the benefit of the players, and only amateur athletes could compete. Pierre de Coubertin, the aristocratic French Anglophile who founded the modern games, repeatedly asserted that the Games were a forum for the young men of the world to unite in peaceful competition through sport. Yet even the official ideology of the Games included more than simply participation for the sheer joy of the experience. The Games would also, Coubertin argued, expose athletes to people with different values, broaden their horizons, and contribute to pacific international relations. Unofficially, Coubertin, who smarted deeply from the humiliating defeat that the Germans had administered to the French in 1870–71, also hoped the example of the Games would strengthen the national character of the French people. Moreover, responsibilities for the management of the Games and the national teams rested with committees of nonathletes. Finally, forces external to the Olympic movement (including national pride, commercial consideration, and boosterism) shaped much of the history of the Games.

Until 1912 the Olympic Games remained a minor event in American track and field competition. The Americans made no concerted effort to field a strong team at the first Games held at Athens in 1896. College athletes sponsored by the Boston Athletic Association reinforced by a few others who paid their own expenses comprised the total American delegation. Harbingers of the use of the Games for nonathletic purposes were evident even at Athens. The Greek royal family blatantly exploited the Games to enhance their power, and the first

---

[18]Charles. W. Paddock, *"The Fastest Human"* (New York, 1932), pp. 48–49, 158.

[19]For general accounts of the games see John Kiernan et. al., *The Story of the Olympic Games,* rev. ed. (Philadelphia, 1977); William O. Johnson, Jr., *All That Glitters Is Not Gold: The Olympic Games* (New York, 1972); and John Lucas, *The Modern Olympic Games* (New York, 1980). Allen Guttman's *The Games Must Go On: Avery Brundage and the Olympic Movement* (New York, 1984) treats a central figure in much of the history of the modern games. On the founding and early history of the modern games, see esp. Richard D. Mandell, *The First Modern Olympics* (Berkeley, CA, 1976) and John MacAloon, *The Great Symbol* (Chicago, 1981).

Games initiated the practice of raising the national flags of the winning athletes at a victory ceremony. The next three Games were essentially sideshows to other more publicized attractions: the Paris Exposition of 1900, the World's Fair held in St. Louis in 1904, and the Franco-British Exposition of 1908 held in London. In addition, the Greeks scheduled what has been called a "rump" Olympics at Athens in 1906.[20] Only fifteen countries competed in the 1900 Games, and only eleven nations participated in the third Olympics held at St. Louis in 1904. Rivalries between the large and patriotically motivated American and British teams marred the London Games of 1908. For the first time, Olympic officials required that all competitors perform as part of a national "team." By 1908 American track and field officials took the Games seriously. They had organized a national Olympic committee that selected teams of first-rate athletes and subsidized them for their trips abroad. At each of these early Games, American athletes tended to dominate track and field, but fared poorly in other forms of competition.

In the 1912 Olympic Games held at Stockholm, Sweden, the Games "arrived," at least as far as the Americans were concerned. Unlike earlier Games, nothing overshadowed the event, and American newspapers gave the Games detailed coverage. The Americans went all-out to win the track and field events. The American Olympic Committee selected the best athletes available, including a native American and several blacks. Jim Thorpe, the great athlete from the tiny Carlisle (Pennsylvania) Indian School, emerged as the hero of the Games. Already well known for his football feats, Thorpe captured the pentathlon and decathlon. He won four of the five individual events in the pentathlon and scored a 700-point margin over his nearest competitor in the decathlon. Unfortunately, Thorpe became a victim of the amateur code. The following year, a Massachusetts newspaper accused Thorpe of playing professional baseball for a minor-league team during the summer of 1909. Thorpe admitted the transgression, and the AAU revoked his amateur status. The International Olympic Committee then deprived him of his Olympic medals. The IOC selected Berlin as the host for the 1916 Games, but the eruption of World War I in 1914 resulted in their cancellation.

World War I was only a temporary setback. After the war the Games became far bigger and more extravagant than the prewar affairs. The 1920 Games, awarded to Antwerp in recognition of the horrendous sacrifices made by the Belgians during World War I, was a modest affair. But each of the following Games—Paris in 1924, Amsterdam in 1928, Los Angeles in 1932, and Berlin in 1936—was more extravagant than its predecessor. Despite a worldwide depression, the Los Angeles promoters in 1932 established the pattern for the expensive and ornate facilities that would become characteristic of the modern games. The local organizing committee determined to make the 1932 spectacle a showcase for the city of Los Angeles and the state of California. To finance the spectacle, the city of Los Angeles floated a $1.5 million bond issue, and the voters of

[20]Mandell, *The First Modern Olympics*, p. 167.

California, in a special referendum, approved the expenditure of $1 million in state funds. At Los Angeles the athletes found magnificent facilities: an 105,000-seat stadium, an indoor auditorium with seats for 10,000, a swimming structure with a seating capacity of 12,000, and the first specially constructed Olympic Village. The Olympic Village provided housing in prefabricated cottages, feeding, and recreational facilities for all of the male athletes at a single location.

Not to be outdone by the Los Angeles buccaneers, the Nazis put on an even bigger show at Berlin in 1936. They built a new 100,000-seat track and field stadium, six gymnasiums, and many smaller arenas. They installed a closed-circuit television system, a radio network that reached forty-one nations, photo-finish equipment, and electronic timing devices. In contrast to Los Angeles, they built sturdy brick and stucco cottages to house the male athletes. The Nazis commissioned Leni Riefenstahl, a brilliant producer, to make a $7 million film of the event. Her film, *Olympia*, subsequently became a classic in cinematography. Altogether the Nazis spent an estimated $30 million, far more than the total costs of all the preceding Games. Obviously, competition was no longer restricted to the athletic field, for the staging of ever more spectacular Olympiads had become a contest as well.

The building of elaborate facilities was an integral part of the increased politicization of the Games. Politicization had begun well before the 1920s and 30s. From the outset, Pierre de Coubertin had promoted the Games as a means of inspiring the youth of France to greater physical prowess and courage and at the same time as a means of encouraging international ideals. The decision to have the athletes compete as national teams rather than as individuals inevitably gave rise to international rivalries. On the eve of the 1908 Games, James E. Sullivan, leader of the American Olympic delegation, bluntly declared: "We have come here to win the championship in field sports, and we are going to do it, despite the handicap from which we are suffering."[21] For the 1908 Games the American press devised an unofficial point system so that national achievements could be easily compared. And the national organizing committees soon found that by appealing to patriotic sentiments they could raise more money to send athletes to the Games.

Political animosities arising from World War I drove the International Olympic Committee to exclude the losers in the war (the Central Powers of Germany, Austria, Hungary, and Turkey) from the Games of 1920 and 1924. Neither did the IOC extend an invitation to the newly established communist regime in Russia to compete in the postwar Games. (Soviet Russia did not participate in the Games until 1952.) Such actions revealed clearly that the Olympic movement was not immune to the exigencies of international politics.

The politicization of the Olympics reached a climax with the 1936 Games. Nazi Germany's blatant anti-Semitism sparked a movement in the United States to boycott the 1936 Olympics. As early as 1933, shortly after Adolf Hitler had

---

[21]As quoted in Peter J. Graham and Horst Ueberhorst, eds., *The Modern Olympics* (Cornwall, NY, n.d.), p. 32.

taken command in Germany, Americans serving on the International Olympic Committee had protested Nazi discrimination against Jews and the AAU had voted to boycott the games unless Germany's policy regarding Jewish athletes be "changed in fact as well as in theory."[22] While the German Olympic Committee took nominal steps to reassure the Americans, Hitler, in 1935, proclaimed the "Nuremberg Laws," which deprived German Jews of their citizenship and legalized social practices designed to preserve the integrity of the "Aryan race."

The issue of boycotting the Games divided American athletic officials into two bitter camps. Avery Brundage, the self-made millionaire president of the American Olympic Committee (AOC), led the advocates of participation while the president of the AAU, Judge Jeremiah T. Mahoney, a Catholic who was disturbed by Nazi paganism and anti-Semitism, led the boycott movement. Both sides published pamphlets, issued press releases, and gave radio interviews. A Gallup poll revealed that 43 percent of the American people favored a boycott. Brundage, in a private letter to a Nazi friend, interpreted the boycott movement as a Jewish-Communist conspiracy. "Jews and Communists," he wrote, "threatened to spend a million dollars to keep the United States out of Germany . . . by use of bribery, corruption and political trickery, and other contemptible tactics."[23] A showdown came at the AAU convention in 1935 where Brundage was able, by a two-and-a-half vote margin, to obtain defeat of a resolution that would have delayed the American decision to enter the Games pending further investigation of German behavior.

Controversy continued at the Games in Berlin. Although the German fans enthusiastically welcomed the American black athletes, a German newspaper contemptuously referred to them as the "Black auxiliary." When Cornelius Johnson, a black, won the high jump with a record leap, Hitler, who had personally congratulated the first two winners in track and field, suddenly left his stadium box. This action led to the potent myth that Hitler had refused to shake the hand of Jesse Owens, the American star of the games, although during the subsequent days, Hitler carefully avoided public congratulation of any winner. Bitterness flared within the American ranks. At the last moment the American track and field coach, Dean Cromwell, dropped two Jewish athletes (the only Jews on the track and field squad) from the 400-meter relay team. Although Cromwell insisted that he substituted other athletes (including Owens) in order to prevent a surprise German victory, the argument was lame. Everyone else believed the Americans could have won easily without the substitutions, and one of the Jewish athletes had times equal to that of one the substitutes.

[22]Richard D. Mandell, *The Nazi Olympics* (New York, 1971; Urbana, IL, 1987), p. 71. For the Nazi Games, see also Guttmann, *The Games Must Go On*, Chap. 6; Arnd Kruger, "The 1936 Olympic Games—Berlin," in Graham and Ueberhorst, eds, *The Modern Olympics*, pp. 168–82; George Eisen, "The Voices of Sanity: American Diplomatic Reports from the 1936 Berlin Olympiad," *Journal of Sport History*, 11 (1984), 56–78; Duff Hart-Davis, *Hitler's Games: The 1936 Olympics* (London, 1986).

[23]As quoted in Kruger, "The 1936 Olympic Games," p. 171.

The 1936 Games revealed that, more than ever before, nations perceived their athletes as their representatives in a struggle for international power and glory. Athletes were national assets, procurable like submarines or bombs. After 1936 many of the nations who sent their athletes to the Nazi Games began to prepare for both war and the 1940 Olympics. Ironically the 1940 Games were scheduled for Tokyo just as the 1916 Games had been set for Berlin. In 1938 the Japanese withdrew their invitation to host the 1940 Games and World War II caused the cancellation of the 1944 Olympics.

MINORITY OLYMPIANS

In the interwar era women finally began to break down the Olympic barrier. Coubertin had consistently opposed the participation of women in the Games. Nonetheless, while excluded from track and field, women had been permitted to enter golf and tennis competition in the Games of 1900 and a few events in the Games of 1912. European rather than American women led the crusade for female participation in track and field. Coubertin staved off a female invasion of the 1920 Games, but the newly organized Fédération Sportive Féminine Internationale (FSFI) responded by sponsoring the first Women's Olympic Games in Paris in 1922. The competition furnished by the new Women's Olympic Games convinced the IOC to override Coubertin's objections. They adopted a five-event track and field program for the 1928 Olympics. As part of the compromise, the FSFI then changed the title of its meets to the International Ladies' Games, which continued to be held until 1934.[24]

American women wishing to participate in international competition faced the almost unanimous opposition of women physical educators. A small contingent of American females, organized by a male physician, competed in the Paris Games in 1922. The Paris Games touched off a complex debate in the United States about the desirability of women competing in highly competitive sports and an equally complex struggle for power between the AAU and various organizations of women physical educators for control of women's athletics. In 1924 the AAU staged the first national indoor and outdoor championships in track and field for women. The 1928 Games had mixed results for the supporters of women's sports. Of the eleven women entering the 800 meter race, five dropped out before the race was completed, five collapsed after reaching the finishing line, and the remaining finisher fainted in the dressing room. The incident fueled the belief that women were incapable of coping with such vigorous, sustained physical activity and the IOC dropped the 800 meter race from future programs.

[24]Betty Spears, "Women in the Olympics: An Unresolved Problem," in Graham and Ueberhorst, The Modern Olympics, pp. 62–83; Mary H. Leigh and Therese M. Bonin, "The Pioneering Role of Madame Alice Millait and the FSFI in Establishing International Track and Field Competition for Women," Journal of Sport History, 4 (1977), 72–83; Cindy L. Himes, "The Female Athlete in American Society, 1860–1940," unpub. Ph.D. diss., University of Pennsylvania, 1984, pp. 206–13.

Nonetheless, two female Olympic competitors, Gertrude Ederle and Mildred "Babe" Didrikson, became national heroes. Ederle, who won a gold and two bronze medals in swimming in the 1924 Games, achieved celebrity status by swimming the English Channel in 1926. She was not only the first woman to swim from France to England, a distance of thirty-three miles, but she accomplished the feat in fourteen hours and twenty-three minutes, smashing the men's record by more than two hours. The newspapers immediately hailed her as "The Grease Smeared Venus," "Queen of the Waves," and as "America's Best Girl." Upon her return to the United States, New York gave her a reception that dwarfed the greeting extended to Sergeant Alvin York upon his return from World War I. Movie, stage, and commercial offers poured in. A pair of songwriters composed a quick tribute: "You're such a cutie. You're just as sweet as tutti-frutti. Trudy, who'll be the lucky fellow?"[25]

Ederle's swim represented victories for women, German-Americans, the United States, and the efficacy of practicing traditional virtues. According to her mother, Gertrude developed her strength from doing household chores; she was a " 'plain home girl,' who preferred sewing and cooking to smoking, drinking and going out with young men." The press, Ederle's family, and the politicians turned the swim into a patriotic occasion; Ederle herself said that "It was for my flag that I swam." German-Americans took a special pride in the feat of an offspring of a German immigrant family; some saw in Ederle hope for a reduction in the wartime antagonisms that had been directed toward German-Americans. That Ederle had bested the male mark for swimming the Channel by more than two hours seemed to belie the assumption that women were the "weaker sex." For women (and many men as well), Ederle blended perfectly such older feminine virtues as modesty and domesticity with exhibitions of strength and independence.[26]

Though never soaring to the heights of public acclaim reached by Ederle in 1926, Babe Didrikson remained in the public limelight for many more years. In 1950 the Associated Press picked her as the Woman Athlete of the Half Century. (Jim Thorpe received the honor as the top male athlete of the half century.) Between 1930 and 1932 she held American, Olympic, or world records in five separate track and field events. In 1930, 1931, and 1932 she was an "All-American" girls' basketball player and led her team, the Golden Cyclones, to the AAU women's national championship in 1931. As a golfer, both professional and amateur, she had no equal; she won thirty-four of the eighty-eight tournaments she entered. Reportedly, she bowled a 170 average, could punt a football seventy-five yards, and for short distances could swim close to world record times.[27]

---

[25]*New York Times,* Aug. 7, 1926.

[26]For the quotations and the interpretations in this paragraph see Himes, "The Female Athlete," pp. 224–37.

[27]See Babe Didrikson Zaharias, *This Life I've Led* (New York, 1955) and William Oscar Johnson and Nancy P. Williamson, *"Whatta-Gal": The Babe Didrikson Story* (Boston, 1977).

Like Ederle, Didrikson amply fulfilled the American dream of success. One of seven children from a lower income, Norwegian immigrant family in Galveston, Texas, she joined the local boys in their games. At Beaumont High School, she participated in all sports available to girls—volleyball, tennis, golf, basketball, and swimming. In 1930 the Employers Casualty Company of Dallas offered her a job (ostensibly as a stenographer) to play for the Golden Cyclones basketball team. The company also sponsored her as the only member of its squad at the women's AAU track and field championships in 1932. In the space of three hours in a single afternoon, she won six gold medals and broke four world records—in the baseball throw, javelin, eighty-meter hurdles, and high jump. At the 1932 Olympics, she broke the world records in the javelin, the eighty-meter hurdles, and the high jump, though the Olympic officials disqualified her high jump because she had "dived" over the bar. Had women been permitted to enter more than three events in the Olympics, Didrikson would undoubtedly have won even more gold medals.

After her success at the 1932 Olympics, Didrikson tried to benefit financially from her athletic skills and celebrity status, but opportunities for women in professional sports were virtually nonexistent. One of her few recourses was to become essentially an exhibitionist, to display her athletic prowess on the road,

MILDRED "BABE" DIDRIKSON (1914–1956)
Shown here at the 1932 Olympic Games held at Los Angeles, Didrikson was perhaps the world's greatest woman athlete of the first half of the twentieth century. Although she won great fame from sports, her success did little to alter prevailing attitudes toward the proper role of women in sports.

often as a sideshow to the main attraction. In 1934, she formed a mixed-gender basketball team that played local men's teams in small tank towns across the nation. The next year she pitched a few innings in spring training games for several major league teams and that summer toured with the bearded House of David baseball team. Although her earnings were substantial for the depression years, she disliked the life of an itinerant athlete. In the late 1930s she turned to a career as a professional golfer.

Didrikson's larger significance is difficult to assess. On the one hand, she demonstrated that women could achieve excellence in sport and even earn money from it. On the other hand, her appearance and behavior aroused deep-seated fears among those concerned about departures from traditional femininity. Paul Gallico described Didrikson in her early years as a "muscle moll," "who never wore make-up, who shingled her hair until it was as short as a boy's . . . and who despised silk underthings as being sissy."[28] Her speech was always candid and sometimes earthy. When touring with the bewhiskered House of David team, a female spectator once asked Didrikson where her beard was. "I'm sittin' on 'em, just like you are!" she replied.[29] Her biographers concluded that "she was used as a kind of bogeywoman by mothers who wished to prevent their budding tomboy daughters from pursuing sports."[30] Perhaps in part due to her marriage to a professional wrestler, George Zaharias, in 1938, and in part to gain greater acceptance as a professional golfer, she cultivated a more feminine image in her later years. In sum, the advent of Didrikson did not herald a revolution in women's sports. That revolution awaited the turbulent 1960s and 70s.

Nor did sprinter James Cleveland "Jesse" Owens, the American hero of the 1936 Olympics, spark a revolution in the status of blacks in sport.[31] Like Didrikson, Owens was from a poor family. The son of Alabama sharecroppers, he migrated with his family to Cleveland, Ohio. In both high school and college he won a wide reputation as a track star. (In most cases even northern colleges excluded blacks from their team sports but welcomed them in the individual sports.) As a sophomore at Ohio State University in 1935 he broke four world records at the annual Big Ten meet. In the 1936 Olympics he competed in twelve events, including preliminary heats, and set or equalled world marks nine times. In 1950 the sports reporters selected him as the best track athlete of the first fifty years of the twentieth century.

Owens's remarkable victories symbolized a kind of savage irony. On the one hand, he gave the lie—at least in the case of sport—to the Nazi argument for "Aryan" supremacy and he was a hero to white and black Americans alike. Yet in 1935 and 1936, twenty-six blacks lost their lives in the United States from lynchings. In 1936 the walls of racial segregation in the United States seemed as unbreachable as ever; no blacks played in major league baseball or professional

---

[28]Gallico, *Farewell to Sport*, p. 239.
[29]Quoted in Himes, "The Female Athlete," p. 251.
[30]Johnson and Williamson, *Whatta-Gal"*, p. 132.
[31]William J. Baker, *Jesse Owens: An American Life* (New York, 1986).

football and few played on integrated college teams. Owens himself preferred the role of the symbol of what a black man could accomplish in sport rather than that of a crusader for black rights.

13
THE RISE
OF ORGANIZED YOUTH SPORTS

The 1890–1950 era witnessed the emergence of mammoth programs of adult-managed sports for youth. Well before 1890 youth had competed in sports, but usually on teams and in games that they themselves had organized or on teams composed largely of adults. After 1890 the Young Men's Christian Association, the Public Schools Athletic Leagues, the city playground associations, and the public high schools, all of which reflected old-stock, Protestant, middle-class concerns, became major sponsors of boys' sports. Females in colleges and high schools also joined the boom in organized youth sports, but without the enthusiastic support of adults.

THE SOCIAL CONTEXT

The drive for adult-directed boys' sports was an integral part of a larger movement to organize and manage the spare-time activities of the nation's youth. The thrust for this larger movement to control the environment of youth stemmed from a heightened concern that the traditional agencies of socialization no longer satisfactorily prepared youth for adult roles in the community. Boys' sports, the leaders of the movement believed, could be an important surrogate for a rural upbringing. They believed also that an organized sports environment could fill the voids left by the disappearance of the household economy, the absence of early work experience, the weakened authority of religion, and the breakdown of the small geographic community. Muscular Christianity furnished the initial rationale for the movement; later, professional "boy-workers" added a theory of play that was grounded in evolutionary theory. The combined ideas of a virile Christianity and an evolutionary theory of play constituted a new sporting ideology. These ideas also shaped the content and institutional structure of the adult-managed boys' sport movement.[1]

Those most concerned for the fate of youth believed that the new urban-industrial society had dealt harshly with the old ways of child-rearing. In particular, the new society had weakened the family as a nurturing institution. Earlier in the nineteenth century, the family had often constituted a household economy. Children had lent assistance to their parents in spinning thread, weaving cloth, making garments, fabricating tools, constructing furniture, baking bread, or perhaps in helping their father pursue his trade. But by 1890, all save the most wretched families purchased many of their essential items in the marketplace. No longer was the home either a place for creating new goods or the location for the father's trade or business. Father now toiled away from home, and the children were left at best with dull, routine chores, with "make-work" that failed to exercise their "constructive impulses in a wholesome way." Relieving the children of productive work in the home, most youth observers believed, had fatal consequences for healthy moral growth. Habits of good conduct could best be nurtured in a family jointly engaged in creative, essential work, not simply from proper moral instruction. "The transmission of morals is no longer safe in the family," Luther Gulick glumly concluded, "because the activities out of which morals arise have been taken away."[2]

Nor could numerous casual contacts with other adults shape the youth's character. Increasingly, the new society segregated teenagers from the general work force. In the early nineteenth century, children fourteen or younger had been expected to leave the family and strike out on their own. Sometimes they became apprentices learning a skill, or they might experiment with a variety of jobs and sporadically attend local academies. But the growing reliance on machinery in the nineteenth century gradually undermined the apprenticeship system. Countless youths were left with dead-end jobs that required few if any skills and offered even fewer opportunities for a better future. While the sons of workingmen had no choice but to continue taking jobs in industry at a tender age, middle- and upper-income parents began to encourage their sons to enter the growing white collar sector of the economy. The key to becoming a lawyer, doctor, accountant, engineer, or business manager seemed to be an extended education, lasting until age sixteen or even longer. Parents who could afford to do so began to withdraw their children from the job market and send them to school.

The push by middle- and upper-income parents for longer periods of formal education coincided with the passage of state laws that had the effect of

---

[1] For the larger movement to organize and manage the spare-time activities of youth, see Joseph F. Kett, *Rites of Passage: Adolescence in America, 1790 to the Present* (New York, 1979), and Paul Boyer, *Urban Masses and Moral Order in America, 1820–1920* (Cambridge, MA, 1978). Specifically on the organized play movement, see the historiographical essay by Stephen Hardy and Alan G. Ingham, "Games, Structures and Agencies: Historians on the American Play Movement," *Journal of Social History*, 17 (1983), 285–301.

[2] Luther Halsey Gulick, *A Philosophy of Play* (New York, 1920), p. 219.

barring younger adolescents from the workforce. In the first two decades of the twentieth century, most of the states, as part of the "Progressive" reform impulse, increased the length of the school term from four months to nine months, extended compulsory school attendance to the age of fourteen or longer, and prohibited children from working at full-time jobs until they were fourteen or even sixteen. "The whole tendency of the times, therefore, is to drive children under sixteen out of work and into school," noted the Fall River, Massachusetts, school board in 1914.[3] Not only did this legislation deny younger adolescents opportunities for employment, but it also made long periods of seasonal work combined with school attendance impossible.

The separation of teenagers from the general work force undermined a traditional source of socialization. Instead of numerous casual contacts with adults through early work experience, youths now spent most of their time in school with other youngsters or in leisure activities that were unsupervised by adults. The school tended to restrict youth-adult interaction to the highly formal student-teacher relationship. The abundance of unmanaged spare time that younger adolescents increasingly enjoyed was a cause of deep concern for parents and youth observers alike. Unless offset by morally uplifting activity organized by adults, the ethical growth of the urban youth was endangered by the pervasive wickedness of the city. Urban children, declared one youth worker, "watch the drunken people, listen to the leader of the gang, hear the shady story, smoke cigarettes, and acquire those vicious habits, knowledge, and vocabulary which are characteristic" of the worst denizens of the city.[4]

Profound suspicions of the burgeoning cities and deep nostalgia for the countryside shaped the attitudes and values of the "boy-workers" in the YMCA, the playgrounds, the Scouts, and the high schools. To them, the cities seemed to symbolize the triumph of the values of the marketplace over the older values of the church, family, and small community. Furthermore, the city was the principal home of alien peoples who held strange beliefs and often violated the behavioral codes of old-stock Americans. Traditional social restraints seemed to evaporate in the cities. Boys were vulnerable to a host of new "perversions"— "the mad rush for sudden wealth," the impulse to mature too quickly, the emulation of the "reckless fashions set by gilded youth," membership in juvenile gangs, impure sexual thoughts and practices, the "secret vice" (masturbation), and fornication. While the city was an unmitigated college of vice for youth, the country was a college of virtue. "The country boy roams the hills and has free access to 'God's first temples,' " asserted F. D. Bonyton, the superintendent of Ithaca schools, in 1904. "What can we offer to the city boy in exchange for paradise lost? His only road to paradise regained is thru the gymnasium, the athletic field, and the playground."[5] Sport, many of the boy-workers came to believe, could serve as an effective surrogate for the lost rural experience.

[3]As quoted in Kett, *The Rites of Passage*, p. 235.
[4]Henry S. Curtis, *The Play Movement and Its Significance* (New York, 1917), pp. 119–20.
[5]F. D. Bonyton, "Athletics and Collateral Activities in Secondary Schools," *Proceedings and Addresses of the National Education Association* (1904), 210.

MUSCULAR CHRISTIANITY AND THE YMCA

To the advocates of the new sporting ideology, modern life had become too soft and effeminate. (See Chapter 8.) Frontiers and battlefields no longer existed to test manly courage and perseverance. Henry W. Williams observed that the "struggle for existence, though becoming harder and harder, is less and less a physical struggle, more and more a battle of minds."[6] Apart from sports, men no longer had arenas for proving their manliness. Theodore Roosevelt worried lest prolonged periods of peace would encourage "effeminate tendencies in young men." Only aggressive sports, Roosevelt argued, could create the "brawn, the spirit, the self-confidence, and quickness of men" that was essential for the existence of a strong nation.[7] In the view of the sport advocates, no game (unless it be boxing) rivalled football in its capacity to instill manliness. The football field "is the only place where masculine supremacy in incontestable," concluded an *Independent* editorial.[8]

In the post-Civil War era, manliness took on additional meanings. Traditionally, manliness meant the opposite of childlike; it signified adulthood, maturity, and self-control. But as the opportunities for the more overt expressions of manliness in the workplace declined and as male social dominance seemed less secure, manliness acquired tougher, more assertive qualities. It included the negation of all that was soft, feminine, or sentimental. Manly men purged longings for ease and comfort; they welcomed strife, strenuous exertion, and physical risks. Their fantasy heroes were daring hunters, cowboys, detectives, adventurers, and athletes rather than tepid businessmen, statesmen, clergymen, or literati.

Sport fiction furnished the most popular vehicle for the transmission of Christian manliness to boys. Thomas Hughes' classic, *Tom Brown's School Days*, published in 1857, inaugurated the new genre of boys' sport fiction. *Tom Brown's School Days*, immensely successful throughout the English-speaking world, spawned a few pale imitations over the next quarter century. Then the 1890s witnessed a virtual flood of boys' sport novels. Beginning in 1896, Gilbert Patten, writing under the nom de plume of Burt L. Standish, introduced the Merriwell series. Over the next twenty years Patten produced 208 Merriwell books, all of which revolved around boyhood manliness. Although a pious man, Patten refrained from preaching explicit Christian doctrines. Instead, he attempted to convince his youthful readers that vigorous participation in athletics would result in personal moral improvement and enhance one's probability of material success. Edward Stratemeyer, the inventor of the Rover Boys along with seven other series, was even more popular than Patten. Stratemeyer and his stable of

[6]Henry W. Williams, "The Educational and Health Giving Value of Athletics," *Harper's Weekly* (Feb. 16, 1895), 166.

[7]Quoted in Joe L. Dubbert, *A Man's Place: Masculinity in Transition* (Englewood Cliffs, NJ, 1979), pp. 116, 117. For discussions of manliness see esp. Elliot J. Gorn, *The Manly Art: Bare-Knuckle Prize Fighting in America* (Ithaca, NY, 1986), and Gorn's references to other works treating manliness.

[8]"The Uncultured Sex," *Independent* (Nov. 11, 1909), 1100.

hack writers stressed adventure, action, humor, and suspense at the expense of moral instruction. By 1920 most of the authors of boys' sport fiction had removed all overt moralizing from their novels, but the "manliness" of Thomas Hughes's original formula remained intact.[9]

In the last quarter of the nineteenth century, the popularity of Christian manliness began to extend beyond the eastern elite to middle-income Protestants, even to those of an evangelical temperament. The favorable response of these groups to muscular Christianity reflected a growing anxiety with the alleged "feminization" of American Protestantism as well as the excessive decorums of Victorian life. Church leaders had long been concerned with their inability to reach both adolescent boys and young men. Women and girls made up the large majority of most Protestant congregations. Furthermore, to those who advocated a virile Christianity, the churches overemphasized the feminine virtues of humility, submission, and meekness. "There is not enough of effort, of struggle, in the typical church life of today . . . ," declared Josiah Strong, a popular exponent of a manly Christianity. "A flowery bed of ease does not appeal to a fellow who has any manhood in him. . . . Eliminate heroism from religion and it becomes weak, effeminate."[10]

By the 1890s, the Young Men's Christian Association had emerged as the outstanding institutional expression of muscular Christianity among evangelical Protestants. Founded by laymen in England in 1851 and subsequently transplanted to the United States before the Civil War, the original purpose of the YMCA had been to offer spiritual guidance and practical assistance to the young men who were flooding into the nineteenth-century cities. But after the Civil War, the local YMCAs began to broaden their program. To attract young men and boys to their spiritual work they offered classes in physical culture, largely in the form of gymnastics and calisthenics. Instead of young displaced males, the main clientele of the YMCAs became young men from the "clerical classes" (bookkeepers, stenographers, clerks, and salesmen), businessmen, a few skilled workingmen, and boys from the middle- and upper-income ranks.[11] By 1892 the YMCA membership had leaped to nearly a quarter of a million, and the organization had 348 gymnasiums directed by 144 full-time physical leaders.

One man, Luther Halsey Gulick, Jr., who began his career with the YMCA, played a preeminent role in all phases of the adult-directed boys' sport

[9]See John Levi Cutler, *Gilbert Patten and His Frank Merriwell Saga* (Orono, ME, 1934); Walter Evans, "The All-American Boys: A Study of Boys' Sport Fiction," *Journal of Popular Culture,* 6 (1972), 104–21; Russel B. Nye, "The Juvenile Approach to American Culture," in Ray B. Browne, et. al., *New Voices in American Studies* (West Lafayette, IN, 1966), pp. 67–84.

[10]Josiah Strong, *The Times and Young Men* (New York, 1901), pp. 179–80. See Barbara Welter, "The Feminization of American Religion, 1800–1860," in William L. O'Neil, ed., *Insights and Parallels: Problems and Issues in American Social History* (Minneapolis, 1973), 305–55.

[11]Luther Gulick, "Young Men of the Cities, II," *Athletic League Letters* (Feb. 1899); Boyer, *Urban Masses,* pp. 115–16; Lawrence W. Fielding and Clark F. Wood, "The Social Control of Indolence and Irreligion: Louisville's First YWCA Movement, 1853–1871," *Filsom Club Historical Quarterly,* 58 (1984), 219–36.

movement. Born of missionary parents in Honolulu, Hawaii, Gulick waged a "determined war" against the "subjective type of religion" fostered by pietistic Protestants.[12] While he rejected the formal religious doctrine of his parents, he retained a zest for embarking on crusades. He discovered his equivalent of a spiritual calling by becoming in turn the champion of muscular Christianity within the YMCA, a major proponent of a new theory of play, the founder of the Public Schools Athletic League in New York City, an organizer and the first president of the Playground Association of America, a leader of the American Boy Scout movement, and the cofounder with his wife of the American Campfire Girls. According to Gulick, he turned to the strenuous life partly as a way of compensating for his personal feelings of physical and psychical inadequacy. Throughout his life he suffered from severe migraine headaches, periods of dark depression, and a weak physical constitution, all of which he attributed to his father, who had been the victim of a nervous breakdown.

Although Gulick obtained a medical degree, he found far more exciting work than medicine in 1887 as an instructor in the physical department of the International Young Men's Christian Association Training School (later renamed Springfield College) in Springfield, Massachusetts. Since most of the general secretaries and physical directors of local YMCAs passed through the regular two-year curriculum or summer school of the training school, Gulick had found an ideal position for reaching a national and even an international audience. In journals he edited for the training school, in numerous articles and books, and in speeches delivered throughout the country, Gulick unrelentingly preached the same gospel: the spiritual life of man rested on the equal development of the mind and the body. Gulick invented the famous emblem of the YMCA, the inverted triangle which symbolized the spirit supported by the mind and the body. Unlike prior YMCA leaders, Gulick welcomed the introduction of sport into YMCA programs. "We can use the drawing power of athletics a great deal more than we are doing at present," he wrote in 1892, but he cautioned that ". . . we must work along our own lines and not ape the athletic organizations, whose object is the development of specialists and the breaking of records."[13]

Under Gulick's aegis, competitive sport, despite formidable opposition, began to supplant gymnastics in YMCA physical programs. The Springfield training school itself furnished an example of athletic activism to the local YMCAs. Throughout the 1890s the school fielded a baseball team. From time to time the college also sponsored competition with outside institutions in track and field, swimming, gymnastics, basketball, and volleyball. In 1890 Amos Alonzo Stagg, a famed Yale football player of the 1880s, enrolled at Springfield. He promptly gathered a team of faculty and students, about half of whom had never played football before, and challenged all the prominent northeastern colleges to games. That fall, "Stagg's Stubby Christians" almost upset mighty Yale before succumbing 16 to 10 in the country's first indoor football game in

[12]See Ethel Josephine Dorgan, *Luther Halsey Gulick, 1865–1918* (New York, 1934).
[13]Gulick, "State Committees on Athletics," *Young Men's Era*, 18 (1892), 1365.

LUTHER HALSEY GULICK (1865–1918)
A pioneer in the Young Men's Christian Association, school sports, and the playground movement, Gulick helped develop a theory of play that exercised a vast influence over organized recreation for youth.

Madison Square Garden. The vigorous sport program at Springfield and the experience of the students there inspired YMCAs everywhere to organize their own athletic teams.

While the physical curriculum of the training school continued to center on such subjects as anatomy and motor development, Gulick added a pioneering course in the psychology of play as well as training in specific sport skills. In his psychology of play course, he asked students to experiment with new games and sports that could be played in the confined space of gymnasiums and that would be appropriate to a certain level of maturity. The invention of both basketball and volleyball resulted from Gulick's inspiration and suggestions. In 1891, James A. Naismith, a young minister from Canada who was a student and part-time instructor at Springfield, put together the essentials of the game of basketball, and in 1895, William G. Morgan, while serving as physical director of the YMCA at Holyoke, Massachusetts, invented volleyball especially for older men who found basketball too strenuous.[14]

The unbridled enthusiasm of the young men and adolescent boys for basketball and other forms of athletic competition presented the YMCA leader-

[14]See Bernice Larson Webb, *The Basketball Man, James Naismith* (Lawrence, KS, 1973) and the journals *Men, Physical Education, Triangle, Young Men's Era,* and *Athletic League Letters,* as well as the *Yearbooks of Young Men's Christian Association.*

ship with a trying dilemma. On the one hand, the organized games obviously increased membership, interest, and the physical prowess of the participants. On the other hand, basketball threatened to convert the YMCAs into full-fledged athletic clubs. As early as 1892, Gulick had warned the association of the dangers of a spectator-centered orientation. Nonetheless, by the mid-1890s, in one local YMCA after another, basketball threatened to drive all other forms of physical activity off the gymnasium floor. "In several places," Gulick reported in 1895, "the game was played with such fierceness last year, the crowds who looked on became so boisterous and rowdyish, and the bad feeling developed between teams so extreme that the game has been abolished in toto."[15] Yet most YMCAs took far less drastic steps. In 1895, the YMCA formed the Athletic League of North America with Gulick as secretary. To curtail excesses the league joined the Amateur Athletic Union, published a monthly newsletter, and developed an extensive body of rules and sanctions.

Ultimately, the league failed to ensure the "purity" of YMCA athletic programs. By 1905, YMCA teams regularly played over 2,000 games with outside competitors. In their contests with the collegians and athletic clubs, the Y athletes enjoyed remarkable success, whether it was in track and field, swimming, or basketball. For example, for over a dozen years the Buffalo German YMCA team totally dominated championship basketball. They won the Buffalo Exposition tournament in 1901 and won the gold medal at the 1904 Olympic Games in St. Louis. Eventually, much to the relief of YMCA officials, the Germans became an avowed professional team. The spirit of rivalry, athletic specialization, and even professional tendencies of YMCA athletics equalled that of the athletic clubs and the colleges. Local YMCAs, despite the repeated admonitions of the Athletic League officials, were guilty of extending to star athletes special privileges such as free memberships, room and board, and generous traveling allowances to compete away from home. Many of the local secretaries and physical directors tried to resist "excessive" athleticism, but others capitulated to the demands of their membership.[16]

In 1911, several years after Gulick had resigned as secretary of the Athletic League and as an instructor at the training school, the YMCA changed the entire focus of its athletic programs. Henry F. Kallenberg, the new physical director at Springfield, recommended a radical break from past practices. The YMCA should, Kallenberg argued, promote a comprehensive sport program that would reach the "mass of young men and boys, [and] discourage prize winning and overtraining."[17] Competition should be restricted to males of a similar age and weight and be restricted to local teams. At Kallenberg's initiative, the league severed its relationship with the Amateur Athletic Union and began to organize

[15]Gulick, "Basket Ball," *Physical Education*, 4 (1895), 1200. See also Gulick, "Abolish Basket Ball," *Men*, 5 (1897), 687.

[16]In addition to *Athletic League Letters*, 1896–1911, see William H. Ball, "The Administration of Athletics in the Young Men's Christian Association," *American Physical Education Review*, 16 (1911), 12–22.

[17]*Athletic League Letters*, June 1911, 1.

local amateur athletic federations composed of Ys, high schools, churches, Turners, and other groups. By 1920 the YMCA had essentially completed Kallenberg's reform agenda. Never again would the YMCAs attempt to compete at championship levels in athletics.

THE EVOLUTIONARY THEORY OF PLAY

In the 1890s, G. Stanley Hall, a pioneer in genetic psychology at Clark University, and Gulick, once a student of Hall's summer school, began to work out an evolutionary theory of play that exercised an immense influence on every phase of the early twentieth-century boys-work. Hall and Gulick believed that humans had acquired the fundamental impulse to play during the evolution of the "race." Each person, as he or she passed from birth to adulthood, recapitulated or rehearsed in an approximate way each epoch or stage of human evolution. The play activities of early childhood—spontaneous kicking and squirming in infancy and running and throwing when a bit older—corresponded to the play of primal ancestors. The track, field, and tag games common to children between the ages of seven and twelve sprang from the hunting instinct acquired during the presavage stage of evolution. Games at this stage were individualistic. Finally, the complex group games of adolescent boys—baseball, basketball, football, and cricket—rested on a combination of the earlier hunting instinct and the new instinct of cooperation, the latter having emerged during the savage epoch of evolution, when savages hunted and fought in groups while subordinating themselves to the leadership of a chief.

That each person recapitulate the history of the race through sports was essential to proper physical, moral, and neural growth. Complex motor behavior became "reflexive" through repetition. Bountiful physical activity in childhood not only developed muscles but also spurred the growth of neural centers in the spinal cord and brain. Directed motor behavior was also the primary agency in shaping moral "reflexes." When the youth repeated via games the evolution of man, he engaged in physical activities that embodied moral principles. "Life for others is rendered far more probable, natural and tangible," Gulick wrote, "when it comes as a gradual unfolding and development of that instinct that has its first great impulse of growth in the games of adolescence."[18] Too often, however, the instincts from which group games sprang could result in the ripening of wicked reflexes, such as the juvenile gang of the city, "the most perilous force in modern civilization," rather than team contests supervised by adults.

Team sport, then, offered an unparalleled opportunity for adults to encourage in boys the healthy growth of moral and religious reflexes. Stemming

[18]Luther Gulick, "Psychological, Pedagogical, and Religious Aspects of Group Games," *Pedagogical Seminary*, 6 (1899). See also Gulick, "Psychical Aspects of Muscular Exercise," *Popular Science Monthly*, 53 (1898), 793–805 and "The Psychology of Play," *Association Outlook*, 8 (1899), 112–16.

from the instinct for cooperation, team sports required the highest moral principles—teamwork, self-sacrifice, obedience, self-control, and loyalty. "These qualities appear to me," Gulick wrote, "to be a great pulse of beginning altruism, of self-sacrifice, of that capacity upon which Christianity is based."[19] The churches and the YMCA sought to deemphasize the teaching of feminine traits to boys and present Jesus in terms of his "noble heroism . . . his magnificent manliness, his denunciation of wickedness in public places, [and] his life of service to others. . . . "[20] Gulick's conception of Christian manliness hardly squared with the injunction of Jesus to turn the other cheek when wronged. On one occasion, he advised that a boy should have the ability and the courage to "punch another boy's head or to stand having his own punched in a healthy and proper manner."[21] Gulick's theory implied a far more radical departure from orthodox Protestantism than he probably recognized. For his ideas not only made the religious and moral life almost exclusively a matter of vigorous activity—almost activity for activity's sake—but also suggested a naturalistic explanation for the origins of human religious sentiments.

In one version or another, the evolutionary theory of play became part of the conventional wisdom of the boy-workers in the first two decades of the twentieth century. G. Stanley Hall repeated it almost verbatim in his classic two-volume work on adolescence published in 1905.[22] Joseph Lee, a prolific writer on play, took as his major premise the notion that play arose from an earlier stage of man's evolution, from the "barbaric and predatory society to which the boy naturally belongs."[23] Henry S. Curtis, a pioneer in both the playground and Boy Scout movements, wrote that athletics "are the activities of our ancestors conventionalized and adapted to present conditions. They are reminiscent of the physical age, of the struggle for survival, of the hunt, of the chase, and of war."[24] William Forbush, an ardent disciple of Gulick and Hall, may have reached the largest audience of all in his *The Boy Problem*, an advice manual reprinted eight times between 1901 and 1912. Each boy, Forbush wrote, repeated the "history of his race-life from savagery unto civilization."[25]

The acceptance by the boy-workers of an evolutionary theory of play had important implications for the use of sport as a socializing agency. First, it seemed to require the creation of special institutions for boys that would be closely supervised by adults. Unregulated activity would fail to encourage desirable social traits. Second, the theory encouraged boy-workers to relinquish the ex-

---

[19]Gulick, "Psychological," 142.

[20]*Athletic League Letters*, June 1901, 65.

[21]Gulick, "The Alleged Effeminization of Our American Boys," *American Physical Education Review*, 10 (1905), 217.

[22]G. Stanley Hall, *Adolescence*, 2 vols. (New York, 1905), I, 202–23.

[23]Joseph Lee, *Play in Education* (New York, 1915), p. 234.

[24]Curtis, "The Proper Relation of Organized Sports on Public Playgrounds and in Public Spaces," *Playground*, 3 (1909), 14.

[25]William Byron Forbush, *The Boy Problem* (Boston, 1901), p. 9.

treme forms of piety associated with the evangelical temperament and emphasize activity at the expense of spirituality or intellectuality. The YMCA became increasingly secular in its programs. Many of the "institutional" or "social gospel" Protestant churches in the larger cities abandoned explicitly spiritual programs for boys in favor of organized activities ranging from dances to baseball matches. Beginning in Brooklyn in 1904, one city after another organized Sunday School athletic leagues. In 1916, through the creation of the Boys' Brigade, Catholics also joined the boys' sport movement.[26] Third, the play theory permitted boy-workers to subordinate ethnic, religious, and social class differences to a presumably universal experience of maturation. Thus the boy leaders saw no need to fashion special programs for boys with distinctive social or cultural characteristics. Finally, the evolutionary theory of play furnished a rationale for the sexual segregation of organized play, a rationale that would influence youth workers and physical educators until past the middle of the twentieth century.

THE PUBLIC SCHOOLS ATHLETIC LEAGUE

In the first two decades of the twentieth century, Gulick, Hall, and their followers found ample opportunities to put their theory of play into practice. After leaving the YMCA training school in 1900 and serving for three years as principal of Pratt Institute High School in Brooklyn, Gulick, in 1903, became the director of physical training of the public schools of Greater New York City. Rather than relying exclusively on traditional gymnastics and calisthenics to nurture physical and moral growth, Gulick quickly determined that "*all* the boys in the city needed the physical benefits and moral and social lessons afforded by properly conducted games and sport."[27] Consequently, he formed the Public Schools Athletic League (PSAL) in 1903. Although the PSAL was financially independent of the school system, it depended upon the city's 630 schools for implementing its program. It won the immediate plaudits of the city's press and the endorsement of such czars of industry and finance as Andrew Carnegie, John D. Rockefeller, J. Pierpont Morgan, S. R. Guggenheim, and Henry Payne Whitney, who contributed munificently to the league's finances.

Underlying the enthusiastic reception of the league was a manifest fear of the city's foreign-born population. The founders were not only concerned with the absence of play experience by immigrant youths, recalled General George W. Wingate, the long-time president of the league, but they "also found the morals of the boys were deteriorating even more than their bodies."[28] The school boys often joined street gangs, engaged in criminal acts, and defied the authority of

---

[26]See George D. Pratt, "The Sunday School Athletic League," *Work With Boys*, 4 (1905), 131–37; "Recreation in the Church," *Literary Digest*, 53 (1916), 256; Richard A. Swanson, "American Protestantism and Play, 1865–1915," unpub. Ph.D. diss., Ohio State Univ., 1967.

[27]Gulick, "Athletics for School Children," *Lippincott's Monthly Magazine*, 88 (1911), 201.

[28]George B. Wingate, "The Public Schools Athletic League," *Outing*, 52 (1908), 166.

their teachers. Above all, the ethnic youngsters exhibited a lack of understanding of American values and institutions. A carefully managed sport program, the founders believed, would reduce juvenile delinquency and "Americanize" the ethnic youth of the ghettos. By 1910, the PSAL, which was hailed as "The World's Greatest Athletic Organization," had at least seventeen imitators in other large American cities.[29] Moreover, in 1905, the league had added a Girls' Branch. But, unlike the boys' division, the Girls' Branch did not permit public interschool competition.

The league's comprehensive athletic program embodied the latest wisdom of the play theorists. To ensure maximum participation of the school boys, the league included three separate forms of competition. By reaching a minimum level of performance in several physical feats, every boy could win the Athletic Badge. A widely heralded means of encouraging overall physical development, the badge test served as a model for a similar program implemented by the Playground Association of America in 1913 and for the President's physical fitness drive which began in the 1950s. The second form of competition, class athletics, pitted the average performance of one school class in certain track and field events against the average of another. Finally, the league sponsored district and city championships in more than a dozen sports. Baseball was especially popular. In 1907, 106 teams competed, and over 15,000 fans attended the championship game held in the Polo Grounds. Class, district, and city champions received expensive trophies.

The introduction of rifle-shooting competition among the high school boys by the PSAL suggested the special fondness that most of the boy-workers had for martial virtues. By 1908, over 7,000 boys competed for marksmanship badges. Each year, President Theodore Roosevelt wrote a letter of commendation to the boy receiving the highest marks, and the E. I. du Pont de Nemours Powder Company awarded prizes to the school team having the highest scores. General Wingate declared that none of the sports conducted by the league "was likely to have as important an influence on the country at large as the system of instruction in military rifle shooting."[30]

"Duty," "Thoroughness," "Patriotism," "Honor," and "Obedience"— these were the official mottoes of the Public Schools Athletic League. To inculcate such values, the league consciously exploited the athletic interests of the students. Each year General Wingate wrote an open letter to the boys warning them of a host of dangers that might adversely affect their athletic performances. Above all, "you must keep out of bad influences of the street if you want to be strong," he wrote.[31] While it may be doubted that Wingate's advice had much influence on the behavior of the boys while they were away from school, the teachers

[29]Albert B. Reeve, "The World's Greatest Athletic Organization," *Outing*, 57 (1910), 107–14; J. Thomas Jable, "The Public Schools Athletic League of New York City: Organized Athletics for City Schoolchildren, 1903–1914," in Steven A. Riess, ed., *The American Sporting Experience* (West Point, NY, 1984), 219–38.

[30]Wingate, "The Public Schools," 174.

[31]Ibid., 169.

quickly recognized that the PSAL could be used effectively to promote discipline in the classroom. "All of the little imps in my class have become saints," wrote one teacher, "not because they want to be saints, but because they want to compete in your games."[32] No student could compete without a certification from his teachers that his deportment and class performance had been satisfactory. Peer group pressure also encouraged student conformity. "Many a big, vigorous boy out of sympathy with his school work," reported another source, "is driven to his lessons by his mates so that he can be eligible to represent his school."[33] Perhaps it was little wonder that the city's teachers volunteered to spend long hours after school and on weekends in planning and supervising every aspect of the league's program. The improvement by the student "on the side of ethics, school discipline, and *esprit de corps* is even greater," concluded a report in 1910, than in athletic proficiency.[34] Nonetheless, the PSAL failed to alter the lives of over two-thirds of the city's adolescent boy population. For these older boys did not attend school and in most cases had already entered the labor market.

THE PLAYGROUND MOVEMENT

The early twentieth-century movement for city playgrounds furnished Gulick and his followers with even broader opportunities for implementing their evolutionary theory of play. Prior to 1900, a few private citizens and charity groups had organized playgrounds—usually consisting of sandpiles and simple play equipment—for preadolescent children in the slums of the larger cities. A turning point came in 1903 when the voters of the Chicago South Park District approved of a $5 million bond issue for the construction of ten parks. Unlike previous efforts, the Chicago system included field houses at each park with a gymnasium for both boys and girls. Moreover, the Chicago authorities hired a professional physical educator, Edward B. de Groot, as director and furnished each park with two year-round instructors to supervise play activities. The managers of the new system sponsored a host of activities ranging from organized athletic leagues to community folk dances. Inspired by the Chicago example and driven by anxieties arising from modern cities, middle- and upper-income taxpayers exhibited a remarkable enthusiasm for supervised recreation programs. Between 1906 and 1917 the number of cities with managed playgrounds grew from 41 to 504.[35]

The same concerns and values that shaped the PSAL also guided the work of playground leaders. The evolutionary theory of play furnished them with ready-made formulas for supervising playgrounds. For example, among the questions on the standard examination administered to all candidates for employment with the New York playgrounds was: "What is meant by the 'club

[32]Reeve, "The World's Greatest Athletic Organization," 110.
[33]Clarence Arthur Perry, *Wider Use of the School Plant* (New York, 1910), p. 308.
[34]Reeve, "The World's Greatest Athletic Organization," 108.
[35]See the literature cited in Hardy and Ingham, "Games, Structures and Agencies."

or gregarious instinct?' How can it be developed and utilized with beneficial results on the playground? What athletic events are appropriate for boys aged 10–14? . . . for boys aged 14 to 16?"[36] Not only were prospective playground leaders expected to master the principles and practical implications of play theory, they also had to be able to exercise the subtle psychological techniques essential for managing youth without resorting to harsh repression. Edward B. de Groot summed up the prevailing conception of the ideal playground director. "The men or women employed for playground service . . . should not be regarded as mere instructors, play bosses, or leaders of games, but rather as thoughtful managers, interpreters of child and adolescent life, chemists of human desires, and captains of the marching legions of young people on the way to a 'square deal' citizenship."[37] The playground leaders abhorred the unsupervised, unstructured play that arose from the spontaneous impulses of children. Henry S. Curtis, in the leading textbook for playground supervisors, wrote that "scrub play," that is, play that the children themselves initiated, "can never give that training either of body or conduct, which organized play should give; for in order to develop the body, it must be vigorous, to train the intellect, it must be exciting, to train the social conscience, it must be socially organized. None of these results come from scrub play."[38]

Despite the enthusiasm of municipal governments for organized recreation, the playgrounds usually failed to extend their control over spare-time activities to those who presumably needed it the most—the ethnic youth in the slums. According to the sweeping claims of the playground leaders, supervised recreation sharply reduced the incidence of juvenile delinquency, but even Henry Curtis admitted that less than 10 percent of the urban youngsters regularly used available playgrounds. The playgrounds appealed most to the children of old-stock families of the middle- and upper-income ranks, youngsters who had been shaped by the same values espoused by recreation leaders. The children of the slums tended to admire physical prowess—particularly as expressed in streetfighting—spontaneity, and defiance of authority rather than the values of self-restraint and cooperation so dear to the playground leaders. Conflicts between recreation supervisors and ghetto youths were inevitable. To attract such youths, the leaders had to make compromises with the values of the slum subculture and remove heavyhanded, detailed supervision. Yet the absence of direction not only ran counter to prevailing playground theory, it could result in the transformation of the playground into an asphalt jungle in which the strongest and most vicious boys ruled the grounds by intimidation. Even in 1920 there were clear harbingers of the typical inner-city playground of the mid-twentieth century, which, except for a few of the toughest adolescent boys in the neighborhood, often stood empty.[39]

---

[36]"Questions for Teachers to Answer," *American Gymnasia*, 2 (1906), 149.

[37]Edward B. DeGroot, "The Management of Park Playgrounds," *Playground*, 8 (1914), 273.

[38]Curtis, *The Play Movement*, p. 81.

[39]See ibid., pp. 31, 83; Howard R. Knight, *Play and Recreation in a Town of 6000* (New York, n.d.), p. 25; L. H. Wier, "Playgrounds and Juvenile Delinquency," *Playground*, 4 (1910), 37–40; Gulick, *A Philosophy of Play*, pp. 223–45.

HIGH SCHOOL SPORTS

Like the YMCA, the PSAL, and the playgrounds, the demand for the adult management of public high school athletics arose from several sources. In the first place, in order to preserve the moral image of their institutions, educators eventually felt compelled to extend their authority over interscholastic competition. High school sport had begun in the nineteenth century at the initiative of the students themselves; students had formed the first athletic organizations, scheduled the first games, managed the finances, and hired seasonal coaches. By the 1890s, in some places, the rage for football in the larger high schools equalled or surpassed that of the colleges. High school authorities could no longer ignore interscholastic sport, for sport imposed on the academic functions of the school. High school sport not only absorbed student interest at the expense of their study, it was guilty of all the same "abuses" as college sport—winning at all costs, use of "ineligible" players, and financial mismanagement. "Athletic contests between different high schools," declared one irate principal in 1905, "cause a reduction in the class standing of the students participating, teach boys to smoke cigarettes, loaf in the streets during school hours, and use unfair methods in order to win, and make liars out of many teachers and students."[40] To curtail such evils, high school educators across the country tried to increase their authority over interscholastic sport. By 1902, when the Fifteenth Educational Conference of Academies and High Schools met, the faculties had already gained basic control of interscholastic sport in Wisconsin, Illinois, and at several of the boarding schools of the Northeast. That year, the conference recommended strict faculty supervision, the limitation of interscholastic athletics to bona fide students, and the formation of associations to regulate competition. By 1923, only three states were without state-wide interscholastic athletic organizations.[41]

The emergence of the "comprehensive" high school in the twentieth century encouraged both the extension of adult control and the growth of school sport. In the three decades before 1920 the comprehensive high school gradually supplanted the academic-oriented high school. In 1893, the Committee of Ten, chaired by President Charles W. Eliot of Harvard, had called for a continuation with only slight modifications of the classical curriculum, a course of study that featured Greek, Latin, mathematics, oratory, and writing. The committee visualized the high school as an academic institution designed to prepare students for entrance into the colleges. In the years following the committee's position came under heavy attack, especially from middle-income parents who wanted their sons to develop the social poise required of white collar occupations and from

---

[40]"Public School Notes," *American Gymnasia*, 1 (1905), 215.

[41]Lewis Hoch Wagenhorst, *The Administration and Cost of High School Interscholastic Athletics* (New York, 1926), p. 9; "The Question of School and College Athletics," *School Review*, 10 (1902), 4–8; Jeffrey Mirel, "From Student Control to Institutional Control of High School Athletics: Three Michigan Cities," *Journal of Social History*, 16 (Winter 1983), 82–99; Timothy P. O'Hanlon, "School Sports as Social Training: The Case of Athletics and the Crisis of World War I," *Journal of Sport History*, 9 (1982), 5–29.

"social" educators who believed the school ought to be a major agency for the preparation of youth for adulthood. By 1917, when a special committee of the National Education Association published *The Cardinal Principles of Secondary Education,* the social educators and middle-income parents had routed the defenders of the classical curriculum.[42]

The proponents of the comprehensive high school shared many of the perceptions and ideas of the boy-workers. They believed that modern industrial life had eroded the traditional socializing institutions. According to *The Cardinal Principles:* "In connection with home and family life have frequently come lessened responsibility on the part of the children; the withdrawal of the father and sometimes the mother from home occupations to the factory or store; and increased urbanization resulting in less unified family life. Similarly, many important changes have taken place in community life, in the church, in the State, and in other institutions. These changes in American life call for extensive modifications in secondary education."[43] To meet these changes the committee recommended two goals for the high school: prepare the students for vocations and teach them the social values essential for coping with modern life. By social values the committee meant "those common ideas, common ideals, and common modes of thought, feeling, and action that make for cooperation, social cohesion, and social solidarity."[44] Vocational preparation required that the school offer a wide range of subjects, expert guidance, and a differentiated curriculum. Inculcating the social values necessary for establishing a genuine community was a much more difficult task, for the students lacked a common curriculum, represented different "racial stocks," and had "differing religious beliefs." Like Gulick, the social educators believed that activity rather than the teaching of moral precepts was the key to developing proper social or moral traits. Thus they advocated that the high school give special attention to the "participation of pupils in common activities . . . such as athletic games, social activities, and the government of the school."[45]

Underlying the attention that social educators gave to the extracurricular activities of their students was an acute awareness of adolescent sexuality, a subject approached with excruciating obliqueness. For example, a report of the National Education Association of 1911 argued that moral training in high school had to differ from that in grammar school because the teenage years were a "time of life when [sexual] passion is born [and] which must be restrained and guided aright or it consumes the soul and body." Formal classroom work was not enough. Only athletics could, Henry S. Curtis wrote, "use the sex energy directly and so ease the strain"; they could "use the time that is often devoted to obscene gossip or experiences" by promoting "a

[42]See Kett, *Rites of Passage,* pp. 235–36, and Joel H. Spring, *Education and the Corporate State* (Boston, 1972), esp. Chap. 6.

[43]*Cardinal Principles of Secondary Education,* Bul. 1918, no. 35 (Washington, DC, 1918), pp. 7–8.

[44]Ibid., p. 21.

[45]Ibid., p. 23.

healthful fatigue and sound sleep;" in short, they could "strengthen the will to resist" sexual urges.[46]

Educational leaders also recognized that interscholastic athletics could be used to solve the problem of controlling the behavior of a heterogeneous mass of potentially rebellious students. Apart from interscholastic athletics, the public high schools had no common goals that could inspire the allegiance of the student body as a whole. Many of the students attended school only because of parental or legal compulsion. Few students found in grades alone an adequate motive for a positive identification with the high school. Grades tended to encourage individual achievement, student competition rather than cooperation. But varsity sport could rally the student body in a common cause; it could create an *esprit de corps*, "a mass spirit in which each individual surrenders himself" to a common goal.[47] Such a communal spirit encouraged a positive attitude toward the high school and a peaceful acquiescence of the students to adult direction.

Moreover, high school sports helped give an identity and common purpose to many neighborhoods, towns, and cities which were otherwise divided by class, race, ethnicity, or religious differences. These geographic entities, like the schools without interscholastic games, lacked collective goals. Varsity sport could coalesce them into a united front. High school sport could become a community enterprise; the entire community might celebrate victories or mourn losses in concert. The result of this identification of the community with school sport was quite evident in teachers' salaries, for school boards typically paid the coach more than any other teacher. "You know that, if a principal is looking for a teacher, one of the first questions he asks frequently is: 'Can this man be of use in connection with athletics?' " reported Edwin H. Hall as early as 1905, "and the man who can be of use in connection with athletics gets more money, gets the place sooner, than another man."[48] Likewise, school boards invariably placed a higher priority on the construction of a gymnasium or a football field than they did a laboratory or library. In the 1920s, high schools, both small and large, built expensive athletic facilities. In Indiana, a hotbed of high school basketball, the seating capacity of a school's gymnasium sometimes exceeded that of the town's population.

The large stake of the community in interscholastic sport tended to subvert the ideals of the comprehensive high school. The actual participation of the student body at large in athletics, according to the principles of the social educators, was essential to the growth of desirable social habits. But school

---

[46]"Tentative Report of the Committee on a System of Teaching Morals in the Public Schools," *National Education Association Proceedings* (1911), 360; Henry S. Curtis, *Education Through Play* (New York, 1915), pp. 225–26.

[47]Webster Cook, "Deportment in the High School," *School Review*, 10 (1902), 629. See also Luther Halsey Gulick, "Amateurism," *American Physical Education Review*, 13 (1908), 103. On occasion social educators and boy-workers advocated an explicitly repressive school atmosphere. Luther Gulick, for example, once asserted that the modern school required the "complete obliteration of individual differences." Gulick, "The Alleged Effeminization," 28.

[48]Edwin B. Hall, "Athletic Professionalism and Its Remedies," *School Review*, 13 (1905), 761.

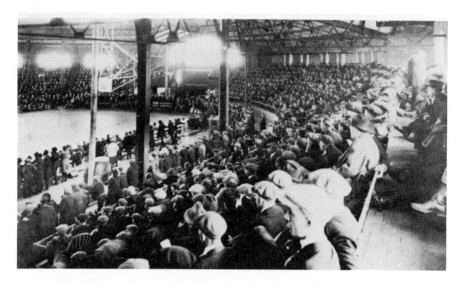

STATE HIGH SCHOOL BASKETBALL TOURNAMENT, CIRCA 1921
This photograph of the Nebraska State High School Basketball Tournament at the
University of Nebraska reflected the growing popularity of high school varsity sports.
Interscholastic sports helped bind together neighborhoods, towns, and cities.

boards, reflecting the will of the community, placed a far higher priority on
fielding a strong varsity team. They were reluctant to furnish the coaches and
facilities required for mass student participation, particularly since, unlike
interscholastic sport, financing would have to come largely from additional
taxes. While intramural sports did experience a minor boom in the late 1910s
and physical education instructors increasingly substituted athletics for gymnastics and calisthenics, the results were pitifully small in terms of the goals of
the social educators. Within the high school, varsity sport tended to glorify
athletic success at the expense of other forms of possible achievement. James
Naismith unwittingly suggested this point while praising the democratizing
function of varsity sport. The athlete "who will perfect himself physically for
the good of the institution is respected, regardless of his ancestry or his
financial standing," wrote Naismith. "Mere manhood is recognized, while lack
of it is sufficient to bar a student from the honors of his fellows."[49] In the high
school status structure, the athlete almost always dwelt in the upper ranks,
usually higher than the most outstanding academic students.

The identification of the community with interscholastic sport presented yet another problem to the conscientious social educator. The pressures
to win resulted in varsity athletics developing a code of ethics independent of
the values of the social educators. Cooperation and fair play might extend to

[49]James Naismith, "High School Athletics and Gymnastics as an Expression of the Corporate Life of the High School," in Charles Hughes Johnston, ed., *The Modern High School* (New
York, 1914), 434–35.

teammates but rarely extended to the opposing team. "Like the unscrupulous lawyer," wrote Alfred E. Stearns, a former school football coach, "the football player has seemingly come to believe that his business is to circumvent the laws of the game, not to obey them." Football coaches, hired above all to win games, subordinated ethical principles to fielding a strong team. Often the football coach "is vulgar and profane," declared Stearns. "Sometimes he is brutal. Seldom does he exhibit, on the football field at least, those qualities demanded of a gentleman."[50] Stearns feared that the high school athlete would carry with him into adulthood the unethical habits developed on the football field. Perhaps the views of Stearns represented the excessive decorum of the old-fashioned gentry. Nonetheless, the requirements of winning rarely allowed the high school coach the freedom to utilize varsity athletics as a training ground for the values of the social educators.

SCHOOL SPORTS OF GIRLS AND YOUNG WOMEN

Neither men nor women perceived an urgent need for adult-managed sports for girls. The beliefs in a separate woman's sphere, the physical delicacy of women, and evolutionary theory all worked against the establishment of programs for girls equivalent to those of boys. (See Chapter 8.) Rejection of the need for highly competitive athletics for girls, however, did not imply the complete rejection of women's sports per se. Indeed, in the 1890–1950 era, play leaders approved of sports specifically designed for girls.

The special character of adult-supervised girls' sports gradually evolved between the 1890s and the 1920s. In the schools, teachers of physical training classes soon discovered that the female students preferred the intrinsic excitement of games over the routine of exercise. Rather than prohibiting games in physical education classes, teachers usually tried to enlist the enthusiasm for games in behalf of larger physical and social goals. The girls themselves, often with the aid of sympathetic adults, organized competitive games. These took the form of intramural contests and even intercollegiate and interscholastic competition.

No sport exceeded the importance of basketball in defining the special character of women's sport in the schools. Soon after Naismith had invented the game in 1891, it became the most popular sport of college women; women loved the freedom of movement and the vigorous competition it offered. In most cases women played on class teams or in physical education classes, but a substantial number of colleges (especially outside of the Northeast) at one time or another had varsity teams. Interscholastic basketball was even more common. Prior to 1925 over half the states had high school championships for girls. Enthusiasm for the sport could run high. Upon returning home from winning the Michigan state championship in 1905, the town of Marshall welcomed their heroines with

---

[50]Alfred E. Stearns, "Athletics and the School," *Atlantic Monthly*, 113 (1914), 148-52.

"bonfires, 10,000 Roman candles, crowds, noise, Supt. Garfield, ex-mayor Porter, and all red-corpuscled Marshall."[51]

While upper-class women had played tennis and golf within the confines of private clubs without causing much controversy, basketball posed a serious threat to traditional female stereotypes. Because they conceived of colleges both as parents in absentia for female students and as training grounds for the development of social graces essential to fulfilling the ideal role of woman, college trustees, administrators, and faculties often objected to the varsity game. Intercollegiate games might entail travel away from campus, "inadequate" supervision, male coaches, performances before audiences of both sexes, sacrificing modesty to the excitement of the game, and exhibiting aggressive behavior "unsuitable" for women. A former University of Nebraska student recalled that it was "not an unheard of thing to meet at a promenade a proud coed blushing behind a black eye received in the afternoon's practice."[52]

Women's physical educators also played a key role in bringing about the demise of varsity basketball for women. Men's varsity sports had grown up independently of male physical educators, whereas in most places (especially at the college level) female physical educators exercised more control over the evolution of women's sports: they found in women's sports opportunities to professionalize their occupation. By insisting that only trained women could properly manage women's sports, they carved out for themselves a restricted occupational domain. The construction of a homosocial network based on shared experiences in teachers' training colleges (normal schools), participation in physical education associations, and personal friendships added to the power of women physical educators.

Control of the rulemaking process assisted the educators in limiting the strenuosity of the game and reducing the tendencies toward the spectator domination of women's basketball. In the 1890s, Senda Berenson, director of physical education at Smith College, developed a modified set of rules for women. The rules of the men's game, she decided, encouraged too much roughness, too much physical and emotional exertion, and the domination of play by the better athletes. Thus she prohibited the players from snatching the ball out of an opponent's hands or talking with one another during play. A player was not allowed to move out of her designated area. To prevent intentional fouling, the women's rules by 1914 awarded an automatic point to the offended team plus a free throw to the victim of the foul. In 1899 a committee of educators led by Berenson induced the A.G. Spalding Company to publish these rules as the "Official Rules" of women's basketball. Several other sets of rules competed with Berenson's and probably as late as 1914, half the girls in the country still played

[51]Quoted in Deobald B. Van Dalen and Bruce L. Bennett, *A World History of Physical Education,* 2nd. ed. (Englewood Cliffs, NJ, 1971), p. 451. For a detailed treatment of girls' sport in the schools, see Cindy L. Himes, "The Female Athlete in American Society, 1860–1940," unpub. Ph.D. diss., University of Pennsylvania, 1984, Chaps. 3 & 4.

[52]Quoted in Robert N. Manley, *The Centennial History of the University of Nebraska* (Lincoln, NE, 1969), p. 305.

SCHOOLYARD BASKETBALL FOR GIRLS
In this early twentieth century photograph in Lincoln, Nebraska, the girls apparently played
by the men's rules. Notice, however, that there were eleven players. The woman on the far
left is described as the "director."

by boys' rules. Nonetheless, despite the apparent opposition of many players and
fans, the distinctive women's game eventually triumphed and prevailed in
educational institutions until the 1960s.[53]

Gradually women educators developed a stand in opposition to all
intercollegiate and interscholastic competition for girls. Pressure came partly
from the "evils" associated with men's athletics. "The spirit of athletics in this
country . . . that one must win at any cost—that defeat is an unspeakable dis-
grace," must be avoided in women's sport, warned Berenson in 1901.[54] Sharing
assumptions similar to those of the boy-workers in the early twentieth century,
they also thought that sports, if properly managed by trained adult women,
could nurture social traits desirable in girls. Team sports might offset extreme
individualism by teaching valuable lessons in cooperation. But varsity sports,
which placed a high priority on winning and the achievement of individual
players, were likely to encourage excessive individualism.

By the early 1920s, all educational groups directly concerned with female
sports had reached a consensus. In 1923, the Women's Division of the National
Amateur Athletic Federation, composed of colleges, high schools, athletic associations, YWCAs, and women's clubs and headed by Lou Henry (Mrs. Herbert)

[53]See Ronald A. Smith, "The Rise of Basketball for Women in Colleges," *Canadian Journal of
History of Sport and Physical Education*, I (1970), 18–36.
[54]Quoted in ibid., 24.

Hoover, went on record against varsity competition. The 1923 platform of the division served as the guiding principle for women's athletics in the schools until the late 1960s. Taking as its premise the motto "a sport for every girl, and every girl in a game," it stated that women's athletics should "be protected from exploitation for the enjoyment of the spectator, the athletic reputation, or the commercial advantage of any school or organization. . . . Individual accomplishment and the winning of championships" should be subordinated to universal participation.[55]

Although the Women's Division made little headway in reforming women's sports outside the schools, they did reduce spectator-centered competition within the schools. Assisted by the financial exigencies of the Great Depression, women educators claimed credit for the discontinuation between 1931 and 1939 of fourteen state-wide basketball tournaments for girls. Countless schools dropped women's varsity sports entirely. A probably not uncommon notice appeared in the New York *Herald Tribune* in 1931: "Acting on the suggestion of . . . [the] girls' physical education instructor . . . the [school] board last night voted unanimously to withdraw the sport [of girls'] basketball from the interscholastic calendar."[56]

Apparently girls' varsity basketball survived mostly in high schools located in smaller, rural communities where physical educators had little or no power. A classic example may have been Iowa. In 1925, educators in the larger school systems induced the Iowa High School Athletic Association to abolish the statewide basketball tourney for girls. However, the smaller schools, led by their high school superintendents and principals, promptly formed a rival organization to sponsor the continuation of a state tournament. "We really want our town to be on the map," explained a small town high school principal in 1928.[57] The publicity and sense of identity that the girls' teams provided to such communities overrode any reservations the administrators may have had about the desirability of varsity sports for girls.

To embody their ideology in practice, physical educators in the Women's Division invented alternatives to interscholastic and intercollegiate athletics. The alternatives took four principal forms: intramurals, telegraphic meets, play days, and sports days, all of which had a player-centered orientation. A survey of seventy-seven colleges taken in 1936 indicated that 74 percent had been involved in a telegraphic meet, 70 percent in a play day, and 41 percent

---

[55]Quoted in Ellen Gerber, "The Controlled Development of Collegiate Sport for Women, 1923–1936," *Journal of Sport History*, 2 (1975), 11. See also Mabel Lee, "The Case for and Against Intercollegiate Athletics for Women and the Situation as It Stands Today," *Mind and Body*, 30 (1923), 246; and Nancy M. Theriot, "Toward a New Sporting Ideal: The Woman's Division of the National Amateur Athletic Federation," *Frontiers*, 3 (1978), 1–8.

[56]Quoted in Gerber, "The Controlled Development," 10. According to a survey taken in 1938 only nine states scheduled state-wide basketball tournaments for girls. See Alice Allene Sefton, *The Women's Division, National Amateur Athletic Federation* (Stanford, CA, 1941), p. 44.

[57]Quoted in John R. Tunis, "Women and the Sport Business," *Harper's Monthly Magazine*, 159 (1929), 217. See also Janice A. Beran, "Playing to the Right Drummer: Girls' Basketball in Iowa, 1893–1927," *Research Quarterly* (Centennial Issue, 1985), 78–85.

in a sports day.[58] Telegraphic meets curbed the competitive spirit between schools by replacing face-to-face competition with telegraphed reports of performances and excluding spectators. Frequently, the colleges competed in only one activity. Play days, which brought together all of the girls from several schools to a single site, minimized competitiveness by arbitrarily selecting girls from several schools to form teams. The play days also featured a wide array of informal contests and placed a high emphasis on social interaction among the girls. Sport days, on the other hand, did permit teams representing the colleges to play, but to ensure a player-centered orientation, the educators altered the rules of such games as basketball and refused to announce winners.

The programs of the educators can be compared with women sports sponsored by business and industrial concerns. Beginning mostly in the 1920s, companies established two kinds of programs. In the first kind of program, as part of a strategy to improve worker efficiency, to court worker loyalty, and to reduce the likelihood of unionization, companies offered sports to all interested female employees. In 1923, at the Hawthorne Works of the Western Electric Company in Chicago, for example, over 500 women participated in bowling, 127 in horseback riding, and 96 in rifle shooting. Each fall the Works scheduled a major track meet for women employees. Although companies provided financial assistance and arranged for playing spaces, the women often managed their own sports programs. Also, unlike women physical educators, women athletes in company sports programs exhibited little if any opposition to the employment of male coaches.

The second kind of program entailed the sponsorship of company teams or of individual female athletes. In most cases, company teams consisted of the better athletes selected from among existing female employees. But other firms were determined to build top-flight teams as a means of advertising. Colonel Melvorne McCombs of the Employers' Casualty Company in Dallas, Texas, systematically recruited high school stars to play on the Company's girls' basketball team; only incidentally were the girls employed in clerical positions. The team grabbed public attention both for its victories and its daring. For the team uniform, McCombs substituted "panties of bright orange satin" and jerseys for the far more conservative bloomers, long stockings, and middy blouses common to girls' teams of the 1920s. According to McCombs, the controversy over the team's brief apparel raised average game attendance from 150 to 5,000. Likewise, Marty Fiedler, a women's sports promoter in southern California, gave women's softball teams such alluring names as Slapsie Maxie's Curvaceous Cuties and the Balian Ice Cream Beauties.[59]

Thus, during the 1890–1950 era, three sharply distinct worlds of women's sports emerged. One existed within the confines of the private social clubs. A second arose inside the schools where women educators excluded male coaches,

[58]Cited in Gerber, "The Controlled Development," 3.
[59]See Himes, "The Female Athlete," pp. 190–206; and Stephanie L. Twin, ed., *Out of the Bleachers: Writings on Women and Sport* (Old Westbury, NY, 1979), pp. xxix–xxx.

placed a premium on maximum participation, held competitiveness to a minimum, and eliminated spectatorship. They thereby avoided the excesses of men's sports, but generated little enthusiasm for sport among female students and limited the opportunities for girls to develop their athletic potential to the fullest. Industries encouraged the establishment of a third world of sports, which provided opportunities for superior athletes to excel and even profit financially from their skills.

14

THE SETTING OF ORGANIZED SPORTS SINCE 1950

"When the Dodgers left Brooklyn [in 1958]," recalled a fan twenty-five years later, "we lost our innocence forever. Love and loyalty, we were shattered to hear, were only so much mush to the people in power."[1] But one man in power, Dodgers' owner Walter O'Malley, had his reasons. No matter that the Dodgers had been one of the most prosperous franchises in major league baseball during the past five years. Ebbetts Field, the home of the Dodgers, seated only 35,000 fans, had parking places for only 700 cars, and was located in a decaying neighborhood. The future of baseball in Brooklyn, O'Malley said, depended upon the construction of a larger sports facility, one that included ample parking and that could be reached easily by motorists. While New York officials dallied, Los Angeles promised this and more. As a site for a new stadium, the city offered Chavez Ravine to O'Malley, 300 acres in downtown Los Angeles with easy access to several freeways. In addition, Los Angeles provided O'Malley with an uncontested media market in the nation's third largest metropolitan area.

The decision of O'Malley to transfer the Dodgers from the East to the West Coast exemplified two of the most fundamental external forces shaping the contours of organized sports in the post-1950 era. One was the rapid growth of new metropolises and the other was the new technological marvel of television.[2]

---

[1] Jim Kaplan, "Perspective," *Sports Illustrated*, 58 (May 23, 1983), MW2. See also Neil J. Sullivan, *The Dodgers Move West* (New York, 1987).

[2] General treatments of sports in the postwar era include Benjamin G. Rader, *In Its Own Image: How Television Has Transformed Sports* (New York, 1984) and Randy Roberts, *Winning Is the Only Thing* (Baltimore, 1988).

THE SPRAWLING METROPOLISES

By 1990 sprawling metropolitan areas, which consisted of one or more large cities, scattered suburbs, and satellite cities, became the homes for three out of four Americans. The thirty-seven largest metropolises alone contained nearly half of the nation's population. Metropolises in the Sunbelt states of the South and Southwest grew much faster than those in the Northeast. Los Angeles, San Francisco, Dallas-Ft. Worth, and Houston climbed into the top ten, pushing aside such older areas as St. Louis, Cleveland, Pittsburgh, and Baltimore.

Professional sports teams soon mirrored these changes. Aided by jet air travel, sports entrepreneurs moved to exploit the new population centers; they relocated existing teams and created additional franchises. In 1950 only 42 major-league professional franchises existed, and these were located mostly in the industrial tier of states that extended from the Northeast to the upper Midwest. By 1990 the figure had swollen to over 100. As early as 1946 entrepreneurs had planted professional football teams in both Los Angeles and San Francisco. In the same year baseball's Pacific Coast (minor) League petitioned unsuccessfully for major-league status, but big-league baseball did not invade the Sunbelt until 1958 when the Brooklyn Dodgers and the New York Giants transferred to Los Angeles and San Francisco respectively. By 1990 no major metropolitan area in the nation was without at least one big-league franchise.

In baseball, relocation preceded expansion. The owners first abandoned the smaller cities that hosted two teams; in 1953 the Boston Braves moved to Milwaukee, in 1954 the St. Louis Browns to Baltimore, and in 1955 the Philadelphia Athletics to Kansas City, leaving behind the Red Sox, Cardinals, and Phillies. Then came the transfer of the Dodgers and the Giants to the Pacific Coast. In 1960 a congressional investigation that threatened to reverse baseball's exemption from the antitrust laws, the threat of competition from a proposed third major league (the Continental League headed by Branch Rickey), and the willingness of investors to pay $1.8 million (plus several million dollars for the purchase of players from other clubs) for a new franchise led both leagues to announce plans for expansion. By 1977 the American League consisted of fourteen franchises and the National League of twelve. (For the expansion of professional football and basketball, see Chapter 15.)

By offering professional franchises subsidized playing areas, the sprawling metropolises often abetted relocation and expansion. To be "big league," cities thought they had to have a professional sports team. To attract such teams, cities increasingly had to provide potential franchises with generous terms. In the 1960s, 70s, and 80s, local governments went on a stadium-building binge. Of the 28 teams in the National Football League, for example, 26 played in city, county, or state facilities. In the early 1960s the price tag on a modest stadium ran to some $30 million, but Houston's Astrodome, the first stadium with a roof for all-season play, cost $45 million to complete in 1965. The cost of the Astrodome paled before that of the Louisiana Superdome, which mounted to at least $300 million before it was finished in 1975. To cover only the operating deficit of the Superdome cost Louisiana taxpayers $8 million annually.

Just as the cathedral represented the spirit of the Middle Ages and the great railroad terminals that of the nineteenth century, supporters of publicly financed sports stadia saw them as the quintessential symbol of the modern city. Not only could the edifices serve as great cultural monuments, enthusiasts argued, but they could stimulate downtown revitalization and lure tourist and investment dollars to the city. Several team owners seized the advantage that such thinking made possible. They presented cities with the ultimatums: either the cities build new stadia (or extend other specified subsidies) or the franchises would move elsewhere.

More than 20 percent of the new structures were built outside the downtown area, usually in a suburban satellite city but within easy access of freeways. For example, the Patriots football team moved out of Boston to Foxboro, Massachusetts, where they renamed themselves the New England Patriots; the Dallas Cowboys encamped at Irving, Texas; the Texas Rangers located at Arlington, Texas; both the football Giants and Jets departed from New York City for the Meadowlands Sports Complex in East Rutherford, New Jersey; and the Detroit Lions moved to Pontiac, Michigan, twenty-five miles from downtown Detroit. Suburban facilities often permitted easier access to cars and to more affluent fans, while providing an escape from the congestion, dirt, and dangers of the inner city.

Critics of public assistance for sports franchises responded that (1) cities could better use the money for the resolution of more pressing problems, (2) building stadia or arenas in the suburbs simply encouraged the further decay of

THE PONTIAC SILVERDOME
The Pontiac Silverdome, located near Detroit, Michigan, reflected the decline of the inner city and the growth of independent suburbs.

downtown areas, (3) corruption in financing and construction resulted in costs far exceeding original estimates, and (4) in effect, all residents subsidized the entertainment of "the advantaged." Yet opponents rarely blocked stadium-building projects. In the late 1980s nearly two dozen of the largest 65 metropolitan areas were building new facilities, many of which were the domed variety. Enthusiasm ran so high for stadia and arenas that several cities even built them before receiving assurance of a major league franchise.[3]

THE INNER CITY

Decaying inner cities and fast-growing suburbs affected metropolitan leisure patterns in other ways. In the first half of the twentieth century, the lives of city dwellers had revolved mostly around the central business district. Even those residing in the suburbs used street railways to make their way downtown to work, shop, and find recreation. For amusement, the inner city offered shopping streets, restaurants, movies, indoor arenas, saloons, and for the pursuit of high culture, concert halls and the theater. Baseball parks, football fields, and amusement parks, though often located outside the central business district, could be cheaply and quickly reached by mass transit.

After World War II, the suburbs pulled both jobs and the more prosperous families away from the inner city. Soaring automobile sales, subdividers with a knack for building houses en masse, the construction of miles and miles of multilane freeways, and federal subsidies to new homeowners transformed cornfields and cow pastures into acres and acres of suburbs. In addition, manufacturers, retail outlets, corporate headquarters, and dozens of other businesses relocated along the beltways and the intersections of arterial highways. By the mid-1960s more jobs existed in the busy suburban rings than in the inner city. In short, the peripheral regions of cities became functionally independent of the older central business districts.[4]

[3]Steven A. Riess examines the historical relationship between urban space and sports in *City Games: The Evolution of American Urban Society and the Rise of Sports* (Urbana and Chicago, 1989). See also Benjamin A. Okner, "Subsidies of Stadiums and Arenas," in Roger G. Noll, ed., *Government and the Sports Business* (Washington, DC, 1974), 325–47; Melvin Durslag, "Pro Sports Move to the Suburbs," *TV Guide* (Aug. 5, 1972), 37–38; Joseph Coniglio, *The Names in the Game: A History of the Movement of Sport Franchises* (New York, 1978); Arthur T. Johnson, "The Sports Franchise Relocation Issue and Public Policy Responses," in Arthur T. Johnson and James H. Frey, *Government and Sport: The Public Policy Issues* (Totowa, NJ, 1985), Chap. 12; David Harris, *The League: The Rise and the Decline of the NFL* (New York, 1986); Pete Axthelm, "RX for Cities: Build a Dome," *Newsweek*, 110 (Dec. 28, 1987), 21: Harrison Donnelly, "High Stakes of Sports Economics," *Editorial Research Reports*, April 8, 1988, 170–83.

[4]I use the term "independent suburb" while recognizing its inadequacy in describing what is essentially a new form of the city. See esp. Robert Fishman, "The Post-War American Suburb: A New Form, A New City," in Daniel Schaffer, ed., *Two Centuries of American Planning*, (Baltimore, 1988), 265–78, and Fishman, *Bourgeois Utopias: The Rise and Fall of Suburbia* (New York, 1987). Fishman calls the new cities "technoburbs."

The creation of the independent suburbs in combination with television spelled disaster for central city commercial recreation. Only the poorer people, most of whom were blacks or Hispanics, remained in the inner city. Unless required to do so for employment, suburbanites rarely went downtown anymore. For example, one-fourth of the residents of a well-to-do Philadelphia suburb in the 1980s made their way downtown less than twice a month while another fifth did so less than twice a year. Without the patronage of the more affluent suburbanites, inner city bars and restaurants closed their doors and movie attendance skidded downward. Attendance at major and minor league baseball, inner city high school sports, and boxing and wrestling all dropped precipitously. Although downtown renewal projects in the 1970s and 80s partly reversed the tide, the relative decline of the central city seemed to be permanent.[5]

For recreation, inner city residents improvised as best they could. As with the working class of the past, ghetto leisure usually divided along gender lines. Women spent much of their spare time watching television, visiting on their front stoops, or, if it was Sunday, attending church services. Men watched television, too, but they were more likely than women to gather on streetcorners, in local bars, or in city parks. With restricted opportunities for recreation and inspired by the athletic stars they watched on television, ghetto youth spent far more time than their suburban counterparts in practicing and playing team sports. In particular, boys and young men devoted countless hours to "pickup" basketball games on outdoor courts. For many inner city youth, developing expertise in sports seemed to offer one of the easiest, most lucrative, and most glamorous routes out of the ghetto.[6]

THE INDEPENDENT SUBURBS

Nothing distinguished the independent suburbs from the inner city more than the automobile. Suburbanites drove their cars to workplaces, schools, and shopping malls. The car became a supreme instrument of pleasure as well. Families drove them to drive-in restaurants, drive-in movies, and even drive-in churches, leading one historian to conclude that postwar suburban life could be summed up as a "drive-in culture."[7] Even working-class families now had available a highly flexible means of escaping on weekends, holidays, and vacations from the cities to the countryside. In addition to one or more cars used for convenience, families purchased record numbers of campers, pick-up trucks, jeeps, and other

[5]See data in Benjamin G. Rader, "The Great Slump in Spectator Sports in the 1950s: The Case of the United States," in J. A. Mangan, ed., *Proceedings of the XI HISPA International Conference* (1985), 158.

[6]See for example Pete Axthelm, *The City Game: Basketball, from the Playground to Madison Square Garden* (New York, 1970) and Rich Telander, *Heaven Is a Playground* (New York, 1976).

[7]Kenneth T. Jackson, *Crabgrass Frontier: The Suburbanization of the United States* (New York, 1985), Chap. 14.

vehicles designed for recreation. For suburban teenagers of all classes, ownership of a car became a rite of passage; they customized their cars, transforming them into personalized art objects.

While the automobile pulled suburbanites back and forth between home and the outside world, television pulled only one way—toward the home. "And so the monumental change began in our lives and those of millions of other Americans," recalled one man about the effects of his family's purchase of their first television set in 1950. "More than a year passed before we again visited a movie theater. Money which previously would have been spent for books was saved for TV payments. Social evenings with friends became fewer and fewer still." By 1956 three out of four families owned television sets; those families watched television on the average of thirty-five hours each week. Novelty alone did not account for the new medium's magnetism; Americans persisted long afterward in spending a staggering amount of their free time watching television. A study thirty years later of Muncie, Indiana, found that the median viewing time for all families was twenty-eight hours per week. The significance of such figures could not be dismissed by the argument that families had their sets turned on without really watching them. Viewers in Muncie, at any rate, could recall substantial amounts of program content.[8]

Television and the automobile, along with central heating, air-conditioning, and more spacious houses and yards, contributed to a general shift in leisure from public places to the privacy of the home. Do-it-yourself projects, home repairs, and conquering the "crabgrass frontier" consumed more of the suburbanite's spare time. "No man who owns his own house and lot can be a Communist," observed one of the mass builders of suburban housing in 1948. "He has too much to do."[9] Indeed, for many, the home became a self-sufficient recreation center, or a "family playpen," as an anthropologist aptly put it. The enjoyment of children and "family togetherness," according to the popular media of the day, became virtually a moral obligation.

Critics often charged that the suburbs were homogeneous, but in fact they were divided by educational levels, occupations, and race. Blue collar working-class families cultivated a life style distinct from white collar families. In the past, both married and unmarried workingmen had spent much of their spare time in a homosocial milieu of saloons, billiard halls, lodges, union halls, and streetcorners. Similar patterns persisted, especially among younger, unmarried workers, in the postwar era suburbs. Even married men frequently continued to gamble, hunt, and fish in all-male groups. But "night(s) out with the boys" became far less common. Husbands stayed home more with their families watching television, working on cars, or doing home repairs. Entire families loaded into cars or campers for weekend boating, swimming, or fishing excursions.

[8]Rader, *In Its Own Image*, p. 35; Theodore Caplow, et. al., *Middletown Families: Fifty Years of Change and Continuity*, (Minneapolis, 1982), p. 23; John P. Robinson, *How Americans Use Time* (New York, 1977), esp. pp. 172–79; Herbert J. Gans, *The Urban Villagers* (New York, 1962), pp. 187–196; Fishman, *Bourgeois Utopias*, pp. 201–02.
[9]William J. Levitt, as quoted in Jackson, *Crabgrass Frontier*, p. 231.

Instead of neighbors or workmates, families more frequently joined relatives scattered over the larger metropolitan area for backyard barbecues and other social occasions. When younger men played softball or bowled, wives usually accompanied them as spectators or as participants. After the games, players and their families often retired together to a local bar or pizza parlor for food and refreshments.[10]

Suburban white collar professionals occupied a quite different world of leisure. They entertained more in the home, had more social interaction with nonfamily members, and belonged to more voluntary associations than did their suburban blue collar counterparts. Country clubs grew in membership and numbers, though at rates slower than those of the 1920s or what might have been expected from increases in population and income. As a partial substitute for the country club, developers of expensive suburban housing sometimes provided residents with clubhouses, swimming pools, tennis courts, and golf courses. With jet air travel at their disposal and infusions of additional income, the more affluent Americans ranged farther away from home for their amusements—to tennis ranches in the Sunbelt, to watering spots in Hawaii, the Caribbean, or the Mediterranean, and to ski slopes in the Rocky Mountains or the Alps.

THE SELF AND THE FITNESS CULT

In the 1970s and 80s white collar suburbanites embarked upon a wide-ranging quest for individual power and fulfillment apart from their occupations. As the society became more rationalized and systematized and more people worked in bureaucracies, the importance of the individual seemed to diminish. As early as the 1960s corporations discovered pervasive problems of morale among executives. Rising absenteeism and declining rates of productivity, especially among middle managers, reflected a growing dissatisfaction with the anonymity and impotence of white collar workers. According to one study, white collar employees, on the average, devoted only about half their potential labor to the job.

Nor did consumption provide an adequate substitute for the absence of satisfactions in the workplace or in personal relationships. Apart from the issue of whether consumption had the capacity to satisfy the deepest needs of the human specie, the very existence of the advertising industry depended on its ability to convince people that they could not achieve fulfillment unless they purchased even more goods and services. To the extent that advertising was successful, then, consumption could never completely satisfy yearnings arising from material wants, powerlessness, meaningless work, loneliness, or sexual deprivation. Many thus sought control over their lives and greater personal fulfillment in arenas other than in work or consumption. They became converts

[10]See esp. Bennett M. Berger, *Working-Class Suburb* (Berkeley and Los Angeles, 1969), Chap. 5, and David Halle, *America's Working Man*, (Chicago, 1984), Chap. 2.

to charismatic religions, experimented with vegetarianism, drugs, psychother-apy, or EST, or they became apostles of a new fitness cult.[11]

The fitness cult of the 1970s and 80s grew out of, but differed significantly from, its turn-of-the-century predecessor. Then, members of the old Eastern elite had urged the strenuous life as a means of rejuvenating their class and thereby enhancing the nation's welfare. But no larger social goal motivated or informed the new strenuosity; the American lifestyle in general focused upon the self rather than upon society. Unlike the earlier campaign for the strenuous life, crusaders for fitness in the 1970s and 80s included both sexes. Women not only took up vigorous exercise to look better, feel better, and to improve their health, but as an assertion of self-sufficiency. By using physical prowess as a means of achiev-ing equality with men as well as to oppose actual male oppression, physical fitness became a part of the women's liberation movement.

Signs of the new strenuosity had become evident in the 1950s and 60s. In response to the Cold War and the abysmal performance of American youth (compared to European counterparts) on fitness tests, President Dwight D. Eisenhower created the President's Council on Youth Fitness in 1956. In the meantime, by 1960 Jack LaLanne's daily calisthenics had climbed to the top of the ratings among daytime television shows. Though John F. Kennedy was physically impaired by a bad back, no previous president, not even Theodore Roosevelt, had projected such powerful images of raw vigor, youth, and good looks. At the White House itself, his brother Robert's house in Virginia, and at the family compound in Hyannisport, Massachusetts, Kennedy's extended family never seemed to rest; they filled every spare moment with an exhausting range of isometric exercises, tennis, swimming, horseback riding, badminton, and a brutal form of touch football. When Marine Corps commandant General David M. Shoup accepted Kennedy's challenge of having his Marines march 50 miles in under 20 hours, thereby duplicating the feat of Roosevelt's 1908 Ma-rines, thousands of nonsoldiers tried it too.

The transformation of physical activities into quantifiable units and the authority of scientific expertise encouraged the new strenuosity. While testing the fitness levels of thousands of potential pilots in the 1960s, Kenneth Cooper, an Air Force physician, developed measurable standards of ideal conditioning. Light calisthenics or short walks were not enough, according to Cooper. Only strenuous activities such as jogging, running, racquetball, cycling, swimming, or

---

[11]For the intricate connections between the new fitness movement and earlier movements see James C. Whorton, *Crusaders for Fitness: The History of American Health Reformers* (Princeton, NJ, 1982) and Hillel Schwartz, *Never Satisfied: A Cultural History of Diets, Fantasies and Fat* (New York, 1986). For the new movement see esp. Patricia A. Eisenman and C. Robert Barnett, "Physical Fitness in the 1950s and 1970s: Why Did One Fail and the Other Boom?" *Quest*, 31 (1979), 114–22; Roberts, *Winning Is the Only Thing*; Marc Leepson, "Physical Fitness Boom," *Editorial Research Reports*, April 14, 1978, 263–80; Jerry Kirschenbaum and Robert Sullivan, "Hold on There, America," *Sports Illustrated*, 58 (Feb. 7, 1983), 60–74; Jack Mc-Callum, "Everybody's Doin' It," ibid., 61 (Dec. 3, 1984), 72–86; Michael Walsh, "Make Way for the New Spartans," *Time*, 122 (Sept. 19, 1983), 90–92; Anastasia Toufexis, "The Shape of the Nation," ibid, 126 (Oct. 7, 1985), 60–61; Karin DeVenuta, "Future Stars Aren't Ready," *Wall Street Journal*, Feb. 26, 1988, 19D.

fast walking elevated the pulse rate to adequate levels. Cooper even told Americans exactly how far and fast they would have to run and walk in a given week in order to become "aerobically fit." By 1972 an estimated eight million Americans, including astronaut-hero John Glenn, followed Cooper's regimen for aerobic fitness, which included not only vigorous exercise but the maintenance of careful personal records of pulse rate, blood pressure, weight, and the times taken to complete the exercises.

In the 1970s, as disillusionment mounted over the Vietnam War, the counterculture, leadership in high places, and the erratic performance of the economy, the enthusiasm for fitness increased. By the late 1970s, the number of Americans who claimed to exercise regularly had jumped to 20 million. As more and more white collar employees replaced their two-martini lunches with jogging, swimming, and working out with exercise machines, YMCAs, YWCAs, and similar organizations experienced a sudden reversal in their long-term membership declines. The number of commercial health clubs multiplied from 350 in 1968 to more than 7,000 in 1986. By 1986, Americans spent more money on exercise devices in the home than they did on golf, camping, and the racquet sports combined. Advertisers and manufacturers quickly moved in to exploit the new enthusiasm. Perhaps no sign of the times was more important than the decision to update the marketing of Barbie, "the ultimate yuppie doll," by including with the doll a workout center, complete with an exercise cycle, dumbbells, slant board, and a locker with towel.

The new strenuosity extended far beyond a desire to achieve simply physical fitness. After having been deskbound by day, "the new Spartans," as they were dubbed by *Time* magazine, sought intense physical experiences, even if it meant aching muscles, pounding hearts, and gasping lungs. While many jogged short distances only a few times weekly, an astonishing number of Americans took up regular long-distance running. In 1970, only 126 men entered the first New York marathon; but by the mid-1980s the organizers accepted 20,000 "official" entries from both men and women while rejecting thousands of others. By then hundreds of cities scheduled marathons in all parts of the country. As if running 26 miles were not enough exercise, the apostles of running invented the triathlon, which included a 2-mile swim, a 112-mile bicycle ride, and a 26-mile run. In 1986 more than a million Americans completed this grueling event. Apart from building or releasing additional sources of energy, improving one's sex life, and reducing anxieties, strenuous workouts, according to its proponents, induced a mystical "runner's high," a trancelike euphoria that could become addictive. A distinctive runners' culture emerged, one that revolved not only around running, but around clubs, special diets, in-group understandings and behaviors, running magazines, and a flourishing equipment industry.

The quest for fitness was often an integral component of a larger effort to reshape the body. To be sure, prosperous Americans had long been preoccupied with bodily beauty, but the postwar media's accent on youth gave the concern a new urgency. Weight lifting and other body-shaping exercises became more popular than ever before. Being fat in America became the greatest single sign of personal failure. "Eating has become the last bona fide sin left in America," concluded columnist Ellen Goodman in 1975.[12] Dieting had its negative side; a Gallup poll in 1986 estimated that 3 million Americans, most of them women, suffered from the eating disorders of anorexia nervosa and/or bulimia. If exercise and dieting failed to obtain the desired figure, the most affluent Americans increasingly resorted to plastic surgery.

Measurably positive results issued from the fitness crusade. The death rate from cardiovascular diseases fell from 511 per 100,000 people in 1950 to 418 by 1985, though part of the decline was attributable to better medical treatment of cardiovascular patients. White collar Americans smoked fewer cigarettes, drank less alcohol, and ate less red meat (beef and pork) while consuming more white meat (poultry and fish) than ever before. Yet the positive effects could be easily exaggerated. Children improved their scores little if at all on push-ups, high jumps, long jumps, endurance runs, and sprints. Although nearly half of the adult population claimed to exercise regularly, probably less than one in ten exercised consistently enough to match the minimum levels specified by physical fitness experts.[13]

THE ADVENT OF TELEVISED SPORTS

Nothing was more central to the history of organized sports during the second half of the twentieth century than television. With the advent of television, the fans at home rather than those in the stadium or the arena became the ultimate arbiters of organized sports. To attract more television viewers and meet the demands of commercial sponsors, television directors employed multiple cameras, replays, slow motion shots, flashy graphics, catchy music, and announcers to create a sporting experience unavailable to the fan in the stands. Likewise, to make their games more attractive television spectacles, the moguls of sports altered the nature of their games. For example, they changed game rules, permitted arbitrary timeouts for television commercials, and in most of the team sports established lengthy playoff systems for the national championships.

Television affected American sports in other ways. It contributed to the further nationalization of sports. In earlier times, newspapers, magazines, movies, books, and radio had allowed Americans everywhere to learn about the feats of Babe Ruth, but television permitted millions to see instantaneously Pete Rose pursue Joe DiMaggio's record for hits in consecutive games. When fans could regularly see sports performed at the highest plateau of excellence on television,

[12]Quoted in Schwartz, *Never Satisfied*, p. 308.

[13]*Newsweek* speculated in 1988 that the fitness crusade may have run its course. It claimed that participation in marathons had dropped by over 15,000 through 1987 and the number doing aerobics fell 4 million below the peak in 1985. The magazine even predicted that the "anorexic look" might be waning in popularity. See Bill Barol, "The Eighties Are Over," *Newsweek*, 111 (Jan. 4, 1988), 40–48.

attendance at local sporting events frequently declined. The new electronic medium also revolutionized the economics of big-time sport. Eventually, no sporting entrepreneur, no matter how rich or imaginative, dared buy a team, stage a sporting spectacle, or even set a date or starting time for a game without first consulting the chiefs of television. And as television pumped additional millions of dollars into sports, professional athletes demanded a larger share of the revenues generated by sports.

During television's pioneer stage, that is, from 1938 (the first sports telecast)[14] to the early 1960s, technology limited the potentialities of televised sports. Before the common use of multiple cameras, perfected color, replay, and slow motion, primitive television cameras more effectively captured the excitement of arena spectacles such as Roller Derby, wrestling, and prize fighting than outdoor games such as baseball and football. Television fans could easily follow two men whose combat was restricted to a small ring. But the small white baseball could sometimes hardly be distinguished from the white dots ("snow") on the black and white screens, and viewers, when they could see the hit ball, could rarely determine its precise location relative to the playing field. Because of its more concentrated action, football fared somewhat better, but the camera, located far from the playing field, could hardly capture the essence of sophisticated plays; mud-covered and grass-stained uniforms sometimes made the teams indistinguishable.

In each of the arena sports, television contributed to a short-term boom and a long-term depression. Prize fighting was the most spectacular instance. In the late 1940s and early 50s television lifted boxing into a new "Golden Age" only to deliver it a blow from which it never fully recovered. In 1944 the Gillette Safety Razor Company signed a pact with Madison Square Garden to sponsor weekly telecasts of fights. In the 1950s the Gillette fights became something of a Friday night institution. Advertisers soon brought fights to television on other nights of the week. Millions of Americans who had never seen a prize fight before became devotees of the ring. Fascinated fans even loved the Golden Glove bouts that usually featured the flailings of inept amateurs.

Then in the mid-1950s the happy union of television and boxing came apart. Old-time fight fans complained that television had created an entirely new form of entertainment. No longer did fighters bide their time until a proper opening occurred or soften up an opponent early in the match with nonlethal blows. Slugging replaced defensive finesse. Furthermore, to continue programming such a busy schedule of fights required an endless supply of winning fighters. "The big thing you were up against is that there had to be a loser, you know? And you couldn't bring a loser back on TV," explained Chris Dundee, a prominent fight promoter from Miami Beach, Florida. "The sponsors didn't want losers, just winners. And let's face it, the sponsors called the shots during

---

[14]The long accepted date for the first American sports telecast has been 1939, but a year earlier a college football game was telecast in Philadelphia. See NCAA Football Television Committee, *Football Television Briefing Book* (Shawnee Mission, KS, 1981), p. 1.

the TV age of boxing."[15] The voracious demand by television for fighters encouraged the monopolization of promotion by the International Boxing Club (IBC). By controlling the key arenas and through his connections with underworld figures, Jim Norris, the president of the IBC, drove independent promoters out of the fight game. Antitrust actions against the IBC, the convictions of Norris and mobsters associated with prize fighting for income tax evasion, and the televised hearings by a Senate Committee on organized crime (which included revelations about boxing) darkened the reputation of a sport that had always had difficulty establishing a positive image.

In the late 1950s boxing's new Golden Age suddenly collapsed. Television and other at-home activities drove down live attendance and destroyed the once prospering smaller fight clubs. In 1948–49, ten to twelve thousand fans regularly watched the Friday night card at Madison Square Garden; by 1957, when the Garden had become little more than an oversized television studio, attendance had dropped to an average of a mere 1,200. By 1958, along "Cauliflower Row," as Eighth Avenue in New York City was known, nearly all the fight clubs had closed. In the early 1950s over 300 fighters had worked out of Stillman's Gym; by 1958, the number using the famous gym had dropped to below 90. Television wiped out over half of the fight clubs located in smaller cities. Likewise television ratings fell disastrously. In 1952, 31 percent of all households watching television had their sets tuned to prime time fights; seven years later the figure had fallen to 10.6 percent. Apart from all the problems that beset prize fighting, boxing simply failed in head-on competition with other kinds of prime time (evening) programming that the networks began developing in the late 1950s.

Initially, radio men, known for their "golden throats" and abilities to describe in abundant and vivid detail the course of a contest, handled television's announcing chores. Even though viewers could see the games for themselves, announcers tended to talk too much, employ too many cliches, and risk their credibility by resorting to hyperbole. Being enthusiastic fans themselves, employed by the networks or the home teams, and dependent upon the commissioners of professional sports leagues for approval, they rarely criticized players, managers or coaches, game officials, or team owners. Nor did they comment on racism or sexism in sports. By the 1960s dozens of athletes, ex-athletes, and even referees had replaced radio men. While the diction of athlete-announcers sometimes bordered on incomprehensibility, producers believed that the athlete's inside knowledge added to the fan's enjoyment.

For baseball aficionados across the country in the 1950s, watching and listening to Jay Hanna "Dizzy" Dean on the CBS Game of the Week became

[15]Quoted in William O. Johnson, Jr., *Super Spectator and the Electric Lilliputians* (Boston, 1971), p. 92. On prize fighting, besides Rader, *In Its Own Image* and Roberts, *Winning Is the Only Thing*, see Barney Nagler *James Norris and the Decline of Boxing* (Indianapolis, 1964); Jeffrey T. Sammons, *Beyond the Ring: The Role of Boxing in American Society* (Urbana and Chicago, 1988), Chaps. 5–7; Steven A. Riess, "Only the Ring Was Square: Frankie Carbo and the Underworld Control of American Boxing," *International Journal of the History of Sport*, 5 (1988), 29–52.

virtually a weekend ritual. Apparently sensing the game could not always hold the viewer's attention, Dean himself took center stage, letting the game provide the background image for the spell of his personality. A former pitching star for the St. Louis Cardinals in the 1930s, Dean came to New York City in 1950 to do Yankee pregame shows on WBAD, the flagship station of the DuMont radio and television network. He was an "instant success" in New York, and in 1955 he joined Buddy Blattner, another ex-big leaguer, to do the Game of the Week. Claiming to have attended a one-room school in Oklahoma only long enough to get into the "Second Reader," Dean enthralled viewers with his country drawl, unusual verbal conjugations, and uninhibited anecdotes. (When Dean heard the school teachers in St. Louis had complained about his syntax, he shot back: "Sin Tax. Are them jokers in Washington puttin' a tax on that too?")[16] When the game became unusually slow or boring, he might bawl out an impromptu version of the "Wabash Cannonball."

THE BATTLE OF THE NETWORKS

During the 1950s, none of the networks considered sports programming critical to their overall success. They put far more of their resources and talent into news, musicals, comedies, Westerns, and popular dramas. But in the early 1960s, ABC broke this pattern. Having been long a laggard behind NBC and CBS, ABC gambled that increased sports programming would give its network greater visibility, bring in new local television stations as affiliates, and improve the audience ratings for all shows. The gamble paid spectacular dividends. Sports telecasts contributed substantively to ABC's sudden rise from third place in prime time audience ratings in the 1950s to the top in the 1970s.

No person was more responsible for ABC's success than Roone P. Arledge. After winning a television Emmy for producing the best children's program, "Hi Mom," in 1959 on NBC, Arledge joined ABC in 1960 to direct and produce the network's football games. Arledge was determined, as he put it, "to get the audience involved emotionally. If they didn't give a damn about the game, they still might enjoy the program."[17] To obtain more audience involvement, he attempted to capture the full ambience of the game setting. He used cranes, blimps, and helicopters to obtain novel views of the stadium, the campus, and the town; hand-held cameras for close-up shots of cheerleaders, pretty coeds, band members, eccentric spectators, and nervous coaches; and rifle-type micro-

[16]Quoted in Rader, *In Its Own Image*, p. 57. See also Curt Smith, *America's Dizzy Dean* (St. Louis, 1978) and Curt Smith, *Voices of the Games*, (South Bend, IN, 1987).

[17]Quoted in Johnson, *Super Spectator*, p. 161. On Arledge and ABC sports see esp. Bert Randolph Sugar, *"The Thrill of Victory": The Inside Story of ABC Sports* (New York, 1978); Ron Powers, *Supertube: The Rise of Television Sports* (New York, 1984); Howard Cosell, *Cosell* (New York, 1974); Frank Deford, "I've Won, I've Got Them," *Sports Illustrated*, 59 (Aug. 8, 1983), 66–82; Jim Spence, *Up Close & Personal: The Inside Story of Network Television Sports* (New York, 1988).

phones to pick up the roar of the crowd, the thud of a punt, or the crunch of a hard tackle. Arledge made the crowd itself part of the performance. Once the fans perceived themselves as potential performers, they began to carry banners, run onto the playing field, and engage in unseemly antics to grab the attention of the television cameras. In the early 1970s shots of women in the stands stripping down to their bras and panties (usually local strippers seeking free publicity) aroused so much protest that ABC began to cut back on its coverage of some of the more bizarre forms of off-the-field behavior.

Arledge also brought his talents to "The Wide World of Sports" and the Olympic Games. In 1961 he began production of Wide World, which was to win more Emmys than any other sportscast. A pioneer in stop-action filming, Wide World consisted of a potpourri of feats and games, including boxing matches, track meets, ski races, surfing, cliff diving, barrel jumping, wrist wrestling, and demolition derbies. The program was especially effective in stimulating public interest in winter sports. Although normally effusive in its enthusiasm for all sports, no matter how trivial, Wide World's occasional interviews by Howard Cosell of Muhammad Ali, Joe Namath, and other more or less controversial sports figures added spice to the telecasts. Arledge also turned the 1968, 1972, and 1976 Olympic Games into television extravaganzas.[18]

One of Arledge's productions, "Monday Night Football," outstripped all other regular sportscasts in popularity. Initiated in 1970, this prime-time sport show altered the Monday-night habits of a large portion of the American people. Movie attendance nose-dived, restaurants closed, and bowlers rescheduled their leagues. Much of the success of Monday Night Football stemmed from Arledge's decision to hire Howard Cosell, already the most controversial sportscaster in the country as a commentator. (As part of the agreement for ABC to do the Monday night games, Arledge had refused to sign the traditional contract providing for "announcer-approval" by league officials.) From the first telecast, Cosell, who had championed Muhammad Ali's resistance to the Vietnam draft and right to retain the heavyweight crown, sparked controversy. Analysts concluded that Cosell was a man the audience "loved to hate." Caustic, unctuous, polysyllabic, and given to making even the most trivial observation sound like something profound, Cosell claimed to "tell it like it is." He even had the audacity to second-guess the wisdom of head coaches. Unlike any other broadcaster, Cosell was able to get away with simultaneously promoting, reporting, and criticizing an event packaged and merchandised by his own network.

Jarred by ABC's successes, in the 1970s and 80s CBS and NBC decided to do battle with the upstart network. The results (detailed in subsequent chapters) were: (1) the money poured into sports by television in the late 1970s and early 80s escalated at a pace far exceeding inflation or the nation's overall economic growth; (2) augmented in the late 1970s by competition from cable television, the quantity of sports available on the cool medium doubled, tripled, and then became practically omnipresent; and (3) to make their contests more attractive to

---

[18]Pete Axthelm, "Let Roone Do It," *Newsweek*, 88 (Aug. 9, 1976), 51.

CARICATURE OF ROONE P. ARLEDGE
More than any other single person, Roone P. Arledge, the long-time director of ABC Sports, was responsible for major innovations in telecasting sporting events.

television and capitalize upon the millions of dollars offered by the networks, all of the major sports made changes in their games.

Apart from intense competition for the television rights to professional and college football and basketball, major league baseball, and the Olympic Games, the networks beamed a galaxy of "synthetic" or "trashsports." "Legitimate sports, for the most part, have limited audiences," explained sportscaster Vin Scully. "But when you give it another dimension—entertainment—you capture a new breed of viewer."[19] In the 1960s ABC's Wide World of Sports pioneered in the telecasts of bizarre or unusual physical activities: high wire acts, the national logrolling championships, wristwrestling championships, and a rattlesnake hunt in Keane, Oklahoma. In the 1970s, as the battle of the networks became more intense, the quantity of sports created especially for television

[19]Quoted in Rader, *In Its Own Image*, p. 128.

increased. Allegedly to find out who was the best all-around athlete in the country, ABC first aired "The Superstars" in 1973. In that program, renowned athletes competed against one another in events outside their specialties.

"The Superstars" begat a large progeny of similar shows. At ABC, viewers soon witnessed "The Women Superstars," "The World Superstars," and "The Superteams." NBC responded with "Dynamic Duos" and "US Against the World" (a celebrity Olympics). At CBS, "The Challenge of the Sexes" spawned "Celebrity Challenge of the Sexes." One contest, a tennis match between Farrah Fawcett-Majors and Bill Cosby on "Celebrity Challenge," drew a whopping 49 percent of the television audience. Since Majors was without even minimal skills in tennis, one critic concluded that the astronomical rating must have resulted from men ogling the actress while she cavorted about in shorts. "The way we are going," asserted Curt Gowdy, a spokesman of the old school of sportscasting, "we'll see Secretariat racing a Wyoming antelope." For a time, there seemed to be no end for the potential of trashsports. "I've got ideas for telecasts in envelopes piled as high as this building," declared Robert Wussler, the president of CBS Sports in 1978. "I'll bet 25 percent of those ideas are good ones."[20] But in the early 1980s viewers tired of the made-for-television spectacles, and the networks responded by less televising of synthetic sports.

Syndicated sports shows, cable television, and communication satellites added vast new dimensions to the fight between the networks for supremacy in sports. From the earliest days of television, independent producers had put together shows, which then would be aired either by one of the major networks or by a special syndicated network of local stations. The launching of the first communications satellite in 1974 and the end of complex legal restrictions on cable television in 1977 paved the way for the so-called superstations and cable network systems. Fans of televised sports rejoiced at the formation of two sports networks: USA Network in 1975 and the Entertainment and Sports Programming Network (ESPN) in 1979. At first both networks concentrated on telecasting local contests or the more obscure college sports, but eventually ESPN landed contracts for college and professional football games as well as big-league baseball games. Yet neither USA nor ESPN were able to prosper by televising sports alone; in the 1980s both networks broadened their programming to include nonsports shows.

In the mid-1980s signs were present that the long romance between television and sports might be cooling. Network ratings told part of the story. Although millions continued to watch televised sports, ratings slipped downward. In particular, professional football, long the darling of the networks, suffered from declines. The networks faced increasing competition from the superstations and the cable television systems for audiences, rights, and advertising dollars. Some long-time sponsors of televised sports reduced their commitments or pulled out entirely. Both car manufacturers and breweries, traditionally two of the most generous sports sponsors, began shifting advertising dollars elsewhere.

[20]Both statements quoted in Randall Poe, "The Angry Fan," *Harper's*, 251 (1975), 95.

Caught in a vise between rising costs for television rights and falling advertising receipts, the networks began to economize. In 1985, when Capital City Communications (a media conglomerate) purchased ABC, it removed Roone Arledge as head of the sports division and abruptly ended the division's free-wheeling spending. "Pretzels, potato chips, and sodas from the machines in the hallway" soon replaced "lavish parties" and "six block limo rides to executive lunches," grumbled an ABC employee. Both NBC and CBS slashed budgets for sports as well, though not as drastically as ABC. The networks suddenly reversed the escalation of rights payments. "The days of quantum leaps have ended, not only for football but for other sports," mourned Cleveland Browns owner Art Modell after having helped negotiate a new contract for National Football League television rights in 1987.[21] Nonetheless, beginning in 1990, CBS and ESPN nearly doubled payments for the rights to major league baseball games.

THE SOCIAL ROLE OF THE MEDIA

Throughout the post-1950 era, the role of televised sports occasioned debate. Everyone conceded that television could provide experiences unavailable to fans in the stands or to radio listeners. To keep viewers riveted to the screen, the directors provided quickly shifting images—from close-ups to long distance shots, from players to spectators, from spectators to cheerleaders, from live action to replays. Close-ups, replays, and slow-motion shots could add to the fan's appreciation of beautifully executed plays. Perhaps for these reasons, a majority of Americans, according to a nationwide poll in 1978, preferred to watch sports (except baseball) on television rather than being in the stands.[22]

Yet, while conceding that television furnished viewers with experiences in some ways superior to those available to the live fan, critics argued that the medium ultimately trivialized and diluted the traditional sporting experience. Dilution and trivialization took the form of too much—too much hype, too many "big plays," too many extraneous sensations, and too many games. Once the miracle of seeing major sporting events and well-executed plays became commonplace, viewers lost some of their enthusiasm. No longer did the sensations arising from the immediacy of the sporting event exert the same poignancy, the same urgency, or the same power to inspire.[23]

[21]*Lincoln* (NE) *Star*, March 16, 1987. See also *Wall Street Journal*, Feb. 13, 1987; William Taaffe, "TV to Sports: The Buck Stops Here," *Sports Illustrated*, 64 (Feb. 24, 1986), 20–27; and William Taaffe, "It's Bottom-Line Time," ibid, 67 (Oct. 12, 1987), 50–73.

[22]Don Kowet, "TV Sports: America Speaks Out," *TV Guide*, Aug. 19, 1978. For largely favorable views of televised sports, see Richard Kostelanetz, "Fanfare for TV Football," *Intellectual Digest*, 3 (Aug. 1973), 53–54, and Joan M. Chandler, *Television and National Sport: The United States and Britain* (Urbana and Chicago, 1988), Chaps. 1–3.

[23]See Rader, *In Its Own Image*; Herbert I. London, "TV Sports: Real Life's Last Stand," *Television Quarterly*, 13 (1976), 57–60; Michael Oriard, "Viewpoint," *Sports Illustrated*, 60 (April 2, 1984), 13–14.

Television affected sports journalism as well. Although survivors of the literary tradition in sportswriting remained in the age of television, in the 1960s sportswriting took a new turn. Since presumably the fans could see for themselves on television the drama transpiring on the field of play, reporters increasingly tried to cover dimensions of the contest hidden from the cameras. This usually meant seeking the opinions of others; thus post-game interviews of coaches and players became a kind of ritual. At worst, stories might consist of little more than quotations of game participants strung together; at best, the stories included analyses of important behind-the-scenes activities.

Other modern sportswriters, influenced by the Vietnam War and the counterculture of the 1960s, attacked modern sports themselves. They conceived their job to be the smashing of the false illusions that surrounded sports and believed that sports should be subjected to the same close scrutiny as other important social institutions. They explored racism, sexism, drugs, religion, gambling, cheating, and violence in sports, as well as its business side. On occasion, the fan might find on the sports pages more about what happened in the courtroom, the boardroom, or the bedroom than what happened on the field of play.[24] But most fans cared little for news about social problems or business; they turned to the sports pages to escape news of wars, politics, assassinations, discrimination, and high finance.

The post-1950 era witnessed the far-reaching influences of television and population changes on American sport. Population growth, especially in the Sunbelt states, encouraged professional leagues to expand the number of their franchises and caused professional teams to relocate in cities that could promise them more patrons, subsidies, and/or media revenues. In the sprawling metropolises the traditional spatial pattern of urban leisure changed. Commercial entertainment in the inner city declined. Instead of seeking entertainment in the inner city, suburbanites looked to at-home, do-it-yourself projects. White collar professionals even embarked upon a new physical fitness crusade. And all classes watched television. The new medium became the ultimate instrument not only in encouraging the privatization of leisure but also in altering the general contours of organized sports.

---

[24]For a biting analysis of sports journalism in the age of television, see Michael Novak, *The Joy of Sports* (New York, 1976), Chap. 14. See also David Q. Voigt, "From Chadwick to Chipmunks," *Journal of American Culture*, 7 (Fall, 1984), 31–37.

15

PROFESSIONAL TEAM SPORTS

At first no one expected the annual Super Bowl, a product of the National Football League and the American Football League merger of 1966, to exceed all other sports spectacles in popularity. Within only a half-dozen years of its founding, the Super Bowl enjoyed a larger national audience than horseracing's venerable Kentucky Derby or baseball's World Series. By the 1980s over half the nation's population watched the game on television. Only an occasional television special attracted so many viewers. Elaborate fanfare and ceremony accompanied the Bowls, and each was given its own Roman numeral, thereby elevating the pageant above the mundane and linking it with the spectacles of ancient Rome. Super Bowl Sunday became an unofficial national holiday, one that was more rigorously observed in many circles than Washington's Birthday, Independence Day, or even drinking on New Year's Eve.

Nothing suggested more dramatically than did the Super Bowl the relative decline of baseball and the growing prosperity of professional football. Although millions continued to listen to baseball on radio, to follow the sport in their daily newspaper, and to watch games on television, in the post-1950 era baseball lost its preeminent position among American sports. By the late 1970s, professional football, a sport unknown to millions prior to midcentury, overtook baseball in popularity—and basketball, once an equally obscure professional team sport, also won a growing following. (See Figure 15-1.)

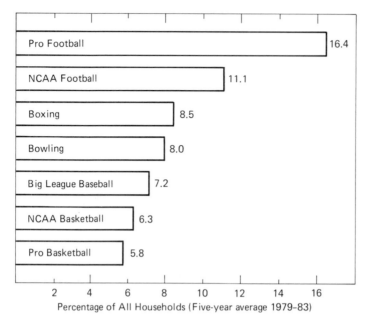

Figure 15-1
National Television Audience for Sports

Pro Football	16.4
NCAA Football	11.1
Boxing	8.5
Bowling	8.0
Big League Baseball	7.2
NCAA Basketball	6.3
Pro Basketball	5.8

Percentage of All Households (Five-year average 1979–83)

THE WOES OF BASEBALL

In the post-1950 era baseball's elaborate superstructure all but collapsed.[1] Literally thousands of semipro teams folded and minor league baseball became a shell of its former self. The major leagues fared somewhat better. Average game attendance at big league games remained below the marks achieved in the 1948–52 seasons until 1978, but even then lagged proportionately behind the population growth of metropolitan areas served by big league franchises. Beginning in the mid-1960s the television audiences for regular season baseball games fell to nearly half of that of regular season professional football games.[2]

Baseball's relative loss of fan support sprang from several sources. Perhaps because of its slow pace and its evocation of a past of farms and small towns, baseball failed to attract many of the nation's youth. By the 1970s, men aged fifty years and over comprised the largest television audience for baseball games. Baseball suffered from more tangible problems as well. After World War II, growing slums surrounded many big league parks. Responding in part to fears for their personal safety and for the security of their cars, the residents of

[1] As a general history critical of major league leadership, see David Voigt, *American Baseball: From Postwar Expansion to the Electronic Age* (University Park, PA, 1983). Defensive but insightful of his era as commissioner is Bowie Kuhn, *Hardball* (New York, 1987). For baseball in general see also Bill James, *Bill James Historical Baseball Abstract* (New York, 1988). All of these books underplay the post-1950 decline in baseball.

[2] Attendance and population data can be conveniently found in the annual editions of *Information Please* or *World Almanac*. On television audiences, see A.C. Nielson, *Televised Sport*, published annually since 1972. For the relative popularity of professional sports, see also Research & Forecasts, Inc., *The Miller Lite Report on American Attitudes Toward Sports* (Milwaukee, 1983).

independent suburbs hesitated to drive into the inner cities to attend games. In the summers, suburbanites chose to spend more of their spare time doing other things than watching baseball games. "Why should a guy with a boat in the driveway, golf clubs in the car, bowling ball and tennis racket in the closet, a trunkful of camping equipment, two boys in the Little League and a body full of energy left over from shorter working hours pay to sit and do nothing but watch a mediocre game?" asked W. Travis Walton of Abilene, Texas, in a letter to *Sports Illustrated* in 1958.[3] Apart from the intrinsic difficulties television had in capturing all of the dimensions of baseball, the sport's long season and many games (compared to football and basketball) meant that only a few games seemed crucial enough to attract large television audiences.

The problem of devising a satisfactory television policy also plagued Organized Baseball.[4] In part, minor league baseball succumbed to the greed of the big league owners. The return of prosperity in the 1940s had stimulated a new boom in minor league baseball. Annual attendance increased nearly three-fold between 1939 and 1949, from 15 to 42 million—then came the invasion of television. Alone, the minor leagues could do nothing to stem the intrusions of big-league telecasts into their home territories. Threatened by antitrust action by the Justice Department and seeking to maximize their own broadcast revenues, in 1951 the major league owners repealed their ban against their games being aired in minor league territories.

Combined with the interest in competing leisure-time activities, the decision to allow unlimited telecasts spelled disaster for minor league baseball. After 1951 nearly everyone who owned a television set could see the big leaguers play for free. Local minor league heroes paled beside major league superstars such as Henry Aaron, Willie Mays, Ted Williams, Bob Feller, and Mickey Mantle. Attendance at minor league games fell from 42 million in 1949, before the advent of nationally televised major league games, to 15 million in 1957 and 10 million in 1969. The number of minor leagues shrank from fifty-one in 1949 to twenty by 1970. In the 1970s, in order to survive, nearly all minor league clubs had to receive substantial subsidies from major league affiliates. By then, college teams began to replace the minor league franchises as a major source of big league recruits.

The television history of the Braves (Boston, Milwaukee, and Atlanta) illustrated the effects of the cool medium on big league owners. Permitting the telecasts of nearly all home games, Boston's attendance fell nearly 81 percent between 1948 and 1952. Faced with financial ruin, the Braves' owner moved the club to Milwaukee in 1953 and permitted telecasts only of selected road games. Although attendance at Milwaukee was consistently above the median for big league franchises, a new set of owners transferred the club to Atlanta in 1966. The

---

[3] *Sports Illustrated*, 9 (Sept. 1, 1958), 26.

[4] See Benjamin G. Rader, *In Its Own Image: How Television Transformed Sports* (New York, 1984), Chap. 4 and pp. 141–44; Ralph Andreano, *No Joy in Mudville: The Dilemma of Major League Baseball* (Cambridge, MA, 1965); Lance E. Davis, "Self-Regulation in Baseball, 1909–1971," in Roger G. Noll, ed., *Government and the Sports Business* (Washington, DC, 1974), pp. 374–375; Kuhn, *Hardball*, Chap. 22; "The Most Powerful Man in Sports," *Sports Illustrated*, 60 (March 12, 1984), 9.

media in Atlanta offered to increase the television-radio rights for Braves games to $1.5 million, nearly a million more dollars than they had received in Milwaukee. In the future, before relocating a franchise, big league owners carefully considered both the population of the proposed site and its potential for broadcast revenues.

Until 1961, when Congress passed the Sports Broadcasting Act, major league baseball was unable to develop a national television package for the regular season games that included all franchises. In 1954 the majors submitted to the Department of Justice a plan for a "Game of the Week" in which the Commissioner of Baseball would negotiate with the networks for the sale of national television rights of the member franchises, but the Justice Department advised that the proposal would violate federal antitrust laws. Organized Baseball acquiesced without taking the issue to the federal courts; apparently the owners feared the possible loss of baseball's unique legal status. At any rate, the networks negotiated packages with individual clubs for national telecasts. Under such circumstances the fans enjoyed a bonanza of televised baseball in the late 1950s, but clubs that could not land network telecasts (usually those located in smaller population areas) suffered from both declining attendance and a reduction in potential broadcasting revenues.

After the passage of the Sports Broadcasting Act of 1961, which exempted package contracts of professional sports leagues from the antitrust laws, the major leagues negotiated contracts with the television networks in which all clubs shared equally in the revenues. The size of the network contracts slowly drifted upward, paralleling the rate of inflation until 1983. In that year, an era when the networks were slugging it out for television rights for the major sports, baseball saw its payments from the networks suddenly increase to $4 million annually per club, more than four times what each franchise had received a year earlier. The 1990–93 package contracts with CBS and cable television shot upward again, totalling $14.4 million annually for each franchise, a figure comparable to the NFL. But, unlike the NFL, which did not permit individual franchises to retain media rights, each major league franchise averaged nearly $6 million annually (in 1987) from local television and radio rights. The franchises located in large market areas such as New York (where the Yankees received $41 million in 1990) garnered far more from television and radio than those in smaller cities such as Milwaukee, where the Brewers earned a mere $3 million from their local contract. These differences in club broadcast earnings resulted in much larger disparities in gross income among baseball franchises than in those of pro football.[5]

THE RESPONSES OF THE BIG LEAGUES

Apart from relocating franchises, expansion, and the building of new parks (see Chapter 14), major league baseball took other steps to counter declining interest

[5]See Rader, *In Its Own Image*, pp. 122–25; Curt Smith, *Voices of the Game*, (South Bend, IN, 1987), p. 444; William Oscar Johnson and William Taaffe, "A Whole New Ball Game," *Sports Illustrated*, 69 (Dec. 26, 1988–Jan. 2, 1989), 34–42.

in the sport. The first step, which entailed the enlarging of the strike zone, was a near-disaster. One theory for this action held that the Rules Committee had become acutely sensitive to the charge that baseball was too slow to sustain the interest of television audiences. "Delay, Dally, and Stall," was the way John Cashman described big league baseball in *TV Guide*.[6] In the early twentieth century the playing time of games averaged about an hour and a half, whereas by the 1960s the typical game lasted over two and a half hours. Pitchers worked more slowly and batters stepped out of the box more frequently; managers had more conferences on the mound and replaced pitchers more frequently than in the past. To counter the slowdown, the big leagues in 1963 instructed the umpires to call as strikes some pitches that had formerly been called as balls. A second theory for the decision was that the leagues had no intention of altering significantly the balance between offense and defense, that the Rules Committee was merely trying to clarify the size of the strike zone by requiring umpires to call pitches at the bottom of the knee strikes. By reducing the likelihood of walks and increasing the incidence of strikeouts, they presumed the pace of the game should quicken.

Whatever the motives, with the new strike zone offensive production dropped precipitously. Although batting averages had been slipping downward prior to 1963 (thirty points between the mid-1930s and the early 1960s), in the 1962–63 seasons alone major league run totals fell by 1,681, home runs by 297, batting averages by twelve points, and bases on balls by 1,345. Pitchers recorded 1,206 more strikeouts than in 1962. The 1963 totals became the standard for the next five years. Carl Yastrzemski won the American League batting title in 1968 with an average of .301, the lowest in major league history. At the very time that the nation seemed obsessed with power, baseball had transformed itself into a series of defensive contests reminiscent of the early twentieth century dead ball era.[7]

From the late 1960s through the 1970s, "The Young Turks," a new, less convention-bound group of owners, tried to undo the damage caused by the 1963 decision. To reverse the decline in hitting, they lowered the pitching mound from fifteen to ten inches (thereby making the curve and the slider less effective) and ordered the umpires to reduce the size of the strike zone. Officially, the strike zone extended from the knees to the armpits, but to be certain of obtaining a called strike, pitchers now had to throw the ball between the knees and the belt.

[6]John Cashman, "The Ump Yells 'Play Ball,' " *TV Guide* (Sept. 18, 1965), 18. On the strike zone controversy, see Leonard Koppett, *All About Baseball* (New York, 1974), pp. 324–34; William Leggett, "The Season of the Zero Hitter," *Sports Illustrated*, 28 (June 17, 1968), 20–23; Peter Gammons, "What Ever Happened to the Strike Zone?" ibid, 66 (April 6, 1987), 36–46; James, *Bill James*, pp. 228–29, 267.

[7]Baseball observers offered a number of additional explanations for the decline in hitting: (1) night baseball, which was introduced in 1935; (2) better pitching, especially the increased use of the slider and of relief specialists; (3) efforts by more players to hit home runs rather than singles ("Home run hitters drive Cadillacs; singles hitters don't," explained Pittsburgh slugger, Ralph Kiner); (4) more coast-to-coast air travel; (5) bigger and better fielders' gloves; and (6) larger, more symmetrical ball parks.

Moreover, in 1973 the American League replaced pitchers in the batting order with "designated hitters." The changes had the desired results; in the 1970s batting averages, runs, and home runs increased. Yet maintaining an attractive balance between offense and defense remained a problem. To reverse a sudden outburst of home runs in 1987, the majors again enlarged the strike zone, cracked down on the use of cork-filled bats, and may have reduced the ball's liveliness as well.

The Young Turks also led the movement for new leadership at the top. In 1969 they hired Bowie Kuhn, an ex-Wall Street lawyer with connections in Washington, as commissioner. They hoped Kuhn would improve baseball's relations with the press, the federal government, and the television networks. Within two years Kuhn signed a contract for the televising of Monday night games, scheduled part of the World Series at night, and delayed the start of the Series until the second Saturday in October so television could beam two weekends of games. In the 1970s and 80s, despite the continuing independence of the owners and the rise of a powerful players union that constricted the much-maligned commissioner's authority, under Kuhn's more aggressive leadership baseball experienced some recovery.

The new commissioner, Peter Ueberroth, who was employed after his spectacular performance in managing the 1984 Olympics in Los Angeles, enjoyed even more success than Kuhn. With the aid of Kuhn, Ueberroth insisted before he took office that the commissioner's reelection would require only a simple majority of all owners rather than three-quarters of the owners in *each* league. In a reorganization of the commissioner's office, the owners relinquished much of

BOWIE KUHN
Bowie Kuhn, Commissioner of Baseball (1969–1984), brought to major league baseball more forceful leadership than had existed since the retirement of Kenesaw Mountain Landis and helped to restore some of baseball's declining popularity.

their own power by making Ueberroth the "sole executive officer" of baseball. Ueberroth also signed a gigantic $1.08 billion, four year (1990–93) television contract with CBS. With the addition of a cable television package, each major league franchise received $14.4 million per year from national television rights.

Reducing the disparities between the performances of teams should have abetted baseball's recovery. If more teams had a viable shot at winning the pennant, it was assumed that no single team would dominate championships over the years and pennant races could be closer fights. On the other hand, television increased the importance of regularly having teams in large market areas in the playoffs and in the World Series. A World Series between teams representing New York and Los Angeles was more likely to attract a large television audience than teams from Kansas City and St. Louis.

Regardless, disparities in performance continued to plague the sport. (See Figures 15-2 and 15-3). In the 1950s and 60s, the New York Yankees dominated the American League pennant races; in a fifteen-year span, they won thirteen flags and lost only two. The superior resources arising from larger attendance, more broadcast revenues, and skilled management accounted for the longevity of the Yankee dynasty. Casey Stengel, the erstwhile field manager of the Yankees from 1949 to 1960, had at his disposal so many good players that he platooned nearly all of his hitters, using left-handed hitters against right-handed pitchers and vice versa. Under new ownership and management in the late 1960s and early 70s, the Yankees suffered a temporary eclipse, but when George

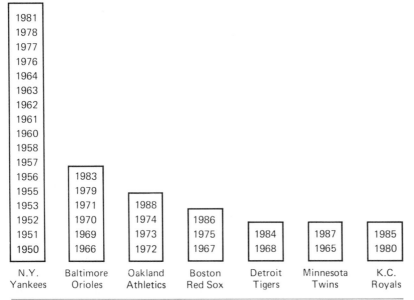

Figure 15-2 Disparity in Competition, Major League Baseball (1950–1988) as Reflected in American League Pennants

*The Milwaukee Brewers, Chicago White Sox, and Cleveland Indians won one flag each while the Toronto Blue Jays, California Angels, Seattle Mariners, and Texas Rangers did not win a single flag.

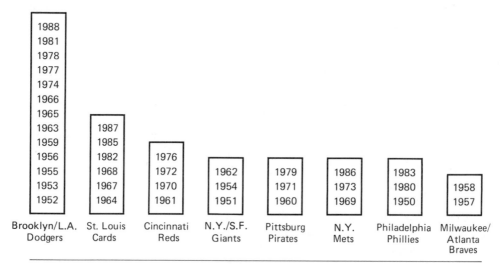

Brooklyn/L.A. Dodgers	St. Louis Cards	Cincinnati Reds	N.Y./S.F. Giants	Pittsburg Pirates	N.Y. Mets	Philadelphia Phillies	Milwaukee/ Atlanta Braves
1988							
1981							
1978							
1977							
1974							
1966							
1965							
1963	1987						
1959	1985						
1956	1982	1976					
1955	1968	1972	1962	1979	1986	1983	
1953	1967	1970	1954	1971	1973	1980	1958
1952	1964	1961	1951	1960	1969	1950	1957

*The San Diego Padres won one pennant (1984) while the Chicago Cubs, Montreal Expos, and Houston Astros did not win a single flag.

Figure 15-3
Disparity in Competition, Major League Baseball (1950–1988) as Reflected in National League Pennants

Steinbrenner, a free-spending construction magnate, gained control of the club in 1973, they won three flags in the late 1970s and another one in 1981. For similar reasons the Brooklyn-Los Angeles Dodgers franchise enjoyed almost equal success in the National League.

The owners had long insisted that the player reservation and draft system were essential to the preservation of competitive balance. Yet, historically, the reserve clause in contracts had failed to prevent the building of dynasties, especially by teams in the larger metropolitan areas. (See Chapter 10.) In 1965 the majors adopted an annual draft of all unsigned high school and college players and in the late 1970s veteran players gained the right to become free agents. Some feared that free agency would give the richer owners, or those in larger market areas, a decided advantage. And indeed some owners, such as George Steinbrenner, spent enormous sums to woo established players from other clubs. But, in fact, free agency appeared to reduce performance disparities. During the first nine years of the 1980s only St. Louis (with three), and Philadelphia, Los Angeles, and Kansas City (with two each) won more than one league flag.

THE EARLY DAYS OF PRO FOOTBALL

Professional football had modest origins. In the 1890s the tough mine and mill towns in western Pennsylvania and Ohio were the cradle for the infant sport. There, local clubs, often formed by the players themselves, began to pay some men a few dollars to risk life and limb to play on Sunday afternoons. A team representing the Panhandle Shop of the Pennsylvania Railroad in Columbus, Ohio, may have been typical of the pre-1920 teams. "The boys worked in the shop until four Saturday afternoon, got their suppers at home, grabbed the rattlers to any point within twelve hours' ride of Columbus, played the Sunday game, took another train to Columbus, and punched the time clock at seven Monday morning."[8] No leagues existed in the pre-1920 era and each team scheduled its own matches.

Unlike college football, the early ambience of the pro sport was ethnic, Catholic, and working-class. Some rosters included a few blacks and Native-Americans. For almost a decade, Jim Thorpe, the hero of the 1912 Olympics and the Carlisle Indian School football great, was the game's premier attraction. The playing of collegians and sometimes high school athletes under aliases, the practice by players of jumping from team to team during the season to maximize their pay, wagering, and charges of game fixing placed the sport outside of respectable circles. Hoping to reverse the game's image and improve its profitability, representatives from mostly smaller Ohio cities gathered at the Hupmobile automobile agency showroom at Canton in 1920. There, led by Joseph F. Carr, a sportswriter, minor league baseball owner, and manager of the Columbus football team, they formed a new pro league that became officially known as the National Football League in 1922.

Until the mid-1950s, NFL teams rarely earned profits. During its first thirty-five years, over forty franchises joined the league, struggled, and then expired. The Great Depression of the 1930s wiped out all the franchises in smaller cities save Green Bay, Wisconsin. Major college games invariably outdrew the pro games. To many Americans, pay-for-play carried a stigma. The league failed to attract many of the top college players. Even though the NFL signed college heroes such as Red Grange and Ernie Nevers in the 1920s, most college graduates could make more money elsewhere or simply bypassed the game because of its negative associations. In the early days, the newspapers all but ignored the NFL. Even in the daily papers located in the larger cities, pages of speculation and reports about college games could be found, but little or no mention was made of pro games.

Yet the NFL somehow survived these handicaps as well as the ravages of the Great Depression and World War II. Creating a more offensive-oriented sport than the collegians may have been part of the reason. The pro rule-makers moved the hashmarks ten yards inside the sidelines and permitted forward passes from any spot behind the line of scrimmage (1933), and allowed free substitutions (1943). The adoption of two divisions in 1933 with a championship game at the end of the season also enhanced interest in the sport. The creation of the College All-Star Game in 1934, which pitted the NFL champion of the

[8]Harry A. March, *Pro Football: Its Ups and Downs*, 2nd. ed. (New York, 1934), p. 65. For pro football see also Tom Bennett, et al., *The NFL's Official Encyclopedic History of Professional Football* (New York, 1977); George Halas, with Gwen Morgan and Arthur Veyesy *Halas by Halas* (New York, 1979); Paul Brown with Jack Clary, *PB: The Paul Brown Story* (New York, 1979).

previous season against recently graduated college seniors, added to the respectability of the pro game, attracted large gates, and gained the attention of the nation's press. In 1936, the NFL adopted a draft, which allowed teams the exclusive right to contract for the services of college players in reverse order of their league standing in the previous season. Ostensibly, the draft would equalize competition between clubs, but it also strengthened the owner's bargaining position with potential players.

At the conclusion of World War II, the fortunes of pro football improved. By 1950 average game attendance had doubled, though the NFL confronted an expensive war with a rival, the All-America Conference between 1946 and 1949. The NFL also signed more college stars to contracts. And on the horizon was television, which promised not only lucrative revenues but the creation of new fans for the sport.

THE MAKING OF PRO FOOTBALL

No one would have predicted in 1950 that pro football would shortly rival baseball for the affection of the American people. A New York Giants halfback, Frank Gifford, who came to the NFL in 1952, returned home to California after that first season and was asked by his friends: "Where have *you* been?"[9] But ignorance of the NFL among sport fans soon changed. By the mid-1960s, no other team sport even approximated professional football's popularity on television.

Superior management accounted for part of the NFL's success. The football owners had much in common. Nearly all of them were Irish-Catholic in origin and shared the long history of financial tribulations that had beset the NFL. Unlike the savagely independent barons of baseball, they were far more willing to delegate authority to the commissioner's office. And unlike the baseball owners, they chose as commissioners men who had experience in the game's business side. In the post-World War II era, both DeBenneville "Bert" Bell and Alvin "Pete" Rozelle provided the NFL with astute leadership. Appointed as commissioner in 1946, Bell, a former owner-coach of the Philadelphia Eagles, established the framework for the powerful NFL headed by Rozelle from the 1960s through the 1980s. The commissioners welded the NFL owners into a single economic cartel, one far more united than in any other professional team sport.[10]

In the 1950s Bert Bell laid the foundations for the NFL's successful marriage to television. The experience of the Los Angeles Rams convinced Bell

---

[9]Quoted in Rader, *In Its Own Image*, p. 83.

[10]See ibid, Chap. 6; Frank Deford, "Long Live the King," *Sports Illustrated*, 52 (Jan. 21, 1980), 100–19, and for detailed analysis of the business side of the NFL's history, David Harris, *The League: The Rise and Decline of the NFL* (New York, 1986).

of the need for restricted telecasts. In 1949 the Rams drew 205,109 fans to their home games. In 1950, when for the first time the club telecast each of its home games, attendance fell to 110,162. In 1951 the Rams again blacked out home games, and attendance promptly doubled. In 1952 Bell rammed through the owners' meeting amendments to the NFL bylaws that made him the virtual dictator of the league's television policy. Although a federal district court judge ruled in 1953 that the new bylaws violated antitrust law, the judge implicitly upheld home-game blackouts. Bert Bell was elated.

By the mid-1950s televised pro football was attracting millions of new viewers. Watching the games filled a gap in the lives of many Americans. On blustery fall Sunday afternoons men now had something to do besides take their dog for a walk or watch an array of "high brow" programs on television. Television helped the novice fan to understand and appreciate the intricacies of the sport. As one fan put it: "You watched a game on television and, suddenly, the wool was stripped from your eyes. What had appeared to be an incomprehensible tangle of milling bodies from the grandstand made sense. [Television] created a nation of instant experts in no time."[11] The central requirement of the game—that the offense must move the ball ten yards in four plays or give it up to the opposing team—set up recurring crises, keeping the viewer's attention riveted to the little silver screen. The pause between plays permitted the viewer to savor the drama. If the situation were third down and long yardage, would the linebackers blitz? Would the quarterback throw or call a draw play?

Technological breakthroughs contributed to pro football's growing popularity. The perfection in the 1960s of instant replays and slow motion shots allowed fans to experience the game in an entirely different way from that of the spectator in the stands. Instant replay (first used by CBS in 1963) and slow motion shots could pinpoint a receiver running a pattern, the vicious blocking of an interior lineman, or the balletlike steps of a running back eluding would-be tacklers. Color television and artificial playing surfaces radically altered the appearance of games. The teams donned bright uniforms with the names of individual players on the backs and logos on their helmets. More than one viewer shared the judgment of critic Richard Kostelanetz, who declared that, compared with telecast games, "live games now seem peculiarly inept, lethargic, and pedestrian."[12]

One game, the 1958 championship tilt between the Baltimore Colts and the New York Giants, seemed to trigger the national mania for pro football that would reach unprecedented proportions in the following decade. With only

---

[11]Quoted in Associated Press, *A Century of American Sports* (Maplewood, NJ, 1975), 17–18. For the role of television in creating professional football, see apart from Rader, *In Its Own Image*, Phil Patton, *Razzle-Dazzle* (Garden City, NY, 1984).

[12]Richard Kostelanetz, "Fanfare for TV Football," *Intellectual Digest*, 3 (Aug. 1973), 54. See also Joan M. Chandler, "TV & Sports: Wedded with a Golden Hoop," *Psychology Today*, 10 (April 1977), 64–76.

seven seconds left in the game, Steve Myhra of the Colts calmly kicked a twenty-yard field goal to tie the game, 17–17. For the first time in NFL history, the championship game went into a "sudden death" overtime. Some thirty million fans watched their screens intently as Johnny Unitas, the Baltimore quarterback, took "The Thirteen Steps to Glory," marching the Colts down the field for the winning touchdown. Television had enabled millions to share in the excitement of a classic sporting contest.

Television also played a key role in the making of a new league, the American Football League (AFL). Rebuffed in their efforts to obtain franchises in the NFL, in 1959 two millionaire Texans, Lamar Hunt of Dallas and K.S. "Bud" Adams of Houston, announced the formation of the new league. The AFL began play in 1960 with eight teams, four of which were in cities already occupied by the NFL. The AFL nearly went down at the outset; it lost an estimated $3 million in its first year, and the undercapitalized New York franchise, essential to the AFL's potential success, threatened to drive the entire league into bankruptcy. In 1960 Harry Wismer, former sportscaster and eccentric owner of the New York team, persuaded the AFL owners to sell the league's television rights to ABC as a package, each franchise sharing equally in the receipts. Although the AFL contract with ABC was modest, it helped to keep the league temporarily afloat.

In the meantime, the NFL inaugurated its own new era. In 1959, Bert Bell died, and the NFL owners, after nine days of heated discussion, made the surprise choice of thirty-three-year-old Pete Rozelle as their new commissioner. Rozelle had learned the game from the vantage point of business rather than as a player or coach; he had served as both chief publicity man and general manager of the Los Angeles Rams. He was to become the most remarkable commissioner in the history of professional sports. In due time, he so won the admiration of the owners that they delegated to him nearly complete authority to handle television negotiations, relations with the Federal Government, and controversies among themselves.

The "Boy Czar" soon got an opportunity to test his skills. In 1961 the NFL signed a television pact with CBS similar to the one that the AFL had made with ABC, but in this instance a federal judge struck it down as a violation of federal antitrust law. Aroused by this adverse decision, professional sports leagues (including major league baseball) turned to Congress for relief. Package or pooled contracts, in which franchises shared equally in the receipts, were essential to the existence of modern sports leagues, the sports magnates argued in congressional hearings. Otherwise, Rozelle testified, the leagues could not avoid disparities in competition. None of the witnesses, however, noted that increased profits for all franchises would be likely to result from the monopolistic practice of pooled contracts. Congress quickly passed and President John F. Kennedy signed the Sports Broadcasting Act of 1961. The act permitted the professional clubs to negotiate the sale of national broadcast rights as a single economic unit. The hasty action of Congress and the President clearly exhibited the clout of professional sport on Capitol Hill.

CARICATURE OF ALVIN "PETE" ROZELLE
Along with the media itself, Pete Rozelle, the long-time commissioner of the
National Football League, helped transform professional football into the
nation's most popular televised sport.

THE GOLDEN AGE OF PROFESSIONAL FOOTBALL

By any measure, the success of pro football from the 1960s to the early 1980s was
staggering. Although owners refused to open their financial records to public
perusal, apparently teams rarely lost money. "Any dummy can make money
operating a pro football club," declared Al Davis, managing partner of the
Oakland Raiders in 1978.[13] By the 1970s, each pro stadium regularly exceeded
90 percent of its capacity in attendance, even for preseason training games. The
average audience for televised games leaped from 11 million in 1967 to nearly
20 million by 1977. Two league policies insured teams against financial failure.

[13]Quoted in Ray Kennedy and Nancy Williamson, "Money in Sports: Part II," *Sports
Illustrated*, 49 (July 24, 1978), 56.

By giving visiting teams 40 percent of the gate receipts the NFL avoided the gross disparities in revenues among franchises characteristic of major league baseball and pro basketball. More importantly, the NFL split television revenues equally among the franchises. As Art Modell, the Cleveland Browns owner, once happily quipped: "We're 28 Republicans who vote socialist."[14]

Much of the happiness of the owners sprang from escalating television contracts that the Sports Broadcasting Act of 1961 made possible. In 1964 Rozelle signed a $14 million pact with CBS that was nearly three times the contract of 1962. Little wonder that Arthur Rooney, Jr., veteran owner of the Pittsburgh Steelers, exclaimed: "Pete Rozelle is a gift from the hand of Providence."[15] Under the 1964 contract, each NFL franchise received over $1 million a year. NBC, a loser in the 1964 bidding war for NFL rights, decided to gamble on the AFL. NBC agreed to pay the new loop $42 million over five years, or about $850,000 annually per team, for television rights.

NBC provided enough money to the AFL so that its clubs could engage in an all-out "Battle of the Paychecks" with the NFL for college stars. Both leagues resorted to clandestine methods to obtain the contracts of top college players, but in 1965 the AFL signed the biggest prize of all, Joe Willie Namath, a slope-shoul-dered quarterback out of the University of Alabama, for the (then) astonishing sum of $420,000 for three years. Art Modell of the rival NFL hooted that the signing of Namath was merely a "theatrical stunt." But the high command of the New York Jets, now headed by David "Sonny" Werblin, recognized the value of a player possessing both athletic talent and charisma. Namath had both. In the first season with Namath at the helm, Jets ticket sales doubled. Soon other players received even higher contracts, making Namath's salary one of the best bargains in pro sports.

The rising costs of player talent drove the leagues to the peace table in 1966. Under terms of the merger agreement, Rozelle became the sole commis-sioner, the combined league established a common player draft to end the bidding war, and the two leagues (or conferences as they were to be known after 1969) agreed to a NFL championship game to begin in 1967. Congress quickly passed a law exempting the merger from antitrust action. Senate Whip Russell Long and House Whip Hale Boggs, both from Louisiana, were chiefly responsible for guiding the legislation through Congress. Perhaps not coincidentally, only nine days after the Football Merger Act became law, the NFL awarded New Orleans an expansion franchise.

The American Football Conference, as it became known after the merger, soon caught up with the senior loop in the quality of play. Vince Lombardi's Green Bay Packers easily disposed of the first two AFC champions. But Super Bowl III in 1969 symbolically established the AFC's parity with the NFC. That year, Namath, leading the New York Jets of the AFC against the Baltimore Colts

---

[14]Quoted in "Scorecard," ibid, 51 (Oct. 15, 1979), 24.

[15]Quoted in Joseph Durso, *The All-American Dollar: The Big Business of Sports* (Boston, 1971), pp. 58–59.

of the NFC, confidently predicted: "We'll win. I'll guarantee it." And the Jets did, 16-7. In the 1970s and 1980s, AFC teams dominated NFC rivals in interconference games.

Television contracts for the games of the combined leagues spiraled upward. By 1970 the merged NFL received nearly $50 million from television. Seven years later, "Pete the Shark," as one of the network negotiators dubbed Rozelle, engineered a whopping $656 million, four-year package with the three major networks. Each team received nearly $6 million annually from the contract, nearly six times what they had obtained ten years earlier. But the 1977 contract paled beside that of 1982. In the midst of an all-out battle between the networks for television rights to major sporting events, the three networks paid $14.2 million per team annually, a huge windfall for each NFL franchise. To put that figure in perspective, the annual television share of the Washington Redskins under the new contract exceeded the team's *gross* revenues for the previous season. As the teams received far more money from television than gate receipts, it was little wonder that some observers conjured up visions of pro football becoming a studio sport. But in the mid-1980s, as the networks began to economize, the era of escalating television revenues seemed to be over. The NFL's 1987 contract with the three networks and ESPN called for the retention of the same total revenues that the teams had received from the 1983 agreement.[16]

As early as 1984 several events indicated that the long era of unity among the NFL franchise holders was falling apart. Against the wishes of the overwhelming majority of owners and Pete Rozelle, Al Davis moved his Oakland Raiders to Los Angeles. The federal courts upheld Davis's right to defy the league. Shortly thereafter the Baltimore Colts moved to Indianapolis and the St. Louis Cardinals to Phoenix. Rozelle's power had diminished, and in 1989 he announced his retirement. Whether the league would continue to function as an effective economic cartel was in doubt.[17]

The success of pro football in the post-World War II era evoked an unusual amount of speculation about the sport's larger significance. One point was certain. Pro football no longer attracted only workingmen and ethnics. According to national public opinion polls, the game appealed most to the "successful," to those who had a college education, lived in the independent suburbs, held jobs in the professions, and enjoyed incomes higher than the national average. Football more than baseball seemed to echo its fans' work experience. Most Americans now worked in large bureaucracies, corporations, or institutes. Football was a bureaucratic or corporate sport; eleven men acted in unison against eleven opponents. Football, unlike baseball, was time-bound; the ever-present clock dictated the pace and intensity of the game. And like modern

---

[16]See Rader, *In Its Own Image*, pp. 121–22; William Taaffe, "The Other Game in New York," *Sports Illustrated*, 65 (Sept. 29, 1986), 32–33; Associated Press wire service story on 1987 NFL television contracts, March 16, 1987.

[17]See esp. Harris, *The League*.

work, football embodied rationality, specialization and coordination; the game required careful planning and preparation.

Yet football suggested that committees, systems, bureaucracies, and technologies were still the tools of men, not their masters. The long completed pass and the breakaway run reflected not only careful planning and long hours of practice, but human potency, natural skill, and grace under pressure. The bone-crunching physicality of the game seemed to compensate for the widespread feelings of individual powerlessness in the 1960s and 70s. The game may have most attracted those who led lives of rigid self-control. But, as in all of human life, fate or luck could be decisive. Even the best made plans and the best of human performance might fall victim to the unpredictable bounce of the oblong ball.

Many observers related football to the larger social upheavals of the 1960s and 70s. To President Richard M. Nixon, perhaps the nation's most conspicuous football fan and a man obsessed with winning and losing, football was a miniature school of life, but without life's everyday ambiguities and moral dilemmas. Nixon believed football furnished a healthy antidote to what was perceived in the 1960s and 70s as excessive individual freedom and lawlessness. He regularly placed long distance calls to stadium locker rooms to congratulate winning teams. Intrigued by the strategy and tactics of the game, he even gave unsolicited suggestions for pass plays, including diagrams, to the head coaches of the Miami Dolphins and the Washington Redskins. He used the specialized vocabulary of football to describe his proposals for ending the Vietnam War and for dealing with the nation's economic problems. Some commentators, on the other hand, insisted that only a nation addicted to the violence of a sport like football could pursue a war as immoral and brutal as the Vietnam conflict.[18]

PACKAGING PRO FOOTBALL FOR TELEVISION

No other team sport was quite so responsive to the needs of television as pro football. "The product [we] provide is, of course, simply entertainment," Pete Rozelle once confessed to a congressional committee.[19] At first, the NFL had refused to interrupt the flow of a game for commercials but by the mid-1970s referees received signals from the television crews to call no fewer than fourteen timeouts while each game was in progress. Commercials added at least thirty minutes to the length of each game. Traditionally, the NFL had all but ignored

[18]The literature is immense, but see Murray Ross, "Football and Baseball in America," in John T. Talamini and Charles H. Page, eds., *Sports and Society* (Boston, 1973), 102–12; Michael Novak, *The Joy of Sports* (New York, 1976), Chap. 5; Allen Guttmann, *Sports Spectators* (New York, 1986), Part II; Guttmann, *From Ritual to Record: The Nature of Modern Sports* (New York, 1978), Chap. 5; Robert M. Collins, "Richard M. Nixon: The Psychic, Political, and Moral Uses of Sport," *Journal of Sport History,* 10 (1983), 77–84.

[19]Quoted in Rader, *In Its Own Image,* p. 149.

the hoopla which had long surrounded college football. But in the late 1970s pro teams urged fans to bring banners, pennants, and towels to wave during the games. By 1980 nearly every franchise hired skimpily dressed female cheerleaders to prance along the sidelines.

Even though the low-scoring, power football of the 1960s and early 70s satisfied millions of spectators, in the 1970s the moguls of the NFL experimented with rule changes to make the game more exciting. Critics charged that the pro games had become too predictable; coaches seemed determined, above all else, to avoid costly mistakes. Some of the problem stemmed from rapid improvements being made mostly in defense rather than in offense. Since a football field consists of a rigidly defined and limited amount of space, the appearance of larger, speedier, and better-trained defensive players reduced offensive capabilities. Faced with stronger and quicker defensive players and required to keep their hands flat against their chests while pass blocking, offensive linemen, unless they violated the rules against holding, found it difficult to protect quarterbacks from defensive pass rushers. In 1975 alone, defensive players knocked seventeen quarterbacks out of action.

To bring more offense to the game, the NFL adopted minor rule changes in 1972, 1974, 1977, and a revolutionary set of changes in 1978. In 1978 the rule-makers permitted pass defenders to chuck, or bump, a potential receiver only once and allowed offensive linemen to extend their arms and open their hands to protect the passer. The next year, *Sports Illustrated* reported that "the offenses are going wild."[20] Within three years, passing yardage nearly doubled, and quarterback sacks fell to an all-time low. Football purists were horrified: "It may be track, it may be basketball," observed Myron Cope, a long-time student of the game, "but it isn't football the way it should be."[21] Gradually, however, defenses reversed the offensive barrage. Game officials began to permit more physical contact with receivers, coaches invented new pass defenses, and defensive players learned how to elude would-be pass-blockers more effectively.

As in baseball, the NFL also confronted disparities in competition. Lopsided games, runaway races for the championships, and having the same teams repeatedly in the playoffs threatened to reduce interest in the sport. The NFL was only slightly more successful than baseball in preventing certain teams from dominating championship play. In the 1960s, Vince Lombardi's Green Bay Packers won six conference titles and five championships. The Dallas Cowboys (1966–1985) and the Oakland/Los Angeles Raiders (1965–1980) set NFL records for the most consecutive winning seasons.

Expanding the number of teams eligible for the playoffs and establishing "position" scheduling reduced the likelihood of dynasties. Beginning in the 1970s, eight teams rather than four participated in the playoffs for the champion-

[20]Paul Zimmerman, "The Name of the Game is Now Armball," *Sports Illustrated*, 51 (Nov. 19, 1979), 36–43.
[21]Quoted in Pete Axthelm, "The Sport That Defense Forgot," *Newsweek*, 101 (Jan. 24, 1983), 61.

ship. The "wild card" berth in the playoffs added excitement. Under this system, one team from each conference, the team that had the best record apart from the divisional champions, joined the divisional winners in the playoffs. In 1977 the NFL introduced the controversial position or "parity" scheduling, which had the effect of pitting more of the weaker teams (according to their records in the previous season) against each other and consequently more of the stronger teams against each other for regular season play. The new system virtually assured that three-fourths of the teams would have a crack at the playoffs up to the final few weeks of the season.

PROFESSIONAL BASKETBALL

Until the 1950s, professional basketball languished in the long shadows cast by college teams, Amateur Athletic Union fives, and the Harlem Globetrotters (an all-black quintet).[22] In the 1920s and 30s only a few barnstorming teams enjoyed more than short-term success. The New York Original Celtics, the most prosperous club of the 1920s, occasionally drew as many as 10,000 fans to Madison Square Garden. In the 1930s the New York Rens, an all-black five, and the Philadelphia Sphas, an all-Jewish quintet, fielded the strongest teams. In 1937 commercial concerns located in cities in the Midwest organized the National Basketball League; in 1949 it joined the Basketball Association of America (BAA) to form the National Basketball Association (NBA).

A turning point in the history of the pro game came in 1946 when a group of big city arena owners decided to form the BAA. At first the owners saw BAA games only as fillers for vacancies in their winter schedule between the more profitable ice hockey and college basketball matches. Until 1951, for example, the New York Knickerbockers typically played less than half of their home games in the Garden. Nor did the BAA teams initially compete seriously for the best college talent. Many of the best players opted to play in the National Basketball League, on AAU teams, or, if black, with the Harlem Globetrotters. Since the 1920s companies in towns where basketball enthusiasm ran high had formed powerful AAU teams composed mostly of college stars. Although they technically held regular jobs for the companies that they represented, these "amateur" players often earned more money than the avowed pros. Until 1950, when Boston drafted Charles Cooper of Duquesne, no black played in the NBA. Apart from likely racial prejudice, the arena owners of the BAA did not want to offend Abe Saperstein, the owner of the Globetrotters, by raiding his near-monopoly on black talent. Saperstein's Trotters often drew larger crowds to their arenas than did their own league games.

[22]For general treatments of pro basketball see Leonard Koppett, *24 Seconds to Shoot: An Informal History of the National Basketball Association* (New York, 1968); David S. Neft, et al. *The Sports Encyclopedia: Pro Basketball* (New York, 1975); Lewis Cole, *A Loose Game: The Sport and Business of Basketball* (Indianapolis/New York, 1978). For the Harlem Globetrotters, see esp. Randy Roberts, *Winning Is the Only Thing* (Baltimore, 1989), Chap. 2.

In the 1950s pro basketball wiped out, or absorbed some of the public following of its major rivals. The emergence of the powerful Minneapolis Lakers, led by towering George Mikan, strengthened the NBA's claim that the league featured the "best of basketball." In the 1950s the NBA began to recruit top black stars and the Globetrotters resorted increasingly to showmanship rather than playing serious basketball. Likewise, in the 1950s, the NBA began to outbid the AAU teams for players. Ironically, a point-shaving scandal in college basketball in 1950–51 also assisted the fledgling NBA. In the wake of the scandal most of the colleges cancelled their games in the big city arenas. In these cities, fans either had to forego their hunger for basketball or attend pro games.

Yet the NBA continued to have problems. Television produced only modest revenues. Part of the reason was the failure of the NBA to field a strong team in New York City, where Ned Irish, the owner of the Knickerbockers, made many ill-advised trades and drafted players for their immediate publicity value rather than their potential. Because of his abrasive personality, Irish was unable to obtain assistance from fellow owners in building a stronger New York franchise. The NBA also had a problem in coping with low scoring and a rough-and-tumble style of play. Pressure from the fans and television induced the NBA in 1954 to adopt a 24-second rule. A team had to take a shot at the basket within twenty-four seconds or relinquish the ball to the opposing team.

Yet experience disclosed that the time-limit rule produced subtle, unforeseen difficulties. The new rule made it hard for fans to get excited about the game until the middle of the last quarter. Since it was difficult for a team to build up a lead and "sit" on it, to the fans it appeared that the players did not exert themselves fully until the last quarter. If a team did have a large lead in the final quarter of the game, then the last portion of the game was likely to be unexciting. On the other hand, if the score was close in the middle of the last quarter, then what transpired earlier seemed, in retrospect, to have been insignificant.

In the meantime the style of NBA play changed sharply. Apart from the jump shot, which became part of the standard repertoire of most players, Bob Cousy of the Boston Celtics introduced a razzle-dazzle style of guard play that featured pinpoint passing (even behind the back) and expert dribbling that foreshadowed the black playground style of the 1960s and 70s. Bill Russell, also of the Celtics, introduced a revolutionary style of play for the big center. Russell, exceptionally quick and agile, not only reduced the effectiveness of the opposing center, but by playing in effect a one-man zone (zone defenses were technically illegal in the NBA) he clogged up driving lanes and prevented easy lay-ins. With Russell in the middle, Boston's other four players could gamble by pressing the ball everywhere, causing numerous turnovers without being victimized by easy shots. Russell's rebounding and precise outlet passes also ignited Boston's vaunted fastbreak offense. With Russell leading the way, Arnold "Red" Auerbach's Celtics captured nine NBA championships between 1957 and 1966. Before retirement in 1969, Russell, as coach of the Celtics, led the team to two additional championships.

Pro basketball shared in the largesse of the sports boom of the 1960s, though by no means as spectacularly as pro football. NBA attendance increased from less than 2 million in 1960 to 10 million in the late 1970s. Network television, however, remained lukewarm toward the NBA. In 1962, NBC even dropped its coverage of regular season games, and in 1964 ABC paid a mere $650,000 for a package of Sunday afternoon regular season telecasts. Rights payments increased slowly, reaching $535,000 per team when CBS won the package in 1974. While the NBA's fortunes with the media had improved, the newly founded American Basketball Association (1967), which had hoped to capitalize upon television to ensure its success, was unable to land a network contract. In 1976 it failed.

As in baseball and football, certain franchises tended to dominate championship play. In the 1970s, in the wake of the decline of the Boston Celtics dynasty, the NBA enjoyed a temporary era of competitive balance; eight different teams won championships. But from 1980 through 1988, with one exception, either the Boston Celtics or Los Angeles Lakers won all the championships. The market areas of the NBA franchise ranged from cities of a half million to nearly eight million. Furthermore, the gate-sharing arrangement favored the large market areas. But, although the home teams retained all gate receipts, the franchises shared the revenues from the NBA's package television contract. Long-term supremacy seemed to flow mainly from the ability of the Celtics and the Lakers to find the right combination of players rather than from distinct financial advantages.

At the close of the 1980s the future of pro basketball remained less certain than that of either major league baseball or the National Football League. The expected rise in television ratings never occurred. The introduction of the three point shot in 1982 and the entrance of popular players such as Larry Bird and Earvin "Magic" Johnson into the league provided a temporary revival of interest, but Sunday afternoon college games frequently had higher ratings than the NBA. Yet in the 1980s (1) the alienation of white fans by the high percentage of blacks in the NBA (some three-fourths) seemed to dissipate, (2) superstation and cable television filled some of the gap left by the absence of network television, (3) average game attendance increased to over 10,000, and (4) the NBA expanded the number of its franchises.[23]

---

[23]See "Rampaging Rookies," *Newsweek*, 104 (Nov. 26, 1984), 121–22; Larry Eldridge, "Anatomy of a Sport's Turnaround," *Christian Science Monitor*, March 6, 1989, 14.

16

COLLEGE SPORTS IN A NATIONAL ARENA

Before World War II, conference championships and the competition between traditional rivals had satisfied all but the most rabid college football fans. Only the military academies, Notre Dame, and to a lesser degree the Ivy League schools had more than a regional following. Even the New Year's Day bowl games were small-time affairs. But no longer. Television, jet air travel, and massive population movements, among other forces, prompted fans and college officials to seek national standing for their teams. A team succeeded nationally only when it ranked high in the wire-service polls and, by the 1960s, appeared regularly on network television. To join the vaunted ranks of the wire-services' Top Ten required large sums of money, winning coaches, fancy athletic facilities, a national recruiting system, and a burgeoning bureaucracy.[1]

THE NCAA BECOMES A CARTEL

In managing college sports as a national, spectator-centered enterprise, the colleges faced a unique problem, one not shared by professional leagues. That problem was the recruitment of athletes. Without a draft, some 120 colleges might

[1]See esp. James V. Koch, "The Economics of Big-Time Intercollegiate Athletics," *Social Science Quarterly*, 52 (1971), 248–60; George H. Hanford, *A Report to the American Council of Education on an Inquiry into the Need for and the Feasibility of a National Study of Intercollegiate Athletics* (Washington, 1974); Robert N. Atwell, et al., *The Money Game: Financing College Athletics* (Washington, 1980); Joseph Durso, *The Sports Factory: An Investigation into College Sports* (New York, 1975); Jim Benagh, *Making It to # 1: How College Football and Basketball Teams Get There* (New York, 1976). This chapter focuses on the 167 NCAA Division 1A schools that (as of 1988) sponsored what might be called "semiprofessional" teams.

compete for the same blue-chip football or basketball player. With the stakes so high, the temptation to cheat in recruiting and retaining top-flight athletes intensified. To equalize and regulate the conditions of competition for athletes and to improve revenues from television, colleges turned to the NCAA. Consequently, in the 1950s the previously impotent NCAA became an unwieldy and a sometimes effective economic cartel.

The years between 1940 and 1953 marked a watershed in the evolution of the NCAA into an economic cartel. Prior to 1941 the colleges had limited the NCAA's authority to the making of playing rules for various sports and the supervision of certain national tournaments. While frequently issuing statements condemning athletic subsidies and unseemly recruiting, the NCAA could only resort to moral suasion to enforce its principles. Traditionally, colleges had accepted the basic premise that, being honorable institutions, they should police themselves. Yet the great football debates of the 1920s and 30s had revealed the utter inadequacy of self-imposed restraints. In 1940 the colleges finally departed in principle from the policy of self-discipline; they ratified a new NCAA constitution that provided for the expulsion (by a two-thirds vote) of members who failed to abide by association rules.

The new constitution had no immediate impact. World War II interrupted intercollegiate sport and the colleges failed to expel a single institution. In fact, with a resurgence of public enthusiasm for college football and basketball after World War II, the competition among colleges to field winning teams reached heights undreamed of in the interwar years. Many of the colleges blatantly violated NCAA rules on recruiting and subsidies. To curb the worst abuses and to regulate and equalize the conditions of competition between colleges, the colleges decided to break with a fundamental principle of amateur athletics—the ideal that no athlete should receive monetary rewards simply for play. The so-called "sanity code" adopted in 1948 permitted the extensions of scholarships and jobs to athletes. But the sanity code did provide one major restriction. The grants or jobs had to be awarded solely on the basis of the athlete's demonstrated financial need.

Soon after the adoption of the sanity code, the colleges confronted a series of shocking revelations that forced them to reconsider all aspects of intercollegiate sports. In 1950 the United States Military Academy acknowledged that all but two members of its varsity football team had been dismissed for cheating on examinations. The guilty cadets had stained the image of the great Army teams that had dominated college football for a decade. The next year, in 1951, the public learned that college basketball was the victim of the biggest scandal in the history of American sport. The New York District Attorney's office accused thirty-three players from seven colleges of "point-shaving"—keeping the margin of points between teams within a range called for by gamblers from whom the players received cash payments. Widespread revelations of illegal recruiting and under-the-table payoffs to football and basketball players by alumni, booster groups, and the colleges themselves soon followed. In 1953 the NCAA reported that Michigan State, which had fielded the nation's top football team in 1952, operated a huge "slush fund" from which football players were paid handsomely. A highly publicized educational survey in 1952 suggested that the University of Maryland had become a "football factory." According to the survey, 54 percent of Maryland's total scholarship funds went to football players.[2]

The apparent failure of the sanity code, the absence of strictures on postseason bowls, and the negative effect of unrestricted television upon attendance induced the colleges to extend additional powers to the NCAA. Many colleges, especially those in the Southwestern and Southeastern conferences, defied the NCAA by continuing to offer "full-ride" athletic scholarships regardless of the athlete's need or academic promise. A showdown vote came in the 1950 NCAA convention when a motion to suspend seven colleges cited for noncompliance fell short of the necessary two-thirds vote. With this setback, the NCAA repealed the sanity code and, in 1952, decided to permit the awards of full scholarships based only upon athletic ability. At the 1952 convention, the colleges also extended to the NCAA the power to impose sanctions upon colleges that violated the association's legislation. For the 1952–53 seasons, the NCAA for the first time placed two colleges, Kentucky and Bradley, on probation. Finally, the convention adopted legislation governing postseason bowls, named a full-time executive director (Walter Byers, who held the post until 1988), and established a national headquarters in Kansas City, Missouri (later moved to a suburb of Kansas City). With the 1952 actions, the colleges had taken the first steps toward converting the NCAA into a major athletic regulatory body.[3]

Television eventually provided perhaps the most important lever for enhancing the authority of the NCAA. The colleges were eager for the additional revenues offered by television as well as the publicity attendant to having their contests televised. Consequently, they at first laid down no restrictions on telecasts. Each college negotiated its own contracts with television stations or networks. By the fall of 1950, football telecasts virtually flooded the country. In September of 1950 the *New York Times* reported: "TV football coverage will offer New York fans a choice of five different games every Saturday afternoon during most of the season and three nighttime games in addition."[4] Apparently many fans decided to stay at home and watch the games. Attendance at college games plummeted; in 1950 it fell 1,403,000 below 1948 totals.

Alarmed college officials responded by forming a television committee within the NCAA. The committee immediately recommended a moratorium on the wholesale telecasts of football games. In 1951 the NCAA authorized the

[2]Donald S. Andrews, "The G.I. Bill and College Football," *Jounral of Physical Education, Recreation and Dance,* 55 (1984), 23–26; Benagh, *Making It to #1,* pp. 192–95; Charles Rosen, *The Scandals of '51: How Gamblers Almost Killed College Basketball* (New York, 1978).

[3]On Walter Byers see Jack McCallum, "In the Kingdom of the Solitary Man," *Sports Illustrated,* 65 (Oct. 6, 1986), 64–78. For the official history of the NCAA see Jack Falla, *NCAA: The Voice of College Sports* (Mission, KS, 1981).

[4]Quoted in Walter O. Johnson, Jr., *Super Spectator and the Electric Lilliputians* (Boston, 1971), p. 90. On the NCAA and television see also McCallum, "In the Kingdom of the Solitary Man"; Falla, *The NCAA,* Chap. 6; Benjamin G. Rader, *In Its Own Image: How Television Transformed Sports* (New York, 1984), Chap. 5, pp. 122–23, 164–69.

telecast of only seven regular season games in each region and negotiated a national network football package with the Westinghouse Broadcasting Company. Although reports of possible Justice Department action against the NCAA for violation of the federal antitrust laws appeared in the press, the Department took no action to prevent this form of economic collusion. Several colleges also threatened to ignore the NCAA. Notre Dame suffered the most from the restrictions of the NCAA. If Notre Dame had been able to sign a separate television contract with a national network, given its large national following, it could have earned much more than through the NCAA package. In the end, all of the colleges decided that it was in their best interests to cooperate. Despite the NCAA "blackout" policy, overall football attendance lagged behind 1948 figures for a decade and television initially generated modest revenues for the sport. Since only those colleges (or conferences to which the colleges belonged) that had their games televised received funds from the networks, the medium contributed to financial disparity among the colleges. The decision to grant to the NCAA control of television also strengthened the organization's hegemony over college sports.

THE SOARING POPULARITY OF COLLEGE FOOTBALL

In the 1960s, television, an exciting style of football, post-season bowl games, and weekly press polls all contributed to the popularity of intercollegiate football. Annual attendance soared from 20 to 30 million in the 1960s and jumped another 10 million in the 1970s. While television ratings lagged slightly behind those of professional football games, they exceeded those of regular season major league baseball games. Bowl games televised at the conclusion of the season became spectacles that grabbed almost as much attention as the World Series, the Super Bowl, or the Olympic Games.

The colleges introduced a new, wide-open style of offense. Clock-stopping rule changes allowed college teams to execute twenty-seven more plays per game in 1968 than in 1964, and a study of the 1970 season found that colleges averaged forty more plays per game than their pro counterparts. The adoption of two-platoon football in the 1960s permitted coaches to perfect more complicated offensive systems. It also resulted in the disappearance of one of the last pretensions of player-centeredness in the sport: the tradition that the players rather than the coaches call offensive and defensive signals during play.

The 1960s produced record highs in scoring, passing, rushing, receiving, and kicking. Quarterbacks sometimes filled the air with fifty or more passes per game, figures that would have astonished football fans of the 1920s and 1930s. The "I formation," a popular offensive system developed by Tom Nugent at Maryland in the 1950s, permitted a team to combine both a potent running and passing attack. Even more remarkable were the triple-option formations that featured quarterbacks as an integral part of the running attack. Oklahoma's wishbone (invented by a Texas high school coach and adopted first at the college level by Darrell Royal at Texas) and Bill Yeoman's veer at Houston regularly produced more than 400 yards rushing per game. Many fans found the college game, with its explosive action, more exciting than the pros.

The weekly press polls for determining the top teams in the nation furnished an additional source of excitement to the fans. Individual journalists had named national champions since the 1890s, but it was not until 1936 that Alan Gould, sports editor of the Associated Press, invented the weekly press poll. To determine the top twenty teams, the Associated Press polled about fifty writers and broadcasters nationwide. By establishing a board of college coaches to name the top teams in 1950, the United Press International joined the polling game. The absence of a system for determining the relative strength of teams or a national champion made the polls a powerful symbolic substitute. Many fans echoed the feelings of Dan Jenkins: "I . . . will assure anyone who is uncertain about it that there is no drama, suspense, excitement, thrill or feeling of necessity in sport that can equal the countdown to an opening kickoff between two great teams or contenders for that elusive, cantankerous, agonizing, dreadful and wonderful thing called No. 1."[5] By the 1960s, a college's standing in the weekly press polls was often more important to fans, players, and coaches alike than the defeat of a traditional rival or a conference championship.

Bowl games, though late arrivals to the college scene, eventually became an exciting climax to the regular season. The parent of college bowls, the Tournament of Roses (Rose Bowl), traced its origins back to 1902. In the depressed 1930s, boosters in southern cities hoped to attract tourists and outside investors by founding the Orange (1933), Sugar (1935), Sun (1936), and Cotton (1937) bowls. Initially, the bowls offered little financial inducement to the top football-playing schools; the inaugural Orange Bowl, for example, paid each team a mere $1,000 to make the trek to Miami on New Year's day. Television changed that. In 1960 NBC paid the Rose Bowl half a million dollars for rights, but by 1983 the figure had escalated to $7 million. That the bowl games often determined the national champions added immensely to fan interest in the contests.

"Pseudoevents"—those created largely or solely by the media—also generated interest in the college game. Walter Camp had named mythical "All American" teams as early as the 1890s, but in the 1960s, the selection of all-star teams of college football players became something of a national ritual. The press services, magazines, broadcasters, and organizations of football fans chose not only all-American teams and all-conference teams, but participants for East-West, North-South, Blue-Grey, and other all-star bowl games. The biggest individual prize became the Heisman Trophy, which had been awarded each year since 1936 by the Downtown Athletic Club of New York City in honor of a former coach and athletic director. A group of sportswriters and sportscasters chose for the award the "outstanding" intercollegiate football player of the year. That the winner of the award nearly always was an offensive back, played on a nationally ranked team, had appeared in nationally televised games, and was the beneficiary of an intensive selling campaign led by the sports information director of

---

[5]Dan Jenkins, *Saturday's America* (Boston, 1970), pp. 45–46.

THE NATION'S NUMBER ONE FOOTBALL FAN
Here, President Richard M. Nixon awarded the National College Football Championship to
the University of Nebraska team of 1971. Nixon was an avid football fan who often placed
calls from the White House to college and professional coaches and players.

his college did not seem to tarnish the glamour of the award. And the recipient welcomed the publicity, the potential commercial endorsements, and the likelihood of a better pro contract that accompanied the award.[6]

The colleges added exciting half-time shows to accompany their games, featuring marching bands, baton twirlers, and card sections. Elaborate, animated card sections first appeared at Oregon State in 1924, but did not become standard fare until the 1950s. The most remarkable change came in cheerleading. Before World War II, most colleges relied upon male "yell captains." But in the 1950s fans began to witness regularly the spectacle of briefly clad coeds leading cheers, doing fast, leggy can-cans, and other Broadway-like chorus line routines. In the 1970s and 80s the cheerleaders added difficult mixed-gender gymnastic moves to their more traditional exhibitions.

College football's popularity strengthened the NCAA's bargaining position with the television networks (see Figure 16-1). ABC, which held the regular season package from 1964 through 1981, increased its payments from $3 million to $29 million annually. Then, as with major league baseball and pro football, the stakes escalated. Beginning in 1982, from a combined package extended by ABC, CBS, and the Turner Broadcasting System, the colleges received $74.3 million annually, more than twice what they had obtained two years earlier. But in 1984 the United States Supreme Court struck down the package contracts, declaring them in violation of federal antitrust law. Subsequently each college was free to negotiate its own television rights independent of the authority of the NCAA or any other regulatory body.

[6]See esp. Neil D. Amdur, *The Fifth Down: Democracy and the Football Revolution* (New York, 1971), Chap. 5.

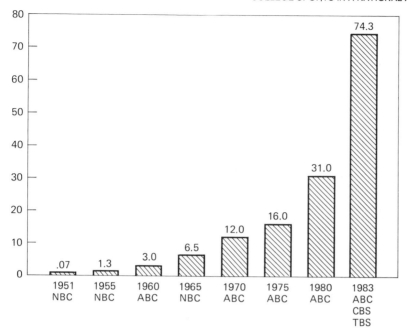

Figure 16-1
NCAA Football Television Rights: Selected Years, 1951–1983 (in millions of dollars)

     The demise of the exclusive package contracts resulted in a hodgepodge of football telecasts originating from national networks, regional networks, or from local stations or cable companies. Without a monopoly on telecasts, the networks were no longer willing to continue the escalation of rights payments. Apparently colleges in high-density population centers, those with a national

COED CHEERLEADERS
Unlike the pre-World War II era, cheerleading in the age of televised sports frequently featured coeds doing Broadway chorus line routines.

following, or those without competition from professional teams benefited most from the new freedom. These colleges could both obtain a share of national contracts and negotiate lucrative deals for regional or local telecasts as well.

JOINING THE TOP TEN

Joining the Top Ten teams in the nation required the generation of vast sums of money, lavish athletic facilities, a national recruiting system, and a burgeoning bureaucracy, in short, the full-scale professionalization of a college's athletic program. Success in joining the Top Ten began with a highly specialized, well-managed bureaucracy. While the number of players in varsity sports rose by 11.8 percent between 1966 and 1972, the number of full-time administrative personnel climbed 35.9 percent. In 1966 the ratio of players to coaches in college football stood at thirty to one; seven years later, it was eight to one. Similar ratio changes occurred in other sports. Athletic directors who once performed multiple roles as business managers, sports information directors, fund-raisers, and coaches all but disappeared from the college scene. Almost no coaches or players applied their skills to more than one sport. In season, athletes in basketball and football frequently spent up to forty hours a week in practices, chalk talks, film sessions, and travel. Out of season, they typically engaged in programs of supervised weight lifting. In and out of season, a 1988 study by the NCAA revealed that athletes devoted averages of thirty hours a week to their sport and twenty-six hours in studying and attending class. Such a regimen made it difficult to sustain the illusion that college players were students who merely happened to be athletes.[7]

Pressures to join the Top Ten intensified efforts to recruit blue-chip athletes. "Recruiting, not coaching, is the name of the game," explained Oklahoma's Barry Switzer, the nation's most successful coach in the 1970s and 80s. Oklahoma has "built its tradition with Texas high school players—and I am proud of it. We've got to get where the players are. Texas has 1,400 high schools playing football. There are just 200 in the entire state of Oklahoma."[8] Schools located in sparsely populated areas had to recruit nationwide, but in the 1970s, even the University of Southern California, which was situated in a rich pool of football talent, extended its recruiting effort to the entire nation.

Effective recruiting required a systematic, well-coordinated effort. Coaches spent hours poring over high school game films and some three months each year jetting about the country visiting callow high school youths. Recruiters relied heavily upon personal contacts. Local alumni, especially if they were celebrities such as state governors, astronauts, singers, actors, and professional athletes, often lent assistance to their alma maters. Colleges tried

[7]James H. Frey, "The Organization of Amateur Sport: Efficiency and Entropy," *American Behavioral Scientist*, 21 (Jan./Feb. 1978), 367–68; *The Final Report of the President's Commission on Olympic Sports, 1975–1977*, 2 vols. (Washington, DC, 1977), II, 345, 354; *Lincoln* (NE) *Star*, Nov. 30, 1988.

[8] Quoted in *Lincoln* (NE) *Star*, Aug. 30, 1979.

to appeal to the rising consciousness of ethnic, religious, racial, and regional concerns. Big-time football powers usually hired at least one black, one Irish-American or another representative of a Catholic ethnic group, and one or more coaches who identified with a region outside of the state in which the university was located. Once a prospective athlete arrived on campus, he might be greeted by the Bengal Babes, Hawk Hunters, Hurricane Honeys, or the Gater Getters, organizations of comely coeds recruited by athletic departments to act as official hostesses.[9]

Recruiters might promise prospective team members legal or illegal benefits. All major colleges offered athletic scholarships that consisted of room, board, and tuition. Without violating NCAA rules, a recruiter could also emphasize to a potential recruit the likelihood after graduation of joining the pro ranks or of landing a good job, the quality of the school's coaching staff, the number of past bowl or past television appearances, or, more improbably, the quality of education offered by the college. Prospects could be shown special athletic dormitories (complete with a television set in each room, recreation rooms, a special dining hall, and a swimming pool), carpeted locker and shower rooms, the latest weight-training equipment, and a staff of private tutors to assist players in their academic programs. At the University of Oklahoma dormitory, known locally as the "Sooner Hilton," two athletes shared a suite consisting of a bedroom, living room, and private bath. On most campuses the players spent four years or more closeted only with fellow athletes.

Illegal inducement took several forms. Alumni and booster groups, often with the tacit approval or at least the knowledge of the coaching staff, might grant cash, cars, clothes, rent-free apartments, use of charge accounts, or high-paying jobs. One of the most common abuses was the sale by college athletes of tickets provided to them by athletic departments ostensibly for their families or close friends. But athletes often sold the tickets, sometimes generating more than a thousand dollars in income. To obtain the admission of an athlete with a poor academic record, coaches might tamper with transcripts. To make up deficiencies in college credits or grades, coaches might arrange for snap courses offered through correspondence or by college extension divisions.

Given the intense competition among colleges for top-flight athletes, the NCAA faced an insuperable enforcement problem. A thin line sometimes separated legal from illegal practices. Coaches often complained that minor infractions were impossible to avoid. Some of the rules seemed petty; for example, a coach could not technically treat his players to ice cream cones from a local Dairy Queen. The rules seemed to weigh heaviest against the poorer black players; for example, a coach could not buy such a player a round-trip airline ticket to return home for vacations. Although the NCAA acted as police,

[9]See esp. Durso, *The Sports Factory*, pp. 57–63; John J. Rooney, *The Recruiting Game: Toward a New System of Intercollegiate Athletics* (Lincoln, NE, 1980); Willie Morris, *The Courting of Marcus Dupree* (Garden City, NY, 1983); Alexander Wolff, "The Fall Roundup," *Sports Illustrated*, 67 (Aug. 31, 1987), 46–56.

prosecution, and judge, it had no subpoena powers. With an enforcement squad that grew to fifteen full-time employees by 1988, it tried to police the complicated athletic operations of more than 900 colleges. Close observers of the college athletic scene, including coaches and athletes, estimated that only a small fraction of the total violations resulted in punishment. Even at that, more than half of the some 140 colleges playing big time football were at one time or the other placed on probation.[10]

Many colleges sought a quick entry to the Top Ten by hiring a coach with a proven record as a winner. To seize the opportunities, coaches broke their existing contracts with no fear of retribution. Such questionable ethics were consistent with the readiness with which colleges dismissed nonwinning coaches. Salaries of winning coaches soared. In 1982, Texas A & M stunned the college football world by luring Jackie Sherrill away from the University of Pittsburgh for $1.7 million over six years. A television show and boosters footed all but $95,000 annually of Sherrill's salary. Wealthy boosters "can make it so attractive that even a high principled guy could be tempted to do anything to be in the top 10 every year," asserted Donald B. Canham, director of athletics at the University of Michigan. "I am fearful that more and more . . . wealthy people are trying to use their money to control a college football team or a basketball team as if it were a professional franchise."[11]

Although in principle the NCAA equalized the conditions of athletic recruitment, glaring disparities in playing strength appeared throughout the era of televised sports. Year after year, the same teams dominated conferences and appeared regularly in postseason bowls. Between 1950 and 1990, the same fifteen colleges held more than 60 percent of the Top Ten positions in the Associated Press season-ending poll. Oklahoma led the parade by being chosen in the Top Ten 26 times, followed by Alabama (21), Nebraska (20), Ohio State, Notre Dame, and Michigan (18), Pennsylvania State (16), Texas and Southern California (15), and Arkansas (13). In the late 1940s and 50s, Charles "Bud" Wilkinson led the Oklahoma Sooners to thirty-one- and forty-seven-game winning streaks. In the 1960s, 70s, and 80s, Oklahoma, led first by Charles "Chuck" Fairbanks and then by Barry Switzer, continued to be the winningest team among big time schools.

Disparities in competition arose from tangible and intangible variables. A few conferences imposed tougher standards than others. By refusing to grant athletic scholarships, the traditionally powerful Ivy League colleges dropped out of big time football competition. In the 1960s and early 70s the once-powerful Big Ten colleges fared poorly against nonconference foes. Until 1973, the conference had prohibited redshirting (the practice of having a player sit out a season to gain

---

[10]See esp. Ray Kennedy, "427: Parts I & II," *Sports Illustrated*, 40 (June 10–17, 1974), 87–100, 24–30; John Underwood, "The NCAA Goes on the Defense," ibid, 45 (Feb. 27, 1978), 20–22, 24, 29; Hanford, *A Report*, pp. 88–89. Between 1952 and 1976 the NCAA placed a total of 64 college football and 61 college basketball programs on probation.

[11]Quoted in Rader, *In Its Own Image*, p. 167.

more strength, size, and skills while on an athletic scholarship) and permitted only one team to go to a postseason bowl.[12] Winning traditions, a skilled coaching staff, and ample revenues also played important parts in creating the disparities, but effective recruitment of superior athletes was the most significant key in establishing winning programs.

Colleges that did not belong to a conference (the "independents") and those located in the Sunbelt enjoyed the most success. For the 1981–88 seasons, independents won six of the eight national championships, and for the 1988 season four of the top five teams were independents. Unlike conference teams, the independents did not have to share media receipts with conference schools. In the 1980s, Nebraska, for example, turned over almost $10 million in media money to fellow Big Eight schools while receiving less than $2 million in return. The Top Ten also increasingly mirrored the massive population shifts to the Sunbelt. Whereas in the 1930s 44 percent of Top Ten schools hailed from the Sunbelt, the figure rose to 63 percent for the 1980s. In the season-ending poll for 1988, 14 of the top 20 college teams were located in the Sunbelt.

COLLEGE BASKETBALL ENTERS THE NATIONAL ARENA

Until the mid-1930s, basketball had been primarily a local or regional, player-centered sport. From its invention in the 1890s it had attracted participants from diverse social groups and of both sexes. They played on organized teams and in YMCAs, churches, city recreation programs, high schools, colleges, and industrial leagues; many more played informally in driveways, playgrounds, school yards, and gymnasiums. In a few places in the 1920s notably in Kentucky, Indiana, and Illinois, high school and college basketball caught on as a popular spectator sport. Yet in most places, football was the king of campus sports; football fans often looked upon basketball as a "sissy" game (it was played in short pants, indoors, and by girls) and sneeringly referred to it as "round ball." College gymnasiums usually held only a few thousand spectators, the colleges scheduled few if any intersectional games, and coaching turnovers were frequent. On most campuses, even track and field generated more excitement than basketball.[13]

Perhaps architecture more than anything else converted college basketball into a sport that attained national attention. To capitalize upon the boxing craze of the 1920s, entrepreneurs in about a dozen cities built large arenas seating several thousand spectators. With the Great Depression and the decline in the popularity of boxing in the 1930s, the owners desperately sought other ways to make their arenas profitable. Intersectional college basketball games displayed

[12]See Benagh, *Making It to #1*, Chap. 14.

[13]For general but essentially unsatisfactory histories of college basketball see Alexander Weyand, *The Cavalcade of Basketball* (New York, 1960); Neil D. Isaacs, *All the Moves: A History of College Basketball* (Philadelphia, 1975); Zander Hollander, ed., *The Modern Encyclopedia of Basketball* (New York, 1969).

potential in 1931 when Mayor Jimmy Walker of New York asked a group of sportswriters to organize tripleheaders in Madison Square Garden for the benefit of the city's relief fund. Despite the Depression, the "Relief Games" of 1931, 1932, and 1933 drew full houses. One of the sportswriters who had organized the relief games, Edward S. "Ned" Irish, decided in 1934 to stage his own college games. He rented the Garden, which held over 16,000 fans, paid the fees to visiting teams, and kept whatever was left over as a profit. To maximize interest among New York residents, Irish usually pitted strong local colleges against the most powerful rivals he could attract from other parts of the nation. The Garden games promoted by Irish served as a catalyst for the transformation of college basketball into a full-fledged spectator sport.

One game promoted by Irish became a legend in basketball history. In 1936 he matched Long Island University, winner of forty-three consecutive games, and Stanford University, led by tall (for that day) Angelo "Hank" Luisetti. Stanford won 45-31, but Luisetti was the bigger story. Luisetti scored fifteen points—all on unorthodox one-handed shots—and became the nation's first basketball hero. His one-handed shots defied years of conventional coaching. "That's not basketball," sneered veteran City College coach Nat Holman. "If my boys ever shot one-handed, I'd quit coaching."[14] Yet the one-handed shot and its derivative, the jump shot, could be shot as accurately, more quickly, and with less danger of being blocked than the standard two-handed set shot. The new shooting styles, along with the elimination of the center jump after each goal in 1937, increased scoring and won the plaudits of fans.

From the late 1930s through the 1940s—World War II notwithstanding—New York was the hub of big-time college basketball. In 1938 the Metropolitan Basketball Writers' Association of New York organized the National Invitational Tournament (NIT), designed to determine the national championship team at the end of each season. The following year, the NCAA founded its own post-season invitational tournament, though until 1951 the NIT remained the premier college tourney. After World War II, Ned Irish extended his promotion beyond the Garden to Philadelphia and Buffalo, thereby offering at least a three-game package to college teams venturing to the East. Irish also increased the number of doubleheaders to twenty-five or more per season. By 1950, the Garden college program drew over 600,000 spectators. It became every schoolboy's dream to play one day in the Garden. For both financial and publicity purposes, appearances at the Garden were obligatory for those college teams striving for national status. Never had the promise of basketball as a spectator sport looked more roseate than in 1950.

Then disaster struck. In 1951 New York District Attorney Frank Hogan revealed that thirty-two players from seven colleges, including players from the strongest teams in the nation, had been involved in fixing point spreads. The Garden was not only the mecca of college basketball; it was the "clearinghouse" for New York's sports gambling establishment. With the invention of the point spread by gamblers, basketball had become a hot attraction for bettors. Rather

[14]Quoted in Zander Hollander, ed., *Madison Square Garden* (New York, 1973), p. 76.

than picking a winning team or giving odds on favorites, the bettor wagered on how many points a particular team would win by. Such a system invited "fixing," for a fixed team did not have to lose the game; it merely had to win by less than the quoted point spread. The revelations of the fixes shocked the entire country. Coinciding in time with the "fall" of China, the commencement of the Korean War, the Soviet detonation of an atomic bomb, and spectacular charges of treason in high governmental places, the basketball scandal contributed to a general climate of suspicion and mistrust.

The scandal had a far-reaching impact upon American sport. Apart from the apparent widespread immorality of college basketball players, the scandal revealed that many colleges, in their mad scramble for opportunities to play in the big city arenas and win national renown, engaged in the "illegal" recruitment and subsidization of players. For example, as many as 500 college players "worked" for munificent salaries in the Catskill resorts where they "incidentally" played basketball in organized leagues. College coaches and presidents reacted to the scandals and revelations of athletic subsidies with dignified horror; many colleges announced that they would no longer permit their teams to compete in the big-city arenas. The scandal ended the Garden's pivotal place in the financial structure of big-time college basketball. Irish's famed Garden doubleheaders collapsed. The scandal also wiped out the powerful basketball programs of New York's metropolitan colleges. After the scandal, the local colleges no longer attracted the best talent in the city; most of them went elsewhere. In the 1950s and 60s, state universities began to fill the vacuum by building large fieldhouses and scheduling intersectional holiday tournaments. Between 1967 and 1977, the colleges built eighty-two new basketball arenas, thirty-nine of which seated in excess of 10,000 people.[15]

THE RISING POPULARITY OF COLLEGE BASKETBALL

Despite the scandal of 1950–51 and an initial lack of interest in basketball by network television, when all levels of the sport were combined, it apparently outdrew football and baseball in live attendance. Estimates in the 1970s placed total annual attendance at 150 million per season. For sports fans, the basketball season bridged perfectly the gap between football in the fall and baseball in the spring. Unlike baseball, competition from other forms of recreation was less intense in the winter months. Since the season was long, a team could easily play several games per week, the costs of fielding a team were small, and the sheer number of games exceeded those of football and baseball combined. The sport appealed to all sizes and types of communities. In the small towns of mid-America, high school basketball often furnished a source of common pride, identity, and purpose, a shared experience equalled perhaps only when a natural disaster struck the community. At the other end of the spectrum,

[15]See Benagh, *Making It to #1*, pp. 192–95; Rosen, *The Scandals of '51*.

basketball flourished in the ethnic and racial enclaves of the sprawling metropolises. In fact, city basketball from the 1930s to the 1970s reflected the ascent of ethnic and racial groups from the ghettos. In the 1930s and 40s, Irish, Jewish, and Italian athletes dominated the rosters of metropolitan high schools and colleges; in the 1950s, blacks began to replace the earlier ethnic groups. By the 1960s, the position of blacks in college and professional basketball had become so conspicuous that observers wondered if the sport was not especially suited to blacks, either because of physical or cultural reasons.[16]

New modes of play also helped account for the growing popularity of basketball in the post-1950 era. Player skills improved remarkably. By the 1970s, dozens of players six feet, six inches tall and taller had reached higher levels of coordination and dexterity than most of the shorter men of the pre-1940 era. In the 1940s, Robert Kurland of Oklahoma A & M, a towering defensive specialist, and George Mikan of De Paul, a prolific scorer, initiated the revolution in height. The next decade produced two more outstanding big men. Bill Russell of San Francisco demonstrated that the tall center could be a dominating force as a rebounder and defender, and Wilton Chamberlain, a center with the University of Kansas who stood over seven feet tall, showed that a big man could be almost unstoppable as a scorer. Rule changes to restrict the impact of the big men (defensive goal tending in 1944 and widening the free-throw lane in 1955) failed. Moreover, the fans loved the "playground style" of play led by the black players from the big-city ghettos, which featured individual moves and spectacular ball handling.

As an enterprise involved in the business of entertainment, college basketball resembled a scaled-down version of college football. While basketball did not generate as much revenue from spectators or television as college football, it cost much less to field a team. Since costs were modest, many more colleges tried to play big-time basketball. Like football, a high rating in the national press polls helped ensure a team a berth in the NCAA or NIT tourneys, a profitable season, and "free" publicity for the college. In turn, the key to a successful team was the recruitment of blue-chip athletes. Unlike football, however, one or two super athletes might reverse the fortunes of an otherwise mediocre basketball team. Thus each year scores of coaches, many of whom were hired more for their recruiting ability than their coaching skills, sought the services of a dozen or so of the most talented high school seniors. Coaches even subscribed to commercial scouting services to assist them in locating the more promising prospects; many colleges hired a black assistant coach so they could make a special pitch to black athletes. Given the intensity of competition for the more promising prospects, the basketball coaches tended to be even more flagrant in violating or ignoring NCAA rules than their football counterparts.[17]

[16]See for example Martin Kane, "An Assessment of 'Black is Best,' " *Sports Illustrated*, 34 (Jan. 18, 1971), 72–83.

[17]See Pete Axthelm, "Scandal on the Court," *Newsweek*, 94 (Dec. 24, 1979), 77.

Basketball could offer a relatively simple and inexpensive means by which an otherwise unknown smaller college could attract national attention. LaSalle, San Francisco, Cincinnati, Loyola (IL), Texas Western, Georgetown, and Villanova all won national titles. In the post-World War II era, more than a score of smaller Catholic-affiliated colleges dropped football and placed the major part of their athletic resources into basketball. Between 1939 and 1987, seventeen different Catholic institutions reached the final four of the NCAA playoffs.

In some instances, basketball programs of smaller colleges suddenly sprang into national prominence. One example in the 1960s and 70s was Oral Roberts University, founded by evangelist Oral Roberts in Tulsa, Oklahoma, in 1965. Roberts, who was also the president of the institution, determined from the outset to make the university a "Notre Dame of the Hardcourts." He candidly explained why: "Many people are not as faithful in church attendance on Sunday mornings as they once were. But 40 million men read the sports page on Sunday morning. In my ministry, we try to reach people where they are. . . . "[18] Each year, Oral Roberts upgraded its schedule; the school built a plush, elliptical basketball arena, and in 1969 the university brought in Ken Trickey, a high-powered recruiter from Middle Tennessee State, as head coach. Never did a team rise so fast to national prominence. Under Trickey in the early 1970s the college twice led the nation in scoring, played in both the NIT and NCAA tourneys, and at one time ranked eleventh in the wire service polls. Although those close to the college basketball scene (especially Trickey's fellow coaches) branded Oral Roberts as an "outlaw school" for its presumed infractions of NCAA rules, the university avoided NCAA sanctions. At the height of the team's success, Trickey, after a controversy with Oral Roberts, left for Iowa State, and Roberts decided to "deemphasize" basketball. But only temporarily. In the late 1970s, Roberts determined again to go "big-time," only to find itself placed on two-year probation by the NCAA in 1978.

Certain institutions with well-established basketball traditions and well-known coaches nonetheless dominated conference championships and the top ten in the national polls.[19] In fact, between 1964 and 1975, the dominance of the University of California at Los Angeles in college basketball far exceeded the feats of any college football team of the era. In that time John Wooden's UCLA team won ten NCAA championships in twelve years, including seven titles in a row. Inasmuch as the NCAA tourney format (where a single defeat eliminated a team) and the limit on the eligibility of a player to three years (after 1972 to four years) made such a feat appear to be virtually impossible, UCLA's success may have represented the most remarkable achievement in sport

---

[18]Quoted in Benagh, *Making It to #1*, p. 5. On Catholic colleges and basketball, see James A. Michener, *Sports in America* (New York, 1976), pp. 231–34 and Frank Deford, "A Heavenly Game," *Sports Illustrated*, 64 (March 3, 1986), 58–70.

[19]Michael E. Canes, "The Social Benefits of Restrictions on Team Quality," in Roger G. Noll, ed., *Government and the Sports Business* (Washington, DC, 1974), pp. 89–90. Canes's data (p. 90) indicated that between 1950 and 1965 basketball teams in the major conferences tended to win successive championships more often than football teams.

history. Wooden's first two championships seemed to be simply the products of astute coaching combined with superior athletes. But after 1965, UCLA was the beneficiary of several of the most promising players in the country. Two of the most spectacular big men to ever play the game—Lew Alcindor (1967–69) and Bill Walton (1971–74)—contributed directly to five of UCLA's ten championships.

By the late 1970s NCAA basketball became a major television spectacle. The annual national tournament ranked only slightly behind the pro football playoffs, the World Series, and college football games in fan interest. Television ratings for the tourney moved ahead of the professional basketball playoffs. To increase the size of the television audience, the NCAA spread out the tournament over several weeks and expanded the number of participating teams. Television revenues escalated rapidly. In 1966 the NCAA and participating colleges had received a mere $180,000 from television; twenty-two years later the figure rose to $58 million. By 1980 each college in the final four of the NCAA tourney received over one million dollars from television rights.

THE TRIPLE CRISIS

Despite rising attendance and television ratings, college athletics in the 1980s confronted what Indiana University's President John Ryan aptly described in 1984 as a "triple crisis."[20] One crisis revolved around the integrity of college athletic programs, another around the academic performance of athletes, and the third around the exploding costs of college sports.

Beginning in 1980, a string of ugly stories leaped to the headlines of the nation's press, all revealing an utter disregard on the part of many college athletic programs for NCAA rules and regulations. In the Southwest reports indicated that Arizona State football players received credits for unattended, off-campus extension courses. Forgery and fakery wrecked the University of New Mexico basketball team. Then came even more startling news. Half of the Pacific-10 Conference schools admitted that they had "laundered" academic transcripts and granted false course credits to student athletes. In 1982 Charles "Digger" Phelps, respected Notre Dame basketball coach, charged that the "going underground" price for blue chip basketball players was $10,000 annually. An NCAA investigation verified that one football recruit received from boosters more than $10,000 in cash to sign with Southern Methodist while others obtained cash and cars. Perhaps it was little wonder that Walter Byers warned in 1984 that the situation was the "most serious" that he had known during his thirty-five years as executive director of the NCAA. In 1986 national

[20]"NCAA Presidents' Panel to Back Studies of Integrity, Finances of College Sports," *Chronicle of Higher Education*, Oct. 17, 1984, pp. 23, 25. Allen Guttmann in *A Whole New Ball Game: An Interpretation of American Sports* (Chapel Hill and London, 1988), Chap. 8, provides a lucid discussion of the social and cultural implications of contemporary college sports. See also James Frey, ed. *The Governance of Intercollegiate Athletics* (West Point, NY, 1982).

columnist George F. Will glumly concluded that American colleges were "our schools for scandal."[21]

For most colleges involved in big-time sports, the recruitment and retention of an athlete for four years of varsity eligibility seemed to come before concern about the player's opportunities in pro sports or whether the athlete obtained an education, let alone a college degree. The colleges recruited hundreds of scholastically handicapped youths who had elementary reading abilities; some were classified as having less than fourth-grade reading skills. Reflective of the situation was Chris Washburn, an outstanding basketball prospect. Even though Washburn failed to answer a single question correctly on the verbal portion of the Scholastic Achievement Test in 1983, more than 150 colleges tried to recruit him. Once recruited, the athletic departments insulated the athletes against serious academic expectations. Only one-third of the NFL players and even fewer NBA players ever earned college degrees. Handicapped by their earlier experiences and perhaps by special treatment within the colleges, black athletes had less chance of academic success than whites. A survey of 1,359 black athletes who entered colleges in 1977 revealed that only 31 percent graduated in six years; 53 percent of the whites obtained degrees. Coaches also frequently ignored or even encouraged the use of steroids to enhance weight, strength, and aggressiveness. Revelation of the apparent absence of concern for the ultimate fate of athletes damaged the moral image of the nation's colleges. (See Table 16-1.)[22]

Table 16–1. Public Attitudes Toward College Sports, 1989

	PERCENTAGE		
	Favor	Oppose	No Opinion
Do Division I colleges place too much emphasis on sports programs	68	25	7
Do colleges hold student-athletes to high enough academic standards	25	65	7
Do you think it's a common practice for colleges with big sports programs to make under-the-table payments to student-athletes	57	28	15
Do you think colleges should be permitted to pay cash to their student athletes or not	18	76	7
Would you call yourself a college sports fan or not	54	45	1

SOURCE: Media General-Associated Press, as reported in *Lincoln* (NE) *Star*, April 3, 1989.

[21]"The Shame of College Sports," *Newsweek*, 96 (Sept. 22, 1980), 54; *New York Times*, March 16, 1982, pp. A1, A22; "Overzealous Boosters Threaten the Integrity of Collegiate Sports," *Wall Street Journal* (Midwest ed.), Dec. 27, 1985; "NCAA Presidents," 23; George F. Will, "Our Schools for Scandal," *Newsweek*, 108 (Sept. 15, 1986), 84; Harrison Donnelly, "College Sports Under Fire," *Editorial Research Report*, Aug. 15, 1986, 590–608.
[22]Will, "Our Schools for Scandal," 84; Dennis A. Williams, "Out of Bounds," *Newsweek on Campus*, Sept. 1985, pp. 8–14; *Lincoln* (NE) *Star*, Nov. 30, 1988.

Recurring financial problems constituted the third crisis in college sports. In the 1960s and early 70s, forty-two colleges dropped football. Throughout the era of televised sports, nearly 90 percent of college athletic programs operated at a deficit. The costs of large programs mounted from some $3 million in the mid-1970s to more than $12 million in the late 1980s. Inflation, nationwide recruiting, lavish athletic facilities (typically more extravagant than those for the pros), large coaching staffs (again, larger than for the pro teams), stadium expansion, installation of artificial turf, construction of new arenas, and the expansion of women's athletics as a consequence of Title IX—all of these contributed to spiraling costs.[23]

In the 1980s, the colleges embarked on a wave of reforms designed to respond to the triple crisis and cap the momentum toward even costlier and more grandiose programs. To curtail the recruitment of academically questionable prospects, the NCAA in 1983 adopted Proposition 48, mandating minimum test scores and high school grade point averages for entering athletes. Next came the creation in 1983 of the NCAA Presidents Commission, a body of 44 college presidents, who nominally seized the reform initiative. The commission pushed through a new set of tougher penalties for rule violators, including the "death penalty," which could cost a repeat offender its entire athletic program. The NCAA accepted the commission's recommendations for sharply curtailing the activities of boosters (boosters could not even phone or write prospects any more) and reducing costs. To cut costs and restrict unseemly recruiting, the NCAA ordered a reduction in the number of athletic scholarships and in the size of coaching staffs, shortened the recruiting season by 60 percent, and cut the number of visits the coaches could make to potential recruits.[24]

The full impact of "The Reformation" of the 1980s remained to be seen. In perhaps the most drastic step in the cartel's history, the NCAA in 1985 levied the death penalty against Southern Methodist's football program, a program that had been guilty of NCAA violations in eleven of the previous fourteen seasons. Proposition 48 reduced the number of academically marginal athletes, but it fell far heavier upon black athletes who came from the ghettos and received inferior educations. Looking ahead, I. Michael Heyman, the chancellor of the University of California, urged a "mutual disarmament" of big-time college athletic programs.[25] Yet the reforms of the 1980s did not fully address the fundamental problem faced by college coaches. Unless the college had a winning tradition, cheating seemed to be the only way to gain entry into the Top Ten.

---

[23]See Durso, *The Sports Factory*, pp. 87–95; "NCAA Presidents' Panel," 23, 25.
[24]Williams, "Out of Bounds," 8–14.
[25]"Scorecard," *Sports Illustrated*, 66 (Jan. 1987), 9.

17

THE INDIVIDUAL SPORTS

As late as the 1948 Olympics, Bob Mathias won the gold medal in the decathlon, which was emblematic of the world's best athlete, after only a few months of training. Such a feat would never be possible again. Twenty-eight years later, Bruce Jenner devoted four years of his life (and of his wife's) to the single-minded pursuit of a decathlon gold medal. Each day, he worked out for six or seven hours. Driven not by the joy of play nor by patriotic sentiment, Jenner frankly acknowledged that he engaged in such arduous training only in antici-pation of future gains. After winning at Montreal, he resolved never again to set foot on a track. By the 1970s even in the most traditionally relaxed sports, rigorous training and large sums of money were essential to success. For example, preparations for the 1983 *America's Cup*, in which a cup was the only tangible reward, cost yachtsmen in excess of $7 million. "I just a little bit deplore that you've got to work for two years—every working day—to prepare for a sailboat race," commented Robert Bavier, president of *Yachting* magazine.[1]

Such incidents heralded a new stage in the evolution of sports with origins in the socially exclusive clubs of the nineteenth century. Well before 1950 spectators had played a central role in determining the character of track and field, golf, and tennis, but after mid-twentieth century the possibilities of fabulous financial rewards for successful athletes in these sports escalated to undreamed-of heights. Under such circumstances, these sports at the championship levels also severed most if not all their connections with private clubs and dropped any

---

[1]"Old Skippers Take New Stock," *Newsweek*, 96 (Sept. 22, 1980), 11.

lingering pretense to amateurism. Even youth sports programs began to resemble their professional counterparts (see Chapter 19).

THE POLITICS OF THE OLYMPIC GAMES

Despite the experience of the 1936 Games and World War II, Olympic officials continued after the war to adhere to the belief that the Games could escape the exigencies of politics and avarice. The International Olympic Committee (IOC) itself had changed little from the days of Pierre de Coubertin; an aristocracy of counts, princes, barons, marquesses, and men of old wealth ruled the organization. No woman or active athlete sat on the IOC. "Sport," said Avery Brundage, the Chicago construction magnate who served as president of the IOC from 1952 to 1972, "... like music and the other fine arts, transcends politics.... We are concerned with sports, not politics or business."[2] Yet this nineteenth-century athlete-centered ideal of the Olympics never fully corresponded with reality. In the postwar years the gap between official Olympic ideology and practice widened. The Olympic Games increasingly became great international media spectacles. Not only athletes and nations, but bureaucracies, business concerns, and even terrorists enlisted sports in behalf of their special interests.

The very structure of the Olympics militated against an athlete-centered orientation. By requiring that athletes compete as representatives of nations rather than as individuals, the Games inevitably became forums for international politics. In the postwar era the combatants in the Cold War and the new nations of the Third World were especially prone to use the Olympics to further their own international political goals. As the Games grew in size, cost, and the power to generate international attention, commercial considerations also shifted the focus away from the individual athletes. Financing the expanded games required ever larger sums from television, corporations, and governments. Moreover, business interests seized upon the Olympics to sell products. Finally, nation-state pressures, pressures from local organizing committees, and the vast sums of money required to finance the Games forced the Olympic movement to place its emphasis upon the success of its organizations rather than the interests of the athletes. Consequently, the Olympic movement tended to define its goals in terms of its size and growth rather than in terms of its athlete-centered ideals.

The importance of external forces first became manifest in the postwar era at the 1952 Games held in Helsinki, Finland. The 1948 Olympics, scheduled in war-ravaged London, had occurred with a minimum of commercialization and political friction. Yet American Olympic and political officials did worry about the Soviet Union. While the Soviets did not enter the 1948 Games, they did

---

[2]International Olympic Committee, *The Speeches of Avery Brundage* (Lausanne, 1968), p. 67. For treatments of the Olympic games in this era see Allen Guttmann, *The Games Must Go On: Avery Brundage and the Olympic Movement* (New York, 1984); Richard Espy, *Politics of the Olympic Games* (Berkeley, 1979); David B. Kanin, *A Political History of the Olympic Games,* (Boulder, 1981); Randy Roberts, *Winning Is the Only Thing* (Baltimore, 1989), Chap. 1; Peter J. Graham, and Horst Ueberhorst, eds., *The Modern Olympics* (Cornwall, NY, nd).

send a battery of observers. When the Soviets announced that they would send a team to the 1952 Games and a Soviet delegate was appointed to the IOC, American worries turned into alarm. To raise funds to counteract the "Red Menace" in 1952, the United States Olympic Committee (USOC) arranged for an Olympic Telethon starring Bing Crosby and Bob Hope. Hope set the tone for the American effort when he cracked: "I guess Joe Stalin thinks he is going to show up our soft capitalistic Americans. We've got to cut him down to size."[3]

Athletic rivalry between the two superpowers dominated the 1952 Helsinki Games. To the chagrin of the IOC, both countries devised ingenious self-serving scoring systems that allegedly demonstrated the athletic superiority of their respective social and political systems. Athletic success, the Americans and Soviets believed, would bolster national self-confidence, enhance the respect of allies and nonaligned nations, and demoralize the opposition. Little wonder that the athletes began to conceive of themselves as surrogate warriors in the Soviet-American battle for prestige and influence. Bob Mathias, the Olympic decathlon champion, captured the mood of the American team: "There were many more pressures on the American athletes [in 1952] because of the Russians than in 1948. They were in a sense the real enemies. You just loved to beat 'em. You just had to beat 'em. It wasn't like beating some friendly country like Australia."[4]

The degree to which the rivalry between the United States and the Soviet Union impinged upon the Olympics usually depended upon the intensity of the Cold War. The Games of 1956 at Melbourne, Australia, and 1960 at Rome reflected a new phase in the Cold War. Repercussions from the Soviet invasion of Hungary and the joint British, French, and Israeli seizure of the Suez Canal from Egypt in 1956 inevitably spilled over into the Melbourne Olympics. The Netherlands, Spain, and Switzerland withdrew from the Games to protest the Soviet action; Egypt, Lebanon, and Iraq pulled out because of the Suez invasion; and refugee Hungarians used the Games to stage several anti-Soviet demonstrations. Yet the IOC determined to remain aloof from the international turmoil. Avery Brundage asserted that "every civilized person recoils in horror at the savage slaughter in Hungary but that is no reason for destroying the nucleus of international cooperation...." He repeated the myth that "the Olympic Games are contests between individuals and not between nations."[5] Neither did the United States use the Games to condemn Soviet aggression against Hungary. By the mid-1950s the classic phase of the Cold War had passed.

In the new phase of the Cold War, Soviet-American athletic relations assumed a somewhat less belligerent character. At Melbourne the United States and Soviet Union track officials announced a tentative agreement for an exchange of track meets to begin in Moscow in 1957. At the Rome Games of 1960 East-West goodwill abounded; Soviet and American athletes openly fraternized. The chair-

---

[3]Quoted in William O. Johnson, Jr., *All That Glitters Is Not Gold: The Olympic Games* (New York, 1972), p. 223.
[4]Quoted in Espy, *The Politics of the Olympic Games*, p. 38.
[5]Quoted in ibid, p. 40.

man of the Soviet Olympic Committee, Constantin Andrianov, was even moved to say "Politics is one thing, sport another. We are sportsmen."[6] (Yet apparently the poor showing of the highly touted American track and field team at Rome led President John F. Kennedy to enlarge the program of the President's Council on Physical Fitness.) In the 1960s and 70s regularly scheduled athletic competition between the Soviet Union and the United States constituted part of a wide-ranging program of cultural exchange between the two nations.

In the 1960s the apartheid (racial segregation) of South Africa replaced Soviet-American conflict as the main Olympic political issue.[7] The newly formed black African states determined to use international sports as a lever to force change in South Africa's apartheid. The IOC barred South Africa from the 1964 Games, but reassured by promises that racism would be eliminated in South African sports, it voted by postcard to readmit the nation's team to the 1968 Games in Mexico City. Almost all of the African nations and several Third World countries promptly withdrew from the Games, and American black athletes, led by San Jose State sociology instructor Harry Edwards, announced a probable boycott. With the 1968 Games seriously jeopardized and to save face, the IOC declared that the international climate of violence made it necessary to bar South Africa from the Games. In 1970 the IOC officially expelled South Africa from the Olympic movement.

Despite the expulsion of South Africa, the black Africans continued to use the games as a political weapon. In May of 1976 New Zealand scheduled a rugby tour in South Africa. The Organization of African Unity announced that its member states would boycott the 1976 Games unless New Zealand were barred. Only forty-eight hours before the opening ceremonies at Montreal, fifteen African nations sent the IOC an ultimatum: either send New Zealand home or they would boycott. The IOC responded that rugby was not an Olympic sport and New Zealand did not practice apartheid. In this instance, the IOC refused to accede to African demands and thirty countries pulled out of the Montreal Games. No action indicated so clearly the absence of concern for the individual athletes. Track and field fans were especially angry because the boycott prevented a classic confrontation between the two top milers of the world—Tanzania's Filbert Bayi and New Zealand's John Walker. Several African athletes paid their own expenses to Montreal and tried to compete under the Olympic flag, but Olympic officials, apparently hoping to woo the African countries back into the Olympic fold, refused to allow them to participate.

The political use of the Games reached grotesque proportions in the 1972 Munich Olympics when a group of Arab terrorists seized the Israeli compound and eventually killed nine Israeli athletes. The tragedy dripped with irony, for the West Germans had hoped to erase the ugly memories of Nazism only to have Jewish blood once again spilled on German soil. But this time the Germans were the would-be rescuers. After having scaled an eight-feet-high

---

[6]Quoted in Johnson, *All That Glitters*, p. 236.

[7]In addition to Espy, *The Politics of the Olympic Games*, see Richard Lapchick, *The Politics of Race and International Sport* (Westport, CT, 1972).

fence and capturing the Israeli compound, the terrorists made five demands for the release of the nine hostages, including the freeing of some 200 Arab guerillas in Israel and elsewhere. The West German negotiators, guided by top Israeli government officials, refused to make any major concessions. In the meantime the terrorists postponed deadlines for the execution of the hostages. Television cameras positioned near the compound zoomed in on the hangmanlike-visage of a terrorist in a stocking cap who seemed to symbolize the total prostitution of the Games to nonsports-centered goals. West German and Israeli officials finally settled upon a desperate plan that was to culminate in an ambush of the terrorists at an airport near Munich. The plan failed. The terrorists killed all of the Israeli hostages, though German authorities captured three of the Arab guerillas and killed the others. Despite the massacre, Olympic officials decided that the Games ought to continue. As a consequence of the Munich tragedy, fears of terrorist attacks also clouded the 1976 Games in Montreal and the 1980 Games in Moscow.

The invasion of Afghanistan by the Soviet Union in 1979 suddenly reawakened the latent antagonism between East and West. Although the United States had not withdrawn from the earlier Games to protest Soviet invasions of Hungary and Czechoslovakia, President Jimmy Carter quickly called for a world-wide boycott of the 1980 Games. Fearing Soviet expansion into the Persian Gulf region, American officials apparently believed that a boycott would serve as a moral condemnation of the Soviets, perhaps induce them to withdraw from Afghanistan, and deal a severe blow to Soviet prestige. Although only Canada, West Germany, and Japan, of the industrial states, cooperated fully with the American boycott, it was the first instance of one of the superpowers withdrawing from the Games. Furthermore, the boycott denied the Soviets access to the immense American television audience. In 1984 the Soviets retaliated by refusing to participate in the Games at Los Angeles. With the absence of one or the other of the superpowers at the Games of 1980 and 1984, the Games lost some of their intrinsic excitement.

THE ESCALATION OF THE STAKES

Commercial considerations, though perhaps not as spectacular as political intrusions, likewise became increasingly important to the Games. Brundage visualized the Olympic movement as "a revolt against Twentieth Century materialism . . . a devotion to a cause and not the reward."[8] But such noble sentiments could hardly square with the realities of the postwar era. Television alone was responsible for altering much of the commercial and financial structure of the Olympics. The medium transformed the Games into a genuine international drama, played upon national rivalries, and eventually became essential to their financial solvency. The contracts between the American television networks and the Olympics grew slowly until the 1970s when they soared to astronomical heights (see Figure 17-1). In 1988 Seoul received $300 million from NBC, $52 million from Japanese television, and $28 million from Western Europe for television rights; in the same year ABC paid $309 million for the rights to the Winter Games in

[8]Quoted in Johnson, *All That Glitters*, p. 24.

THE SOVIET JUNIOR OLYMPIC TEAM IN AN AMERICAN DEPARTMENT STORE
This photograph of members of the Soviet Junior Olympic team examining sales items at a department store in Lincoln, Nebraska, suggested the possibility that international sports competition could broaden understanding between nations. Yet political considerations often intruded, as when the United States boycotted the Olympic Games of 1980 and the Soviet Union, the Games of 1984.

Calgary. Television receipts came to constitute about two-thirds of the host city's revenues from the Games. ABC's coverage of the 1968, 1972, and 1976 Games contributed immensely to the Games becoming television extravaganzas. ABC brought to the Games the technical expertise gained from producing "The Wide World of Sports" and college football. Apart from good Nielsen ratings, the networks believed that telecasting the Games enhanced their image and provided valuable "lead-ins" to their fall programming.

Figure 17-1 Television Contracts with American Networks for the Summer Olympic Games (in millions of dollars)

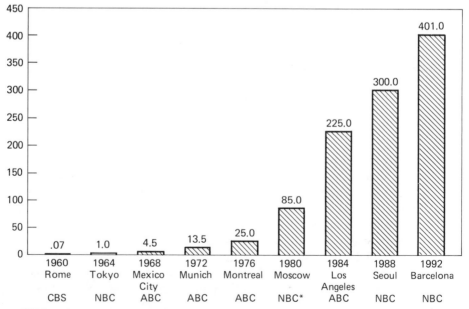

*NBC made a partial payment of this sum before the United States withdrew from the Games.

Television provided host cities opportunities to present themselves as showcases of modernity. Each host city hoped the Games would attract tourists, improve the city's image, and promote trade. The 1964 Winter Games at Innsbruck, Austria, and Summer Games in Tokyo were the first since the Berlin Games of 1936 to exploit fully the opportunities presented by the Olympics. The Austrians used the Winter Games to promote the sale of their ski equipment and to transform Innsbruck into a major sports center and tourist attraction. While the Tokyo Games served as a stimulus for badly needed urban renewal, the Games also helped launch Japan as one of the world's top trading nations. Scheduling the 1988 Games in Seoul likewise symbolized the growing power of South Korea in world trade. Yet the costs of hosting the Games mounted to staggering heights. Only large infusions from television, subsidies from governments, and/or skillful franchising and sales of Olympic-related privileges (as exemplified by Peter Ueberroth at Los Angeles in 1984) could prevent large financial losses to the host cities.

Corporations found the Games to be a wonderful opportunity to sell their products. They spent large sums to have their wares identified with the Olympics. Traditionally, American athletes had not been issued coordinated apparel, but in 1964 clothing firms began providing free, coordinated outfits for the entire American team. Clothing manufacturers believed that the Olympic team outfits exerted a particularly strong influence on the purchases of youths, especially in the fall season following the Games. By the time of the 1976 Games, Olympic fans could purchase official Olympic butter, beer, sugar, gasoline, cameras, watches, and a host of other products. At Montreal, Coca-Cola alone paid $1.3 million to supply athletes with free, Olympic-endorsed soda.

By the 1980s, the IOC, the international bodies that supervised competition at the Games, the host city organizing committee, and the national Olympic committees had become absorbed in the tasks required to maintain their own existences. The Olympic movement had become a huge network of bureaucracies. The IOC itself reflected the trend toward bureaucratization. Until 1964 the permanent staff of the IOC consisted of only the president and two part-time assistants in Chicago (Brundage's home) and a chancellor and two part-time assistants in Lausanne, Switzerland, the IOC headquarters. Until 1960 the expenses of the IOC had been less than $10,000 per year. But by 1980 the administrative head of the IOC (Monique Berlioux) received an annual salary of $100,000, and the Lausanne office included more than thirty-five full-time employees. A similar bureaucratization occurred in the United States, where the USOC typically spent well over half its budget on administration.[9]

Until the 1972 Games, Americans accepted a hypocritical system of amateur athletics and an uncoordinated Olympics program without great concern. Except for a two-week interlude every four years, the media and most Americans simply ignored the Olympic Games. Television, more than anything

---

[9]See Espy, *The Politics of the Olympic Games*, pp. 163–171; *Final Report of the President's Commission On Olympic Sports*, 2 vols. (Washington, DC, 1977), II, 422, 442; Anita Verschoth, "Carrying the Torch," *Sports Illustrated*, 54 (April 13, 1981), 70; E. M. Swift and Robert Sullivan, "An Olympian Quagmire," ibid, 69 (Sept. 12, 1988), 38–40.

else, spurred American interest in the Games. The drama of the 1972 Munich Games with its monumental blunders (the failure of two American sprinters to show up for the second round of the quarterfinals of the 100-meter dash), sparkling heroes (American swimmer, Mark Spitz, and the tiny Soviet gymnast, Olga Korbut), and tragedy (the seizure of the Israeli compound by Arab terrorists) riveted the American people to their television sets as nothing had done since the assassination of President John F. Kennedy and the murder of Lee Harvey Oswald in 1963.

At both the 1972 Munich Games and the 1976 Montreal Olympics, television magnified the victories of the Soviet bloc countries and made millions of Americans acutely aware for the first time of the deficiencies in their nation's Olympic effort (see Table 17-1). Americans had long complained that the Soviet bloc nations directly and fully subsidized their athletes, thereby enjoying an advantage in Olympic competition. But Communist successes sprang from more than subsidies. Unlike the United States, the Communist nations made sport an integral part of state policy. They invested millions of dollars in sports centers, training programs, and research. East Germany, a nation of only 17 million people, won more gold medals in the 1976 and 1988 Summer Games than the United States with a population of more than 240 million. In fact, in each of the Games since 1968, the combined medals of East and West Germany exceeded those of either the United States or the Soviet Union.

In response to the poor showing of American athletes in 1972 and 1976, President Gerald Ford appointed a special commission to study the American system of amateur athletics and make recommendations for a total overhaul. "In international sport," the presidential commission concluded, "American performances are deteriorating. Against athletes from nations [to] whom Olympic medals are as precious as moon rocks, U.S. competitors seem to have steadily diminishing chances of success."[10] The resultant Amateur Sports Act of 1978 represented a sharp departure from the traditions of American amateur sports. To eliminate the long-standing disputes between amateur sports governing bodies for hegemony over the American Olympic effort, the act empowered the USOC to act as a coordinating authority. This provision sharply trimmed the

Table 17–1. Leading Olympic Medal Winners, Summer Games, 1952–1988 (total medals)

NATION	OLYMPIC YEARS									
	1952	1956	1960	1964	1968	1972	1976	1980	1984	1988
USA	76	74	71	90	107	93	94	*	174	94
USSR	69	98	103	96	91	99	125	195	*	132
E. Germany	—	—	—	—	25	66	90	126	*	102
W. Germany	—	—	—	—	25	40	39	*	59	40
Germany*	24	26	42	50	—	—	—	—	—	—

*Until the 1968 Games, Germany had a combined team. The USA and West Germany did not compete in the 1980 Games. The USSR and East Germany did not compete in the 1984 Games.

[10]*Final Report,* I, 6.

power of the once-powerful Amateur Athletic Union. Subsequently, the USOC set up permanent quarters in Colorado Springs, Colorado, for research and athletic training. For several months of each year, promising Olympic hopefuls in several sports could now train at Colorado Springs with all expenses paid.

The nation also moved closer to a complete and open subsidization of athletes competing in Olympic sports. Until the mid-1970s, amateur athletes technically could not benefit monetarily in any way from sports. However, nearly all of the world-class athletes received some sort of subsidy. Those attending colleges usually enjoyed athletic scholarships and athletes in the military often received additional time off for training. Since at least the 1920s, promoters of track and field meets in both the United States and Europe had paid well-known athletes generous "travel" expenses to participate in their meets. In the 1960s, endorsements of sporting equipment became something of a world-wide scandal. Manufacturers offered Olympic participants free equipment plus cash payments to prominently display skis, vaulting poles, clothing, and shoes before the ever-present television cameras. "Most of us are aware," acknowledged Jack Kelly, president of the Amateur Athletic Union, "that as many as two-thirds of the athletes signing the Olympic oath are committing perjury."[11]

Gradually practice and principle came closer together. In 1974 the IOC modified its strict rules. It permitted "amateur" athletes to receive their regular salaries when in training for international competition even though the athletes might not actually be working at a job. Additional changes in IOC rules and the Amateur Sports Act of 1978 allowed Olympic hopefuls to accept guaranteed appearance money, earn "Grand Prix" points on the international track circuit (which could be translated into dollars), serve as highly-paid consultants to corporations, and even do television commercials without losing their eligibility. Suddenly, several of the world-class athletes in Olympic sports began to earn as much money as professional athletes in team sports.

Unlike avowed professionals, however, the Olympic athletes could not receive the money directly. Funds first went to the national sports organization to which the athlete belonged. For example, The Athletic Congress (TAC), the governing body of track and field, placed athletes' earnings in a trust fund that could be technically tapped only for essential living and training expenses. But TAC was generous in its definition of living expenses, allowing athletes in effect to earn as much as they could. Such an artifice made it possible to retain the tissue-thin illusion of amateurism while in fact providing for a system of professional sports. Whether the professionalization and centralization of the American Olympic effort would produce more athletic victories over the Communist countries remained to be seen. The results in the 1988 Winter Games in Calgary and the Summer Games in Seoul did not provide much basis for optimism.[12]

[11]Quoted in Johnson, *All That Glitters*, p. 38.
[12]See *Final Report;* The Athletic Congress of the USA, "TACTTRUST Agreement," Indianapolis, IN, Sept. 1, 1982; Jack Fall, *NCAA: The Voice of College Sports*, (Mission, KS, 1981), pp. 92–96. On the performance at Seoul, see E. M. Swift, "Mandate for Barcelona," *Sports Illustrated*, 69 (Oct. 10, 1988), 154.

TELEVISION AND THE ASCENT OF GOLF

In the era of televised sports, golf entered a new "golden era," or as some observers would put it, "The Age of Arnold Palmer." In the 1950s golf's ambience was still that of the country club and summer resorts, but in the 1960s golf rather suddenly experienced a revival of spectator interest. The number of active players and courses doubled, and the professional tour achieved unprecedented popularity and prosperity. In 1956 the television networks collectively carried only five and a half hours of golf for the entire year, but by 1970 viewers could see nearly that much weekly, and earnings had soared to more than $6 million. Golf furnished the Associated Press "Athlete of the Decade" for the 1960s— Arnold Palmer.[13]

Signs of the new golden age of golf were apparent in the 1950s. Ardent fans admired the precisionist play of Ben Hogan and Sammy Snead, perennial winners of major championships in the late 1940s and 50s. In the nation's capital, the new president, Dwight D. Eisenhower, unlike two of his golf-playing predecessors (William Howard Taft and Warren G. Harding) made no secret of his addiction to the game. To sharpen his putting skills, the president had a real green constructed outside his office. He played at every opportunity, with golfing pros, business tycoons, or entertainment celebrities, either in the Washington, D.C. area or at the Augusta, Georgia, National Course where club members built him a vacation cottage. At the other end of the continent Hollywood celebrities took up golf with equal ardor. Often as part of a gimmick to hawk local real estate, Bing Crosby, Bob Hope, Perry Como, Danny Thomas, Andy Williams, and Jackie Gleason, among others sponsored new professional tournaments. The association of golf with a popular president and a host of celebrities lent to the sport a glamour perhaps unequalled by any other sport.

Then in the 1960s came the potent combination of television and Arnold Palmer. Palmer brought to golf high drama and a charismatic personality. The son of a club pro from the Latrobe, Pennsylvania, Country Club, Palmer's first major victory came in the 1954 National Amateur; four years later he attained some national prominence by winning the Masters, the first of four triumphs on Bobby Jones's home course at Augusta. Then came the U.S. Open at Denver in 1960. Before a nationwide television audience on a searingly hot afternoon, he established his reputation for the Palmer "charge," "a heart-attack approach to golf that demanded the situation look hopeless before one really begins to play."[14] Entering the last round of the tourney while trailing by seven strokes and fourteen players, Palmer exploded, scoring one birdie after another to finish with an epic 65, a score low enough to take the title. Golf fans never forgot the 1960 Open, but Palmer added to his own legend by fashioning an incredible string of come-from-behind victories. He won at Palm Springs with a final round of 65, at

---

[13]See Ray Kennedy and Nancy Williamson, "Money in Sports: Part II," *Sports Illustrated*, 49 (July 24, 1978), 43; Herbert Warren Wind, *The Story of American Golf*, rev. ed. (New York, 1975), Part Seven.

[14]Joseph Durso, *The All-American Dollar: The Big Business of Sports* (Boston, 1971), p. 185; See also Mark H. McCormack, *Arnie: The Evolution of a Legend* (New York, 1977).

Pensacola with a 67, at Hartford with a 67 that got him to the playoff which he won, and at Mobile with a 67. Few experiences in sport equalled the sheer drama of the Palmer charge.

Not since the historic feats of Bobby Jones in 1930 had a golfer created so much national excitement. Golf fans loved Palmer and he reciprocated their affection. He acted and looked like a "regular guy" who needed the help of the fans. Unlike the typically stony-faced pros, Palmer's face registered his emotions. He celebrated his good shots with a wide disarming grin and by raising his club high in the air as if to say "We did it"; bad shots produced painful grimaces. Long after Palmer stopped winning many championships, "Arnie's Army," as the immense throngs who accompanied him were dubbed, continued to follow him around the course as he played. He exuded trust and was an advertising agency's dream. Palmer's capitalization on his popularity seemed to enhance his heroic stature. His manager, Mark McCormack, a Cleveland lawyer who was to become the most successful of the sports managers, made Palmer into a one-man conglomerate, a corporation that produced and endorsed a galaxy of products, many of which were unconnected with golf. Even as late as 1987, when Palmer was more than twenty years past the prime of his career, estimates placed his earnings from product endorsements ($8 million annually) higher than that of any other athlete in the world.

In the mid-1960s Jack Nicklaus challenged Palmer's supremacy as a player but never his popularity. Nicklaus became the winningest and perhaps the greatest golfer of all time. He won the U.S. Amateur twice, the Masters six times, the U.S. Open three times, the British Open three times, and the PGA four times. His style of play amazed the world of golf. No one had ever been able to drive the ball so consistently down the fairway with distance, height, and accuracy. A stunned Bobby Jones acknowledged: "Jack Nicklaus plays a game with which I am not familiar."[15] Several tournaments even redesigned their courses to present Nicklaus with more formidable challenges.

Television was the other key to golf's new golden era. Although golf matches were expensive to telecast (more than double an NFL football game), the cameras could easily capture the bucolic scenery; even when most of the nation was blanketed with snow, viewers could be transported to sylvan, semitropical sites. Although televised golf was punctuated by numerous lulls and suffered from intrinsic difficulties in obtaining a proper perspective between the ball and the course, the drama of thousands of dollars riding on a single putt could equal the more intense moments in other sports. Even though television audiences consistently fell far below the major team sports, sponsors believed that televised golf reached an especially affluent, male clientele.

Television was mainly responsible for altering the economics and governing structure of pro golf. With growing infusions of money from television, the pro tour purses grew rapidly (see Figure 17-2). By 1987 the leading money winner garnered more than a million dollars a year, and twenty-one players

[15]Quoted in Frank Deford, "Still Glittering After All These Years," *Sports Illustrated*, 49 (Dec. 25, 1978–Jan. 1, 1979), 26.

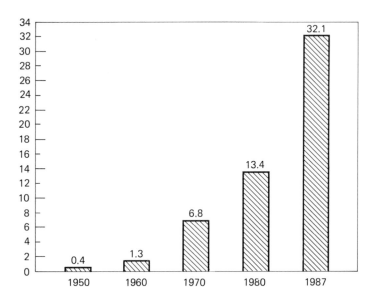

Figure 17-2
Growth of PGA Tour Purses
(in millions of dollars)

enjoyed lifetime tour earnings of more than $2 million each. Primarily to seize the opportunities made available by television, the touring pros in 1968 threatened to break away from the PGA, which was comprised mostly of club pros. The warring factions finally reached a settlement; it called for the establishment of a separate division with the PGA (initially called the Tournament Players Division but later renamed the PGA TOUR) with its own commissioner. Rather than private promoters, the player-controlled PGA TOUR gained a large measure of control over the world's major tournaments.[16]

In the 1970s the prize money and public exposure of women's professional golf lagged far behind that of the men's game. In 1946 a handful of women formed the Women's PGA (changed to Ladies' Professional Golf Association in 1948). The LPGA sponsored the United States Women's Open from 1948 to 1953 when the USGA took charge of the tourney. Purses remained pitifully small. In 1948, for example, the ladies' tour consisted of only nine tournaments and Babe Didrikson Zaharias, the leading money-winner, garnered only $3,400. As late as 1970, the women's tour offered only $345,000, divided among twenty-one events. Then television suddenly took an interest in the game. Nancy Lopez aided the sport, capturing the attention of the entire sporting world, when she reeled off five consecutive tour victories in 1978, a feat not accomplished since Arnold Palmer in the 1960s. Prize money grew to $5.1 million in 1980. The leading money-winner in 1987 earned nearly a half million dollars in prize money.[17]

Golf at the grass-roots level grew in popularity in the 1950s and 60s, slowed in the 70s, and then spurted again in the 80s. Some analysts blamed the "curse of slow play" for the slackened interest in the 1970s; critics said that slow play arose from amateur efforts to imitate the deliberate style of the pros that they

[16]See Herb Graffis, *The PGA* (New York, 1975), Chap. 26 and *Official PGA Tour Book, 1988* (Ponte Vedra, FL, 1987).
[17]*New York Times*, Dec. 30, 1979, S7.

watched on television. Regardless of the cause, on weekends at most courses playing eighteen holes required five or more hours. Some golfers shifted to tennis or racquet ball where brisk matches could be played in an hour and a half or less. Raging inflation in the 1970s also slowed growth. Private clubs suffered financial squeezes, forcing them to close their doors or raise fees to new heights. Nonetheless, in the 1980s the construction of new courses by municipalities, resorts, and real estate developers, and a growing interest in the sport by blue collar workers stimulated a new era of growth.[18]

TENNIS—OPEN TO ALL

Patterns of competition in tennis, one of the last bastions of the player-centered era and one of the most conservative of sports, changed little from the 1930s to the mid-1960s.[19] "Social climbers," more interested in using tennis as a means of earning a social reputation than in promoting tennis as a spectator sport, continued to dominate the management of the game. Consequently, the ambi-

GOLFERS, LINCOLN, NEBRASKA, COUNTRY CLUB, 1975
A sport long identified with the nation's elite, television contributed to a rapid growth of the sport in the post-World War II era.

[18]See "Country Clubs Fall Short of the Green," *Business Week* (March 6, 1971), 77–78; Wind, *The Story of American Golf*, pp. 517–518; Ron Givens, "Hail the Size of Golf Balls," *Newsweek*, (Aug. 18, 1988), 71.

[19]See United States Lawn Tennis Association, *Official Encyclopedia of Tennis* (New York, 1972) and Rich Coster, *The Tennis Bubble—How It Grew and Where It's Going* (New York, 1976).

ence of tennis remained stuffy, formal, and pompous. The tennis establishment permitted and encouraged "shamateurism," usually in the form of paying amateurs liberal "expense" allowances for appearing in tournaments. Most players could make more money by remaining nominal amateurs than they could by becoming avowed professionals. Professional tennis could support only two or three players in a decent fashion. Beginning with the formula established by Bill Tilden in the 1930s, a handful of pro players embarked each year upon international tours, but these itinerant pros played in relative obscurity—in matches that the public often perceived as mere exhibitions. On the other hand, the absence of the best known players in the great amateur tournaments at Forest Hills and Wimbledon robbed the tourneys of potential excitement. To be successful as a spectator sport, tennis needed to shed its "country club" image and develop a format which would feature classic confrontations between the world's greatest players, regardless of whether the players were professional or amateur.

"Open" tennis seemed to be a solution. In the 1950s Jack Kramer, winner at Forest Hills in 1946 and 1947 and Wimbledon in 1947 and the best known figure in American tennis, launched an intensely personal campaign for the open game. Tournaments open to both pro and amateur players, with prize money, Kramer reasoned, would not only erase the blatant hypocrisy endemic to big-time amateur tennis but would generate a renewed public interest in the sport. At the same time, tennis officials within the United States Lawn Tennis Association (USLTA) worried about falling tournament receipts and the drastic decline in the performance of American amateur players. Between 1953 and 1968 American men failed to capture a singles title at Forest Hills; a series of great Australian players (Australia had a population approximately equal to New York City) dominated the sport.

The decision of an Australian, Rod Laver, winner of the Triple Slam—British, American, and Australian championships—to turn pro in 1963, when the game most needed a star gate attraction, and the establishment of a small but successful pro circuit in 1964 were important turning points in the movement for open tennis. While the USLTA wavered in its support for the open game, the British, French, and Australian associations joined the movement. Only the International Lawn Tennis Federation (ILTF), controlled by the national associations of the smaller nations, resisted the open game. By announcing that Wimbledon would be an open event in 1968, the British unilaterally defied the ILTF and thereby inaugurated a new era of tennis. The next year the United States championships at Forest Hills also opened its gates to the pros. Faced with a virtually united front of the largest tennis playing nations, the ILTF finally capitulated.

Open tennis, television coverage of the big tournaments, the emergence of a new set of American stars such as Stan Smith, Arthur Ashe, Jimmy Connors, Billie Jean King and Chris Evert, and bourgeoning purses all contributed to a heightened public interest in tennis. "The big purses," said Smith, "made people watch who didn't know a lob from a volley, and suddenly a lot of people realized tennis was good for spectators, and good to play."[20] Although television ratings remained below that of the team sports and golf, production costs were far less than the other sports and advertisers suspected that televised tennis matches reached an exceptionally affluent market. Between 1970 and 1973 the networks tripled the amount of time devoted to the sport and NBC paid a record $100,000 for the rights to televise each of eight World Championship Tennis tournaments. Televised tennis reached a peak in 1975. That year the networks telecast fifty matches and CBS paid $600,000—a sum exceeding an NFL telecast—to cover a match between Jimmy Connors and John Newcombe.[21]

Open tournaments with larger purses marked a decline in the monopolies of the national associations and the ILTF and the rise of a new set of private promoters. The promoters engaged in a vicious, cutthroat competition for profits. In 1970 Lamar Hunt, Texas millionaire and owner of the Kansas City Chiefs football team, bankrolled World Championship Tennis, which, for a guarantee, would provide pro tours anywhere in the world with a tournament of competing stars. The same year Jack Kramer established the Grand Prix, nominally under the jurisdiction of the ILTF, which awarded points to players for high finishes in major tournaments and prize money to top winners at the conclusion of the season. The top winners then played in a Masters tournament for bonus money. Largely because of the international character of tennis, neither the promoters nor the players established a single economic cartel to govern the sport.

Several observers forecast that tennis would replace football and golf as the major "growth" sport of the 1970s. The early years of the decade seemed to confirm their prediction. Apart from the professional game which was suddenly the beneficiary of unprecedented purses for tournaments, rich endorsement contracts, millionaire stars, and an abundance of television coverage, tennis became the "in" sport of upper middle income groups. According to a Nielsen survey, 34 million people played the game in 1975 compared to 10.6 million in 1970. In the first three years of the decade sporting goods companies tripled, then quadrupled their sales of tennis gear; in 1973 the manufacturers, unprepared for the sudden boom, even ran short of balls. The demand for tennis instruction, especially in more or less exclusive social circumstances, reached new heights. John Gardiner, who started the country's first tennis ranch in 1957, pioneered in intensive instruction in a resort setting. Gardiner's program included professional instruction in basic strokes and tactics, the use of videotape replays, and rapid-firing, ball-throwing machines. Hundreds of indoor tennis centers sprang up across the country. In 1961 only one indoor facility operated in the Chicago area; by 1974 there were forty-three centers.[22]

But tennis never regained the momentum of the early 1970s. The construction of new resort and indoor facilities tapered off, the sale of tennis equip-

[20]Quoted in Judson Gooding, "The Tennis Industry," *Fortune*, 87 (June 1973), 126.

[21]See William Leggett, "Serving Up Tennis to a Fault," *Sports Illustrated*, 42 (March 24, 1975), 54.

[22]Gooding, "The Tennis Industry," 124–133.

ment slumped, and, except for Wimbledon and the United States Open, the networks cut back sharply on television coverage. "Unless there's better organization and focus," predicted NBC's Don Ohlmeyer in 1979, "[tennis] . . . is going to die on television in the 80s. There's eight million tournaments and only two that mean anything—Wimbledon and the U.S. Open."[23] Whether the manic court behavior of stars such as John McEnroe attracted or repelled fans was uncertain, but the failure of American men to do well in the late 1980s reduced the television audience for the sport.

[23]Quoted in *New York Times*, Dec. 30, 1979, S7.

18

BLACKS AND WOMEN DEMAND EQUAL OPPORTUNITY

A symbolic turning point in the racial desegregation of American sports came on March 19, 1966. In the presence of 14,253 basketball fans at the University of Maryland's Cole Field House and before a nationwide television audience, number-one ranked Kentucky sought their fifth NCAA championship against upstart Texas Western College of El Paso. By 1966 nearly every major college team had been integrated, but at Kentucky their venerable coach, Adolph Rupp, had held out. Rupp recognized that black athletes had innate talent, but he thought blacks lacked the initiative, intelligence, and self-control to play basketball at the championship level. On the other hand, all five starters on the Texas Western Miners were black. Playing a ball-control offense, the Miners led all the way, winning by a score of 72 to 65.

An era had passed. Between the end of World War II in 1945 and the victory of Texas Western in 1966, overt racial segregation collapsed on many fronts.[1] Well before the Supreme Court decision in 1954 (*Brown* vs. *Topeka Board of Education*) that undercut the superstructure of Jim Crow laws and practices in the United States, both professional and college teams began to eliminate traditional racial barriers. By 1966, thousands of blacks played on teams in the North and the South. In the early 1970s even Adolph Rupp began recruiting blacks. But, while blacks had taken a giant step forward, women continued to be denied equal opportunities in sports. A revolution in women's sports awaited the post-1966 era.

[1]For general treatments, see Randy Roberts, *Winning Is The Only Thing* (Baltimore, 1989), and Arthur R. Ashe, Jr., *A Hard Road to Glory*, 3 vols. (New York, 1988), III.

JACKIE ROBINSON AND BRANCH RICKEY
In this publicity photograph, Jackie Robinson signed a contract offered by Branch Rickey
to play professional baseball. By playing with the Brooklyn Dodgers, Robinson broke a
"color ban" that had existed in the major leagues since the 1880s.

THE ORIGINS OF DESEGREGATION

"Brooklyn announces the purchase of the contract of Jack Roosevelt Robinson
from Montreal," read a terse press statement released by Branch Rickey, general
manager of the Brooklyn Dodgers, on April 9, 1947.

The announcement revealed nothing of the larger significance of the
event. It did not mention that Robinson was black, that he would be the first black
to play in the major leagues since the 1880s, or that breaking the "color ban" in
the National Game might be of incalculable symbolic importance. No one knew
that the racial integration of Organized Baseball would herald the beginning of
a black breakthrough in many other sports, or that it would lead essayist George
F. Will forty years later to conclude that Robinson was "one of the two most
important blacks in American history."[2] (The other was Rosa Parks, who refused
to move to the back of a Montgomery bus in 1955.)

The late 1940s witnessed a collapse of racial segregation in other sports.
In the fall of 1946 blacks played for both the Los Angeles Rams in the NFL and

[2]George F. Will, "The Fuse That Lit the Fire," *Newsweek*, April 13, 1987, 88. For Robinson
and the early history of baseball's integration, consult Jules Tygiel, *Baseball's Great Experiment: Jackie Robinson and His Legacy* (New York, 1983).

the Cleveland Browns in the All-America Conference. In 1947 the Missouri Valley Athletic Conference dropped its racial bans; the next year more than a dozen blacks joined Valley Conference teams. In 1949 the American Bowling Congress opened its lanes to blacks. In 1950 two blacks joined the NBA and Althea Gibson played at Forest Hills. The PGA finally admitted the first black athletes in 1961, but then only as a consequence of a California court order.

The desegregation of sports arose from a combination of pressures: increasing agitation by blacks from outside the world of sports, assertions of black political power, international circumstances, shifting attitudes of whites toward blacks, and quests for additional profits by sports entrepreneurs. Outside the sports world, resistance to segregation, especially by the rapidly growing number of blacks in the northern cities, had been mounting since the 1920s. In the 1930s Nazi racism exposed in glaring relief the contradictions between official American principles and actual racial practices. Not wishing to have American racial prejudice and discrimination publicized when the nation was about to wage war against Nazi Germany, President Franklin D. Roosevelt issued an executive order in 1941 banning discrimination in hiring "because of race, creed, color, or national origins" by the national government and its war-related contractors. But severe labor shortages in World War II did even more than the poorly enforced executive order to expand opportunities for blacks.

Urban blacks learned that trading black votes for black rights could be a highly effective tactic. Since the northern cities lay in highly competitive, two-party states with large electoral votes, a solid black vote could tip the balance in elections. As early as 1942 in New York, a state in which black voters could decisively affect elections, the legislature passed the Quinn-Ives Act to ban discrimination in hiring. In New York City Mayor Fiorello LaGuardia established a special committee to study race relations, including the discrimination against blacks by New York's major league baseball clubs. Thus the political circumstances in New York City were favorable to Rickey's assault on segregated baseball. In fact, local political pressure may have induced Rickey to sign a black player sooner than he intended.

Inside the world of sports two black athletes—Jesse Owens and Joe Louis—both of whom had moved from the South to northern cities as youths, enhanced black pride and won the admiration of many whites. The success of Owens, the hero of the 1936 Berlin Olympics, seemed to be the perfect answer to Nazi racism, but it also highlighted the existence of racial discrimination in the United States. The discrepancy between racial practice at home and propaganda against Nazi racism abroad was not lost upon American blacks nor their white sympathizers. The career of Joe Louis, the victor in 1938 over the darling of the Nazis, Max Schmeling, revealed a similar discrepancy.[3]

[3]On Louis see among others Barney Nagler, *Brown Bomber* (New York, 1972); Anthony O. Edmonds, *Joe Louis* (Grand Rapids, MI, 1973); Gerald Aston, *"And a Credit to His Race"* (New York, 1974); Dominic J. Capeci, Jr. and Martha Wilkerson, "Multifarious Hero: Joe Louis, American Society and Race Relations During World Crisis, 1935–1945," *Journal of Sport History*, 10 (1983), 5–25.

The sharp decline in public interest in boxing after the retirement of Gene Tunney in 1928, the nonthreatening image of Louis, and international tensions all contributed to the circumstances that gave Louis a shot at the title and won him a large following among both whites and blacks. Five different men had held the championship between 1928 and 1937. Heavyweight boxing needed a new hero and Louis, with his superb boxing skills and powerful knockout punches, was, except for his race, the most likely candidate to fill the need. The promoters of Louis consciously determined to avoid the image problems that had beset Jack Johnson: they imposed upon Louis a rigid code of personal conduct. "The colored boy is clean, fine and superb, as modest and unassuming as a chauffeur or as the man who cuts and rakes the lawn once a week," declared a sportswriter.[4] Unlike Johnson, Louis inspired little racial fear among whites.

Louis also benefitted immensely from the international climate of the 1930s. By defeating ex-champ Primo Carnera of Italy in 1935, at the very time that the Italian Fascist dictator Mussolini was blatantly overrunning defenseless Ethiopia, Louis won the plaudits of both white and black America. In 1936 Louis lost by way of a knockout to Max Schmeling, who had briefly held the crown after Tunney's retirement. One year after his humiliating defeat, Louis defeated James J. Braddock for the championship. In 1938 he fought Schmeling again in a fight freighted with international tension. Only two months before the fight Hitler had annexed Austria. Approximately two-thirds of the people in the United States heard the fight on the radio. Louis knocked out Schmeling in the first round. Americans everywhere rejoiced. Louis further improved his standing among whites by voluntarily joining the Army in World War II. When he announced his retirement in 1949 he had held the heavyweight crown for nearly twelve years and twenty-five defenses—both records for any weight divisions.

In view of the establishment of the principle of nondiscriminatory hiring in World War II, the passage of several state nondiscrimination laws, American condemnation of Nazi racism, and the heroics of Jesse Owens and Joe Louis, the continuation of racial segregation in baseball appeared to be at odds with a new phase in the history of white-black relations. During the 1930s urban black newspapers, a few influential white sportswriters, and the American Communist Party began to attack the ban. Not only would integration aid the "Negro cause," they claimed, but it would open an enormous new pool of talent to big league clubs. Baseball spokesmen issued contradictory responses. One was simply a denial that the color ban existed. Another was a suggestion that integration would decimate the Negro leagues and therefore harm blacks. In the 1930s and 40s both a Negro National and American League existed. Since the teams in these leagues often played in major league parks, the big league owners had a vested interest in their survival. The shortage of players in the major leagues in World War II led to several attempts to arrange tryouts for black players; finally in 1945 a few blacks did "try out" for the Dodgers, Boston Red Sox, and Boston Braves. But none of the black players received a contract. However, a year earlier, in 1944,

[4]Quoted in Edmonds, *Joe Louis*, p. 64.

Commissioner of Baseball, Kenesaw Mountain Landis, who had secretly sabotaged efforts to integrate the National Game, died. His replacement, former governor A. B. "Happy" Chandler of Kentucky, was sympathetic to integrating baseball.

RICKEY AND ROBINSON INTEGRATE THE NATIONAL GAME

In the meantime, unknown to the public, Branch Rickey, prepared to end baseball's color ban. A devout Methodist, Rickey personally disliked segregation, and was also aware of the potentials for improving his team by recruiting blacks. "I don't mean to be a crusader," he wrote to sportswriter Arthur Mann in 1945. "My only purpose is to be fair to all people and my selfish objective is to win baseball games."[5] Rickey worked out a careful plan for the introduction of a black player into the major leagues. So that he could scout black talent without being detected, he announced the formation of a new all-black league. He sought a black athlete who would be assured of making the club and be able to wear a "cloak of humility" in the face of expected abuse from white players and fans. Except for a rather hot temper, Jackie Robinson fitted Rickey's requirements perfectly. Robinson had attended UCLA for nearly four years and had been an army officer in World War II. He was an active Methodist, who did not smoke, drink, or womanize. Finally, he was a gifted athlete: he had starred in football, basketball, golf, track, and swimming at UCLA. In 1945 he played baseball for the Kansas City Monarchs of the Negro National League. After receiving assurances from Robinson that he would not retaliate against white insults, Rickey signed him to a contract to play for Montreal, a Dodger farm club in 1946. Robinson won the International League's most valuable player award and moved up to the parent club in 1947.

Jackie Robinson was an instant hero of blacks. "When times get really hard, really tough, He [God] always send you somebody," said Ernest J. Gaines's fictional heroine Miss Jane Pittman. "In the Depression it was tough on everybody, but twice as hard on the colored, and He sent us Joe [Louis] . . . after the war, He sent us Jackie."[6] At games in spring training, in the International League, and in the National League, blacks came out in droves to see Robinson play. Thanks largely to Robinson, five National League teams set new season attendance records in 1947. But racial integration spelled disaster for the black leagues. The Negro National League dissolved after the 1948 season and the Negro American League fielded only four teams in 1953 before expiring in 1960.

No uniform white reaction greeted Robinson. Before he arrived in Brooklyn, southern players on the Dodgers circulated a petition demanding that Robinson not be promoted to the majors, but organized opposition dissipated when Harold "Pee Wee" Reese, a southerner and the team captain, refused to

[5]Quoted in Tygiel, *Baseball's Great Experiment,* p. 52.
[6]Quoted in ibid, p. 196.

sign, and Rickey agreed to trade discontented players to other clubs. A threat of wholesale suspensions by National League President Ford Frick stopped a rumor that the St. Louis Cardinals players planned to boycott games with the Dodgers. At the personal costs of persistent headaches, bouts of depression, and smoldering resentments, Robinson eased the way for his acceptance by publicly ignoring racial slurs. Instead of direct retaliation, he channeled his energies onto the baseball field where he played magnificently. That Robinson had won over many whites became evident at the end of 1947 when he was ranked second only to popular singer Bing Crosby as the nation's most admired man. After completing the 1948 season, Robinson in effect declared his independence from Rickey's strictures. From then to the end of his career in 1956, he was as outspoken and as aggressive as any of the white players.

In the international arena, baseball's example of interracial harmony quickly became a weapon in the Cold War. In 1949, when Paul Robeson, a popular black singer and a former college football star, told a Paris audience that American blacks would never bear arms against the Soviet Union, the United States House of Representatives Un-American Activities Committee invited Jackie Robinson to repudiate Robeson's statements. Rickey urged Robinson to cooperate. Seated before the committee, the Dodger star denounced American racism. "I am not fooled because I've had a chance open to very few Negro Americans," Robinson said. But at the same time Robinson took issue with Robeson. "I've got too much invested for my wife and child and myself in the future of this country . . . ," he told the committee, "to throw it away for a siren song sung in bass."[7] The newspapers lavished praise on Robinson for his denunciation of Communism and Robeson while ignoring or downplaying his critique of American racism. For the remainder of his life, Robinson remained painfully embarrassed by the use made of his testimony.

Robinson's successes did not result in the immediate full-scale integration of baseball. A few weeks after Robinson joined the Dodger organization, Rickey signed four other blacks, but no other team followed his example. The pace with which blacks joined major league clubs was agonizingly slow; the Boston Red Sox did not employ a black player until 1959, twelve years after Robinson's debut in Brooklyn. By the early 1950s fears mounted among whites that blacks might dominate big league baseball; many if not all clubs had unwritten understandings to restrict the total number of blacks. Driven in part by the profit motive, franchise owners tried to calculate whether increasing the number of black players would result in more wins and thereby increase attendance or whether it would adversely affect identification of whites with their teams and thereby reduce attendance and revenues. The net effect of such a consideration was that blacks had to outperform whites in order to make team rosters. In 1959 the National League had twice as many blacks as the American League.

[7]Quoted in ibid, p. 334. See also Ronald A. Smith, "The Paul Robeson-Jackie Robinson Saga and a Political Collision," *Journal of Sport History*, 6 (1979), 5–27.

The integration of other sports was also slow. Although no historical study has been made of race relations in pro football, it apparently integrated more rapidly than baseball. At any rate, the percentage of blacks on pro teams depended in part on the number of blacks playing on college teams. In the 1940s and 50s several ugly racial incidents marred relations among colleges. As white colleges selectively recruited those blacks who they perceived would best "fit in" the dominant white society, tokenism frequently sufficed as integration. Not until the mid-1960s, when the civil rights movement reached its heyday, did tokenism begin to fade from the intercollegiate scene.[8]

MUHAMMAD ALI

Partly because of continued racial discrimination, black athletes, somewhat tardily, joined the civil rights movement. While Robinson had breached the color ban in the National Game well before the momentous Supreme Court decision of 1954, black athletes were conspicuously absent from the "sit-ins" of the early 1960s, the Freedom Riders, and the March on Washington in 1963. Perhaps they had more to lose than nonathletes such as the black students who were prominent in the civil rights movement. By conforming to white expectations and the authoritarian structure of sports, a few blacks had clawed their way to athletic fame. To protest racism in sport or elsewhere might have jeopardized their newly won status. Nonetheless, a new stage of militancy in the civil rights movement in the mid-1960s, rising black expectations, and the controversy swirling around Muhammad Ali finally spawned a widespread black athletic revolt.

Initially, Ali's career furnished few indications that he would become a focal point of the massive social and cultural unrest of the 1960s. As Cassius Clay, he had won the light heavyweight gold medal at the 1960 Rome Olympic Games by defeating a more experienced Russian boxer. Asked by a Soviet reporter about racial prejudice in the United States, he responded with remarks that could have been authored by the State Department's press secretary. "Tell your readers we got qualified people working on that, and I'm not worried about the outcome," he said. "To me, the U.S.A. is still the best country in the world, counting yours." Ali soon began a rapid climb to the heavyweight championship. His good looks, enthusiasm, and loquacity attracted more than the usual attention given to an aspiring heavyweight. Ali exhibited a penchant for self-promotion; he told a reporter that "Cassius Clay is a boxer who can throw the jive better than anybody you will probably meet anywhere."[9] Prior to his fight with Sonny Liston for the heavyweight crown in 1964, he proclaimed, "I am the greatest!" Unlike the more reticent black athletes who had preceded him but reminiscent of Jack Johnson,

---

[8]See Adolph H. Grundman, "The Image of Intercollegiate Sports and the Civil Rights Movement: An Historian's View," *Arena Review*, 3 (1979), 17–24.

[9]For the Ali quotations see "Through the Years with Ali," *Sports Illustrated*, 45 (Dec. 20–27, 1976), 111, 113.

Ali brought to the attention of the nation a more expressive, candid, self-indulgent black cultural style. His style would soon affect the behavior of other athletes, both black and white.

After his defeat of Liston, Ali shocked boxing fans by renouncing his "slave name" of Clay in favor of Ali and announcing his conversion to the Black Muslim faith. To counter its negative reputation for shady connections, the world of boxing had always tried to cloak its athletes in the mantle of orthodox religion, conventional morality, and patriotism. By rejecting Christianity and joining a militant black religious sect opposed to racial integration, Ali completely defied these conventions. Nearly all whites feared the Muslims; in a series of press and television reports the sect had been depicted as violent, disciples of black racial superiority, and as exceptionally disciplined. Ironically, the fact that Ali, consistent with his new faith, renounced coffee, liquor, drugs, and sexual liaisons with white women failed to allay white fears. Indeed, it seemed only to intensify them.

Ali's proclamation of his conversion to Muslimism coincided with mounting social conflict. In the summer of 1964 riots broke out in Harlem, three white civil rights activists were murdered in Mississippi, and the Senate adopted the Gulf of Tonkin resolution, which opened the way for a large troop buildup in Vietnam. Ali became increasingly iconoclastic; he expressed an utter contempt for past boxing heroes, declaring them slow, inept, and ugly. His outrageous doggerel sometimes satirized American ideals. Ali's fight with Floyd Patterson, a former heavyweight champion, took on the character of a "holy war": Christian versus Muslim, loyal American versus one whose loyalty was suspect. Patterson, a recent convert to Roman Catholicism, was determined, as he put it, "to give the title back to America." Ali dashed all such hopes. He totally outclassed Patterson, mocking and humiliating him before the referee finally called a halt to the mismatch in the twelfth round. To militant black writer Elridge Cleaver, Patterson had been the "leader of the mythical legions of faithful darkies who inhabit the white imagination," while Ali was a "genuine revolutionary, the black Fidel Castro of boxing," who had inflicted "a psychological chastisement on 'white' white America similar in shock value to Fidel Castro's at the Bay of Pigs."[10]

When shortly thereafter Ali refused to be inducted into the Army on religious grounds, was preemptorily on that account stripped of his livelihood by the custodians of boxing, and faced a possible prison term, he became one of the most powerful symbols of the troubled decade. While he was under suspension and while court appeals were being prepared, Ali may have become the best-known American in the world. He inspired blacks everywhere, as well as opponents to the war in Vietnam, participants in the counterculture, and civil libertarians. On the other hand, supporters of the war and adherents to traditional values found in Ali a highly visible target for their frustrations and anger.

---

[10]Quoted in Gerard O'Connor, "Where Have You Gone, Joe DiMaggio?" in Ray B. Browne, et al., *Heroes in Popular Culture* (Bowling Green, OH, 1972), p. 87.

Ali's actions placed other black athletes in an uncomfortable position. As a measure of the degree of their militancy, coaches and reporters repeatedly asked black athletes what they thought about Ali. Often the black athletes tried to weasel. Ali's aggressive anti-Christianity, his opposition to the war, his pronouncements against liquor, drugs, "race-mixing," and sex genuinely bothered many black athletes. Yet his bravery infused many others with additional courage. They began to ask: Had Ali been a white and a Christian, would his title have been taken from him? Would he have been indicted? Were black athletes as free as whites to develop their skills and fulfill their ambitions? Were they the victims of racism and exploitation? Ali's actions helped trigger a larger black athletic revolt.

THE BLACK ATHLETIC REVOLT

The most dramatic phase of the black athletic revolt arose in the "amateur" sports, especially track and field. In 1967, the year after Ali had been stripped of his title, Harry Edwards, a black sociology instructor at San Jose State College, inspired and organized a movement to boycott the 1968 Olympic Games. As a condition for their participation, the boycotters demanded that Ali's crown be reinstated, Avery Brundage be ousted as president of the IOC, South Africa and Rhodesia be barred from the Games, black coaches be added to the American team, and that the New York Athletic Club be desegregated. The protestors first aroused national attention by boycotting the 100th Anniversary Track and Field Games of NYAC held at Madison Square Garden in 1968. For many years the annual meet had been a showcase for black athletes who later starred on the U.S. Olympic team. The NYAC, now, according to one reporter, a "crusty old Irish-dominated club," refused to admit blacks and had only a few Jewish members. Surrounding the Garden, the demonstrators chanted "Muhammad Ali is our champ!" The boycott was a success. The Soviets pulled out and most black and many white athletes refused to compete in the event.[11]

Edwards had less success in organizing a boycott of the 1968 Olympics. While he obtained the support of prominent black civil rights leaders and broadened the purpose of the boycott to include a dramatization of the general plight of American blacks to the rest of the world, he could not generate universal support among the black athletes themselves. Apparently less than half of the black athletes likely to make the Olympic team favored the boycott. Consequently, Edwards made the boycott voluntary and recommended that those who did decide to compete should protest in their own fashion. Lew Alcindor, the hero of ULCA's championship basketball team, did pass up the games, but most athletes opted for participation. At the Games sprinters Tommie Smith, a gold

[11]Pete Axthelm, "Boycott Now–Boycott Later," *Sports Illustrated*, 28 (Feb. 26, 1968), 24–26; "The Angry Black Athlete," *Newsweek*, 72 (July 15, 1968), 56–60; Harry Edwards, *The Revolt of the Black Athlete* (New York, 1969), pp. 64–70.

medalist, and John Carlos, a bronze medalist, mounted the victory stand and, while the National Anthem played, bowed their heads and raised their gloved fists in the air in a Black Power salute. The United States Olympic Committee quickly suspended Smith and Carlos from the team; the committee then gave them only forty-eight hours to leave Mexico.

While the Mexico City boycott fizzled, the success of the NYAC boycott, Ali's disbarment, and the Smith-Carlos demonstration helped mobilize an increasing militancy among black athletes. Between 1967 and 1971 racial protests occurred on at least thirty-seven campuses. Since black athletes were especially conspicuous symbols on many campuses, they often experienced pressure from radical student groups—both black and white—to join various "liberation" movements. Often specific complaints touched off the revolts. To protest the Mormon Church's views toward blacks, black athletes at the University of Wyoming asked coaches to permit them to wear black armbands in a game against Brigham Young University. The head coach dismissed all the blacks from the team. When head football coach Ben Schwartzwalder (a pioneer in recruiting black athletes) of Syracuse University refused to hire a black assistant coach, the black players walked out of spring practice. Schwartzwalder suspended them but eventually lost his job. In the course of the revolt, black athletes formulated a long list of more general grievances. Among them were "stacking," absence of black coaches, concern by the white coaches only for athletic performances and eligibility of black athletes (not their educations), expressions of racial prejudice by coaches and white teammates, and restrictions on personal freedom.[12]

The sudden militancy of black athletes, joined by a few white athletes, shocked coaches everywhere. During the campus unrest of the 1960s, athletes had been the most conventional and conservative of all students; on several campuses they had led the physical beatings of radical demonstrators. To many coaches, the black protest exhibited a lack of gratitude for the opportunities offered by sports for blacks to escape the ghettos. Moreover, coaches had traditionally exercised an unbridled authority over the public and private lives of their charges. Any relinquishment of that authority, they believed, would reduced the likelihood of winning. They were especially sensitive to symbolic challenges. Nothing irritated and frightened coaches more than the sight of long hair and beards: to them these styles signified personal license, the rejection of traditional manliness, and, in the instance of blacks, racial pride. For a time, coaches everywhere issued orders against such symbolic challenges to their authority.

Yet the net effect of the revolt was minimal. Reforms sometimes took the form of gestures rather than substance. Athletic departments hired black coaches, both to placate and recruit black athletes. As the popular culture as a whole adopted fashionably long hair and more liberal dress styles, most coaches compromised their codes of dress and appearance. The traditional crew cut of the athletes suddenly disappeared. The image of Ali changed. By the mid-1970s

---

[12]See issues of *Sports Illustrated* from 1969 and 1970; Edwards, *The Black Athlete*, Appendix B; and Neil Amdur, *The Fifth Down: Democracy and the Football Revolution* (New York, 1971).

Wilfrid Sheed argued that even "the squares love him now. He has become their kind of nigger: self-reliant, keeps to his own kind, harmlessly entertaining. . . . His naughtiness seems almost old-fashioned by now and ready for the nostalgia bank."[13] The token reforms, the rapid decline in general student and black unrest in the early 1970s, the built-in turnover of student athletes, and the changed cultural climate brought a quick end to the black athletic revolt.

THE CONTINUATION OF DISCRIMINATION

Rather than a matter of active protest, the position of blacks in sport in the 1970s became the subject of lively speculation and debate. Scholars and others asked why there was a disproportionately large number of blacks in the big-time team sports. Martin Kane, a senior editor of *Sports Illustrated*, inaugurated a running debate by asserting that blacks had distinctive physical features that gave them decided advantages over whites in certain sports. Harry Edwards promptly challenged this genetic explanation; he insisted that the differences in black-white numbers in certain sports and in their performances was culturally induced. Blacks believed that sport offered an unusual opportunity for upward social mobility. Thus black youth on the whole spent more time in preparation for sports than their white counterparts.[14]

Racial discrimination continued, but in new forms. Blacks tended to be relegated to certain playing positions and excluded from others, a phenomenon known as "stacking." In 1976, for instance, 52 percent of the major-league outfielders were black, 4 percent of pitchers, 4 percent of catchers, none of the shortstops, 17 percent of the third basemen, 39 percent of the second basemen, and 50 percent of the first basemen. Stacking also existed in professional football. Blacks were more likely to be found playing at a wide receiver or running back position than at quarterback or in the middle of the offensive line. On defense, blacks usually constituted a majority of the cornerbacks and safeties, but few of them played linebacker positions. Sport sociologists speculated that white management discriminated in favor of whites when choosing players for "central positions," those positions that required more leadership, cooperation, coordination, and personal interaction between players. Perhaps this pattern was self-perpetuating, for blacks may have concluded that their chances of succeeding would be improved if they prepared themselves for noncentral positions. At any rate, by the late 1980s the incidence of stacking had somewhat diminished.[15]

[13]Wilfrid Sheed, "Muhammad Ali—King of the Picture Gods," in Tom Dodge, ed., *A Literature of Sports* (Lexington, MA, 1980), p. 296.

[14]For general summaries of research on discrimination in sports see Jay J. Coakley, *Sport in Society: Issues and Controversies*, 2nd ed. (St. Louis, 1978), Chap. 11.

[15]"Scorecard," *Sports Illustrated*, 69 (Dec. 26, 1988–Jan. 2, 1989), 24. In the 1988 college bowl games, 15 of the 34 starting quarterbacks were black. Nonetheless, in 1988, 78 percent of the black players in major league baseball (not including pitchers) played first base or the outfield.

Nor did blacks receive equal rewards for equal performance or equal opportunities in sports-related activities. In all professional team sports blacks earned less in endorsements and off-season activities. The Equal Opportunity Commission reported in the fall of 1966 that black athletes appeared in only 5 percent of 351 commercials associated with New York sports events. Blacks in the 1970s and 80s enjoyed more success, though probably less than their numbers would warrant. No black owned a professional franchise and few held positions as game officials, managers, coaches, or executives. As of 1989 only three blacks had served as big league baseball managers. The number of black assistant coaches in the NFL climbed from fourteen in 1980 to forty-one in 1988, but that this number represented only 14 percent of all assistants and that there were no black head coaches did not give the NFL much basis for crowing about its successes in promoting racial equality or opportunity off the playing field. Neither did the colleges do much better. In 1987 *Sports Illustrated* reported that of the nearly 300 Division I schools, there were only two black athletic directors, three black head football coaches, and twenty-nine black head basketball coaches.[16]

Ironically, the very success of blacks in sports may have perpetuated a cruel hoax on thousands of black youth. The exploits of blacks as depicted by the media left the impression that sports were a reasonably good ladder of social mobility. But in fact only a tiny percentage of blacks won spectacular rewards from sports. Of some 700,000 boys (both black and white) who played high school basketball and one million who played interscholastic football each year, only 15,000 and 41,000 respectively made it to the college ranks. The NFL drafted about 320 players each year; about 150 made the permanent rosters. Of those who did, their average playing career was about 4.2 seasons. The NBA annually drafted about 200 college players; about 50 made the teams, and they had an average pro career of only 3.4 seasons. The odds against a youth making it to the pros were thus astronomical, something like 15,000 to 1. Unaware of the odds against them, sports may have actually hampered the social ascent of black males. Instead of preparing for and pursuing career alternatives, thousands of black youths devoted an inordinate amount of time to sports.[17]

WOMEN'S SPORTS IN TRANSITION

As with black players, aspiring women athletes confronted limited opportunities to display and profit from their skills. In the post-World War II era, earlier beliefs and practices that constricted women's roles retained widespread public acceptance. The upper and middle classes tended to approve only of sedate sports, sports that confined physical contact between players and featured physical grace, such as tennis, golf, and swimming. Furthermore, from the 1920s to the

[16]Ibid, 68 (Feb. 8, 1988), 9; ibid, 67 (Nov. 16, 1987), 15.
[17]See Coakley, *Sport and Society*, pp. 260–69.

1960s the nation's educational institutions, which were major training grounds for male sports, essentially prohibited varsity sports for women. Only in the "industrial" sports did women have opportunities approximating those of men (see Chapter 13).[18]

Well before the women's sports revolution of the 1960s and 70s, industrial and business concerns provided working class women with opportunities for play (and sometimes pay) at the highest levels of excellence. The Amateur Athletic Union expanded its program of national competition for industrial women's sports: in swimming (1916), track and field (1924), basketball (1926), and gymnastics (1931). Although women in industrial programs initially won most of the medals in national track and field meets, later black students, most notably from Tuskegee Institute and Tennessee State, dominated national competition and comprised most of the female members of the American Olympic team. Between 1956 and 1978, Tennessee State captured twenty gold medals at the Olympic Games as well as thirty AAU titles.[19]

Industrial concerns were even more conspicuous in women's basketball. Using the sport as part of their advertising campaigns, industries and business concerns located mostly in the South and the Midwest sponsored nearly all of the teams that played in the national AAU tournaments. When not on the road playing games, the women held down full-time jobs for the firms that they represented. A few itinerant women's professional teams appeared as early as the 1920s. The most famous and enduring team was the Red Heads, organized in 1936. Reportedly by 1947, despite a five-year break during World War II, the Red Heads had played before two million basketball fans in forty-six states. The team, with the players sporting wigs or dyed red hair, combined the display of quality basketball with showmanship in a fashion similar to the Harlem Globetrotters. Playing by men's rules and against local men's teams, the Red Heads won a high percentage of their contests.[20]

Bowling also illustrated the key role played by industry in the pre-1970s era. In the first decade of the twentieth century, commercial concerns, especially in the Midwest, began to sponsor bowling leagues for women and men. Interest was sufficient in 1907 for the World Bowling Congress to conduct a women's tournament in conjunction with the men's event. In 1916 women, mostly employed in industry, formed the Women's National Bowling Association (later renamed the Women's International Bowling Congress) which scheduled national tournaments and had a membership of almost 5,000 within a decade. World War II touched off a new surge of women's bowling, as employers

[18]For general treatments, see Bil Gilbert and Nancy Williamson, "Sport Is Unfair to Women," *Sports Illustrated*, 38 (May 28, 1973), 88–98; Stephanie L. Twin, ed., *Out of the Bleachers: Writings on Women and Sport* (Old Westbury, NY, 1979), Intro; Ellen Gerber, et al., *The American Woman in Sport* (Reading, MA, 1974); Reet Howell, ed. *Her Story in Sport* (West Point, NY, 1982), Parts III–IV.

[19]Cheryl Bentsen, "The Tigerbelle Tradition," *WomenSports*, 5 (Feb., 1978), 52–53.

[20]See Elva Bishop and Katherine Fulton, "Shooting Stars: The Heyday of Industrial Women's Basketball," *Southern Exposure*, 7 (Fall 1979), 50–56; William Johnson and Nancy Williamson, "All Red, So Help Them Henna," *Sports Illustrated*, 40 (May 6, 1974), 76–91.

organized thousands of women's teams and leagues. In the 1950s automatic pin setters initiated yet another wave of growth in women's bowling. Relieved of dependency upon the free time of young boy pinsetters, housewives could now bowl during the day. Women's bowling grew much faster in the Midwest than in the East. Easterners often looked upon bowling as a disreputable sport associated with the lower classes and beer drinking. Consequently, from 1916 to 1961 midwestern women completely dominated bowling at the championship levels. Although by the 1970s the number of women bowlers apparently equalled that of men, the prize money available to women remained only a fraction of that which could be won by men.[21]

Industry was equally important to the growth of women's softball. Starting from a base in southern California, interest in the sport had so grown that by 1933 the Amateur Softball Association scheduled national tournaments for both men and women. Industrial concerns sponsored nearly all the teams participating in these tournaments. Play by defense workers in World War II and technological advances in outdoor lighting, permitting play at night, provided an immense stimulus to the growth of women's softball. Estimates placed the total number of women's teams at more than 40,000, a figure representing nearly one-fourth of all teams.[22]

The war also witnessed an effort to form a professional baseball-softball league. In 1943 Philip K. Wrigley, chewing gum magnate and owner of the Chicago Cubs, organized the All-American Girl's Baseball League when he became concerned that major league baseball might be disbanded during the war. (Initially the league required underhanded pitching with a standard-sized baseball.) At one time or another the league consisted of ten franchises located in middle-sized cities in the Midwest. The promoters carefully cultivated a feminine player image. Each team hired a chaperone and instructed the girls in proper posture, etiquette, and "how to take a called third strike." In 1948 attendance reached a peak of nearly a million spectators, but competition from minor league baseball and television brought about the demise of the league in 1954.[23]

The existence of highly competitive sports sponsored by business concerns may suggest an exaggerated picture of the extent of women's sports. Even in the industrial leagues men had far more opportunities to compete than did women. Moreover, women who played in industrial leagues risked charges of being unfeminine or on the other hand, of flaunting their sexual attractions. Frequent condemnation for the unladylike atmosphere, masculine playing strategy, brief wearing apparel, and the use of male coaches beset those women who dared to play in the industrial sports leagues.[24]

---

[21]Gerber, et al., *American Woman*, pp. 95–99.

[22]Ibid., pp. 117–21.

[23]Ibid., pp. 118–19; *Newsweek*, 28 (July 1946), 68–69.

[24]See Maria Sexton, "Women in Sport," *Wooster* (OH) *Alumni Magazine* (Aug. 1978), 9.

THE WOMEN'S SPORT REVOLUTION

At mid-twentieth century, the possibilities for major changes in women's sports seemed remote. Yet in the 1960s and 70s came a sports revolution for women. Spurred on by athletic competition with the Soviet Union, a revived feminist movement, legislative and court mandates, and a growing commercial exploitation of women's athletics, women began to scale the walls of gender discrimination.

If women were to obtain equal opportunities to play as well as rewards from sports equivalent to men, it was essential that the nation's educational system alter its stand. As early as 1941 Gladys Palmer of Ohio State University invited physical educators to form a women's intercollegiate athletic association. Palmer wanted to broaden the competitive opportunities for women "who have attained above average to superior skill in certain sports."[25] She almost singlehandedly organized the first women's intercollegiate golf tournament at Ohio State in that same year. Thirty coeds participated. But the national body of women physical educators quickly responded with a resolution condemning Palmer's efforts to organize women's intercollegiate competition. According to a survey in 1943, two out of every three women disapproved of national tourneys. Nonetheless, the number of colleges sponsoring some form of varsity sport gradually crept upward, from 16 percent in 1943 to 26 percent in 1951.

The Cold War between the United States and the Soviet Union furnished a more important impetus for breaking down the resistance to women's varsity sports. The State Department, the United States Olympic Committee, and the AAU became increasingly concerned in the 1950s and 1960s about the poor showing of American female athletes in the Olympic Games. For the 1952 Games the American women's track and field team consisted of only ten athletes and a manager-coach. The team had no high jumpers or discus throwers and only one hurdler, one shot-putter, one broad jumper, and one javelin thrower. In 1956 the situation had hardly improved when the United States sent only ten women athletes to the Games; in contrast the Soviet team included women who held or shared world records in five of the nine women's events.[26]

To improve the performance of the female contingent of the team, the USOC had to turn to the high schools and colleges. In 1958 the USOC created a Women's Advisory Board, a board composed of representatives from the AAU, former women Olympic athletes, and sympathetic physical educators. Another turning point came in 1960 when Doris Duke Cromwell, heiress of the Duke tobacco fortune, donated a half million dollars to the USOC to promote women Olympic competitors. With these funds the Women's Board and the Division of Girls' and Women's Sports (DGWS) of the national physical edu-

---

[25]Quoted in Virginia Hunt, "Governance of Women's Intercollegiate Athletics," unpub. Ed.D diss., University of North Carolina at Greensboro, 1976, p. 19.

[26]Mary Snow, "Can the Soviet Girls Be Stopped?" *Sports Illustrated*, 5 (Aug. 27, 1956), 6.

cation association set up a series of national institutes for the training and coaching of women athletes. Nonetheless, most educators hoped that the female performance on the American Olympic Team could be improved without the colleges and high schools committing themselves to varsity track and field programs.

In addition to the experience gained by women in building a stronger Olympic team, the revival of the feminist movement in the 1960s struck a responsive chord. In the same years that the civil rights movement intensified, opposition to the war in Vietnam mounted, and many of the nation's youth embarked upon experimental life styles, women began to demand the same opportunities as men to fashion their own destinies. Emboldened by the new cultural ferment and their involvement in the Olympics, a small band of women's physical educators inched their way toward the establishment of full-fledged varsity sports programs for women. In 1964 the DGWS devoted an entire program at the national convention of men and women physical educators to "Competition for the Highly Skilled Girls" and adopted a statement essentially reversing the famous 1923 position on intercollegiate sports for women. Two years later a group of women within the DGWS formed the Commission of Intercollegiate Athletics for Women which became the Association of Intercollegiate Athletics for Women (AIAW) in 1971. Threatened by the prospect of the NCAA entering the arena of women's sports, the Commission scheduled the first set of national championships for 1969. Only one thing was missing for women's sports to make major inroads in the schools. That was funding. Title IX of the Educational Amendments Act of 1972 appeared to offer a partial solution to that problem.

Title IX, the result of women's lobbying in Congress (but strongly opposed by the NCAA), in effect simply outlawed any sexual discrimination by school districts or institutions of higher education that received federal aid. Its provisions thus applied to nearly every school in the nation. Exactly how the act was to be applied to sport remained a source of running controversy in the 1970s. Male athletic directors insisted that equal funding for women would destroy the major revenue-producing sports of men's football and basketball. Consequently neither men nor women would have enough funds to maintain sports programs. In response to cross pressures from women's groups and the NCAA, the Department of Health, Education, and Welfare (HEW), which was responsible for administering Title IX, repeatedly revised its regulations for implementation of the act. One point did emerge clearly: colleges and high schools would have to commit much more of their resources to women's sports than they had in the past.[27]

[27]See for example, Cheryl M. Fields, "What Colleges Must Do to Avoid Sex Bias in Sport," *Chronicle of Higher Education*, 19 (Dec. 10, 1979), 1, 14; Patricia Huckle, "Back to the Starting Line: Title IX and Women's Intercollegiate Athletics," *American Behavioral Scientist*, 21 (Jan./Feb. 1978), 379–92; Joan S. Hult, "The Female American Runner," in Barbara L. Drinkwater, ed., *Female Endurance Athletes* (Champaign, IL, nd), 1–39.

THE RESULTS OF THE REVOLUTION

The newly found riches made available by Title IX to women had far-reaching implications for women's sports. Before Title IX women probably received less than 1 percent of the total national intercollegiate budget; by 1987 the women's percentage may have exceeded 16 percent. Should women push for sexually integrated sports or sexually separate but equal sports programs? In the early 1970s in several places across the country girls tried out for boys' teams; the successful effort to sexually integrate Little League Baseball aroused the most public furor. But given the general physical differences between the sexes (especially beginning at puberty) and the real fear that men might absorb complete control of women's sports, women sport leaders generally chose a separate but equal world of women's sports. To have done otherwise might have sharply reduced the total number of women who would have been able to participate in varsity-level sports and probably would have resulted in the male management of high school and college sports.[28]

Yet those women who pushed for total equality and a more androgynous society noted that separate women's sports programs were reminiscent of the official racial policy of the United States prior to the Supreme Court decision in 1954. In 1954 the Court had concluded that the "separate but equal" doctrine when applied to race was intrinsically unequal. If boys and girls were separated in sport, sport might encourage sexual stereotyping and reinforce distinctive sexual roles rather than provide a training ground for the elimination of sexism. While Title IX did not lead to sexually integrated varsity sports, it did encourage integrated physical education classes and experiments with integrated intramural sports programs.

Circumstances rather than a clearly formulated philosophic stance led to the bulk of the money resulting from Title IX being used for varsity sports rather than athletic programs for all female students. After all, the establishment of varsity sports furnished highly visible, if not conclusive, evidence that an educational institution was attempting to comply with Title IX. Between 1972 and 1977 nearly every high school and college in the country rushed to form varsity teams in a half-dozen or more sports. By 1980 nearly two million girls participated in a varsity sport during their high school years, a jump from 294,000 in 1970–71. Once priority was given to varsity sports, the women confronted an additional issue. Should they imitate the spectator-centered character of men's sports or attempt to build a world of player-centered sport for women? The overwhelming majority

[28]See "Comes the Revolution," *Time*, 111 (June 16, 1978), 15; Carole A. Oglesby, ed., *Women and Sport: From Myth to Reality* (Philadelphia, 1978); Judith R. Holland, "Women in Sport: The Synthesis Begins," *Annals of the American Academy of Political and Social Science*, 445 (Sept. 1979), 80–90; Joan S. Hult, "The Philosophical Conflicts in Men's and Women's Collegiate Athletics," *Quest*, 32 (1980), 77–94; Susan E. Jennings, " 'As American as Hot Dogs, Apple Pie and Chevrolet': The Desegregation of Little League Baseball," *Journal of American Culture*, 4 (1981), 81–91; Coakley, *Sport in Society*, Chap. 10.

AMATEUR WOMAN GOLFER, 1970s
Compare the dress and wistful appearance of this woman
golfer of the 1970s with the female cyclist on page 127.

BILLIE JEAN KING (1989)
Photographed here as the Chief Executive Officer of Domino's
Pizza's Team Tennis program, King was a leader of women's
tennis both on and off the court. In the 1970s, she was the most
important athletic symbol of the larger women's liberation
movement.

of women physical educators, including those who were in the inner circle of the AIAW and those who favored varsity sport, hoped to avoid the "evils" of men's sports. Thus they opposed athletic scholarships, recruiting, and the supremacy of a winning-at-all-costs ethos.

Yet inexorably the women's sports programs moved toward a spectator-centered orientation. A 1973 court case in which a woman athlete charged that the prohibition on athletic scholarships by the AIAW discriminated against women forced the AIAW to permit the awards of athletic grants-in-aid. Soon afterwards every major college began awarding athletic scholarships. By the late 1970s the number and money value of women's scholarships (as compared to men's) became the principal test for compliance with Title IX. The availability of scholarships firmly launched women's sports into the mainstream of intercollegiate athletics. By the end of the 1970s women's basketball, in particular, began to resemble men's programs, even to the extent of widespread charges of the extension of illegal inducements to star players. By then the influence of women's physical educators on varsity sports had sharply declined. Administratively on most campuses women's sports either constituted a separate department from physical education or a division within the men's athletic programs. And coaches, especially in women's basketball, found their jobs dependent upon the won-lost record of their teams. By deciding to compete directly with the AIAW in the sponsorship of women's intercollegiate sports in 1981, the NCAA drove the AIAW out of existence in the following year. After 1982 the overall direction of women's intercollegiate sports rested in the hands of the male-dominated NCAA.

In 1984 the Supreme Court knocked the props from under the application of Title IX to women's sports. In its Grove City College decision, the court ruled that Title IX applied only to those specific programs that received federal funds. Since few women's sports programs obtained any of their funding directly from the federal government, the ruling potentially negated the revolution caused by Title IX. Within a year after the decision, the Department of Education's Office of Civil Rights suspended sixty-four investigations, more than half of which involved college sports. But in 1988 the legal history of women's sports took another decisive turn. By an overwhelming majority Congress passed the Civil Rights Restoration Act, which barred any institution that received federal aid from discriminating in any of their programs on the grounds of race, age, disability, or gender. The 1988 legislation not only restored the gains made by Title IX but apparently resolved many of the problems of interpretation that had plagued the history of Title IX.[29]

THE SYMBOLIC IMPORTANCE OF WOMEN'S TENNIS

Apart from colleges and high schools, the tennis court furnished the other major battlefield in the struggle to establish a separate-but-equal world of women's

[29]Craig Neff, "Equality at Last, Part II," *Sports Illustrated*, 68 (March 21, 1988), 70–71.

sports. Traditionally, tennis had been a bastion of genteel sexism. Women had been permitted to play the sport by the American social elites, but only within the confines of genteel expectations of female behavior. In mixed doubles the male player played the most conspicuous and dominant role. Proper decorum, circumspection, and subordination had been imposed on women players, even though the emphasis placed upon winning by such players as Suzanne Lenglen in the 1920s and Maureen Connolly in the 1940s had threatened to upset the delicate role assigned to women players. In the 1960s and 70s Billie Jean King, a California player from a working-class family, led the crusade against sexism in tennis. King was not only a superb player, but she was confident, articulate, and assertive. She "gave soul" and "personalized" the "bringing of tennis—classiest of sports—to the people." She, more than any single person, helped erase the stiff formality and pomposity from the sport.[30]

King led the women in demanding a separate but equal world of opportunity for women in professional tennis. Although women's matches sometimes attracted audiences as large as those of the men, until the 1970s the prize money available to women was only about 10 percent of the men's purses. With the advent of open tennis several promoters, assuming that women could not draw financially rewarding gates, had dropped women from their tournaments. Neither Lamar Hunt's World Championship Tennis circuit nor Jack Kramer's Grand Prix circuit offered competition for women. In response to their exclusion, King and seven other players collaborated with Gladys Heldman, publisher of *World Tennis* magazine, to form in 1971 the Virginia Slims, a separate circuit for women. At the urging of Heldman, the Philip Morris Tobacco Company decided to underwrite the circuit and promote it as part of the revived feminist movement. The Slims acquired a substantial television contract and by 1975 awarded nearly a million dollars in prize money. By threatening to withdraw from Forest Hills and Wimbledon, the women also obtained far more equitable portions of the purses. As an arena offering opportunities to women in professional sport, tennis was the most lucrative of all sports. In 1971 King became the first woman athlete to earn $100,000 in a single year; four years later Chris Evert won more than $300,000.[31]

King's significance, like that of Muhammad Ali, extended far beyond the world of sport. She became one of the most important symbols of the revived feminist movement of the early 1970s. Harassed by reporters for her frank pursuit of tennis as a profession and her decision not to have children, she insisted upon her right to be a full-time professional athlete. "Almost every day for the last four years," she told a reporter, "someone comes up to me and says, 'Hey, when are you going to have children?' I say 'I'm not ready yet.' They say, 'Why aren't you at home?' I say, 'Why don't you go ask Rod Laver why he isn't at home?' "[32] To those many Americans who held traditional notions of femininity such remarks

---

[30]See Robert Lipsyte, *SportsWorld: An American Dreamland* (New York, 1975), pp. 222–30; Billie Jean King with Kim Chapin, *Billie Jean* (New York, 1974).

[31]King, *Billie Jean*, Chap. 6.

[32]Quoted in Lipsyte, *SportsWorld*, p. 223.

seemed revolutionary. For a woman in sports to equate herself with a man inspired feminists and aroused the wrath of many males.

A 1973 tennis match between King and Bobby Riggs became a dramatic focal point for both the women's struggle for greater opportunity in sport and for the feminist movement in general. By 1973 women had made substantial gains in acquiring equal purses in tournaments, but fifty-five year old Bobby Riggs, a former triple-crown winner at Wimbledon (1939) and a long-time sports hustler, publicly claimed that women players were inferior to men and thus overpaid. He boasted that despite his age he could defeat the best of the women players. He first challenged King, but she refused, arguing that regardless of the outcome such a match could not benefit the cause of women's tennis. Nonetheless, Margaret Court, another top-flight women's player, accepted the challenge of Riggs. On Mother's Day, 1973, a nervous Court, who had recently become a mother— this fact became part of the hype for the match—lost to Riggs, 6-2, 6-1. To the surprise of television producers, the audience rating for the match topped the WCT championship match played the same day.

The victory by Riggs, when reinforced by his flamboyant male chauvinism, appeared to jeopardize the advances made by women's tennis. King, as the militant leader of women in tennis, now felt compelled to play Riggs. The offer of more than $100,000 in television rights and endorsements plus an additional $100,000 if she won no doubt influenced her decision. In a circuslike atmosphere, she confronted Riggs in Houston's Astrodome before a crowd of 30,472, the largest audience ever to attend a tennis match. Millions more watched on prime time television which, via satellite, extended its coverage to thirty-six nations. Advertised as "The Battle of the Sexes," King routed Riggs, 6-4, 6-3, 6-3.

The victory of King, along with the achievements of hundreds of other women in sports, contributed perhaps as much as did the increased numbers of women entering the professions to the erosion of traditional feminine stereotypes. In the face of rapidly improving performances in swimming, track and field, and dozens of other sports, beliefs in the innate physical weakness of women became more difficult to sustain. In the grueling Olympics marathon, for example, Jean Benoit's time in 1984 was faster than all the male marathoners who had competed prior to 1952, and Florence Griffith-Joyner's time in the 100-meter race in 1988 was only two-tenths of second slower than Jesse Owens's world-shattering mark in 1936. Women athletes dispelled the ancient myths about their special susceptibility to injuries and that sports reduced their capacities for child-bearing. Success in sports may have also encouraged in women a greater sense of mastery, of control over their destiny, that extended beyond sports to nonsporting dimensions of their lives.[33]

[33]See for example, Joanna Bunker Rohrbaugh, "Femininity on the Line," *Psychology Today* (Aug. 1979), 30–42; Jane Gross, "Women's Old Images Fading Rapidly," *New York Times*, Oct. 29, 1982, B11–B12.

19

THE ATHLETES

In the 1970s and 1980s, the age of heroes seemed to be over. The titles of magazine articles struck ominous notes: "Where Have Our Heroes Gone?" "What's Happened to Our Heroes?" "Heroes: Do We Need Them?" "Death of Heroes," "Youth Heroes Have No Haloes," and "What Price Heroes?" Nearly every author particularly mourned the passing of sports heroes. "Where Have You Gone, Joe DiMaggio?" lamented Simon and Garfunkel in their hit song "Mrs. Robinson." CBS's popular television series "Sixty Minutes" did a special using the same title. Perhaps even more striking was the apparent decline of heroes among the young. In a 1977 survey of 1,200 junior-high-school children, the most common response to the question "Who is your hero?" was "None." Answers farther down the line in this and other polls revealed the devaluation of the traditional hero. When students did name heroes, they most often cited rock musicians, television's Bionic Man or Woman, and Evel Knievel, a television stunt man.[1]

The concern for the demise of heroes reflected in part mass nostalgia, the inclination of each generation to believe that those who held center stage in their youth were more noble than those who succeeded to such lofty positions later. Yet it also represented an important emotional response to genuine changes in the status, behavior, and images of athletes in the age of television. In professional

[1]See Gerard O'Connor, "Where Have You Gone, Joe DiMaggio?" in Ray B. Browne, et al. *Heroes in Popular Culture* (Bowling Green, OH, 1972), pp. 87–99; William Oscar Johnson, "What's Happened to Our Heroes?" *Sports Illustrated*, 59 (Aug. 15, 1983), 32–42; William J. Bennett, "Let's Bring Back Heroes," *Newsweek*, 90 (Aug. 15, 1977), 8.

sports, players achieved astronomical salaries, obtained long-term, no-cut contracts, organized labor unions, fomented strikes, and signed collective bargaining agreements, all of which shattered illusions that had long segregated the world of sports from the outside world. With journalism bent upon the full exposure of the private lives of would-be heroes, the American people learned that athletes were human, that they were prone to the frailities characteristic of young men or women who had suddenly become exceptionally well-paid celebrities.

HEROES AND CELEBRITIES

In the post-1950 era, the images projected by athletes reflected not only their performances and behavior but also the changing currents of society and culture at large. The athletic heroes of the 1940s and 50s, men such as Joe DiMaggio, Joe Louis, Mickey Mantle, and Willie Mays, became prominent during a widespread quest for national unity and personal security that had arisen out of the anxieties of the Great Depression, World War II, and the Cold War. Each hero, like many of their predecessors, had won a share of the American dream under adverse circumstances: DiMaggio came up from the fishing wharves of San Francisco, Louis from a Detroit ghetto, Mantle from the red-dirt country of Oklahoma, and Mays from the cotton patches of Alabama. Without the exposure of iconoclastic journalism or the full glare of television, these athletes seemed to have been nurtured on Frank Merriwell stories and traditional virtues. According to a 1958 story in the *New York Times Magazine*, professional ball players eschewed late hours, poker games, pinball machines, and chewing tobacco. They obeyed the Boy Scout Law, babysat, subscribed to the *Wall Street Journal*, and "would not think of tripping their mothers, even if Mom were rounding third on her way home with the winning run."[2]

But in the divisive 1960s, sports idols no longer commanded universal reverence. As the quest for national unity and personal security gave way to struggles by individuals for personal liberation and fulfillment, to specific groups seeking a larger share of the promise of American life, and to other groups desperately trying to hold on to what they already had, athletes were less likely to be representatives of national values. Instead, each major social grouping claimed its own athletic champion. Muhammad Ali represented militant blacks, Billie Jean King militant females, Vince Lombardi militant traditionalists, and Joe Namath a militant quest for freedom from traditional social constraints.

Professional football, as the nation's most popular sport, offered perfect heroes for two major segments of the American population in the 1960s. Those troubled by the cultural unrest of the decade idolized Vince Lombardi. As with Knute Rockne, tragedy cut short Lombardi's career; he died from cancer in 1969 at the age of fifty-seven. Like Rockne, Lombardi was a winner. Under Lombardi's

[2]Gay Talese, "Gray-Flannel-Suit Men At Bat," *New York Times Magazine*, March 30, 1958, 15. See also Peter Schrag, "The Age of Willie Mays," *Saturday Review*, May 8, 1971, 15–17, 42.

guidance, the Green Bay Packers won ninety-nine games, six conference titles, and five NFL championships. His Packers resembled a paramilitary organization. "He's the general and we're the privates," one of his players aptly said. But Lombardi brought to football more than the modern methods of cold, efficient rationality; he was an emotional man who laughed and wept publicly. He truly conceived of his team "as one big family." He implicitly condemned the counter-culture. "Everywhere you look," he said, "there is a call for freedom, independence . . . [but] we must learn again to respect authority, because to disavow it is contrary to our individual natures."[3]

"Broadway Joe" Namath, who was lionized both on and off the field, was the perfect antithesis of Lombardi. If Lombardi represented a father figure, then Namath symbolized the rebellious youth of the 1960s. Johnny Sample, a team-mate of Namath's, said: "Our heroes were a new breed of players. Men like Joe Namath who wore their hair long and bragged about how good they were had replaced men like Johnny Unitas, the clean-cut All-America type."[4] Namath projected multiple, ultimately contradictory, images. On one hand, he seemed to be the hippie of the sports world: he wore long hair and a Fu Manchu mustache and could not abide schedules, strict discipline, authority, or Commissioner Rozelle. Yet he publicly apologized to Rozelle, shaved off his mustache for a price (a commercial on television), proudly wore a Persian lamb coat, and openly celebrated his indulgences—blonde "broads," alcohol, and parties. Supposedly putting to rest the ancient belief that sex the night before a big game impaired one's performance on the field of play, Namath was Hugh Hefner's ultimate playboy.

In the 1970s, the continuing war in Vietnam, the Watergate scandal, the inability of the Federal Government to solve such problems as inflation, unemployment, energy shortages, and pollution, the propensity of post-Watergate journalism to revel in the sordid details of the lives of would-be heroes all contributed to a decline in public confidence. Decisions by committees of experts, bureaucracies, and computers, some suggested, made the individual hero obsolete. The astronauts may have been the logical heirs of Charles A. Lindbergh, but their heroism was submerged in complex team efforts.

Television made myth-making, which is essential to hero-making, more difficult than in the past. For one thing, it reduced the distance between the potential hero and the hero worshipper. Physical distance had disguised imperfections and permitted fantasies; with television the fan could feel like a Lilliputian examining the craters in Gulliver's face. For another thing, televi-

---

[3] Quoted in Leonard Shecter, "The Toughest Man in Pro Football," *Esquire*, (Jan. 1968), 140. A widely-shown 1968 sales training film entitled "Second Effort," starring Lombardi, and Howard Cosell's 1970 "Run for Daylight" television documentary contributed to the Lombardi legend. Lombardi also inspired a vast literature. See esp. Jerry Kramer with Dick Schapp, *Instant Replay*, (Cleveland, 1968), Michael O'Brien, *Vince: A Personal Biography of Vince Lombardi* (New York, 1987); Leverett T. Smith Jr., *The American Dream and the National Game* (Bowling Green, OH, 1975), pp. 209–56.

[4] Quoted in O'Connor, "Where Have You Gone, Joe DiMaggio?" 95.

sion produced a diffusion of images. Instead of a clear profile of the solitary hero generated by the imagination, television served up a bleary succession of endless candidates for heroism. In earlier times professional athletes had hawked products, but to be a shill for chewing tobacco and breakfast cereals in print was an entirely different matter from doing so on television. The image of O. J. Simpson, star running back of the Buffalo Bills, barreling down the sidelines competed with images of Simpson futilely trying to hit a backhand shot on "Celebrity Tennis," and leaping through airports for Hertz Rent-A-Car advertisements. In an age of multimedia roles, the line between the athletic hero and the celebrity tended to vanish. A player might be as well known for his or her activities off the field as he or she was for performances on the field.[5]

Finally, reducing the performances of athletes to a tiny screen made them seem less noteworthy. On television, completing a long pass, returning a wide groundstroke on the tennis court, and scooping up a hard-hit ground ball looked deceptively easy. A wide-ranging survey on the attitudes of Americans toward sports in 1983 found that 45 percent of the respondents sometimes felt that, given the right training, they could do as well as the athletes on television. The figure shot up to a startling 74 percent among those aged fourteen to seventeen and was 25 percent even among those sixty-five and over. Given such perceptions, no wonder many spectators refused to elevate athletes into heroes.[6]

INTERLEAGUE COMPETITION FOR PLAYERS

The invasion of sports by the realities of the outside world contributed to the diminution of the aura surrounding athletes. In the past, the actors in sports dramas had often conveyed the impression that they hitched their own purposes to something larger than themselves, to something that demanded a special endurance, sacrifice, and courage. But in the 1960s athletes had become more politicized, and in the same decade talk and images of money began to pervade sports as never before. In time, reports of strikes, free agents, and soaring salaries sometimes overwhelmed the stories of the games themselves.

Nothing contributed more to the demolition of the myth that sports were somehow insulated from the outside world than the process by which the professional athletes in team sports escaped their serflike relationships to owners. By striking down the reserve clause in baseball and similar player reservation systems in other sports, the federal courts released the players from perpetual bondage. The pro athletes organized unions, fomented strikes, and signed collective bargaining agreements. In the 1970s and 80s players' salaries suddenly escalated to undreamed-of heights. By then, players received incomes

---

[5]See Benjamin G. Rader, *In Its Own Image: How Television Has Transformed Sports* (New York, 1984), Chap. 11

[6]Research & Forecasts, Inc., *The Miller Lite Report on American Attitudes Toward Sports* (New York, 1983), p. 140.

commensurate with celebrities in popular music, television, and the movies. Three conditions—the increased incidence of competition among franchises for player talent, the demise of the traditional player reservation systems and the formation of player unions were mainly responsible for these radical changes.[7]

In the past, direct competition for the services of players had been rare. Whenever team sports franchises could do so, they resorted to the reserve clause and the draft to avoid the rigors of bidding against one another for talent. Ordinarily this system broke down only when rival leagues formed. If leagues bid against one another for players, then salaries and fringe benefits improved. Yet historically such periods of open market competition had been brief. New leagues either had insufficient funds to compete for players, folded within a few years, or merged with an existing league. And the players who jumped to a new league not only risked the possibility that the loop might fold but also the likelihood that the existing leagues would mete out harsh penalties if they wished to return. (In some instances they were banned for life.)

Without interleague competition, players were in a poor position from which to bargain. Average salaries might not reflect either inflation or owner profits. For example, while the median income of baseball players in 1963 was nearly $13,000, a figure that compared favorably with the incomes of physicians, lawyers, and dentists, the actual purchasing power of the big league players apparently declined between 1946 and 1963. Competition between the National Football League and the All-America Football Conference in the late 1940s pushed up the average football salary to about $8,000 by 1949. But with the collapse of the All-America league in 1949, NFL salaries grew far more slowly, reaching an average of $9,200 by 1959, an increase that failed to keep pace with the inflation rate for the 1949–1959 era.[8]

The rivalry between the NFL and the American Football League revealed even more dramatically the effects of interleague competition on player salaries. When the AFL signed a lucrative television contract with NBC in 1964, it obtained the financial means to launch a bidding war with the NFL for players. The salaries of the more prized veterans and draftees immediately skyrocketed. Joe Namath received $420,000 to sign a three-year contract with the New York Jets in 1964. But after the NFL–AFL merger of 1966 owners held the line on salaries and in 1968, Kenny Stabler, who had shattered all of Namath's passing records at

[7]For general accounts see esp. Paul D. Staudohar, *The Sports Industry and Collective Bargaining*, (Ithaca, NY, 1986); James B. Dworkin, *Owners Versus Players: Baseball and Collective Bargaining* (Boston, 1981); James B. Dworkin, "Balancing the Rights of Professional Athletes and Team Owners: The Proper Role of Government," in Arthur T. Johnson and James H. Frey, *Government and Sport* (Totowa, NJ, 1985), Chap. 2. For a view of baseball from the standpoint of management, see Bowie Kuhn, *Hardball* (New York, 1987).

[8]Ralph Andreano, *No Joy in Mudville: The Dilemma of Major League Baseball* (Cambridge, MA, 1965), p. 140; "Player Association Testifies on NBA-ABA Merger," *Audible*, 4 (July 1972), 3; Leonard Koppett, *Sports Illusion, Sports Reality* (Boston, 1981), pp. 52–53. James G. Scoville, "Labor Relations in Sports," in Roger G. Noll, ed., *Government and the Sports Business*, (Washington, DC, 1974), 200–01, on the other hand, argues that average NFL salaries in the 1950s increased slightly faster than family incomes.

Alabama, received only a $20,000 bonus and a $25,000 annual salary to sign with Oakland. In the late 1960s the salaries offered to new draftees fell from one-third to one-half. As late as 1968 one in five NFL players made less than $15,000 per season.[9]

Even after the players had formed a more effective union and the courts had struck down football's player reservation system, interleague competition continued to be the largest single determinant of NFL salaries. Throughout the post-1950 era, the signing of American players by Canadian Football League (CFL) teams exerted some pressure on NFL salaries. However, the CFL employed quotas to limit the number of American-born players on their teams and the Canadians never had the financial resources to compete with the NFL in an all-out war for talent. The players also benefited from the competition with the NFL furnished by the short-lived World Football League (1974–75) and United States Football League (1984–85).

The formation of the American Basketball Association (ABA) in 1967, caused professional basketball salaries to escalate as well. In an earlier era of no interleague competition for players (1952–57) the median salary increased one-third, but in a subsequent era of competition with the ABA (1967–71), NBA median salaries jumped from $25,000 to $40,000, or 60 percent.[10] Aware of the effect of the football merger of 1966 on player salaries, the NBA and the ABA athletes adamantly resisted a basketball merger. In 1970 the NBA Players Association filed a class action suit in the federal courts enjoining a merger as well as the application of the draft and the reserve system to the joint leagues. Eventually, in 1975 the players approved a merger of the NBA and ABA, but only upon the condition that the classic forms of the draft and the reserve system be abolished.

THE PLAYER ASSOCIATIONS

The cultural unrest of the 1960s, expectations of higher salary stemming from the general prosperity of professional sports, and the almost simultaneous appointment of new executive directors of the player associations in baseball, basketball, and hockey helped induce a growing player militancy. In the 1960s and 70s the militancy led in two directions. One path led to the formation of more powerful player associations while the other led to the federal courts.

The players organized the most effective unions in baseball and basketball. With the teams playing many games and the number of players totalling only about 100, the basketball players knew each other better and could communicate more easily with each other than could football and baseball players. The high proportion of blacks in the NBA, who had been inspired by the civil rights

[9]"Scorecard," *Sports Illustrated*, 28 (April 8, 1968), 20; "Pro Football's Average Wage Ranks Lowest," *Audible*, 4 (July 1972), 1; "Real Salary Down," ibid, 5 (April 1973), 2.
[10]Scoville, "Labor Relations in Sports," 198.

movement and common experiences of racial prejudice, and the selection of Oscar Robertson, a highly respected black superstar, as president of the Players Association, created a unity among the basketball players unmatched in any other professional team sport. The players hired Lawrence Fleisher, an experienced labor lawyer, to revamp their moribund association. Fleisher immediately imposed a trade union-like discipline upon the players.

To the surprise of nearly everyone, the baseball players formed an equally, if not more, effective union. Many more men were involved (some 600) and for many years baseball players enjoyed the distinction of being the best paid athletes in professional team sports. The team owners initially dominated the Major League Baseball Players Association (MLBPA), which had been founded in 1953. But in 1966 the players took a historic step by hiring a full-time executive director, Marvin J. Miller, a long-time employee of the United Steelworkers. Miller brought to the organization discipline, factual knowledge, and a keen, painstaking mind. "To a disinterested observer," concluded Robert H. Boyle in 1974, "Miller comes on like a David with an ICBM in his sling while the owners stumble around like so many befuddled Goliaths."[11] Ironically, the owners' undisguised contempt for Miller helped unite the players behind the MLBPA.

MARVIN J. MILLER
Executive director of the Major League Players Association (1966–1983), Miller transformed the moribund association into a powerful agency of the players.

[11]Robert H. Boyle, "This Miller Admits He's a Grind," *Sports Illustrated*, 40 (March 11, 1974), 23.

In the late 1960s and early 70s the MLBPA won a series of victories. The owners agreed to (1) increase minimum salaries, (2) adopt a grievance procedure that led to outside arbitration rather than to the Commissioner of Baseball, (3) the right of players to have counsels or agents represent them in contract negotiations, and (4) a larger player pension fund. In 1972 baseball experienced its first real strike, one that delayed the start of the season for nearly three weeks. Ostensibly, the strike revolved around issues of how the players' pension fund would be funded, but in the background hovered the general agreement that would be negotiated in 1973 and the status of the reserve clause that was before the Supreme Court. Apparently Miller seized the opportunity to demonstrate to the owners that the players could execute a successful strike. The players held firm, voting 663–10 to strike, while owner unity vanished. Miller not only obtained his demands in 1972, but he forced the owners to make major concessions in the 1973 negotiations.

Of utmost importance in the 1973 agreement was the acceptance by the owners of salary arbitration, a procedure by which those players who had two years of experience in the majors could have their salaries decided by an "impartial" arbitrator. After having heard testimony by both sides about the player's performance and the salaries of other players whose performance was roughly equivalent, the arbitrator then chose one of two figures, one proposed by the player or one proposed by the owner, as the player's future salary. The twin forces of arbitration and free agency (gained by the players in 1975) drove up baseball salaries to astonishing rates (see Table 19-1).

Players had the most difficulty in organizing an effective union in the sport that prospered the most—pro football. They confronted several obstacles. First, as did other professional athletes, many players subscribed to the "amateur myth," that is, they assumed that the team owners, the commissioners, and the players all placed the welfare of their sport ahead of personal concerns. Therefore, the formation of unions entailed on the part of the players a frank dissolution of this trust. Second, football owners could, without damaging team performance, replace one or more players more easily than their counterparts in baseball and basketball. Third, having the shortest career expectancies of any professional athletes, the players were reluctant to take actions, especially strikes, that might take valuable time away from their careers. Fourth, unlike the baseball owners, the football moguls comprised a close-knit cartel headed by a powerful commis-

Table 19-1. Salary Averages of Professional Athletes for Selected Years, 1967–1988

SPORT	1967	1975	1980	1988
Baseball	$19,000	$46,000	$135,000	$433,000
Basketball	20,000	107,000	185,000	535,000
Football	25,000	42,000	69,000	227,000

SOURCES: (1967)—Ray Kennedy and Nancy Williamson, "Money in Sport," *Sports Illustrated*, 49 (July 17, 1978), 46; (1975)—*Lincoln* (NE) *Star*, May 5, 1976; (1980)—*Washington Post*, April 13, 1980; (1988)—*Lincoln* (NE) *Star*, Sept. 7, 1988, and phone conversations with player association offices on Sept. 11 and 13, 1988.

sioner, Pete Rozelle. Finally, because of fewer games and more athletes, communications between NFL players was more difficult than in the other sports.

Suffering from these handicaps, the National Football League Players Association (NFLPA) enjoyed less success than the baseball and basketball unions. Organized in 1957, the NFLPA was essentially dormant until 1968. Even then, the association employed only one full-time person and he was without union experience. Nonetheless, the union won small victories in both 1968 and 1970. When the NFLPA decided to "strike" the summer training camps in 1968, the owners retaliated by "locking out" veteran players. Apparently pressured by potential losses of television revenues, the owners decided to end the strike-lockout. They agreed to increase the minimum league salary from $5,000 to $12,000 and to double their contributions to the players' pension fund. Hoping in 1970 to secure a larger chunk of Rozelle's new $45 million contract with the television networks, the NFLPA made a new set of demands. The players exhibited a remarkable solidarity; only twenty-one of some 1,300 veteran players reported to the preseason camps. After a month-long lockout-strike during the preseason, the owners nearly doubled their payments to the players' pension and disability funds.[12]

The next strike in 1974 was clearly a setback for the NFLPA. After the strike-lockouts of 1968 and 1970, the owners embarked on a campaign apparently to crush the players' association. Several owners took punitive action against the union's player representatives. "A player rep's chance of being traded, waived, or cut [from the squad] is about three times as high as that of a player who minds his own business. . . . " reported Gwilym S. Brown of *Sports Illustrated* in 1971. "In addition, reps have been demoted to the taxi squad, benched, and pressured."[13] During the strike of 1974, the NFL played the preseason games without the veteran players. The owners seemed determined to finish the season with strikebreakers, even though attendance at exhibition games had dipped to record lows. The owners also threatened to dismiss striking players. "I have to think that there will be a terribly large turnover on our squad," remarked Wellington Mara, the owner of the Giants.[14] Unity among the players weakened, and in early August, led by Dallas Cowboys star, Roger Staubach, the veterans, especially the white players, began to cross the picket lines. Forty-five days into the preseason, the NFLPA suspended the strike. The NFLPA and the NFL did not reach a new agreement until 1977.

FREE AGENCY

While none of the player associations had been able to abolish the player reservation systems or player drafts through strikes or negotiations, between 1975 and 1977 the federal courts undercut the entire set of strictures on player freedom.

---

[12]*Monthly Labor Review*, 93 (Oct. 1970), 56.
[13]Gwilym S. Brown, "Owners Can Be Tackled Too," *Sports Illustrated*, 34 (March 22, 1971), 19.
[14]Quoted in "Scorecard," ibid, 41 (Aug. 12, 1974), 11.

But instead of establishing a system of complete freedom for the players to sell their services to the team of their choice, the player associations used the right of free agency as a bargaining chip in their negotiations with management. In each team sport, unions and owners eventually settled on modified draft and player reservation systems.

The first breakthrough came in basketball. In 1975, in the face of a challenge by the players, the NBA sought judicial approval of its draft and reserve systems. The following year the court denied their appeal and strongly hinted that the NBA's player control system was illegal. Rather than take the issue to court, the NBA negotiated a contract in 1976 that permitted players to change teams. The team losing a player, however, would be compensated by the team that received the departing player. The 1981 contract replaced a compensation system with a "first-refusal" process. When an athlete had played out his option, his original team had the right of first-refusal, that is, the right to match any offer from another team. Unable to control the upward spiral of salaries stemming from the practice of first-refusal, in 1984 the owners negotiated a salary cap for each team. Limited initially to a total team salary of $3.6 million, salary caps restricted the possibilities of the owners making large offers to free agents. Nonetheless, the combination of interleague competition between 1967 and 1975 and the increased freedom for players to become free agents spurred the salaries of basketball players to record highs (see Table 19-1).

The venerable reserve system in baseball fell in a more indirect fashion. In 1975 the MLBPA filed grievances on behalf of Andy Messersmith and Dave McNally alleging that, since the two athletes had played the prior season without a written contract, both were free agents. As provided by the agreement between the owners and the players, the issue went to an arbitration panel. By a vote of two to one the panel held that the two players were free agents. The owners promptly appealed the decision to a federal district court and the United States Court of Appeals. In both instances the courts ruled in favor of the players. Suddenly the reserve clause was extinct. Using the legal right of free agency as a bargaining wedge for other demands, the players' union proceeded to negotiate a series of contracts calling for a modified reserve system.

In the 1980s the free-spending baseball owners sought to achieve contracts with the MLBPA that would place a salary cap on arbitration awards and thus curb their own impulses to bid up salaries by signing free agents. If a team that gained a player as a free agent had to compensate the team that lost the player with a player or players of equal caliber or with money representing the player's value, it was assumed the owners would be far more reluctant to sign free agents. But the owners failed to obtain a compensation system that would have negated the effects of free agency on salaries. A seven-week strike over the amount of player compensation in 1981 resulted in a union victory. In 1985 the players went out on strike again, this time mainly over the issue of placing limits on salary arbitration awards. The MLBPA won again.

Unable to negotiate a compensation system with the players' union that would have ended the bidding wars among themselves for free agents, the owners in 1985 apparently reached a secret gentlemen's agreement. They suddenly stopped signing free agents. For the first time in recent baseball history, the ascent of salaries levelled off. However, in 1987, an arbitrator found that the owners had violated their contract with the players by a "concerted conduct" to limit the market for free agents. He ordered compensation awards to those players who had become free agents during the time that the owners practiced this restraint. An Associated Press study in late 1988 indicated that club owners had resumed their war for free agents. "The marketplace has gone crazy," concluded Boston general manager Lou Gorman.[15]

In football the players were less successful in using free agency as a bargaining tool. Technically, football did not have a career-bound reserve system. A player could "play out" his option, that is, he could play for one year after his contract had expired and become a free agent. Hypothetically, at that point, he could look forward to bids for his services from other NFL teams. But if a free agent did sign with another team, the team had to grant compensation to the player's original team. If indemnity terms could not be agreed upon by the two teams involved, then Commissioner Pete Rozelle was empowered to make awards to the team losing a player. Under this so-called "Rozelle Rule," the commissioner could compensate the original team with current players, future draft choices, or both. Such a system reduced the prospects of signing free agents. Not knowing how much an indemnity might cost them and wishing to avoid open bidding for player services, the owners rarely signed free agents. In fact, until the abolition of the Rozelle Rule in 1975, Rozelle had awarded indemnities in only two instances.

In 1975 a federal court found the Rozelle Rule violated antitrust law, but it also permitted the NFL and the NFLPA to negotiate a player reservation system. In other words, any player reservation system would have to be the product of a contract negotiation rather than a unilateral decision of the owners. In 1977, in return for better pensions and medical insurance, the NFLPA essentially bargained away free agency; it permitted the retention of a compensation system. Of the 295 players who became free agents during the first three years of the new contract, only four signed with new teams. Given the absence of open bidding for free agents, NFL salaries rose more slowly than those in basketball and baseball (see Table 19-1). In their 1982 negotiations the NFLPA decided upon a new ploy; the union demanded that 55 percent of the gross revenues of teams go to player salaries. A seven-week strike failed to obtain player demands, but competition with the United States Football League for players did force NFL salaries upward. In the 1987 negotiations the players decided to make free agency the main issue. A disastrous twenty-four day strike followed, which even left in doubt the future existence of the NFLPA.[16]

[15]Ibid, 66 (Jan. 12, 1987), 108; ibid, 67 (Sept. 20, 1987), 9; ibid, 68 (Feb. 1, 1988), 10; *Lincoln* (NE) *Star*, Dec. 15, 1988.

[16]Pete Axthelm, "Sorry Surrender in the NFL," *Newsweek*, (Oct. 26, 1987), 68; Darrell Christian, Associated Press analysis, Oct. 16, 1987.

THE IMPLICATIONS OF THE NEW STATUS

Given the salary explosion, unions, strikes, free agency, and the propensity of the media to expose all, the public did not perceive athletes in quite the same way as they had done at mid-century (see Table 19-2). Sports fans worried lest the big salaries, the outside endorsements, and the long-term contracts destroy the players' drive to compete and damage the cooperation so essential to success in team sports. "Regardless of what the athlete says, if he has total security and is put in a tough spot, he may go through the motions and say, 'The hell with it. I've got mine,'" said Thomas Tutko, noted sports psychologist in 1978. "Players often seem to put their own welfare ahead of their team," declared Rick Barry, NBA superstar in the same year. "They are now all hungry to score points. They read that the high scorers are making the money and it's true. . . . I'll tell you what money has done. It's changed the philosophy of the game. Pro basketball is not played as well today as it was ten years ago. Players don't know the fundamentals."[17]

Sports "are modeling greed, egotism, self-centeredness," said Thomas Tutko. "We're modeling things that potentially threaten the fiber of the country. There's no such thing as loyalty to anybody."[18] Many shared Tutko's grim conclusion. When running back Herschel Walker decided to pass up his senior year at the University of Georgia in 1983 and join the professional ranks, *Newsweek* implored: "Say it ain't so, Herschel." For money Walker had cut all ties with and responsibilities to his college. "He was so straight—the quintessential All-Everything," continued *Newsweek*. "And everybody not only admired Herschel Walker, they believed. In the sublime order of things, he would finish out his record-shattering college career, gathering still more honors, the very perfect gentle scholar-athlete, and move with dignity into the professional game."[19] In a major cover story, *Time* magazine conveyed a similar sense of betrayal.

Other fans disliked the increasing incivility of the players. The assault on civility may have begun with Muhammad Ali, but when Ali asserted that he was

Table 19–2.   Spectator Attitudes Toward Professional Athletes, 1982

	PERCENTAGES		
	Agree	*Disagree*	*Undecided*
Athletes are overpaid	76	20	4
Athletes are more dedicated to their own good than to the game	50	42	8
Athletes should be tested for drugs before each game	71	27	2

SOURCE: Research & Forecasts, Inc., *The Miller Lite Report on American Attitudes Toward Sports* (New York, 1983).

[17]Quoted in Ray Kennedy and Nancy Williamson, "Money in Sports: Part 2," *Sports Illustrated*, 49 (July 24, 1978), 44.

[18]Ibid.

[19]Charles Leershen, "Herschel Walker's Biggest Story," *Newsweek* (March 7, 1983) 82.

the greatest, one sensed that he was mocking white America. No one detected a higher purpose in the conspicuous displays of churlish pouting and bad manners of dozens of other athletes. In the 1970s and 80s even the once sedate sport of tennis became a stage for the rude, vulgar, loud, and whining displays of John McEnroe. Television daredevil, Evel Knievel, angered by the remarks of a sportswriter, proceeded to break the offender's arm with a baseball bat. The absence of restraint reflected in part a shift in American sensibility, but it also suggested that the athletes were uncertain about why they were celebrities. Was it their feats on the playing field or their uncivil behavior that captured the attention of the media?[20]

In the 1980s, the widespread use of drugs by athletes also bothered fans. Athletes used drugs to obtain "highs," tolerate pain, and improve performance. Despite warnings of long-term, serious side-effects, virtually every world-class weight-lifter, shot-putter, and discus-thrower turned to anabolic steroids. Revelations suggested that large numbers of linemen in both college and professional football also used the same drug. Many other athletes turned to the "glamour drug" of cocaine, which resulted in the shocking deaths of several well-known athletes. Initially sports organizations at all levels tried to minimize the seriousness of the problem, but as the 1980s closed nearly everyone recognized that more vigorous steps had to be taken to curb drug usage lest the credibility of sports be completely eroded. Concern over the problem even led the United States and the Soviet Union to sign a pact in 1988 calling for the drug testing of athletes.

Athletes, at least those in pro football, faced the likelihood of permanent, disabling injuries as well. A questionnaire sent to 1,000 former NFL players in 1988 revealed that 78 percent of them suffered from physical disabilities related directly to having played football. Injuries, excessive weight gain (both during and after a player's career), high cholesterol diets, and the use of steroids and other drugs, may have shortened life spans. Though no systematic study has been made of longevity in sports, the NFL Players Association claimed that of 78 vested players (those who played at least four seasons) who had died between 1960 and 1988, the average age had been a mere 38.2 years.[21]

YOUTH ATHLETES

In the post-1950 era the professional model of athletics increasingly extended to all levels of sports, including even the preadolescent and adolescent youth programs. Only the professional youth workers tried to stem the tide. They continued to adhere to the idea that games should be both nonspectator-centered and conducive to the physical, mental, and moral maturation of their young charges (see Chapter 13). But in the post-1950 era, as the inner cities decayed, the

[20]See "The Dubious Charm of Media Brats," *New York Times*, May 11, 1975, D-25.
[21]Gene Wojciechowski and Chris Dufresne, "Responses Vary on Effects NFL Has on Ex-players' Lives," *Lincoln* (NE) *Star*, June 28, 1988. The survey was done for the *Los Angeles Times*.

influence of the reformers in the YMCAs, YWCAs, city recreation departments, and schools declined. In the meantime, the programs of untrained adult volunteers, which were scaled-down facsimiles of professional sports, grew rapidly. Relative to time and place, professional physical educators continued to exercise some influence over high school sports, but, in the main, they too tended to take on the characteristics of the professional model.

In the post-1950 era, high school sports in the towns, smaller cities, and the independent suburbs prospered while those in the inner city declined. To prevent violent outbursts among fans and sometimes the players in the late 1960s and early 70s, some inner city schools closed down varsity programs or scheduled contests only during the daytime hours. In terms of attendance as a ratio of population, the secondary schools in smaller towns fared much better than in the larger cities or in the independent suburbs. In the grim industrial and mill towns of Ohio and the desolate prairie towns of west Texas, no single activity exceeded the capacity of high school football in binding communities together. Basketball performed a similar role for Indiana towns.

In those places where interscholastic sports assumed important community functions, they invariably resembled collegiate or professional counterparts. Perhaps the most extreme instance was Massillon, Ohio, an economically depressed steel mill city of some 30,000 people. In the 1980s, the varsity football team of Massillion-Washington High School had a booster club of 2,700 members, a lighted-stadium that held 20,000 spectators, and a 109-page *Official Football Media Guide*. The school also employed a statistician, a trainer, and a football information director—all full time—as well as a head coach and ten assistant coaches. High school football could be an equally serious matter for Texans.

CONSOLING A LITTLE CHIEFS BASEBALL PLAYER, 1970s
Not all coaches of preadolescent youths were as sensitive to the feelings of their charges as this coach apparently was.

When Highland Park, a trendy suburb of Dallas, reached the Texas state football finals in 1985, the residents chartered nine Boeing 727s to shuttle themselves 300 miles to the championship games.[22]

In the 1980s signs appeared that high school basketball might become a national spectacle. Beginning in 1918, the University of Chicago's famed coach, Amos Alonzo Stagg, had sponsored a national interscholastic tournament that gained considerable attention, but the tourney collapsed during the Great Depression of the 1930s. In the 1980s, *USA Today*, a popular nationwide tabloid, began to publish weekly high school rankings, and during the yuletide more than a dozen cities held tournaments that attracted teams from all parts of the nation. Most of the tournaments had local television contracts and some even had corporate sponsors. With national rankings and with tournaments in far-away exotic settings, the emphasis on winning inevitably increased. In some places, competition for star players resulted in scandals arising over the transfer of athletes from one school district to another. Other high schools permitted students to "redshirt"; they held back students for a year in school so that he or she could gain an additional year of athletic maturity.[23]

At the preadolescent level, the programs of adult volunteers in the post-World War II era grew phenomenally. Untrained volunteers founded the Pop Warner Football League in 1929 and Little League Baseball in 1939; for both, survival was doubtful until after World War II. In 1947, when the United States Rubber Company became the sponsor and financial angel of Little League, the league had only sixty teams and some 1,000 players. Then Little League suddenly took root, flourishing mostly in the small and medium size cities without municipal recreation programs and in the newly-built independent suburbs. Within a decade nearly a million boys played on 19,500 teams in forty-seven states and in twenty-two nations abroad. Pop Warner grew almost as rapidly; by the 1970s it suited up a million players annually.[24]

Unlike earlier adult-managed youth programs, no ideology shaped Little League Baseball, Pop Warner football, and a dozen similar programs. Carl Stotz, the lumber company employee in Williamsport, Pennsylvania, who founded Little League, explained that he dreamed up the game in response to his own frustrations as a youth with unsupervised, chaotic play. The colorful team uniforms, use of a regular baseball, outfield fences, dugouts, and even a player

---

[22]Mark Russell, "Football Bores You?" *Wall Street Journal,* Nov. 1, 1984, 1, 16; Paul Duke, Jr., "Teams Make Towns Winners. . . . " ibid, Feb. 26, 1988, 4D. See also James S. Coleman, *Adolescents and the Schools* (New York, 1965); Jay J. Coakley, *Sport and Society,* 2nd ed. (St. Louis, 1982), Chap. 6; Peter Davis, "A Town Divided," *Sports Illustrated,* 56 (March 1, 1982), 50–62.

[23]See C. Robert Barnett and David Helmer, "The Champs," *River Cities Monthly,* March, 1980, 7–16; "Hoosier Madness," *Sports Illustrated,* 3 (Dec. 19, 1955), 23, 45–46; "Scorecard," ibid, 70 (Jan. 9, 1989), 11, 14.

[24]See esp. Hy Turkin, ed., *The Official Encyclopedia of Little League Baseball* (New York, 1954); Kenneth Rudeen, "The Little League, Parts I and II," *Sports Illustrated,* 5 (Aug. 19–Aug. 26, 1957), 56–62, 54–59; "The World of Pop Warner," *Newsweek,* 66 (Dec. 6, 1965), 102–03. For perhaps a typical conflict between suburbanites over Little League, see Herbert Gans, *The Levittowners,* (New York, 1967), pp. 120–21.

draft system all provided for adult volunteers a vicarious experience of the unfulfilled fantasies of their own youth. Uninhibited by a theory of play, the volunteers tried to simulate professional team sports. Ironically, while several states prohibited state high school championships in football and usually strictly limited the number of miles a team could travel, eight- and nine-year-olds trekked all over the nation to play in such "midget" bowls as the Junior Liberty (Memphis), Junior Orange (Miami), Auto (Grosse Pointe, Michigan), and even the Honolulu Bowl. No national championships existed in high school sports, but Little League Baseball held an annual World Series at Williamsport, Pennsylvania.

Critics, especially recreation professionals, frequently complained that the volunteers placed too much emphasis upon winning. Preadolescent youths had not matured enough, they argued, to engage in highly competitive games. Indeed, reports regularly surfaced in the media of apparent excesses. Untold numbers of preadolescents submitted themselves to a regimen of diet pills and low calorie diets in order to make weight limits in junior wrestling or junior football programs. The experience of coaching sometimes turned otherwise humane and reasonable men into angry, violent tyrants. "They want to win at any cost," reported Charles Ortmann, a former Michigan All-American who quit as chairman of a midget football program at Glen Ellyn, Illinois. "They tell their players, 'Go out there and break that guy's arm.' They won't even let all their kids play."[25] An overwhelming majority of the parents of participants agreed that there was too much emphasis upon winning and not enough upon the physical and psychological development of their children, but they believed that the alleged benefits to the children outweighed the costs.[26] In response to widespread criticism, several volunteer programs introduced reforms, such as requiring that all youngsters be permitted to play at least briefly. Yet the reforms failed to transform the main outlines of volunteer youth sports programs.

At the championship levels, the individual sports also became more serious for pre-teenage youth in the post-1950 era. Earlier, youth had rarely given tennis, track, gymnastics, figure skating, skiing, or swimming much of their attention or time. Perhaps during the summer months, they might take a few lessons at the country club to which their parents belonged or participate in a Y or city recreation program. Otherwise they simply played for fun or in a few meets scheduled over the summer. But in the 1960s and 70s television made celebrities of athletes such as Jimmy Connors, Chris Evert, Mark Spitz, and Olga Korbut. Within a decade following the 1972 Olympics, the level of competition in the individual sports took a sudden jump. In tennis, tiny teenage girls developed powerful, dependable ground strokes. Track and field records seemed to fall daily. The record time in swimming that won Mark Spitz the gold medal in the 100-meter race in the 1972 Olympics would not even have qualified him for

---

[25]Quoted in John Underwood, "Taking the Fun Out of the Game," *Sports Illustrated*, 43 (Nov. 17, 1975), 92.

[26]Research & Forecasts, Inc., *The Miller Lite Report*, p. 58.

the event in the 1980 Olympics. In diving, gymnastics, and figure skating, the execution of new, complex maneuvers (some of which were previously thought to be impossible) were necessary before one could even qualify to compete at the international level of competition.

Achievement of these advances came largely from early, systematic training. Those who aspired to national or international competition in individual sports had to begin as preadolescents, training three or four hours daily with careful supervision by individual coaches. On weekends and during the summer months, children engaged in regular competition, often embarking on long trips away from home. They might also live for varying periods at special athletic camps or compounds. No one knew what the long-range effects of such rigorously focused childhoods might be. Disturbing reports occasionally surfaced of early "burn out," suicides, and aimlessness in later life. Yet surveys of children competing at the national and international levels indicated that most of them performed well above average in their schoolwork and seemed better adjusted psychologically than nonsporting youth of a comparable age.[27]

[27]See for example, Emily Greenspan, *Little Winners: Inside the World of the Child Sports Star* (Boston, 1983).

20

AMERICAN SPORTS

From a broad perspective, American sports have evolved from the informal folk games of the colonial era to the highly organized sports of the age of television. Folk games arose from the daily routines of the people rather than from entrepreneurs of entertainment. Sometimes they combined work and play. Unwritten customs governed play; the way a particular game was played might vary radically from one place to another. The contestants rarely trained for or earned a living from their games. In most instances no sharp line separated the players from the spectators. Although folk games were frequently transformed into organized sports in the nineteenth and twentieth centuries, such games never completely disappeared from American life. Children, as in the past, remained especially ingenious in designing games that could be executed within the constraints of the space and the number of players available. And varieties of informal bat and ball games, pickup basketball games, and impromptu games of running and jumping were reminiscent of the folk games of early America.

In the middle decades of the nineteenth century, organized sports increasingly supplemented and to some degree replaced folk games. Entrepreneurs or the athletes themselves formed organizations, adopted written rules, extended competition beyond local areas, drew sharper distinctions between fans and players, attracted the attention of the media, and began to preserve records of their performances. The athletes trained more rigorously. Commercial boxing, wrestling, pedestrianism, and numerous other diversions became vital parts of the Victorian counterculture. In addition, nineteenth-century Americans formed literally thousands of voluntary associations for the playing of games. Organized cricket, baseball, yachting, football, tennis, and golf, for instance, had origins in private, socially-exclusive clubs. Although experiencing important changes since the nineteenth century, these sports retained forms familiar to Americans in the age of television.

In the 1890–1950 era organized sports became entrenched in American society. For growing numbers of Americans, regardless of occupation, social class, ethnicity, or religious persuasion, their leisure experiences entailed the purchase of amusements. They bought tickets to prize fights, intercollegiate football games, and major league baseball games. Organized sports thus became part and parcel of the larger consumer culture. Much of the traditional suspicion of sports dissipated. Indeed, Americans ranging from the old patricians to a generation of experts in play and the human body developed a powerful sporting ideology. Partly in response to this ideology, Americans embarked upon a campaign to provide organized sports to the nation's youths.

In the post-1950 age of television, spectators in their homes rather than in the stands determined the main contours of organized sports. The sheer quantity of sporting experiences made available by television reached proportions unimaginable to previous generations. Television contributed as well to a growing nationalization, even internationalization, of American sports. Intercollegiate sports entered a national arena of competition, and even pre-teenagers competed at championship levels internationally in gymnastics, tennis, golf, and ice skating.

Thus, by the closing decade of the twentieth century, American sports comprised aspects of both the old and the new. Remnants of the old could be found everywhere. Children still played folk games; country clubs continued to serve as socially exclusive voluntary associations; prize fighting remained nearly as chaotic as it had been during the age of John L. Sullivan; and the rules of major league baseball differed little from what they had been in 1900. Yet much was new. Everything was, or at the least seemed, much bigger, and with the advent of television millions worldwide shared sporting experiences instantaneously.

The importance of sports to American culture was manifest. It could be measured by the many hours that fans spend riveted to television screens, by the column inches in newspapers devoted to sports, and by samplings of cocktail conversations. Novelists, poets, and dramatists increasingly turned to sports for motifs, and scholars began to execute minute investigations of the psychological, philosophical, and social significance of sports. In the twentieth century, sports have joined with the electronic media, bureaucratic structures, and mass consumption as a major pillar of a new social order. Spectator sports have become, along with the church, the family, the local community, subcommunities based upon status, ethnicity, or race, and older systems of mutual class obligations, one of the sinews that holds modern society together.

PHOTO CREDITS

INDEX